D0398004

FORTITUDE

Hesketh, Roger Fleetwood,
Fortitude : the D-Day
deception campaign /
2000. WITHDRAWN
33305012417907
MH   12/11/00

FORTITUDE

The D-Day Deception Campaign

ROGER HESKETH

Introduction by Nigel West

SANTA CLARA COUNTY LIBRARY

3 3305 01241 7907

First published in the United States in 2000 by
The Overlook Press, Peter Mayer Publishers, Inc.
Lewis Hollow Road
Woodstock, New York 12498
www.overlookpress.com

Copyright © 2000 by St Ermin's Press and Roger Hesketh
Introduction copyright 1999 by Westintel (Research) Ltd

First published in the U.K. by St Ermin's Press/Little, Brown

All Rights Reserved. No part of this publication may be reproduced or
transmitted in any form or by any means, electronic or mechanical,
including photocopy, recording, or any information storage and
retrieval system now known or to be invented without permission in
writing from the publisher, except by a reviewer who wishes to quote
brief passages in connection with a review written for
inclusion in a magazine, newspaper, or broadcast.

Library of Congress Cataloging-in-Publication Data

Hesketh, Roger Fleetwood, 1902-1987
Fortitude : the D-Day deception campaign / Robert Hesketh ;
introduction by Nigel West.
p. cm.
Originally published: London : St. Ermin's, 1999.
Includes bibliographical references and index.
1. Operation Overlord. 2. World War, 193901945—Campaigns—France—
Normandy. 3. Normandy (France)—History, Military—20th century. I. Title.
D756.5.N6 H47 2000   940.54'21421—dc21   00-055749

Manufactured in the United States of America
FIRST EDITION
1 3 5 7 9 8 6 4 2
ISBN 1-58567-075-8

Contents

Illustrations, Maps and Charts

Introduction

by Nigel West

Strategic deception is now recognised as an essential component of any major military undertaking, and without exception the textbooks agree that the ingenious scheme, codenamed FORTITUDE, dreamed up to mislead the enemy over the long-expected invasion of Europe in 1944, was the most successful ever executed.

The challenge facing the Allies was their inability to conceal D-Day's objectives. The Nazis anticipated an amphibious assault on the French coast, and the Wehrmacht's military analysts saw the situation in much the same terms as their British and American counterparts, so the only issues to be resolved were limited to the exact timing and the precise location of the attack. The ultimate target was the capture of Berlin, which suggested the shortest route between Britain and the Continent, but on the way there were other considerations. The capture of a seaport intact was vital for the huge logistical support demanded by an army on the move, and it was presumed that exploiting the Channel's narrowest point would allow maximum air cover over the combat zone and ensure that the troops arrived in the best condition, without enduring a long sea voyage. In addition, there was the political dimension introduced by the V-1 buzz bombs, which were scheduled to rain on London in June 1944, and thereby make the seizure of their launch sites an important priority.

On this logic the Pas de Calais seemed the obvious target area, a coastline boasting several useful ports, sufficiently close to Dover and Folkestone to guarantee almost immediate resupply of fuel, armour and ammunition, and continuous air support from the many RAF airfields in Kent. As for the timing, the weather and tides would be key factors, and there was little doubt about the imminent conflict.

From the German standpoint, the defence preparations had been made to allow Field Marshal Rommel considerable flexibility. The entire coast, from Holland to the Spanish frontier, had been fortified in depth and mobile armoured reserves had been located at strategic points to counter-attack while the invaders were at their most vulnerable, still fighting their way off the beaches. Although Allied air superiority restricted the opportunities for aerial reconnaissance, and improved signal security procedures prevented much information leaking over the airwaves, the High Command (OKW) did have what it perceived to be the great advantage of a sophisticated network of agents operated by the Abwehr which reported from numerous locations across England.

German confidence in its intelligence organisation was misplaced, for the spies that had been established in Britain had, without exception, fallen under the control of the Security Services, MI5. Every agent that had been infiltrated into the country had been picked up and, in the counter-intelligence argot, 'turned'. In the example of GARBO, a colourful Catalan, he and his handler had embroidered his messages to include almost two dozen entirely notional sub-agents, all compiling detailed reports based on their purported observations, and drawing hefty expenses. To exploit this remarkable accomplishment, a highly secret deception unit had been created under the innocuous title of London Controlling Section, which acted as a clearing house to co-ordinate all Allied efforts to mislead the OKW about where, and when, the troops would storm what Hitler had termed 'Fortress Europe'.

Led by Colonel John Bevan, LCS consisted of a small group of imaginative officers who masterminded a scheme of breathtaking audacity. SHAEF (Supreme Headquarters Allied Expeditionary Force) had long decided that, for such a hazardous assault to succeed, it would require whatever element of surprise could be extracted. Accordingly, SHAEF had opted to concentrate the landings in Normandy. In defiance of conventional military doctrine, the planners proposed to construct an entire harbour offshore, floating the concrete quays over from Devon, and lay an underwater fuel pipeline along the sea floor from the Isle of Wight. The planners calculated that whatever was lost by sacrificing air cover and the longer sea crossing would be outweighed by the advantage of landing unexpectedly in Normandy. As well as supervising and manipulating the whole of the enemy's espionage system in Britain, LCS could count on two other clandestine assets. The first was access, through ULTRA, to German communications, which had enabled SHAEF to develop a comprehensive enemy order of battle and monitor its command structure. The second was a co-ordinated plan to use the local resistance groups to wreck the French landlines so as to increase the enemy's reliance on wireless. Combined with the sabotage of selected bridges and railways, the purpose was to handicap the enemy's ability to respond to the landings and ensure that the code-breakers at Bletchley Park anticipated the OKW's every decision.

It fell to LCS to make the project work, for if just one piece of the jigsaw failed to fit, the enemy might begin to suspect the deception and take the appropriate counter-measures. Tens of thousands of lives were in the balance, and a heavy responsibility fell on those devising FORTITUDE and on those charged with executing it. Once the overall strategy had been agreed, with the intention of reinforcing the German predisposition to expect a landing in the Pas de Calais, the various different components came into play. MI5 case officers handling a small group of trusted double agents were briefed, arrangements were made to generate false wireless traffic in East Anglia, and dummy landing craft and tanks were assembled in the Thames estuary to be photographed by enemy aircraft.

The quiet genius behind FORTITUDE was Roger Hesketh, a brilliantly intuitive, Eton- and Oxford-educated barrister, who, at the end of the war, prepared a classified account of the whole extraordinary story for very limited circulation within Whitehall. Naturally modest and reticent, Hesketh, later to be elected to Parliament in 1952 for his home town of Southport, retained several copies of the document, but never considered publishing it until 1973, when he was astonished to discover that the *Daily Express* journalist Sefton Delmer had been given access to it to write *The Counterfeit Spy*. While his account concentrated on the exploits of a double agent codenamed CATO, who was quite obviously GARBO, it obviously relied heavily on Hesketh's *Fortitude*, with absolutely no acknowledgment. Outraged, Hesketh discovered that Delmer had been assisted by Colonel Noel Wild, one of his wartime subordinates, who had apparently also obtained a copy of Hesketh's report. There was an exchange of fierce letters, and the result was a new edition of *The Counterfeit Spy* in which the author conceded his debt to Hesketh, together with permission from the Cabinet Office to release his own original document. Alas, with *Counterfeit Spy* having been distributed so widely, there was no room for *Fortitude*, and it was never released, despite several attempts to do so before Hesketh's death in 1987.

It was Hesketh's wish that *Fortitude* should be made public with minimal deletions, but there were several security constraints placed on him. He was anxious not to compromise the identities of individual double agents who had made such a necessary contribution to the operation's success, and GARBO's true name, Juan Pujol, was not disclosed until he was persuaded to reveal himself on the fortieth anniversary of the landings in June 1984. Similarly, BRONX (Elvira Chaudoir) and BRUTUS (Roman Garby-Czerniawski) remained under MI5's protection, as did the double agents in Iceland controlled by the Secret Intelligence Service, COBWEB (Ib Riis) and BEETLE (Petur Thomsen).

The need for discretion has now been lifted, all the double agents having emerged from obscurity to claim, half a century after D Day, their rightful place in history. Undoubtedly the true hero of this remarkable achievement is Hesketh himself, an amateur architect who devoted much of his life to his beautiful Lancashire home, Meols Hall, built on the estate which had been in his family since the twelfth century. It was his discerning eye for detail that ensured that there was not the slightest clue in the material carefully prepared for German consumption which might undermine their confidence. At stake was the ability of the Allied troops to establish a beachhead in Normandy and divert the enemy's attention to northern France before the feared crack SS panzer divisions could be deployed. Failure meant a crushing defeat and a lengthening of the war; success would save tens of thousands of lives and hasten the liberation of Nazi-occupied Europe.

As is now well recognised, the deception persuaded the OKW firstly that the Normandy landings were nothing more than a diversionary feint, intended to draw the defenders away from the real area, and secondly that the main thrust would fall in the Calais region a short time afterwards. Exactly how this masterpiece of trickery was achieved is to be found in the pages that follow.

Foreword

I wrote my history of Operation FORTITUDE during the three years following demobilisation in 1945. At that time it was considered inappropriate to record the names of those directly concerned in the implementation of the plan despite the fact that the work was to be classified as a top-secret document. This classification remained unchanged until 1976, when, subject to a few very minor deletions, I was given permission to publish.

I had hoped that this would provide me with the opportunity of paying my own belated personal tribute to all those, most of whom were employed in the secret agencies, whose skill and ingenuity contributed so vitally to the success of the Operation. But I am informed that official policy lays it down that the names of those who serve the secret agencies cannot be revealed, it being a tradition of the service that any credit which they earn must redound to the service as a whole. The names of those to whom the anonymity rule does not apply are included in both this Foreword and in the text of the book itself.

When General Morgan's planning staff (COSSAC) was set up in April 1943, a section known as Ops (B), with Lieutenant-Colonel John Jervis Read in charge, was formed to deal with deception. At the time of its formation I was posted to it with the task of dealing with any parts of a deceptive operation which it was felt could best be promoted by controlled leakage, or as we usually then called it 'Special Means'. As COSSAC had no troops of its own, it was obliged, where physical deception was concerned, to enlist the help of the appropriate fighting service or other outside agency for the execution of any deception plan. For controlled leakage, any information that we might want to pass to the enemy was to be channelled through the London Controlling Section (LCS). In the event, COSSAC only sponsored one deceptive operation, namely COCKADE, and it became my task to present COSSAC's requirements to a sub-committee of LCS known by the name of TWIST, which sat under the chairmanship of Colonel John Bevan, who was, of course, the head of the London Controlling Section as a whole. This committee then decided what channel would be the most appropriate for conveying the misinformation to the enemy and would see that it was despatched accordingly.

In January 1944, when General Eisenhower took over command, COSSAC was absorbed into SHAEF and Ops (B) was enlarged, being divided into two sub-sections, the one dealing with physical deception and the other with Special Means. Colonel Noel Wild, who had served under Brigadier Dudley Clarke, the officer in charge of deception throughout the North African campaign, became head of the section with Colonel Jervis Read as his deputy. The latter also continued as head of the sub-section dealing with physical deception, while I was given charge of the Special Means sub-section.

At this time, Colonel Bevan, realising that from then onwards the bulk of the controlled agents' work would be the implementation of FORTITUDE, decided that the right course would be to abolish the TWIST Committee and allow us to work directly with B1A. This was the section of MI5 which managed the controlled agents, who by this time were proving themselves to be by far the most effective channel for controlled leakage.

In the field of deception an important change in command and control was brought about by the FORTITUDE Directive of 26th February, 1944, issued by General Eisenhower. This made the Joint Commanders (Admiral Ramsey, General Montgomery and Air Chief Marshal Leigh Mallory) responsible for the detailed planning of FORTITUDE SOUTH. In practice this virtually meant, so far as we were concerned, 21 Army Group. Shortly afterwards General Thorne, GOC Scottish Command, was given a similar responsibility for the Army's share of FORTITUDE NORTH. On the other hand Eisenhower retained full control of the implementation of both operations by Special Means. Thus, from February until mid-summer when SHAEF resumed undivided control of FORTITUDE SOUTH, the basic function of the physical deception staff at SHAEF was one of co-ordinating the plans of the Joint Commanders in the South with those of GOC Scottish Command in the North, the latter having become the executants, while the function of the Special Means sub-section was to adapt the plans, both North and South, to suit the needs of the channels made available to them and through those channels to plant the story on the enemy. This demanded the closest co-operation between SHAEF and 21 Army Group in the field of deception, for whereas the latter had charge of the conduct of the Operation as a whole, the Special Means sub-section of Ops (B) was now responsible for the implementation of the plan by controlled leakage. This meant that every troop location or movement that we wished to pass to the enemy had to have 21 Army Group's prior approval. During the weeks immediately preceding the invasion, a despatch rider, usually my late brother Cuthbert, who served in the Special Means sub-section of Ops (B), travelled almost daily between Norfolk House and Southwick Park near Portsmouth, where Field Marshal Montgomery's headquarters were then housed, in order to have our requirements cleared by the Army Groups Deception Staff, known as G (R), and under the control of Colonel David Strangeways.

At the time when the FORTITUDE Directive came into operation, SHAEF had already prepared and issued a plan for FORTITUDE SOUTH, but soon after the Joint Commanders had taken charge this was superseded by a new plan embodying certain important changes which General de Guingand, Montgomery's Chief of Staff, had been advocating for some time, chief of these being the need to add greater weight to the post assault phase with the object of holding the German 15th Army in the Pas de Calais for as long as possible after the invasion. This was the plan which the Special Means sub-section at SHAEF was now required to feed to the enemy. It will be seen that the plan (Appendix V of this book) tabulates in chronological order the movements of every formation taking part in the Operation, the purpose being to provide a framework within which the agents' movements, real or imaginary, could be made to synchronise with those of the troops, again real or imaginary, that we wished to be brought to the enemy's notice. It also helped in co-relating the release dates of the agents' messages. I had worked out this method of presentation during the previous summer for the TWIST Committee in connection with COCKADE and its three subsidiary Operations, TINDALL, WADHAM and STARKEY.

During the three months immediately preceding the Normandy landings, the Special Means sub-section consisted of a major seconded from MI5, my brother, whose transfer from MI Liaison at the War Office had been arranged by Colonel Wild, a secretary supplied by MI5 who also kept our special registry, and myself. My brother, having before the war taken the Army Interpreters' examination, was familiar with German military technical terms.

Once we had established our direct link with B1A and the Special Means plans had been approved, the next step was to decide which agent was best suited for each task. As soon as the choice had been made, the Case Officer in question would come across from St James's Street to Norfolk House, where we would decide on the general sense of the message in hand, after which he would translate it into the particular idiom of the agent under his charge and then send it off. In fact, as my researches after the war were to prove, practically the whole of the Special Means cover plan was put over by two agents GARBO and BRUTUS (see Appendix XIII, 'British Controlled Agents' Share in compiling German Intelligence Reports during the Year 1944'), which meant that in practice one was closeted in our room at Norfolk House almost every day with their respective Case Officers, and I would go as far as to say that it was during these long sessions that the details of the plot were hammered out and the final form in which it was presented to the enemy determined. It should also be mentioned that the major from MI5, before being posted to the Special Means sub-section at SHAEF, where he now took part in these daily meetings, had himself been BRUTUS's Case Officer and had done much to establish his credibility in the eyes of the enemy. The contribution made by these three Case Officers to the success of the Operation would be hard to overestimate. Others came as and when the services of the agents they controlled were required. We did put a certain amount of traffic through TATE, but for some reason, unlike GARBO and BRUTUS, hardly any of his messages found their way into the German Intelligence summaries. Appendix XIII of this book reveals that during the year 1944, out of a total of 208 passages in the OKH Lagebericht West or the Ueberblick des Britischen Reiches whose inclusion can be attributed to the work of British-controlled agents, 86 came from GARBO, 91 from BRUTUS and only 11 from TATE. TRICYCLE made one useful contribution with his visit to Lisbon in March 1944 when he took with him a false Order of Battle which Berlin accepted as genuine. But enemy reaction to the lesser agents was minimal.

In June 1944 the establishment of Ops (B) was enlarged to make provision for the fact that there would be two operating centres, one in France and one in London. But by the end of July, although we continued to churn out plans until well into the New Year, the days of Strategic Deception were over.

The interrogation of senior German officers after the war had ended was carried out by my brother and myself. In March 1946 we met Field Marshal von Rundstedt and his Chief of Staff General Blumentritt at the Bridge End prisoner-of-war camp in South Wales. An account of that interview is recorded in Chapter XXII of this book. The interrogation of Field Marshals Keitel and Jodl and of Colonel Krummacher at Nuremberg in the following month were conducted by my brother alone. His visit to Nuremberg convinced him that it was GARBO's message, despatched on the evening of the 8th June, 1944, which changed the course of the battle in Normandy and no subsequent research led him to modify that view.

On the 18th April, 1946, he wrote me a letter from Nuremberg which I subsequently showed to the late Sefton Delmer, who quoted it in full on pages 187 and 188 of his book *The Counterfeit Spy*, first published in 1973. It runs as follows:

TOP SECRET. International Military Trials, Nuremberg.
My dear Roger,

I saw Keitel last night. He agreed that the halting of 1 SS Pz. Div. would have been an OKW decision as they were very hesitant and nervous about moving anything from the P. de C. at that time. He could not however recollect the incident, nor could he say for certain what the 'bestimmte Unterlagen' were. He suggested that it might have been air recce of shipping movements on the south coast, or some other report from the

Marine or Luftwaffe. When he saw the RSHA message he as good as said, 'Well there you have your answer.' He read through the comment at the end and explained to me that it would have been written by Krummacher and that it exactly represented the frame of mind of the OKW at that moment, which was such that the RSHA report in question would have had just the effect of persuading them to countermand the move of those forces. He added, 'This message proves to you that what I have been telling you about our dilemma at the time is correct.' Later he said, 'You can accept it as 99% certain that this message was the immediate cause of the counter order.'

This morning I managed to get hold of the OKW War Diary and I enclose an extract from it which I think will interest you. The rest of the sheet is a list of things which have recently been sent to London, the first one being in fact the War Diary, which I will try to get hold of when I get back as it covers the whole of 1944.

I am going to Regensburg tomorrow and return here on Monday to pick up a note which Keitel has promised to write in amplification of what he said yesterday. Then I hope to get the aeroplane on Tuesday to London.

Yours ever,
Cuthbert

ROGER HESKETH

Preface

In his report to the Combined Chiefs of Staff on the operations in Europe of the Allied Expeditionary Force, General Eisenhower remarked: 'Lack of infantry was the most important cause of the enemy's defeat in Normandy, and his failure to remedy this weakness was due primarily to the success of the Allied threats levelled against the Pas de Calais. This threat, which had already proved of so much value in misleading the enemy as to the true objectives of our invasion preparations, was maintained after 6th June, and it served most effectively to pin down the German Fifteenth Army east of the Seine while we built up our strength in the lodgment area to the west. I cannot over-emphasise the decisive value of this most successful threat, which paid enormous dividends, both at the time of the assault and during the operations of the two succeeding months. The German Fifteenth Army, which, if committed to battle in June or July, might possibly have defeated us by sheer weight of numbers, remained inoperative throughout the critical period of the campaign, and only when the breakthrough had been achieved were its infantry divisions brought west across the Seine – too late to have any effect upon the course of victory.' This report seeks to explain why the Germans were persuaded to make such a fatal miscalculation. The interrogation of senior German commanders and the examination of captured documents have revealed with remarkable clarity the causes of our success.

FORTITUDE was the code name given to a series of deceptive operations carried out in support of the invasion. The present narrative opens with the appointment of General Morgan as Chief of

Staff to the Supreme Commander Designate in April 1943 and is continued until the end of the war with Germany.

A variety of methods were employed to deceive the Germans. Some succeeded, others failed. It has not been thought necessary to spend a great deal of time in examining methods which did not achieve their object. These have been studied in so far as it enables us to understand why they failed.

Where the ground has already been covered in an existing report, and this applies mainly to the technical aspects of deception, repetition has been avoided, a reference to the relevant report being given.

It is always tempting for those who set out to deceive and who see their objects fulfilled, to claim the credit for their attainment when, in fact, the motive force lay in another quarter. Every effort has been made to complete the chain of cause and effect so that the reader can judge for himself to what extent the Germans were influenced by the action of Allied deceivers and to what extent they were impelled by other considerations. At all times the writer has kept before him the boast of Æsop's fly as he sat upon the axle-tree.

R. F. HESKETH
February 1949

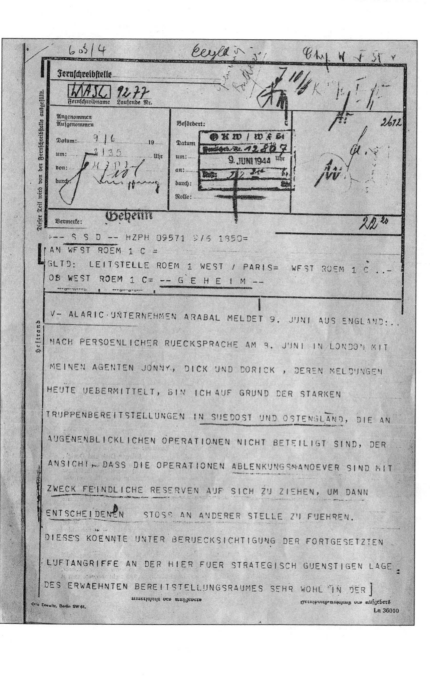

Geheim

Fernschreibstelle

WASC 9277
Fernschreibname   Laufende Nr.

Angenommen
Aufgenommen

Datum: 9/6   19

um: 2135   Uhr

von:

durch:

Befördert:

OKW / WFst
Fernschbr.Nr. 12807
9. JUNI 1944 Uhr

Datum:

um:

an:

durch:

Rolle:

2672

Vermerke: Geheim   22²⁰

+-- S S D -- HZPH 09571 9/6 1850=

AN WEST ROEM 1 C =

GLTD: LEITSTELLE ROEM 1 WEST / PARIS= WEST ROEM 1 C .-

OB WEST ROEM 1 C= -- G E H E I M --

V- ALARIC UNTERNEHMEN ARABAL MELDET 9. JUNI AUS ENGLAND:.

NACH PERSOENLICHER RUECKSPRACHE AM 9. JUNI IN LONDON MIT

MEINEN AGENTEN JONNY, DICK UND DORICK , DEREN MELDUNGEN

HEUTE UEBERMITTELT, BIN ICH AUF GRUND DER STARKEN

TRUPPENBEREITSTELLUNGEN IN SUEDOST UND OSTENGLAND, DIE AN

AUGENENBLICKLICHEN OPERATIONEN NICHT BETEILIGT SIND, DER

ANSICHT, DASS DIE OPERATIONEN ABLENKUNGSMANOEVER SIND MIT

ZWECK FEINDLICHE RESERVEN AUF SICH ZU ZIEHEN, UM DANN

ENTSCHEIDENEN   STOSS AN ANDERER STELLE ZU FUEHREN.

DIESES KOENNTE UNTER BERUECKSICHTIGUNG DER FORTGESETZTEN

LUFTANGRIFFE AN DER HIER FUER STRATEGISCH GUENSTIGEN LAGE

DES ERWAEHNTEN BEREITSTELLUNGSRAUMES SEHR WOHL IN DER

Otto Drewitz, Berlin SW 61.   Ln 36010

GEGEND PAS DE CALAIS ERFOLGEN, INSBESONDERE DA BEI EINEM

SOLCHEN ANGRIFF DIE NAEHER GELEGENEN LUFTSTUETZPUNKTE

FORTGESETZT STAERKSTE UNTERSTUETZUNG DURCH

LUFTSTREITKRAEFTE EINES SOLCHEN UNTERNEHMENS ERLEICHTERN

WUERDEN.=

RSHA, MIL. AMT, BR B NR 2495/44 G ROEM 1 H WEST / 1 V. 0.5.

TRANSLATION

Garbo's message of 9th June, 1944, as received by teleprinter at OKW and seen by Krummacher, Jodl and Hitler.

Message received at 2230 hours on 9th June, 1944, sent by Garbo.

'V-man Alaric network Arabal reports on 9th June from England:

After personal consultation on 8th June in London with my agents Jonny,* Dick and Dorick, whose reports were sent to-day, I am of the opinion, in view of the strong troop concentrations in South-East and Eastern England which are not taking part in the present operations, that these operations are a diversionary manœuvre designed to draw off enemy reserves in order then to make a decisive attack in another place. In view of the continued air attacks on the concentration area mentioned, which is a strategically favourable position for this, it may very probably take place in the Pas de Calais area, particularly since in such an attack the proximity of the air bases will facilitate the operation by providing continued strong air support.'

Krummacher underlined in red the words 'diversionary manœuvre designed to draw off enemy reserves in order then to make a decisive attack at another place', and added at the end –

'confirms the view already held by us that a further attack is to be expected in another place (Belgium?).'

This message was seen by Jodl, who underlined the words 'in South-East and Eastern England'. His initial in green may be seen at the top of the message. The green hieroglyph in the upper left-hand square indicates that Jodl considered it of sufficient importance to show to the Fuehrer, while the letters 'erl' (erledigt) which appear in pencil immediately to the right indicate that it was seen by Hitler.

* Misprint for Donny.

'It was prettily devised of Æsop: "The fly sat upon the axle-tree of the chariot-wheel and said, 'What a dust do I raise!'" So are there some vain persons that, whatsoever goeth alone or moveth upon great means, if they have never so little hand in it, they think it is they that carry it.'

FRANCIS BACON, *Essay on Vainglory*

I

Early Planning

The decision to invade France in 1944 was taken at the Casablanca Conference in January 1943. General Morgan was appointed Chief of Staff to the future Supreme Commander and established his headquarters at Norfolk House, St James's Square, in April of that year.[1] On 26th April he received a directive from the Combined Chiefs of Staff which, besides instructing him to prepare plans for a full-scale assault against the Continent as early as possible in 1944 and for a return to the Continent in the event of German disintegration at any time, also demanded 'an elaborate camouflage and deception scheme extending over the whole summer with a view to pinning the enemy in the West and keeping alive the expectation of large-scale cross-Channel operations in 1943. This would include at least one amphibious feint with the object of bringing on an air battle employing the Metropolitan Air Force and the Eighth US Air Force.'[2] The deception plans which were prepared in compliance with that instruction and which received the name of COCKADE do not strictly lie within the scope of this report. Nevertheless, as they had a bearing upon subsequent events, a short account is included.

COCKADE had two distinct objects: to contain German forces in North-Western Europe, thus preventing them from being used on the active fronts, and to destroy German aircraft. The plan comprised

---

1. General Morgan and his staff were generally known by the abbreviated title COSSAC.
2. COS (43) 215 (O), dated 26th April, 1943 – War Cabinet Chiefs of Staff Committee – Directive to General Morgan.

three connected operations: TINDALL, the threat of a landing in Norway; STARKEY, of a landing in the Pas de Calais; and WADHAM, of one in the Bay of Biscay. STARKEY and WADHAM, so the story ran, were to be complementary operations. After the bridgehead in the Pas de Calais had been established by British forces, an American landing was to take place in Western France with the object of opening Brest, which could then be used to land troops sailing direct from the United States. The forces in the United Kingdom being held inadequate to support all three plans, the French and Norwegian assaults were presented as alternative undertakings. STARKEY was the most important part of COCK-ADE inasmuch as it included an elaborate embarkation exercise[3] by 21 Army Group in which the landing craft actually sailed to within a few miles of the French coast, as well as real air attacks against the Pas de Calais. TINDALL and WADHAM relied mainly on the use of wireless, dummy devices and controlled leakage.

The STARKEY assault took place on 8th September. In accordance with the prearranged story, the preparations for TINDALL, which had been progressing in Scotland throughout August, were cancelled on the 25th of that month in favour of the cross-Channel attack. It was thought that this would give emphasis to the latter. When STARKEY failed to materialise as a real operation, a public announcement explained that it had only been a large-scale exercise. Meanwhile TINDALL was revived in the North and continued until November.

In its attempt to bring the German Air Force to battle STARKEY failed. It should, however, be remembered that in the real invasion which took place a year later the Germans did not commit their Air Force until after the first landing had taken place. The measure of success which it achieved in containing German forces in Western Europe is fully considered in the 'Historical Record of Deception in the War against Germany and Italy',[4] to which the reader in search of further information is referred.

In the summer of 1943 it was argued that STARKEY would help the cover operation for the real invasion which was again to threaten

---

3. Known as HARLEQUIN.
4. Held by the London Controlling Section, Ministry of Defence.

the Pas de Calais in the following year. 'It will be of the utmost importance to pin all . . . reserves for as long as possible. To this end, every artifice must be employed to draw his (*i.e.* the enemy's) attention to his most sensitive spot – the Pas de Calais. Operation STARKEY, it is to be hoped, will have some effect this year.'[5] Whether STARKEY was really an asset to deception in 1944 may be doubted. We ended by admitting that it was only an exercise. To conduct and publicise a large-scale exercise against an objective that one really intended to attack during the following year would hardly suggest a convincing grasp of the principle of surprise.

The only other bearing which COCKADE had upon the deceptive operations of the following year was to implant in the German mind a belief in one, and perhaps two, imaginary armies: the Sixth at Luton, and less certainly, the Fourth at Edinburgh.[6] These were represented as having grown out of, and as being more or less synonymous with, Eastern and Scottish Commands. The Fourth Army later became a valuable part of the FORTITUDE Order of Battle. The Sixth Army we did not need again, but never succeeded in destroying. It remained a part of the German version of the Allied Order of Battle until the end of the war.

It was not until OVERLORD had been written and submitted to the British Chiefs of Staff at the middle of July 1943 that attention was turned to deception plans for 1944. At that time the view was held that preparations for the cover operation should not lag behind those which were being made for the real one. Thus the production of a cover plan for OVERLORD appeared to be a matter of immediate concern. In order to appreciate the reason for this sense of urgency and, indeed, to understand many of the opinions expressed and decisions made at that time, it will be necessary to try and recapture something of the general attitude towards deception which prevailed in the summer of 1943.

---

5. Operation OVERLORD, COSSAC 23 (48), dated 15th July, 1943, para. 47. OVERLORD was the code name for the cross-Channel invasion.
6. The Fremde Heere West map of the United Kingdom, published on 31st December, 1943, gives the Sixth Army at Luton. At Edinburgh an army is shown, but without number.

In any theatre of war, deception must operate in the main through the Intelligence channels which have already been established by the enemy. It is thus the first task of the cover planner to decide which channels are likely to work and which, if they do work, the enemy is most likely to rely upon. The whole nature of one's deception plan will depend upon the initial assessment that one makes in this respect. The most important sources of Intelligence upon which the Germans might have been expected to rely for information about what was happening in the United Kingdom were aerial reconnaissance, wireless intercept and espionage. In all three fields we credited them with an efficiency which, as we now know, they did not deserve. Let us consider the prospect as it then appeared. Admittedly, the value of air photographic reconnaissance depends upon comparison of photographs taken at frequent intervals, and such reconnaissance over the United Kingdom had only been sporadic for a considerable time; yet the invasion was still nearly twelve months away. In the intervening period it might, and indeed was expected to, increase very greatly. Without a guarantee from the Air Ministry, which the latter was not prepared to give, COSSAC could not ignore the danger. So with spies; it was morally certain that there were no *bona fide* German agents at large, but it would have been practically impossible for the Security Service to guarantee that the country would not be flooded with spies during the coming months, some of whom would be bound to escape detection. With wireless intercept, the case was even stronger. Holding the entire Western European coast line, the enemy could place his stations in a continuous arc stretching from Norway to France, and thus appeared to be ideally placed for intercepting wireless traffic in the United Kingdom. Our belief in the efficiency of the German 'Y' Service may have been due to battle experience which had revealed its success at short range; it may also have arisen, in part, from pure lack of evidence; yet that such a belief was held is shown by the following quotation which is typical of many: 'In the case of the British forces, except those arriving from the Mediterranean, it is known that the enemy already possesses an accurate estimate of the number of formations in the United Kingdom, the greater part of this information having been obtained, or at least confirmed, by his

"Y" Service.'[7] One body of evidence which seemed to support this view was provided by the German publication *Das Britische Kriegsheer*. A copy of this manual dated 10th April, 1942, had fallen into Allied hands some time previously. An examination of its contents had disclosed not only a very fair knowledge of those parts of our Order of Battle which had only come into being since the outbreak of war, but also, by implication, a good deal of information about the location of our forces. This could be deduced from an analysis of inaccuracies in the work. For instance, the 76th Infantry Division was located at Norwich at the beginning of 1942. Its nine battalions were correctly listed with one exception: in place of the 1st Battalion of the Leicester Regiment, the 18th Battalion of the Welch Regiment was included. In fact, the Welsh battalion had no connection with the 76th Infantry Division, but happened to be engaged in aerodrome defence at Norwich at that date. A number of similar instances were found. These clearly pointed either to the personal observations of a spy or to intercept. The matter was submitted to the Security Service at the time, who gave it as their opinion that this was undoubtedly attributable to intercept.[8]

These opinions on the excellency of German Intelligence methods were by no means confined to the staff at COSSAC. Thus, in a note written by the Secretary to the Chiefs of Staffs Committee on 22nd April, 1943, the following view was expressed: 'Broadly speaking, deception has three phases. First, the preparation of the deception

---

7. Chief of Operations (B) Section to Chief of United States Operations Branch COSSAC. COSSAC/00/6/5/Ops, dated 5th October, 1943.

8. After the invasion had been launched. a later edition of *Das Britische Kriegsheer* came into our possession. A comparison of this with the previous edition of 1942 showed that the Germans had discovered very little in the intervening period. This was probably due to an improvement in signals security in the British Army, and in particular to the adoption by all British forces in the United Kingdom in July 1942 of the 'link' procedure, which made it more difficult for intercept to establish chains of command as well as to identify the individual formations and units contained in each group. This procedure was invented by the Germans and had been adopted by British troops in the Middle East some time previously. Had we possessed a more up-to-date edition of *Das Britische Kriegsheer* in the summer of 1943, we might not have thought quite so highly of the German intercept service.

plan; secondly, the execution of the plan in terms of movements of men, ships, &c., and thirdly, measures to ensure that the movements become known to the enemy. The first and third phases present no difficulty. As regards the first phase, the responsibility for the preparation of the cover deception plan . . . has been vested . . . in General Morgan. As to the third phase, namely, ensuring the enemy gets to know of the deception movements and is deceived by them, this is a matter for the Controlling Officer.[9] . . . It is the second phase, namely, the execution of the deception which is complicated. The executive orders for troops to march and for troops and aircraft or Air Force personnel to move for deception purposes, must come from the Naval, Army and Air Commanders-in-Chief concerned.'[10] Had the security of the United Kingdom been accepted as absolute, the Controlling Officer could have made his channels say whatever they liked and there would have been no need for the troops to march in order to support his statements. As it was, the troop movements were to form the backbone of the whole deception plan, the Controlling Officer's part in the business being merely 'to ensure that the movements became known to the enemy'. In a later passage, the same letter proposed a meeting of all Commanders-in-Chief concerned, possibly under the chairmanship of the Prime Minister, and recommended that it should 'be explained to the Commanders-in-Chief that effective deception involves the actual movements of stores, craft, troops and possibly Air Force personnel. These movements must inevitably interfere with normal training and movement.'

Having accepted this view as to the capabilities of the German Intelligence Service, the need for vast and complicated physical preparations followed inevitably. All the normal invasion preparations which would be visible from the air – landing craft, camps, hard standings for vehicles and so on – must be physically represented in those places where we wished the enemy to believe that we were concentrating and embarking our invasion forces. Furthermore the false preparations must look realistic at the ground level in order

---

9. The London Controlling Officer was the adviser to the British Chiefs of Staff on deception in all theatres.
10. COS (43) 208 (O), dated 22nd April, 1943.

to deceive the spy. At the same time the activities of the Controlling Officer would be restricted by the extent of these physical preparations. His channels could not report a movement of troops which had not been sufficiently represented to deceive the German Air Force, 'Y' Service and uncontrolled spy, lest his report should be contradicted and the channel discredited. That is why the real and the cover operations had to go forward together. Unless a cover plan was produced quickly, its requirements in the shape of physical resources and demands on manpower would go by default. It was essential that the needs of both should be assessed at the same time and a fair division made.

Here, however, another difficulty arose. It was felt that it would not be easy to write a cover plan until the broader strategy of deception had been decided upon. A decision in the higher sphere was dependent upon the results of the Teheran Conference, which was not due to meet until later in the year. The problem was temporarily solved by dividing the planning into two parts, one 'strategical' and the other 'tactical'. Roughly speaking, 'strategical' meant keeping German forces out of France, while 'tactical' meant keeping them away from the Normandy bridgehead. The strategical plan could wait for Teheran, while the tactical plan could be proceeded with immediately. The development of this plan will now be considered.

II

Appendix Y

The success of a seaborne assault depends on the ability of the attacker to sustain a more rapid rate of reinforcement by sea than the defender is able to do by land. The Germans, well aware of this, had organised their coastal defences on the assumption that the attackers would be dependent on the early capture of deep-water ports in order to maintain their ascendancy in the bridgehead. An examination of this problem by the staff of GHQ Home Forces, made during the previous year, had revealed the notable fact that no group of French ports could, on any reasonable calculation of the time that it would take to put them into working order, provide the capacity to support a single operation on the required scale. This meant that maintenance over open beaches, perhaps for months on end, would have to supplement the flow of men and supplies through the ports. If beach maintenance could be developed on a scale that would make us independent of existing ports for an extended period, we should have gone far towards circumventing the enemy's entire system of coastal defence, whose first aim was to deny us the use of these harbours. The beaches at Caen provided facilities for such development and at the same time satisfied the other basic requirements of a seaborne assault. It was this that determined the choice of Normandy as the objective for OVERLORD and which gave rise to the demand for the MULBERRY harbours.

The decision to invade west of the Seine placed in the hands of the deceivers a gift of priceless value: a cover objective which possessed all the more obvious attractions for an assault landing. So long as one overlooked the vital and determining factor of port capacities, the Pas de Calais had most things in its favour: a short sea passage, excellent air cover and possibilities of strategic development.

As originally planned[1] OVERLORD was to have employed some thirty operational divisions in the United Kingdom, with a subsequent build-up of from three to five divisions a month from the United States. The assault was to have been made by three divisions, two follow-up divisions being landed on the second tide. The first phase of the operation was to have been completed with the capture of Cherbourg fourteen days after the initial landing, troops on the right flank driving west to cut off the Cherbourg Peninsula and then advancing northwards to the port itself. In the second phase the Allied forces were to have advanced south-west to cut off the Brest Peninsula with the object of capturing the Brittany ports and turning them into American bases.[2] Subsequently, as the battle moved eastwards towards Germany, it was anticipated that the British would take over newly captured ports, relinquishing the more westerly ones to the Americans, thus securing for the latter the shortest available sea route for direct shipment from the United States. This arrangement would bring the Americans on the right flank and the British on the left, which in turn would demand that the American base installations and ports of embarkation should be in the West of England and those of the British in the East.

Of the three assault divisions due to take part in OVERLORD, the 3rd British Infantry Division was to train throughout the winter with its naval assault force in the Moray Firth. The 3rd Canadian

---

1. After General Eisenhower's return to England in January 1944, the scale of the attack was enlarged to comprise five divisions in the assault and three in the follow-up. This was made possible by postponing the attack against the south coast of France which, until then, was to have been made concurrently with OVERLORD.

2. This remained the broad policy of the campaign until the first week of August 1944, when 'the chances of delivering a knock-out blow were so favourable' that the capture of the Brittany ports was subordinated to the encirclement and destruction of the German Seventh Army and Panzer Group West. (Report by the Supreme Commander to the Combined Chiefs of Staff on the Operations in Europe of the Allied Expeditionary Force, 6th June, 1944, to 8th May, 1945. First paragraph of chapter headed 'Battle of the Falaise-Argentan Pocket'.)

Infantry Division was to be similarly employed in the Solent and surrounding waters, and the American infantry division, not yet specified, in the Plymouth area. Of the two follow-up divisions, the American formation would be located in the Bristol Channel during the spring of 1944, and the British in the Thames Estuary and Humber. On about 1st April, 1944, a month that is to say before the projected date of the invasion, the 3rd British Infantry Division was to concentrate in the South of England, its assault force sailing down the east coast, through the Straits of Dover, and coming to anchor at Portsmouth. This journey would take about a fortnight. At the same time, the two follow-up forces would move south. Fourteen days before the invasion the position would be as follows: three assault forces would be located respectively at Portsmouth, Poole and Plymouth, while the follow-up forces would be found on the south coast of Cornwall and in the Thames Estuary.

The high regard in which we held the German Intelligence Service led naturally to the conclusion that the invasion preparations which were already being set in motion could not be hidden from them for long. 'After January 1944 it would be impossible to conceal from the enemy that a large-scale operation was pending. All that the cover plan could do in the cross-Channel area was to lead the enemy to believe that the assault was elsewhere than was in fact planned.'[3] It would be the task of deception to move the apparent 'centre of gravity' of the Allied invasion preparations from the South-West to the South-East.

Although planning proceeded on the assumption that all our activities would be more or less accurately observed, it was agreed that the most significant pointer to our intentions would be provided by the landing craft associated with the assault divisions.[4] Whatever the Germans might think before the assault force sailed from the Moray Firth, once it had been observed to pass through the Straits of Dover – and any hope of concealing that part of its journey was thought to be out of the question – it seemed inevitable that they

---

3. Extract from Principal Staff Officers' (43) 12th Meeting, COSSAC, dated 19th August, 1943.
4. COSSAC/2356/Ops, dated 5th October, 1943. Chief of Ops (B) Sub-Section to the Controlling Officer.

should draw the conclusion that we intended to attack somewhere to the west of the Straits where all our assault craft would then be concentrated. It was against this background that the formulation of a cover plan was undertaken.

Though an introductory passage emphasises, in general terms, the need for employing every artifice to draw the enemy's attention to the Pas de Calais as a major condition affecting the success of the operation, it is curious to note that the only specific demand for deceptive action made in the OVERLORD outline plan is for two 'major diversions', one against the Pas de Calais and the other against the Mediterranean coast of France, both to begin about D minus fourteen.[5] This perhaps surprising limitation of deception to a relatively minor role may be partly explained by the fact that when OVER-LORD was being written in the summer of 1943, minds were much preoccupied by the growing strength of the German Fighter Air Force. Not only was this diversion against the Pas de Calais 'to contain the maximum forces both ground and air in that area', but it was also to 'form part of the general air plan for the reduction of the German Fighter Force'.[6] When, two months later, STARKEY failed to tempt a single German aircraft off the ground, the hopes of achieving decisive results in this way were abandoned and the disadvantages of pursuing such a course were recognised. 'The Germans would very soon realise that the landing of such a force without a follow-up was only a diversion; the threat to the Pas de Calais could not then be maintained and the German air and ground forces would be available to reinforce the main assault areas. As this is clearly to our disadvantage, all idea of making a diversionary landing with the object of bringing on air battles has been omitted.'[7] The objects of this cover plan thereafter became and subsequently remained:

---

5. COSSAC (43) 28 Operation OVERLORD, dated 15th July, 1943, Part I, Selection of Lodgement Area, para. 37.
6. OVERLORD, Part II, Outline Plan for Opening Phase, para. 7.
7. COSSAC 43 (39). Second draft for Head Planners dated 16th September, 1943, para. 3, repeated in all subsequent drafts. The cover plan now under consideration was at first given the code name TORRENT. This was changed to Appendix Y in October 1943.

'(*a*) To induce the German Command to believe that the main assault and follow-up will be in or east of the Pas de Calais area, thereby encouraging the enemy to maintain or increase the strength of his air and ground forces and his fortifications there at the expense of other areas, particularly of the Caen area.

'(*b*) To keep the enemy in doubt as to the date and time of the actual assault.

'(*c*) During and after the main assault to contain the largest possible German land and air forces in or east of the Pas de Calais for at least fourteen days.'[8]

The plan was divided into three phases: the preliminary phase, from the time that the plan was issued until the sailing of the naval assault force from the Moray Firth; the preparatory phase, from the departure of that force for the south coast until the touch-down of the assault; and the post-assault phase, from the invasion date until our forces were firmly established in France. In order to convey the desired impression in the vital matter of landing craft, the proposal was to make the Germans believe that we had enough assault craft for one more assault and one more follow-up division than we really possessed; four assault divisions instead of three; three follow-up divisions instead of two.[9] This was to be achieved by the creation of specially trained assault wireless deception units and by the construction of dummy landing craft. The imaginary assault force was to train somewhere on the Scottish coast like the force operating with the 3rd Infantry Division. The imaginary follow-up division was to be located in the neighbourhood of Rosyth. On 1st April, when 'S' Force, the naval assault force training with the 3rd Infantry Division, moved south, the two imaginary forces were also to be shown coming down the east coast, but instead of accompanying 'S' Force through the Straits of Dover, they were to put in to the Thames Estuary, dummy craft being floated out so as to denote

---

8. Appendix Y to COSSAC (43) 28, dated 20th November, 1943, para. 5.

9. It was proposed also to muster the necessary wireless resources to represent another assault force for the purpose of covering the departure of the 3rd British Infantry Division from Scotland.

their arrival to German reconnaissance aircraft. Thus, a fortnight before the invasion took place, it was hoped that the enemy would have the following picture: four assault divisions, one in the Thames Estuary, two in the Isle of Wight area and one in the Plymouth area; and three follow-up divisions, two in the Thames Estuary and one on the south Cornish coast. This result is obtained by adding the real to the imaginary. Portsmouth and Southampton, so it was argued, were as conveniently placed for an attack on the Pas de Calais as against the Seine bay. The presence of one assault and two follow-up divisions east of the Straits would give a bias in favour of the former.

Hardly less significant than the assembly of landing craft, though perhaps less easy for the enemy to observe, would be the location of short-range fighter aircraft. 'The progressive build-up of short-range aircraft in the South-West and South of England after the New Year will be an increasing indication of impending operations threatening the Cherbourg–Caen–Havre area.'[10] This danger was to be overcome by the display of dummy aircraft in the South-East and by wireless deception.[11]

Finally, there was the general disposition of forces in Southern England to reckon with. 'It will be necessary at the same time to ensure that the apparent size of the military and air forces, and preparations in East and South-East England are enlarged by discreet display and other deceptive methods on a scale commensurate with the display of craft in that (*i.e.* the Southern) area.'[12] Without waiting for the completion and acceptance of the plan, COSSAC had already in September 1943 requested GHQ Home Forces, to issue a new camouflage policy to Commands which, it was hoped, would tend to move the balance of our visible preparations from West to East. For Southern and Western Commands a policy of total concealment was inaugurated, while Eastern and South-Eastern Commands were to pursue what was described as a policy of 'discreet

---

10. Appendix Y, para. 11.
11. There was also a somewhat elaborate proposal that the Germans should be persuaded to believe that the real concentration in the South had been made for deceptive reasons.
12. Appendix Y, para. 10.

display'. This studied neglect was to be achieved, not by relaxation of camouflage discipline, but by the omission of technical camouflage advice.

As we were then assuming the presence of German spies and counting on a sustained programme of air reconnaissance, it was accepted that the army could only make its contribution to this great deceptive display by employing real troops, in a false role, and by actually carrying out in the Eastern and South-Eastern counties all those visible preparations which are normally associated with the mounting of a seaborne assault. During the preliminary phase 'the apparent capacity of the sector exclusive Thames Estuary–inclusive Yarmouth should be increased to one and a half divisions per day',[13] and in the preparatory phase, that is to say, when the real forces were moving to concentration, 'large-scale movements will be carried out with formations not immediately required overseas into the East and South-East sectors, to full capacity of these sectors, to simulate the movement of these forces overseas. These movements will be synchronised with the concentration and movement of the expeditionary force in other sectors.'[14]

Accepting the view that all these activities, real and false, were under constant observation, it would indeed have been difficult to deceive the enemy about the date of the invasion. It is, therefore, not surprising to find that the plan devotes little space to this aspect of the problem. Admittedly, as a consideration affecting timing, it says that, 'in order to achieve surprise, cover activities should normally lead the enemy to believe that the main operation is not due to be launched until about D plus twenty', but it then enumerates several good reasons why this would be difficult to achieve. For example, 'the arrival of Naval forces in the south coast from Rosyth about D minus fourteen will make the imminence of the operation difficult to conceal', and 'it will be difficult, if not impossible, to conceal the final loading of the assault forces, as this must be done by day as well as by night'.[15] Generally speaking, it seemed best to aim simply at the fulfilment of the second object of the plan, 'to

---

13. *Ibid.*, para. 34.
14. *Ibid.*, para. 42.
15. *Ibid.*, para. 12.

keep the enemy in doubt as to the date and time of the actual assault'.

Let us now turn to the post-assault phase. That this was to be regarded as a very subsidiary affair may be judged both by its anticipated duration and by the size of the force engaged. 'For about fourteen days after D Day, a force of not less than one assault, one follow-up and four build-up divisions will be represented in Eastern and South-Eastern Commands.'[16] The passage quoted goes on to say that the force would be made up of formations not required overseas during the first fourteen days, including two United States divisions carrying out normal full training in Eastern Command, and formations not forming part of the expeditionary force. Failing real formations, the force was to be made up by deceptive methods, including wireless and the use of dummy equipment. Thus, real divisions were to be used if available, sham ones *faute de mieux*.

The first draft of the plan appeared on 4th September. After undergoing seven revisions, it was submitted in its final form to the British Chiefs of Staff on 20th November, 1943. The latter preferred not to give their approval until the main deception plan for the winter of 1943–4 had been agreed. A request was therefore made for permission to issue it on a provisional basis only, so that it might be studied by those concerned with the preparation of the detailed plans for OVERLORD, with which it would have to be closely co-ordinated. The Chiefs of Staff were also asked to approve certain items of the plan, preparations for which, if they were to be ready in time, would have to be put in hand forthwith. These were three in number: the introduction of wireless silence periods,[17] the adoption of specific measures to lead German aircraft and ground observers into the belief that the Eastern counties had a greater capacity for the accommodation of invasion troops than was in fact the case, and the adoption of the general camouflage policy of concealment in the

---

16. *Ibid.*, para. 55.
17. A security measure introduced 'so that the final and inevitable silence will lose significance'.

West and display in the East. The last-named was in fact a request for confirmation of a policy which had already been adopted. Approval to these requests was given on 30th November, with the proviso that the visible preparations in the East of England should be delayed for as long as possible.

III

BODYGUARD and FORTITUDE

It will be remembered that the formulation of a strategic or 'overall' deception plan was dependent upon decisions taken at the Teheran Conference. This conference met late in November and accordingly, on 6th December, the London Controlling Officer was instructed to prepare a deception plan for operations against Germany in 1944.[1] This was accomplished during the ensuing three weeks and the plan was passed by the British Chiefs of Staff on Christmas Day of 1943.[2]

The object of BODYGUARD, as the London Controlling Officer's plan was called, was 'to induce the enemy to make faulty strategic dispositions in relation to operations by the United Nations against Germany'.[3] It provided the basis for current deception in Europe as well as a framework for the cover plans which would be initiated in due course by the theatre commanders in support of their own operations. While the Supreme Commanders in the North-Western European and Mediterranean theatres were made solely responsible for their own operational cover plans, they were also given a share in carrying out the 'overall' strategic programme. The aim of this long-term deception was to persuade the enemy to dispose his forces in areas where they might cause the least

---

1. CCS 426/1, dated 6th December, 1943, para. 9 (E).
2. It received the approval of the Combined Chiefs of Staff on the 23rd January, 1944.
3. COS (43) 779 (O) (Revise), dated 25th December, 1943. See Appendix I.

interference with operations in France[4] and on the Russian front.
Italy was excluded because the campaign there was itself a containing operation. To SHAEF[5] three specific tasks were given. They
were to persuade the enemy to believe that Allied plans existed to
take advantage of a withdrawal or serious weakening in any part of
North Western Europe. This, it was felt, would help to keep their
garrison troops at full strength. They were to induce a belief in a
coming Allied attack on Northern Norway, to be carried out with
Russian support in the spring, with the immediate object of opening up a supply route from Sweden; that we intended to enlist the
active co-operation of Sweden for the establishment of air bases in
Southern Sweden, whence we could cover an amphibious assault
against Denmark from the United Kingdom in the summer. Lastly,
since it would be 'impossible wholly to conceal the gradual build-up
of Allied forces and other preparations in the United Kingdom
during the next few months',[6] they should try to indicate that
Anglo-American strategy was dictated by caution and that there
was no intention of invading the Continent until the late summer.

The later invasion date was to be suggested in a number of ways.
Shortage of landing craft was to be emphasised; the number of
Anglo-American divisions in the United Kingdom available for an
offensive was to be represented as less than was in fact the case;
American divisions in the United Kingdom were to be reported as
arriving incompletely trained; every effort was to be made to conceal
the return of Allied divisions from the Mediterranean.[7] All this
would show that we were behindhand with our mounting programme. On the other hand, the scale of the assault, when at last it

---

4. When the plan was written it was supposed that a real landing, Operation
    ANVIL, would be made on the south coast of France at the same time as
    OVERLORD. This accounts for the omission of any reference to deceptive
    operations in that region.
5. On the appointment of General Eisenhower as Supreme Allied Commander
    in the North-Western European Theatre, COSSAC became merged in the
    new organisation which was designated Supreme Headquarters Allied
    Expeditionary Force.
6. BODYGUARD, para. 7 (a).
7. The concealment of the return of these divisions was the subject of a special
    plan known as FOYNES. This is examined elsewhere.

did come, was to be greatly exaggerated,[8] thus magnifying the task which still lay ahead.

In addition, as has already been stated, the Supreme Commander was required to provide a cover plan in direct support of OVER-LORD. 'As soon as our preparations for OVERLORD . . . clearly indicate to the enemy our intention to undertake a cross-Channel operation the Theatre Commander must implement his tactical cover plan to deceive the enemy as to the strength, objective and timing of OVERLORD.'[9]

The SHAEF deception plan which embodied all these requirements, both strategic and tactical, received the name of FORTITUDE. Work on this plan was begun as soon as BODYGUARD had been approved by the British Chiefs of Staff.[10] Let us consider the stages of its growth. The objects of FORTITUDE, which remained substantially unchanged from the appearance of the second draft on 11th January until the final plan was approved on 23rd February, were: 'to induce the enemy to make faulty dispositions in North-West Europe before and after the NEPTUNE[11] assault, thus—

(*a*) reducing the rate and weight of reinforcement of the target area,

(*b*) inducing him to expend his available effort on fortifications in areas other than the target area,

(*c*) lowering his vigilance in France during the build-up and mounting of the NEPTUNE forces in the United Kingdom,

(*d*) retaining forces in areas as far removed as possible from the target area before and after the NEPTUNE assault.'[12]

---

8. The assault was to be made by fifty divisions with twelve divisions afloat.

9. BODYGUARD, para. 5 (*b*).

10. The earlier drafts appeared under the code name MESPOT. The name was changed to FORTITUDE on 18th February, 1944.

11. NEPTUNE was the code name used in any OVERLORD document which mentioned the target date or the target area.

12. SHAEF (44) 13, dated 23rd February, 1944, Plan FORTITUDE, para. 5. The reader may think that the distinction between objects (*a*) and (*d*) is a very fine one. The plan is reproduced at Appendix II.

The plan proposed to give effect to these objects by encouraging a belief in three distinct operations.

First, there were to be the operations for the reoccupation of abandoned territories. 'From 1st February, 1944, balanced forces are being held in readiness to occupy any part of North-West Europe in the event of German withdrawal or collapse.'[13] Second, there was to be the Norwegian campaign. Third, the attack across the Dover Straits. The intermediate task of promoting belief in a postponed attack was not treated as a separate problem, but was woven into the story of the cross-Channel assault.

The 'reoccupation' operations required no further elaboration. On the other hand, SHAEF did not find the Norwegian assault as proposed by BODYGUARD wholly acceptable. 'Sweden would be unlikely to concede her southern airfields to the Allies with Germany still in occupation of Southern Norway, and as an assault on Denmark demands the prior occupation of the Stavanger–Oslo area, the target for a deceptive operation should be extended to include this area.'[14] This meant having two assaults, the original one on Narvik, to secure the supply route to Sweden, and another against Stavanger, as a stepping stone to Denmark. The next question to settle was the most suitable date for the attacks. It had been decided, in January, to postpone the real invasion from 1st May to 1st June. On the calculation that a German division would take about three weeks to move from Norway to France, it seemed that OVERLORD would receive the greatest benefit from the Norwegian threat if the Germans could be made to expect these attacks at the beginning of May. By that date the weather would be suitable and it would still allow reasonable time for the subsequent assault on Denmark in the late summer. Accordingly 1st May was chosen for both the Norwegian operations.

Finally, there was the Supreme Commander's tactical cover plan to deceive the enemy as to the strength, objective and timing of OVERLORD. The fear that preparations for invasion would sooner or later give OVERLORD away unless we took preventive measures, though

---

13. FORTITUDE, para. 16.
14. *Ibid.*, para. 6.

still as real as ever, had by now undergone some change. It will be remembered that in August 1943 the view had been officially expressed that after January 1944 it would be impossible to conceal from the enemy that such an operation was pending. January had arrived, however, and the worst fears had not been realised. Opinion now began to regard the month immediately preceding the invasion as the really dangerous time. 'By NEPTUNE D minus thirty, the movement and administrative preparations and the concentration of air forces will be nearly complete and the concentration of craft and shipping will be between 70 per cent and 80 per cent complete for Operation NEPTUNE. Although the German Command would not necessarily expect immediate invasion by such a force against their present scale of resistance, the preparations and the type and location of the forces will begin to threaten the NEPTUNE area unless preparations for the concentration of similar forces are made in the East and South-East of England.'[15]

Although BODYGUARD had stipulated as objects of policy during the 'intermediate' period a late summer invasion and an exaggerated striking force, it gave the Supreme Commander a perfectly free hand with his tactical plan to deceive the enemy as he thought best, and although it still recommended him to choose a date for the imaginary assault later than the real D Day,[16] it robbed this recommendation of its force by suggesting that when the time for tactical deception had arrived, a policy of 'postponement' would tend to lack plausibility. 'When the enemy realises that cross-Channel operations are imminent, the story indicating that no cross-Channel attack will occur until late summer will tend to lose plausibility. At this juncture the tactical cover plan prepared by Supreme Commander, Allied Expeditionary Force, will come into force with a view to deceiving the enemy as to the timing, direction and weight of OVERLORD.'[17] It is, of course, legitimate to point out that if such a policy were ever going to help us to influence German dispositions in our favour, it could only do so if it were sustained until the

---

15. FORTITUDE alias MESPOT. (Third draft), dated 17th January, 1944, para. 11.
16. BODYGUARD, para. 15.
17. *Ibid.*, para. 14 (*a*).

eve of the invasion. The Germans were hard-pressed on other fronts. The fact that they believed, in the spring, that we intended to attack in July rather than in June would have availed us little if they had ceased to hold that view when the cross-Channel operations were imminent. In any case, the policy of postponement was in effect the first instalment of the OVERLORD cover plan, since it related to the invasion armies, and as such was almost bound to colour any stories that came later. As will now be seen, the Supreme Commander's plan upheld both the policy of postponement and that of an augmented striking force, with consequences which will presently be considered. 'With a target date of 15th July, 1944, a cross-Channel operation will be carried out by a total force of fifty divisions, with craft and shipping for twelve divisions. The assault will be made in the Pas de Calais area by seven divisions, two east and five south of Cap Gris Nez. The follow-up and immediate build-up will be a further six divisions. The force will be built up to a total of fifty divisions at the rate of about three divisions per day.'[18] Antwerp and Brussels were to be captured, and from this bridgehead an advance was to be made to the Ruhr.

It soon became evident that between the desire to divert attention from the invasion preparations and the desire to suggest the 15th July as the date for the attack against the Pas de Calais, there lay an irreconcilable conflict. No one could alter the timing of the real preparations for OVERLORD; they had to be ready by 1st June. If we were going to make sham preparations in the South-East in order to 'shift the centre of gravity' towards the Pas de Calais, these presumably would have to be advanced *pari passu* with the real preparations, but then what became of 'postponement'? 'In order, however,' says the plan, 'to minimise our state of preparedness as a whole, the preparations in the East and South-East should indicate a target date of 15th July 1944.'[19] It was always rather difficult to see how this would work out. Assuming that the Germans, by the interpretation of their air photographs and by other means, were able to gauge with any degree of precision the imminence of the operations

18. FORTITUDE alias MESPOT. (Third draft), dated 17th January, 1944, para. 22.
19. *Ibid.*, para. 11.

for which the observed preparations were being made, then, in the South and South-West, they would have seen preparations which indicated 1st June. In the East and South-East, on the other hand, the correct interpretation would be an attack on 15th July. Taking one's stand at 1st May, 1944, the argument would appear to have been that if the enemy saw the invasion thirty days away in the South and seventy-five days away in the South-East, he might somehow or other strike a balance and give it a date between the two. Of course he might equally well have said that the invasion against Normandy was coming in thirty days and the invasion against the Pas de Calais in seventy-five days. This weakness was at once pointed out by Major-General N. C. D. Brownjohn,[20] who put the argument even more strongly by suggesting that if the plan were executed as proposed, the delayed preparations for FORTITUDE SOUTH would not be discernible to the enemy at all before the real invasion. 'It is believed that the discrepancy between concentration for Operation NEPTUNE and the preparations being made in East and South-East England is too great since, if a target of 15th July is taken in the East and South-East, no substantial physical preparations will be apparent to the enemy. It is believed more practicable to state that during this period the preparations in the East and South-East should proceed concurrently with those made for Operation NEPTUNE and should indicate a target date not later than that for the forces being deployed in the NEPTUNE area. This treatment is somewhat inconsistent with the story, but the change is believed necessary, as otherwise no threat will be apparent to the Pas de Calais area prior to D Day.'[21] The point was also taken up later by Major-General C. S. Napier.[22] 'It has often been pointed out that the desire to indicate a state of unpreparedness up to D Day and the desire to conceal the target area by threatening the Pas de Calais before[23] D

---

20. Assistant Chief of Staff, G-4 Division, SHAEF.
21. SHAEF 519/1/Q, dated 21st January, 1944, from AC of S, G-4 Division to AC of S, G-3 Division.
22. Chief of Movement and Transportation, SHAEF.
23. The original text says: 'after D Day', but this is clearly a misprint for 'before'. There would have been little hope of concealing the real target area after D Day.

Day conflict. If the idea of suggesting D plus forty-five as the real target date is not dropped about D minus twenty-one at latest, there is a risk of prejudicing . . . concealment of the target area because unreadiness in South-East England as compared with completed preparations elsewhere might be interpreted as indicating the absence of a threat to the Pas de Calais. I am aware how difficult the problem is and that the present proposals for activity in South-Eastern Command after D minus thirty are probably the best attempt at a solution, if we really must adhere to the attempt to give an impression of unpreparedness. But at every turn we come up against the practical difficulty of this attempt.'[24]

In spite of these opinions, D plus 45 remained the target date for the false operation.[25] On the other hand there appears for the first time, in the Fourth draft issued at the end of January, a paragraph which brings us at least a step towards a resolution of the conflict. This paragraph was introduced at the instance of 21 Army Group. It says: 'If before NEPTUNE D Day, however, it becomes evident that the enemy does not believe in the later target date, preparations in the East and South-East should be accelerated and the threat to the Pas de Calais be fully developed.'[26] 21 Army Group, who, as prospective executants of the operation, were at this time taking an active interest in the progress of the plan, held the view that it might be necessary to make the attack on the Pas de Calais seem both obvious and imminent if in the critical days preceding OVERLORD the secrecy of the real operation appeared to be breaking down. Writing to SHAEF on 25th January, 1944, Major-General F. de Guingand, General Montgomery's Chief of Staff, said: 'I consider that the enemy should be led to believe that from now on our target in Northern Europe is the Pas de Calais area. Once our efforts have failed to make the enemy believe that our attack will not take place before the late summer, we should

---

24. SHAEF/4060/Mov/18th February, 1944. Chief of Movement and Transportation, SHAEF, to BGS Plans and Ops Section, G-3 Division, SHAEF.

25. FORTITUDE alias MESPOT. (Fourth draft), 30th January, 1944, para. 23.

26. *Ibid.*, para. 12.

concentrate on telling him that the Pas de Calais area is our *early* objective.'[27]

When the planning of FORTITUDE began, any attempt to deceive the Germans after the invasion had started was still regarded as a minor affair. The story was to be that 'a force of one assault, one follow-up and four build-up divisions is assembled in and behind the Thames Estuary and the south-east coast ports to carry out a subsidiary operation in the Pas de Calais area with the object of drawing German forces away from the main target area.'[28] On 25th January, however, General de Guingand raised the post-assault phase to a level of importance which it had not hitherto enjoyed. In criticism of the paragraph already quoted he said: 'I do not agree with the object which has been given for the attack on the Pas de Calais. If we induce the enemy to believe the story, he will not react in the way we want. I feel we must, from D Day onwards, endeavour to persuade him that our *main* attack is going to develop later in the Pas de Calais area, and it is hoped that NEPTUNE will draw away reserves from that area.'[29] This change being accepted, the final draft of FORTITUDE expanded the post-assault story from a modest diversion to a grand attack. Thus: 'The operation in the NEPTUNE area is designed to draw German reserves away from the Pas de Calais and Belgium. Craft and shipping for at least two assault divisions are assembled in the Thames Estuary and south-east coast ports; four more assault divisions are held in readiness in the Portsmouth area and will be mounted in craft and shipping from NEPTUNE. When the German reserves have been committed to the NEPTUNE area, the main Allied attack will be made between the Somme and Ostend with these six divisions in the assault.'[30] In accordance with the 'pre-invasion' story which remained unaltered, the Germans were supposed, before the invasion took place, to believe that there were

---

27. 21 Army Group/25/COS, dated 25th January, 1944. Chief of Staff, 21 Army Group, to DACOS, G-3 Division, SHAEF.
28. FORTITUDE alias MESPOT. (First draft), dated 3rd January, 1944, para. 30.
29. 21 Army Group/25/COS, dated 25th January, 1944. Chief of Staff, 21 Army Group, to DACOS, G-3 Division, SHAEF.
30. FORTITUDE, para. 28.

two assault divisions east of the Straits of Dover and five along the south coast. After the invasion had begun, according to this new story, the landing craft on the south coast, having taken their five assault divisions to Normandy (and not to the Pas de Calais, as previously supposed), would return to England for the four additional ones destined for the Pas de Calais. The two imaginary assault forces east of the Straits, having already been established in pre-invasion days, would continue to exercise their threat during the later phase.

The postponed target date had already been criticised on the ground that it would make it difficult before the invasion effectively to shift the centre of gravity of our preparations from West to East. The decision to represent the Pas de Calais operation, *after the real invasion had been launched*, as the main one placed another difficulty in the way of pursuing the 'postponement' theme. If, before the invasion, we sought to show ourselves weak and unprepared, what would be left to carry out the second and greater invasion when the first and lesser attack was seen to have engaged the bulk of our forces? From this point of view the proposal to increase the invading force to fifty divisions was an advantage. But this advantage was cancelled by encouraging a belief in the later target date through a simulated reduction of our strength before D Day. The only way of bringing the two stories into line would have been to suggest a very greatly accelerated rate of reinforcement from the United States between the beginning of June and the date chosen for the imaginary assault. But this would have placed a wholly unrealistic burden on shipping space. FORTITUDE sought a partial escape from this impasse by dropping the story of an actual reduction in strength and relying solely on the argument of incomplete training. 'In order to emphasise a later target date of 15th July, 1944, we should minimise the state of preparedness of the NEPTUNE forces by misleading the enemy about their state of training, organisation, equipment and their location.'[31] For the rest the gap was to be closed by the arrival of American divisions during the operation. This, however, was no real solution, for ill-trained troops could be regarded as little better than no troops. Thus the policy of postponement militated at once against the diversion of the

---

31. FORTITUDE alias MESPOT. (Third draft), dated 17th January, 1944, para. 13.

enemy's attention from Normandy *before the invasion* and against the promotion of belief in a greater assault against the Pas de Calais *after the invasion*. To this unsolved problem we shall return.

FORTITUDE received the approval of the Combined Chiefs of Staff on 26th February, 1944. The draft Appendix 'Y' plan, which had been in the hands of the Joint Commanders for two months, was now relegated to the status of a staff study.

Finally it remains to be seen how command and control of the two major threats comprised in FORTITUDE were apportioned. The responsibility for co-ordinating and controlling the execution of the plan as a whole was retained by the Supreme Commander. On the other hand, it was considered that OVERLORD and its tactical cover plan, the threat to the Pas de Calais, were so interdependent that the commanders responsible for the detailed planning of the one should also have charge of the other.[32] On these grounds the FORTITUDE directive of 26th February, 1944, laid down that: 'The Allied Naval Commander, Expeditionary Force, the Commander-in-Chief, 21 Army Group and the Air Commander-in-Chief, Allied Expeditionary Air Force, will be responsible to the Supreme Commander for directing towards the Pas de Calais the threat created by the forces under their control and for concealing the state of readiness of these forces so as to indicate NEPTUNE D plus forty-five as the real target date. They will also be responsible for making preparations to continue the threat against the Pas de Calais.'[33] When the bridgehead was established, these responsibilities would revert to SHAEF.

Conduct of the Norwegian campaign[34] and control of the arrangements for reoccupying the abandoned sectors were retained by SHAEF, who also reserved to itself the handling of controlled leakage in respect of all three operations.

---

32. This opinion had been expressed as early as September of the previous year, see COSSAC (43) 39 (2nd draft for PSO's), dated 29th September, 1943, Appendix C, Command and Control.
33. SHAEF 24 (41), dated 26th February, 1944. Plan FORTITUDE Directive to Joint Commanders. See Appendix III.
34. Control of the Army's share in the Norwegian operations was delegated shortly afterwards to the General Officer Commanding-in-Chief, Scottish Command.

IV

Organisation and Technical Resources

There were three main considerations, the solution of which was to determine the organisation of the Deception Staff at SHAEF. First, should it come directly under the Supreme Commander, or should it form a section of the Operations Division? Second, should the head of the Deception Staff also command the specialist troops who would execute the cover plans? Third, should he directly control the Special Means[1] channels?

When General Morgan's staff was established in April 1943, a section known as Ops (B)[2] had been formed within the Operations Branch to write the cover plans. As COSSAC was endowed with no executive powers, the command of specialist troops could not in any case have been considered at this stage. So far as Special Means channels were concerned, these remained, as yet, in the hands of the Controlling Officer.

It being felt that these arrangements might not prove adequate in the coming year, some discussion took place during the summer of 1943, and it was to the Mediterranean that attention was now turned and guidance sought in the experience of 'A' Force, which had been active in that theatre since the time of General Wavell's campaign.

---

1. The name given to all forms of controlled leakage.
2. Ops (B) at that time consisted of one General Staff Officer, first grade, who had to rely, for the most part, on the assistance of officers borrowed from the other sections of the Operations Branch and lent, on a part-time basis, by the Intelligence and Administrative Branches. The Naval and Air Staffs also nominated officers to advise on matters relating to their respective Services.

The Commander of 'A' Force acted as adviser on deception to the Service commanders in the Middle East. As such he was independent of the Operations Staff. He had under his command specialist troops and he directly controlled[3] all Special Means channels. His staff was divided into two sections, 'Operations' and 'Intelligence'. The former was concerned with the physical aspects of deception, such as camouflage and wireless; the latter performed an Intelligence function in the collation of enemy information regarding ourselves and an operational function in deceiving the enemy through controlled leakage.

In July 1943 the Controlling Officer recommended that the Head of Ops (B) should, following the Mediterranean example, come directly under the Chief of Staff. 'Experience in other theatres shows the need for a deception staff to be a distinct section within the General Staff and directly under the Chief of Staff. Though it should not come directly under Ops or "I" it must, however, establish the closest touch with these sections and with senior officers in other branches of the Staff.'[4] At COSSAC, however, the opposite view was held. '"A" Force is possibly rather a private army and I see no reason for this being directly under the Chief of Staff, although on certain occasions it should have direct access. Real, cover and deception plans and operations should all be made or conducted by the Operations Branch of the Staff. I think it would be a mistake if it can possibly be avoided to differentiate in any way between real and deception operations or to depart from normal staff channels.'[5] *A fortiori*, this ruled out any question of commanding specialist troops.

In 1943 all Special Means requirements were canalised through the London Controlling Section. A committee known by the name of TWIST, of which the Controlling Officer was chairman, sat weekly and allotted tasks to the various channels held at their disposal. It was

---

3. It must be understood that where controlled enemy agents were concerned there was always a technical and administrative as well as an operational control. It is the latter only that we are here concerned with. The technical control of the Mediterranean agents remained at all times with SIME (Security Intelligence Middle East), as in the United Kingdom it did with MI5.
4. LCS (43) Org./2, dated 21st July, 1943.
5. COSSAC/2361/Ops, dated 26th July, 1943, GSOI Ops (B) to COSSAC.

supposed that this system would continue in 1944, and when recommending that Ops (B) should be divided on the 'A' Force pattern
into 'Operations' and 'Intelligence' elements, the Controlling Officer
had specifically stated that since 'all implementation by secret means
is in the hands of LCS', there would be no need for a large Intelligence
staff. By contrast it seemed to him that the operational element might
have to be stronger than was the case in other theatres. The authority
of a commander-in-chief in the United Kingdom was limited, since
considerable control was exercised by Service and non-Service
Ministries and other departments, many of which might be concerned with the execution of real or deception plans. The
co-ordination of such widespread interests, in so far as they affected
deception, would fall upon the operational side of the Deception
Staff, which should accordingly be strengthened.

After this exchange of views, the question of organisation lay dor-
mant for several months and it was not until January 1944, when
COSSAC became absorbed in the newly created SHAEF, that the
matter was brought up again for consideration.[6] Opinion at SHAEF
still favoured the retention of Ops (B) as an integral part of the
Operations Division and continued to set its face against any proposal
that the head of the Deception Staff should also command specialist
troops: 'The Commander of Force "A" controls directly his own cover
and deception units; and in addition he and his subordinates act as
advisers to the various military commanders. . . . In the United
Kingdom organisation, on the other hand, the cover and deception
staff at Supreme Headquarters and at 21 and First Army Groups forms
an integral part of the G-3 staff;[7] the special cover and deception units
coming directly under the command of the Army Group
Commanders. We feel that the advantages lie with the United
Kingdom set-up. The Deception Staff, forming an integral part of the

---

6. At this time, owing to the expansion of the Staff, Ops (B) Section became Ops
   (B) Sub-Section.
7. Although these arrangements may have been contemplated at that time both
   by 21 Army Group and First United States Army Group, at neither
   Headquarters was the Deception Staff in fact to form part of the Operations
   Division, as will be seen hereafter. At the American Army Group Headquarters
   the Deception Staff did not yet exist.

Headquarters, are likely to be more fully in the operational picture, and more likely to influence the G-3 Staff and Commanders in their decisions. The burden of administering the special units rests with the Army Groups, who can deal with them in their stride. In this respect no change is recommended.'[8] On the other hand, where Special Means was concerned, a unanimous change of opinion is to be observed. As early as 3rd January, 1944, the Controlling Officer had made it clear that in his opinion the TWIST Committee did not provide an ideal solution: 'The directive to the Controlling Officer from the Chiefs of Staff includes the following: "You will control the planting of deception schemes originated by Commanders-in-Chief by such means as leakage and propaganda." In practice this means that the cover plan prepared by SAC, UK, will be planted by LCS through channels available to LCS and in accordance with the characteristics of these various channels. It would seem desirable to have SAC Deception Staff more closely associated with this detailed implementation and in these circumstances it is felt that SAC, LCS and MI5 (B1A)[9] should form a small combined Intelligence Staff, which will be responsible for "planting" the story on the enemy. The exact form in which this should be done is a matter for discussion and will obviously depend to some extent upon SAC, UK's deception establishment. As a first step, it would seem advisable for representatives of SAC, LCS and B1A to meet twice weekly to review the existing situation and decide on any immediate action which may be necessary. This Committee would in fact take the place of TWIST.'[10] On 15th January the Controlling Officer translated these views into action. Just as SAC, UK, should co-ordinate the activities of all forces in the United Kingdom, whether under his command or not, in implementing real plans, 'equally SAC, UK, should co-ordinate the output of all deception material concerned with deception plans covering real operations for which SAC, UK, is responsible. For this purpose a permanent liaison between MI5, MI6,

---

8. SHAEF 18209/Ops, dated 27th January, 1944, Cover and Deception Organisation. AC of S, to DCOS, G-3 Division, SHAEF.

9. This sub-section of MI5 controlled the German agents that we were employing to pass information to the enemy. They constituted by far the most important LCS channel.

10. Memorandum by London Controlling Officer, dated 3rd January, 1944.

LCS and SAC's Deception Staff will be set up at HQ, SAC. *SAC will thus instruct directly MI5, MI6 and LCS with regard to deception material for channels controlled respectively by them and the necessary co-ordination between all channels will be secured at the Headquarters of SAC.* The TWIST Committee will cease to exist.'[11] This was accepted by SHAEF. 'It has been clear for some time that SHAEF must take over control of the "planting the story". In fact, a measure of control has already been taken over (since 12th January) in that the Ops (B) Sub-Section at SHAEF have agreed to hold regular meetings with LCS and MI5 to initiate the planting of the story for OVERLORD.'[12] Henceforth LCS was to be regarded, to use the Controlling Officer's own words, 'as the authority through which co-ordination of implementation . . . of European cover plans should be conducted. In other words, SAC, UK, Deception Staff, Main Headquarters "A" Force and JSC, Washington, should, when necessary, communicate to one another through LCS and not directly with one another.'[13] These arrangements continued to work satisfactorily until the end of the war.

Thus, of the three main issues referred to at the beginning of this chapter, the first two had gone contrary to, and the third, in accordance with, the 'A' Force precedent.

To meet these changed conditions and to provide a staff that would be capable of undertaking the larger tasks which now lay ahead, a new and increased establishment[14] was approved in January 1944.

---

11. Summary of the conclusions reached at a meeting between MI5 and LCS on 15th January, 1944.

12. SHAEF 18209/Ops, dated 27th January, 1944, Cover and Deception Organisation. AC of S, to DCOS, G-3 Division, SHAEF.

13. CO/363/4 Preparation and Implementation of Deception Plans covering OVERLORD and ANVIL, dated 15th January, 1944.

14. The only reason for giving details of organisation is to show how many people it took to do the work and what each person did. The succession of Ops (B) establishments which were approved from time to time do not provide a true guide. Sometimes they were not filled, sometimes they were filled by officers who worked in some other branch of the Staff, and sometimes officers held on some other establishment were lent to the Sub-Section. In these circumstances the writer feels that it is best to ignore them and simply to say how many were in fact employed in the Sub-Section at different times, giving their ranks and the nature of their tasks.

The Sub-Section now had at its head a British colonel, newly posted from 'A' Force. The British lieutenant-colonel who had been head of Ops (B) since its formation became Deputy Chief as well as head of the Operational or Physical Deception element.[15] In the latter capacity he had under him two majors, one British and one American. The Intelligence or Special Means element was placed under the charge of the British major, who had hitherto been attached to Ops (B) from the Intelligence Branch. He had as assistants a British captain and, a little later, a British major lent by B1A. The Physical Deception Staff made use of the G-3 pool for clerical work. The Special Means Staff, on account of the secret nature of its activities, was supplied by MI5 with a civilian secretary and kept its own separate registry. ANCXF and AEAF provided, respectively, a commander and a wing-commander who acted as advisers both to Ops (B) and to the Joint Commanders.

In June 1944 Ops (B) was enlarged, mainly by the addition of American officers. An American lieutenant-colonel became Deputy Chief, the former Deputy Chief continuing to fulfil his second role as head of the Physical Deception Staff. The Physical Deception

---

15. The conventional division of a deception staff into 'Operations' and 'Intelligence', though useful as a method of diverting curiosity from highly secret practices, was by no means – at least in the case of the SHAEF Deception Staff – an accurate description of their functions. In the accepted sense of the terms the functions of both were operational, one controlling deception by physical devices and the other deception by Special Means. If, in theory, it was the function of the Intelligence element to supply the operational element with intelligence, this was not the practice partly no doubt because during the most critical periods they were not even located in the same building; also because the very small size of the 'I' Staff would in any case have prevented it. In fact they both gleaned what intelligence they required as best they could. It may be mentioned in passing that the information most often required was about our own side and not about the enemy, a kind of inverted intelligence, for we were, after all, posing as a part of the enemy's Intelligence Service. That meant that our links with the Intelligence Division were slender as compared with those that we built up with Staff Duties, Training, Movements and Transportation and other branches of the operational and administrative staffs. For the sake of clarity, the two sides of the Ops (B) Sub-Section will therefore be referred to throughout this report as the 'Physical Deception Staff' and the 'Special Means Staff'.

Staff was strengthened by the addition of an American major, and later, in July, of two American captains.[16] The British major in charge of Special Means was promoted to lieutenant-colonel and, soon afterwards, his assistant to major, while the burden of the civilian secretary in charge of the Special Means registry was eased by the addition of two ATS officers. The organisation did not undergo any further notable change until September 1944, that is to say after FORTITUDE had come to an end. This rearrangement, which was made when Ops (B) went overseas, will be alluded to briefly in a later chapter.

The official cover plans, which received the approval of the Supreme Commander through his Chief of Staff, were drafted by the Physical Deception Staff under the direction of the Chief or Deputy Chief of the Sub-Section. Drafts were revised at meetings to which members of other branches of the Staff and representatives of the other Services were invited. The Special Means plans, on the other hand, received no approval beyond that of the Chief of the Sub-Section. For in theory at least they were no more than adaptations of the official plans, prepared by the Special Means Staff with the object of serving the stories to the controlled channels in a palatable form.

The Deception Staffs at the two Army Groups did not follow the SHAEF example. 21 Army Group adhered very closely to the 'A' Force pattern, and the Deception Staff, at first known as Ops (D) but re-christened G (R)[17] on 22nd February, 1944, came directly under the Chief of Staff. The head of G (R) was also the Commander of 'R' Force, a mixed force of specialist troops trained to perform a variety of deceptive tasks.[18]

At the time of which we are speaking, the American Army Group was still in embryo and as yet had no organisation for deception. Although the problem of forming and training an American deception staff was the subject of discussion throughout the winter months and officers with experience of the subject were already attached to ETOUSA, it was not until 26th March, 1944, that the new 'Special

---

16. One of these captains was transferred to the Special Means Staff in August 1944.
17. 21 Army Group 00/217/Ops (D), dated 22nd February, 1944.
18. This arrangement was instituted by General Paget in November 1943. 21 Army Group/1835/1/G (SD), dated 27th November, 1943.

Plans Section' was formed. At first it came under ETOUSA and worked in close co-operation with 21 Army Group, its function being to help the latter in deceptive operations where United States troops under command of 21 Army Group were involved. Later in the year it took its place under the American Twelfth Army Group, when the latter went overseas. The American organisation lay somewhere between that of SHAEF and 21 Army Group. On the one hand it was not, like Ops (B), a sub-section of the Operations Division, but came directly under the Chief of Staff; on the other, it had no troops under command but had to make its demands through normal channels to the heads of the army services for the use of specialist troops in aid of deceptive operations.

The delegation of command and control in respect of FORTITUDE has already been described. Let us now consider its effect upon the work of the Deception Staffs. The Joint Commanders had been made responsible for the detailed planning and control of FORTI-TUDE SOUTH in its physical aspects. Similarly the Army's share of FORTITUDE NORTH had gone to the GOC-in-C, Scottish Command. Thus from February until the middle of July, when SHAEF resumed the undivided control of FORTITUDE SOUTH, the main function of the Physical Deception Staff was one of co-ordinating the plans of the Joint Commanders in the South with those of the GOC-in-C, Scottish Command in the North, the latter becoming the executants. The function of the Special Means Staff was to adapt the plans, both North and South, to suit the needs of the channels under their control and then to plant them on the enemy.

Such was to be the organisation and distribution of responsibility for the development of the plans and for the control of the operation. Before proceeding further let us see what technical resources the Deception Staffs had at their disposal. Most of the technical processes by means of which FORTITUDE was carried out have been the subject of special reports to which reference is made in the footnotes. It is only necessary here to enumerate the principal methods employed and to point out their respective capabilities and limitations in order that the reader may appreciate how far each was able to contribute to the FORTITUDE story.

In view of the great importance attached to physical deception in the early days of cover planning, it was natural that COSSAC should lose no time in making its demands upon the Service Ministries in order that requirements could be met in time. The need for deceptive wireless being regarded as paramount, negotiations for marshalling the necessary resources were opened in the autumn of 1943 with the Admiralty, the War Office and the War Department at Washington. By the spring of 1944 there were in the United Kingdom four separate signals organisations available to carry out the wireless deception programme of FORTITUDE: 'No. 5 Wireless Group' to represent British land forces, '3103 Signals Service Battalion' for American land forces, 'Fourth Army' for British formations taking part in FORTITUDE NORTH, and the 'CLH' units to represent naval assault forces.

In forming No. 5 Wireless Group the War Office (Signals 9) introduced a number of original features. All traffic was recorded in advance, and the equipment required for that purpose was provided. A mechanism was devised which made it possible for one wireless transmitter to simulate six. Thus the wireless traffic of a divisional headquarters with its brigades might be represented by sounds emanating from a single wireless truck. This unit was equipped to provide the essential wireless communications of three divisions, either armoured or infantry. Becoming operational in February 1944, it was immediately placed under the command of 21 Army Group and so remained until its disbandment at the end of the war.[19]

To satisfy United States requirements, a complete wireless deception unit, 3103 Signals Service Battalion, arrived from the United States in the early spring of 1944 fully equipped and trained. The official claim for this unit was a capacity to represent a corps of one armoured and two infantry divisions. In fact, by omitting links below the divisional level, it was able in FORTITUDE SOUTH to represent no less than three army corps and nine divisions as well as

---

19. For further particulars of No. 5 Wireless Group and its subsequent activities see 'History of G (R) 21 Army Group and HQ. "R" Force, April, 1945', 'Notes on Wireless Deception for Operation OVERLORD 32/Security/15 (Signals 9), August 1944' and '"R" Force Wireless Activity 1st November, 1944 to February, 1945'.

the headquarters of an army group and an army. Unlike No. 5 Wireless Group, it used normal equipment. Traffic passed directly between operators without the intervention of recording apparatus, the wireless trucks moving through the country just as the formations which they represented would have done. When the Battalion first reached England it came under ETOUSA. Later it was placed under the command of Twelfth Army Group.

Scottish Command had no ready-made specialist signals unit to carry out the wireless programme required by FORTITUDE NORTH and therefore had to improvise. A team was made up from the 2nd British Corps and the 9th British Armoured Division, both formations being then in process of disbandment, to which were added personnel from Scottish Command and from certain miscellaneous small units. This unofficial group, which became active in March 1944, received the name of 'Fourth Army', the imaginary force which it represented. Like the American battalion it operated with normal signal equipment. In FORTITUDE NORTH it was able to represent one arm and two army corps. As the services of this improvised force were still needed after FORTITUDE NORTH had come to an end, it was given an establishment in July 1944 and received the name of 'Twelfth Reserve Unit'. As such it operated under War Office control.[20]

The formation of three 'CLH' units was undertaken by the Admiralty in the autumn of 1943. Each unit was designed to represent the naval force associated with an assault division. Like No. 5 Wireless Group, the 'CLH' unit operated numerous circuits from a single van but not on the recording system. Two of these units were ready for action at the end of March 1944. The third became active at the beginning of June. They remained at all times a part of the Signals Division of the Admiralty, being lent to commanders as required.[21]

20. An account of the organisation and activities of Twelfth Reserve Unit and of its predecessor 'Fourth Army' will be found in the SHAEF Deception Library Files relating to FORTITUDE NORTH and in the Library File entitled 'Organisation of Twelfth Reserve Unit'.
21. A full account of the 'CLH' units will be found in 'CLH/A/160–172/44, dated 7th July, 1944, Naval Report Operation NEPTUNE, Radio Deception'.

Unlike the Navy and the Army, the Air Force employed no specialised troops for wireless deception, but made its contribution by detailing operators for each particular task.

Two matters of general policy affecting the conduct of wireless deception in support of FORTITUDE call for attention. The first relates to controlled leakage, the second to dummy traffic. On the ground that it would place too great a responsibility on script writers and operators, and would tax their ingenuity unduly,[22] controlled leakage in FORTITUDE wireless traffic was at all times forbidden. This decision, of course, limited the scope of wireless as a vehicle of deception. It meant that the enemy could not be given the designation of an imaginary formation by this means, nor could it reveal intention except in so far as this could be deduced from the type and grouping of formations and the character of training.

Throughout FORTITUDE the use of dummy traffic was forbidden on the ground that the German cryptographers might deduce from the general pattern of the groups that behind the cipher there lay nothing but a random series of letters. The opposite view was held in the Mediterranean theatre. There it was thought that any increase of 'live' traffic added 'depth' to the cipher material and so made it easier for the enemy to break it. Wherever the true answer may lie, there can be no doubt that the use of live traffic involves a great deal of extra and very highly skilled work. It also exposes one to the danger of a leakage in the traffic, resulting from a slip on the part of an operator, which cannot arise with dummy messages.

In the field of camouflage and visual misdirection, the only extensive use that FORTITUDE made of special equipment was in the employment of dummy landing craft. These were supplied by the

---

22. This argument did not apply to No. 5 Wireless Group where traffic was recorded, since each recording could be perfected at leisure. 21 Army Group did in fact make some use of controlled leakage in deceptive operations after it had gone overseas. 'The encoding and phrasing of messages and conversations was often intentionally insecure in order to reveal the germ of the special idea it was desired to convey.' ('"R" Force Wireless Activity, 1st November, 1944, to 12th February, 1945'. Operation TROLLEYCAR TWO, Annexure 27 to Appendix 'E'.)

War Office (SWV8).[23] Between the middle of May and the middle of June 1944 two hundred and fifty-six were displayed. The few dummy aircraft used in FORTITUDE NORTH were supplied by the Air Ministry. Sir John Turner's department at the Air Ministry was responsible for installing and operating decoy lighting apparatus at fictitious embarkation points on the east and south-east coasts.

Both American and British Army Groups had under their command camouflage companies and specialist troops trained in the art of sonic warfare. Although these were used extensively overseas, they played no significant part in FORTITUDE.

Having completed this short catalogue of the physical resources, we must now examine the 'Special Means' channels in somewhat greater detail and discover the processes whereby controlled misinformation could be planted on the enemy.

'Special Means', as has already been explained, was the non-committal name given to all those channels which the Controlling Officer used for passing false intelligence to the Germans. Theoretically, there is no limit to the number of backstairs methods by which one can misinform the enemy; in practice, the only channels that were being used at all extensively at the end of 1943 were the German agents controlled by the British, the neutral embassies and legations in London, upon whose members it was sometimes possible to plant false information, and our own diplomatic representatives abroad, who could be asked, as the occasion arose, to repeat in the countries to which they were accredited the stories which we wished the enemy to believe. A certain amount of deception was practised by introducing false items of news into letters addressed to prisoners of war for the benefit of the German censors, while the Deception Staffs in Washington, in the Mediterranean and elsewhere were always willing to lend their services. The Special Operations Executive (SOE), the organisation controlling sabotage and the activities of resistance groups in enemy-occupied countries,

---

23. They were known by the code name 'BIG BOB'. For further details see 'Operation QUICKSILVER THREE – "BIG BOB", May to September 1944', dated 3rd November, 1944, and issued by the Director of Special Weapons and Vehicles, the War Office.

and the Political Warfare Executive (PWE), the British propaganda organisation, were both accounted possible deception channels at the disposal of the London Controlling Officer.

The agencies which controlled the three main channels referred to above were, for deception through the British Diplomatic Service abroad, the Foreign Office; for deception through the neutrals in London, MI5 (Diplomatic Section); and for the controlled agents, MI5 (B1A). When the TWIST Committee was abolished, SHAEF entered into direct relationship with MI5 in respect of the two last-named channels, but continued to deal with the Foreign Office through the London Controlling Officer. The latter also handled requests for help from other operational theatres.

SHAEF did not revive the TWIST Committee at Norfolk House, but found it easier to deal with each agency on a day-to-day footing. Before many weeks had passed, it became evident that the controlled agents provided far the best medium for the passage of false information to the enemy. With the diplomatic channels one could never be quite sure whom the story would reach and in what form it would arrive. As instruments of deception they lacked precision. Thus while visits between the Special Means Staff at SHAEF and B1A were soon of daily occurrence, meetings with LCS and MI5 (Diplomatic Section) became increasingly rare. By March attempts to plant stories on the neutral diplomatists in London had been given up altogether. On the other hand, the Foreign Office remained an occasional channel for strategic deception in support of FORTITUDE.

The point has now been reached at which we must examine the inner working of section B1A.[24] Before doing so, however, it will be necessary to make a few observations on the German Intelligence Service, without whose co-operation the double-cross system in the United Kingdom could not have existed.

The German Intelligence Service suffered to some extent from that dual control which affected the whole German conduct of the war and which arose from the struggle for supremacy between the

---

24. Much of what follows is based upon the official history of B1A, *The Double-Cross System in the War of 1939 to 1945* by J. C. Masterman, printed by MI5 in September 1945.

fighting services and the Party. So far as espionage was concerned, the matter was temporarily settled by a 'gentleman's agreement' arrived at in 1939 between Heydrich, the Party man and head of the RSHA,[25] and Canaris, the head of the Abwehr, whereby the latter was left in sole charge of the German spy system. The Abwehr, which combined the functions of security and secret services, possessed a widespread and well-established organisation with its Leitstelles in occupied countries and its Kriegsorganizations in the neutral capitals. As Himmler's power increased the Secret Intelligence Branch of the RSHA known as Amt VI, in spite of the agreement of 1939, began to run its own spies. But it displayed a singular ineptitude in the art of espionage; it put its agents in touch with each other and in other ways broke the most elementary rules. The Abwehr at least proved itself capable of administering a large network of British-controlled agents in the United Kingdom. The RSHA could not even do that. All the spies that we used in FORTITUDE were Abwehr agents. In spite of this, the Abwehr was now suffering eclipse on the home front. In the spring of 1944 Canaris was dismissed, being replaced by Hansen, and on 1st June, five days that is before the invasion, the whole Abwehr was taken over by the RSHA. This might have been a very serious thing for deception, and it caused a good deal of anxiety at the time. In the event, however, it turned out to be a gain rather than a loss. Although all the Abwehr chiefs were swept away, the machine was preserved, a course which the RSHA could in fact hardly avoid as it had nothing to put in its place. Now Schellenberg, the head of Amt VI, who replaced Hansen after the *coup d'état* of 20th July, was a more influential man than any of his Abwehr predecessors and for him to claim possession of our controlled agents could be nothing but an added strength to the Allied cause. There was some fear of the 'new broom' when Amt VI took control. It was thought that they would submit the easy-going Abwehr organisation to a close scrutiny, in which case we might have some difficulty in preventing our channels from falling under suspicion. As it turned out, however, the RSHA preferred to let well alone.

The old Abwehr's activities had not ended with the maintenance of the British-controlled network. It also purported to glean information

---

25. Reichssicherheits-Haupt-Amt.

about what was going on in this country from an equally spurious type of spy. Certain individuals, residing in neutral capitals, having persuaded the Abwehr that they controlled networks of agents operating in the United Kingdom, were able, by the exercise of ingenuity and imagination, to supply the Germans with a constant stream of intelligence which had little foundation in truth. They do not usually appear to have been actuated by any feeling of hostility towards the Central Powers, nor by a wish to help the Allied cause, but were moved either by a desire for personal gain or to avoid the inconvenience and hardship of active service.[26] These gentlemen generally met with a success which the quality of the information that they supplied would scarcely seem to have justified. To us they were always a nuisance and often a real danger. Sometimes, by intelligent guesswork, they came alarmingly near to the truth; at other times they talked such nonsense that they lowered the credibility of agents in general in the eyes of the military commanders, but unfortunately seldom went quite far enough to discredit themselves.

The fact that B1A effectively controlled all German espionage in the United Kingdom, and this was probably so from the beginning of the war, was only gradually realised. 'Dimly, very dimly, we began to guess at the beginning of 1941 that we did, in fact, control the enemy system, though we were obsessed by the idea that there might be a large body of German spies over and above those whom we controlled.'[27] The potential value of B1A's organisation as a vehicle for deception could not be fully appreciated until this state of affairs had become known, and it is true to say that in the early days of the war the main object of catching spies and 'turning them round' was not so much to help the deceivers as to prevent the Germans from

---

26. Recent evidence reveals that one or two of these uncontrolled agents had a few meagre sources of genuine intelligence in the United Kingdom. Although final judgment must be reserved, there is nothing at present to show that the Germans acquired any useful information in this way, or that the security ring round the British Isles was effectively penetrated at any time. It seems likely that the agents in question regarded these genuine contacts as an insurance – something which could be quoted if at any time their masters challenged the more extensive but more or less imaginary sources of intelligence which they had superimposed on these slender foundations.

27. *The Double-Cross System in the War of 1939 to 1945*, page 16.

knowing what was going on here, in other words to improve security. By controlling the agents who were already here, one had a better chance of catching the new arrivals. Also, so long as the Germans felt that they had a network upon which they could rely, there would be no need to replace it. The view of B1A was that as the Allies turned to the offensive and important operations came to be launched from this country, the value of their controlled agents as instruments of deception would increase, while the time that they were obliged to devote to their counter-intelligence role would, with the perfection of security arrangements in the United Kingdom, tend to diminish correspondingly. Their first notable contribution to operational deception was made in 1942, when measures were taken to conceal the landing in North Africa. They also played a part in COCKADE in 1943. It was always felt, however, that their great opportunity would come with OVERLORD.

In the absence of a deception policy, it becomes difficult at times to find enough for double-cross agents to say, that is, enough of the right quality. Once there is a deception plan, one has one's material ready-made, high-class and abundant, even if wholly inaccurate; but there was seldom enough of this, at least before the days of FORTITUDE, to satisfy the keen appetites of all the controlled agents. One had to maintain a reasonable standard of interest in their messages, yet by doing so there was always a danger of giving away a vital secret. 'It will readily be believed', writes the historian of B1A, 'that the ultimate responsibility for allowing any message to pass to the enemy is a dangerous power. In communicating with the enemy almost from day to day in time of war we were playing with dynamite, and the game would have been impossible unless the "approving authorities" had been willing to assume this ultimate responsibility.'[28] A solution was found in the creation in January 1941, under the auspices of the Directors of Intelligence, of the XX Committee, which held weekly meetings from then until the end of the war with Germany. The essential purpose of the Committee was to decide what information could safely be given to the Germans. It also acted as a clearing-house where the work of the various agents could be compared and kept within a reasonable measure

---

28. *Ibid.*, page xiii.

of consistency. In addition it weighed the needs of different departments and, if necessary, reconciled those of one with another. The members of the XX Committee, as representatives of the Directors of Intelligence or of the other departments affected, such as the Foreign Office and the Home Defence Executive, were in effect the approving authorities. Messages requiring approval were submitted at the weekly Committee meeting.

After each meeting of the Committee its members had the opportunity of seeing the officers in personal charge of the controlled agents and of agreeing with them the precise wording of any messages that were to be sent on their behalf so as to make sure that the style of the agent employed was not departed from and at the same time that the meaning was not obscured. Every controlled agent had such a 'Case Officer'. The Case Officer lived the life of the individual who had been placed under his care, was responsible for his domestic affairs and had to see that his messages were in character and that the reported episodes of his imaginary life were not contradictory. As deception began to play a larger part in the agents' traffic, a tendency developed for matters to be settled directly between the Case Officer and the approving authority of the Service or Department whose interests were being served by the deception. This arrangement was more expeditious since it avoided the necessity of having to wait for the next meeting of the Committee. The Committee was, of course, informed of all that happened.

By the time that SHAEF was constituted an approving authority this had become the established practice. During the weeks immediately preceding and following the invasion it would probably be true to say that messages in support of FORTITUDE constituted as much as three-quarters of the whole traffic sent. The substance of these messages was worked out, the traffic of the various agents dovetailed together and the final drafts approved by means of daily meetings between the Special Means officer at SHAEF and the Case Officers affected. On one or two occasions of particular importance the agent himself joined in the consultations.

When the partnership between Ops (B) and B1A was first established in January 1944, the detailed plans had not, of course, yet been written. We only had BODYGUARD and FORTITUDE to guide us and these dealt in broad trends rather than in detailed and precise facts. At this time the traffic was therefore supplemented by a method which had been introduced during the previous summer, when shortage of military material had been even more acute. This means of providing a constant flow of information on military subjects was found in the Field Security Report. Through the agency of GHQ, Home Forces, all the Field Security Sections in the United Kingdom were told to put themselves in the position of a German spy and to send in a fortnightly report of observations which, in their opinion, would have helped a spy to draw conclusions about the invasion. This was represented to the Sections as a security measure and copies were sent to the War Office (MI11), who, incidentally, found them to some value. The real object, however, was to give our controlled agents something to say. We could pick items from these reports which had all the attributes of realism because they had in fact been seen. B1A also employed an officer with a motor-car, who could supply local colour about places which the agents had visited in imagination only.

V

The Double-Cross Agents

At the beginning of 1944 B1A controlled fifteen agents of whom seven had the use of wireless transmitters, the rest having to rely upon communication by letter. Complete biographies will be found in the records of MI5. It is only necessary here to give short accounts of those who played a sustained part in the execution of FORTITUDE.

GARBO, a Spaniard by birth, was a political idealist. Service under Franco during the Spanish Civil War had convinced him that both sides in this quarrel were equally hostile to his own Liberal sympathies. It was to England, so he felt, that Europe must look for the maintenance of Liberal principles. In 1940 he approached the British authorities in Madrid and offered to work for them as an agent either in Germany or Italy. His offer was rejected. He then turned to the Germans, who accepted his services and placed him under the control of Kuehlenthal, head of the Abwehr in Madrid. Armed with an espionage mission supplied to him by his new employers he again approached the British. Being still unable to attract their interest, he settled down in Lisbon after the manner of other uncontrolled agents and from there kept up a correspondence with the Germans upon the footing that he was in England actively engaged in espionage on their behalf. At last, in the spring of 1942, after many vicissitudes, the British agreed to employ him and in April of that year he came to England. Being totally unacquainted with this country, he had during his sojourn in Lisbon committed himself to statements which required some ingenuity on the part of his Case Officer to explain away or weave into the subsequent development of the story. When giving the Germans an account of a visit to Glasgow he had remarked, 'There are people here who would do anything for a litre of wine.'

The most notable feature of his correspondence from Lisbon was the introduction of imaginary sub-agents. This system was greatly developed after his arrival in England and, indeed, became an underlying characteristic of the case. The imaginary sub-agent has some decided advantages in the world of deception. He can be created at will in any guise to suit any requirement. In building his character, one is not tied by the enemy's knowledge of his previous life and circumstances. If the sub-agent turns out to be wrong, the agent himself can blame the former's stupidity and so exonerate himself. This technique was brought to perfection by GARBO, who would seldom engage a new imaginary sub-agent without having previously consulted his German masters on the subject. He would also set them intelligence tests, in which they were not always successful.

By February 1944 GARBO had no fewer than twenty-four fictitious sub-agents each clothed with a character and a story of his own. Let us work our way round the chart entitled 'The GARBO Network'. Of the four agents, One, Two, Three and J(1), whom GARBO had recruited when he was still in Lisbon, only Three and J(1) remained. One had resigned after having become embroiled in STARKEY during the late summer of 1943. Two had died of a lingering illness in November 1942 because his place of residence at Bootle, near Liverpool, gave him inconvenient opportunities for watching the Allied convoys sailing to North Africa. Three, a Venezuelan of independent means, plays an important part in our story. Appointed Deputy-Chief by GARBO at the end of 1943, he had been let into all the secrets of the organisation. As he lived in Glasgow, GARBO relied on him for reports from Scotland. In order to cover the ground, Three decided to set up his own small network in the North. Of the three sub-agents that he recruited, only one took any active part in FORTITUDE, namely 3 (3), a Greek seaman deserter and an ardent Communist whom Three engaged on the pretext that he would be assisting Russian espionage against this country. 3 (1), the aviator, can be passed over as he played no part in the story. 3 (2) was a young officer in the 49th British Infantry Division whom Three had met in the train. During the autumn of

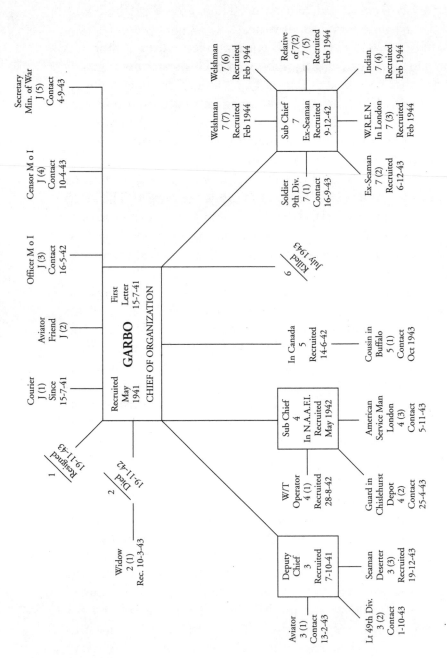

The GARBO Network

1943, when the 49th Division was still in Scotland, it had been proposed to represent it as an assault division for FORTITUDE
SOUTH. As this was changed later, 3 (2)'s usefulness automatically
ceased. This officer was an unconscious agent, that is to say, he had
no idea that Three was working for the enemy, and the latter had to
rely upon his indiscretions for information.

The origins of the sub-network of Agent Four, a Gibraltarian
waiter, are bound up with a rather mysterious story concerning the
caves at Chislehurst. For many months GARBO had been hinting at
strange developments in these caves which were in some way connected with the coming invasion. Four worked underground in the
NAAFI there and one of his sub-agents, 4 (2), was employed as a
guard at this great depot.[2] Four's other two agents, who were in no
way connected with the caves, were of greater value to the network.
Agent 4 (1), the wireless operator, provided the organisation with its
sole means of wireless communication with the German control in
Madrid. This man, a peace-time amateur and strong friend of the
Republican Party in Spain, believed that the encoded messages which
he sent and received were passing between Dr Negrin in London and
the Spanish Communists. GARBO pointed out that by this device
he and his network would be protected if the transmitter were found.
4 (3), the third member of Four's sub-network, was an American sergeant employed in an unspecified military headquarters in London.
Though playing his part unconsciously, he made an important contribution to FORTITUDE and disclosed military secrets not often
vouchsafed to soldiers of his rank. GARBO described him as being
'sociable, jocular and fairly talkative'. His political outlook was said
to be 'anti-Communist and, to a lesser degree, anti-English
Imperialist, following in part the ideas of Randolph Hearst, sustain-
ing an admiration for Franco as Catholic crusader and first leader in
the struggle against the Bolshevik'.

[Note 1 is missing in the original.]

2. The Germans took GARBO's reports about the Chislehurst caves seriously,
even if their interest was sometimes tinged with incredulity. When the invasion
came, a suitable occasion for exploiting the story did not present itself and the
Germans were ultimately informed, in August 1944, that the caves had been
used for storing arms for the Maquis.

Agent Five, a brother of Three and therefore also a Venezuelan, had gone to Ottawa in the summer of 1943 after having exposed himself to danger on a mission to the Isle of Wight and South Wales during the previous year. His cousin, 5 (1), lived across the border in Buffalo, USA. It was hoped that they might be useful for reporting invasion preparations on the other side of the Atlantic. In fact, this was never found necessary. In the later months of the war, however, Five provided a valuable refuge for members of the network who were escaping from the law. Agent Six, having been killed in North Africa in July 1943, does not concern us.

The sub-network of Agent Seven, the largest in the organisation, was specifically recruited to support the threat to the Pas de Calais.[3] Seven was an ex-seaman who lived in Swansea. He was described as 'a thoroughly undesirable character', his incentive for working being purely mercenary. Foreseeing that it would be necessary to post agents along the south and south-east coasts as observers for the coming invasion, GARBO had asked Seven to find suitable candidates from amongst his Welsh friends. On 6th December Madrid was informed that Seven had had the good fortune to meet the leader of a small subversive organisation in Swansea whose members felt that by helping the enemy they would be advancing their own cause. 'A friend of Agent Seven', wrote GARBO to his master, 'has been a member of the "Welsh Nationalist Party", but he had advanced ideas and he was not pleased with the Liberal sentiment of the Party, maintaining that the emancipation of his country would depend entirely on the establishment of what he calls "Aryan World Order Movement" to collaborate with all the Aryans all over the world. On account of this he left the Party more than two years ago and joined an Indian, a friend of his, who has lived for many years in this country, forming a group which he calls "Brothers in the Aryan World

---

3. In the summary of Agent Seven's sub-network which follows no account is taken of 7 (1), a soldier in the 9th British Armoured Division, who had no connection with the others in the group. An 'unconscious' agent, this man's position was very similar to that of the young officer in the 49th Division. It had been supposed in the autumn of 1943 that the 9th Armoured Division would play a prominent part in the deceptive operations of the coming year. As with the 49th Division this proved to be an incorrect forecast. Thus 7 (1) does not appear in the ensuing narrative.

Order". As its position, owing to being clandestine, is very dangerous, they have had little success, as only about twelve revolutionary
members are affiliated, and their activities are very limited and rather
ridiculous.' The members were said to spend most of their time in
making lists of names of Communists and Jews who must be elimi-
nated when their aspirations were achieved.

Besides the leader of Aryan World Order, whom GARBO designated 7 (2), and his Indian friend, now called 7 (4), four other
members of the group agreed to join the spy ring. These were 7 (3),
the secretary and mistress of the Indian, lately enlisted in the WRNS,
and 7 (5), 7 (6) and 7 (7), who were merely described as Welsh
Fascists, 7 (5) being a relative of 7 (2). None of the sub-agents working under Seven knew at this time of GARBO's existence. At the
same time Seven believed that he controlled the whole of GARBO's
spy system in this country and had no knowledge of the rest of the
organisation.

In addition to those agents already described, it will be seen that
there were five more bearing the letter 'J' followed by a number.
J(1), as already stated, had been invented by GARBO before he came
under British control. When, in 1941, he was pretending to be in
England, he had to explain how he was still able to communicate
with Madrid. He therefore told them that he had persuaded an official of one of the airlines, who travelled frequently between England
and Portugal, to post his letters for him in Lisbon. At the same time
he told the Germans to put their letters to him in a safe deposit at
one of the Lisbon banks of which, he told them, this same official
had the key and would collect them in due course. J(1) was the official who assumed this role of courier. As GARBO could no longer
post and collect letters himself after he had come to England, the task
was then undertaken by a British Secret Service representative in
Lisbon, this arrangement being continued until the end of the war.
Of the remaining four, J(2) and J(4) may be passed over as they
played little or no part in FORTITUDE. J(3) and J(5), on the contrary, can claim a large share in the development of the story. A note
written by GARBO's Case Officer in February 1944 tells us that J(3)
'could possibly be identified as the head of the Spanish Section of the
Ministry of Information. For a time GARBO was employed by him
on translation work for the MOI. He is suited for the passing of

high-grade information of a political or strategic nature. He has frequently been quoted by GARBO as one of his best sources. He believes GARBO to be a Spanish Republican refugee and treats him as a close personal friend. He is an unconscious collaborator.' J(5) he described as 'a secretary in the Ministry of War, probably working in the Offices of the War Cabinet. She is carrying on an affair with GARBO, whom she believes to be a Spanish Republican. Unconscious collaborator who has already been very indiscreet and could pass on very high-grade political information. This source has been quoted by Madrid, when reporting to Berlin, as "The Secretariat of the Ministry of War".'

In viewing the GARBO network as a whole, the most important thing to remember is that apart from GARBO himself every one of the characters was imaginary. The methods of communication were by wireless to Madrid with the aid of 4 (1)'s transmitter and by letter through the courier J(1). A second letter service by means of a courier was arranged by Seven, but was never used to any extent. If GARBO had been put out of action, the network could still have continued to operate through the deputy, Three, who knew all its ramifications. Had the system collapsed entirely at the centre, Seven could in all probability have continued to employ his sub-network, communicating with Madrid by means of the courier service that he claimed to have established. Thus the organisation was practically indestructible.

GARBO would never give the Germans the names of his sub-agents because, as he pointed out, this exposed them to an unnecessary risk of compromise. The Germans, on the other hand, gave them all pseudonyms for their own convenience; thus Three's group of agents came to be known as the BENEDICT network, Four's group as the CHAMILLUS and Seven's as the DAGOBERT, each agent within the network having his own designation. It is not necessary to give all these code names,[4] but the reader may care to remember that 7 (2), 7 (4) and 7 (7) were known respectively to the Germans as DONNY, DICK and DORRICK. These names reappear later in a highly significant context.

*

---

4. Facetiously, the Germans bestowed on 7 (5), the sub-agent whom GARBO sent to observe troop movements in Devonshire, the code name DRAKE.

We will now turn to the case of BRUTUS. Though less bizarre in his methods than the Spanish agent, he probably ranks equally with him as a channel for strategic deception. BRUTUS was a Polish officer who escaped to France after the end of the war against Poland in 1939. He set up an espionage network in that country, which continued to work with great success in the Allied cause until November 1941, when, as the result of treachery by sub-agents, he was arrested and his organisation rounded up. He was kept in prison for several months where tentative approaches were made by the Germans in the hope that they might persuade him to collaborate with them. In the spring of 1942 he allowed them to suppose that their efforts to convert him were gaining ground, and in July he accepted a mission to go to England as a German spy. He was provided with crystals for constructing a wireless set and given an escape story to explain his release from prison. On arrival in this country he immediately told the authorities about his mission, was accepted as a double-cross agent and soon afterwards established wireless contact with the enemy. Although there was reason to believe that he was highly regarded by the Germans, the Directors of Intelligence did not feel justified in allowing him to be used for deception. Not only did BRUTUS work in reality at Polish Headquarters, but the Polish Deuxième Bureau had knowledge of the true facts of the case and were in a position to monitor his traffic. In February 1944, as nothing untoward had occurred and in view of the great potentialities of the case, this decision was reversed and in March BRUTUS joined the FORTITUDE team. His chief characteristics were a keenly trained eye for military observation and an extremely retentive memory. In December 1943 he recruited an imaginary wireless operator, an elderly retired member of the Polish Air Force. BRUTUS informed the Germans that this individual, who was given the code name CHOPIN, had lost his family in Russia and would be working principally from idealistic motives.

The third controlled agent who stood in the first rank at this time was TRICYCLE. At the beginning of the war TRICYCLE was a Yugoslav subject and a lawyer by profession. His political sympathies were markedly pro-French and pro-Allied. He was recruited by the

Abwehr in Belgrade in August 1940 through the intermediation of
JEBSEN alias ARTIST, who has been described by TRICYCLE's
Case Officer as one working for the Abwehr on a half-commission
basis. TRICYCLE immediately reported the approach which had
been made to him to the British Embassy in Belgrade and thereafter
acted throughout under British instructions. He was placed under
the control of the KO in Lisbon and reached this country in
December 1940. On arrival, he was made assistant to the Yugoslav
Military Attaché and the Germans were informed of this. Unlike
most of the British double-cross agents, he maintained direct personal contact with his German masters, giving them verbal reports
and receiving lengthy questionnaires on his periodic visits to
Portugal. As the Germans believed that TRICYCLE was making
these journeys in their interest, he had to explain why the British
authorities allowed him to go. He therefore told them that the British
were organising an escape route for the use of airmen in Yugoslavia
who were trying to reach this country. The journey would be made
via Portugal. The British authorities had invited him to co-operate in
the scheme. If he were willing to do so, they would arrange for his
passage to Lisbon. TRICYCLE pointed out to his masters that this
was an opportunity not to be missed and if they could, in fact,
arrange from time to time for the escape of an airman from
Yugoslavia his chances of repeating his visits would be improved. The
Germans, appreciating the cogency of his arguments, fell in with the
scheme. After TRICYCLE had come to England, ARTIST himself
came over to the Allied side, but kept up his close relations with the
Abwehr. When TRICYCLE was interviewed by his controller in
Lisbon, ARTIST would attend the meeting, and if TRICYCLE
seemed to be getting into difficulties, would throw in a question
seemingly suspicious but, in fact, skilfully calculated to draw the
conversation away from the dangerous topic. Besides being able to
communicate by means of these personal reports and by secret writing, TRICYCLE had the use of a wireless transmitter. This
transmitter was operated by another agent, FREAK. FREAK and
TRICYCLE worked very closely together and can practically be
regarded as a single channel.

Contemporary opinion would probably have placed TATE, another
wireless agent, as next in degree of importance. TATE, a confessed

Nazi, was dropped by parachute in September 1940. After his arrest he was imprisoned for some time, but when B1A had gained the impression that he was anxious to co-operate, he was released and allowed to live in a house to the north-west of London with a guard. Wireless contact with his German masters in Hamburg was established in October 1940 and had continued ever since. This was somewhat surprising because he had been given an extremely low-grade cipher; indeed, his traffic was constantly being reported to MI5 by the British Monitoring Services. This defect did not appear to strike the enemy. It did, on the other hand, lead some members of the XX Committee to think that the case was unsafe and should be closed. In 1943 an incident occurred which was even more damaging. Through an oversight, a German prisoner of war who knew that TATE was under British control was repatriated. The arguments for bringing TATE's career as a double-cross agent to a close were strong. While the decision as to his continued employment still lay in the balance, the Germans provided him with a better code. This new mark of confidence had its effect and it was ultimately decided to retain his services and to include him as a member of the FORTITUDE team. Wireless agents were at a premium, their great advantage over the letter-writers being speed and certainty of communication. Furthermore, we knew that a ban on foreign mail was to be imposed in due course, which would make the letter-writers almost valueless during the weeks immediately preceding the invasion.

The only other wireless agent was TREASURE. She was never rated very highly and probably would not have been used at all but for the fact that she had a transmitter. TREASURE, a temperamental French lady of Russian origin, had lived most of her life in Paris, where she had gained a reputation at one time as an artist and later as a journalist. Before the war she had been approached by a German journalist friend, a member of the Abwehr, and asked by him if she would supply intelligence reports on the Civil War in Spain. This she had refused to do. After the fall of France she got in touch with this man again and told him that she was willing to work for the Germans. After receiving the usual training, a wireless set and a control in Paris, she was sent to Madrid en route for England. Here she made contact with the British authorities, disclosed her mission and put herself at the disposal of the Allies. She arrived in England in August 1943 and took up her residence in Bristol.

All the remaining agents employed in FORTITUDE were letter-writers only, and none of them occupied a position in the first rank. BRONX, the daughter of a South American diplomatist, lived in a smart cosmopolitan circle and was able to quote the opinions of those whose names and pictures appeared in the columns of fashionable newspapers.

GELATINE, an Austrian lady, also had a wide circle of friends. Her predilection for the company of the opposite sex made her useful for reporting such things as the stopping and reopening of Service leave. She was constantly being cheated of her assignations.

SNIPER, a Belgian Air Force sergeant-pilot and rather a drab character, worked at the Belgian Air Force Headquarters in London, a fact which was known to the Germans. His mission was to obtain technical Air Force information. He differed from the other agents inasmuch as he received communications from his control in Brussels by wireless but had to send his answers by letter.

To understand the case of MULLET and PUPPET, a little background history is required. HAMLET, a well-to-do Austrian Jew, had settled in Brussels before the war. In 1941 he received permission from the Germans to set up a company in Lisbon to exploit in Portugal certain inventions of which he held the patent rights. He also established relations with the Abwehr and agreed to supply them with intelligence reports, using his Lisbon business as a cover for espionage. He then proceeded to adopt the familiar expedient of establishing an imaginary network of agents and, by the end of 1942, he was able to convince the Germans that his organisation had representatives in England and the USA. HAMLET's next step was to offer his soi-disant espionage organisation to the British. Arrangements were now made, with British connivance, for the appointment of two businessmen, MULLET, an Englishman, and PUPPET, an Austrian, to represent HAMLET's commercial interests in London. These gentlemen were portrayed to the Germans as well-placed spies, with a good business cover, employed by HAMLET. Of course they were really British double-cross agents working back to the Germans through HAMLET. Communication was made by writing in invisible ink between the typewritten lines of MULLET's business correspondence.

The other B1A agents who were operating at this time either took no part in FORTITUDE or such a minor part that their inclusion here has not been considered necessary.

In addition, there were two controlled agents in Iceland, COBWEB and BEETLE. As MI5's jurisdiction was limited to British soil, the control of these agents came automatically under MI6. All matters affecting these two agents were therefore settled between SHAEF and an MI6 representative. COBWEB and BEETLE, both of them young Norwegians and both wireless agents, had been landed in Iceland by submarine. They worked independently and did not know of each other's existence.

We had one triple-cross agent in the team. At the beginning of the war TEAPOT, a German who lived near Hamburg, was the manager of a co-operative food store with numerous branches all over Germany and a branch in Istanbul. While visiting the latter place he professed anti-Nazi sentiments and was recruited by the British as a straight agent at the end of 1943. It was soon afterwards discovered that he was in actual fact a German counter-espionage agent. Nevertheless it was felt that he might still have his uses, and so the British, feigning ignorance of his treachery, continued to employ him. From the point of view of deception his value lay in the fact that the Germans might be expected to draw conclusions as to our intentions from the nature of our apparently unsuspecting questions. Communication was effected by means of a wireless link between MI6 and TEAPOT's residence near Hamburg.

Finally, there was PANDORA, not strictly a double-agent channel at all but included here for convenience. It had long been suspected that HEMPEL, the German Minister in Dublin, provided the Germans with military intelligence. Anonymous letters were therefore written to him from time to time, ostensibly from the pen of some fanatical Irish anglophobe. Into these letters could be inserted occasional items of deception.

VI

First Steps

BODYGUARD had given SHAEF the task of making the Germans believe in the 'reoccupation' operations, in the attack on Norway and in a postponed cross-Channel assault. It had also called for a cover plan to deceive the enemy as to the 'timing, weight and direction of OVERLORD', when invasion preparations could no longer be concealed. FORTITUDE had translated these requirements into the terms of an operational plan, while the FORTITUDE directive had allocated responsibility for executing each part of the plan. FORTITUDE SOUTH, the cross-Channel threat, had gone to the Joint Commanders. In the execution of FORTITUDE NORTH, the threat to Norway, SHAEF and Scottish Command were to collaborate. Both these threats were to be supported by Special Means, operating under SHAEF control. This still left the 'reoccupation' operations and the 'postponement' policy. The latter, having been embodied in the Pas de Calais threat, would not, under the terms of the FORTITUDE directive, come into operation until the Joint Commanders felt that the time was ripe. Yet BODYGUARD had introduced it as a feature of the strategic programme to which effect should be given at once and which should not have to wait until the Joint Commanders' plan was set in motion. In the event it fell to the lot of Special Means, after the New Year, to see that these two requirements of BODYGUARD were satisfied.

When it came to the test, the task of informing the Germans that 'balanced forces are being held in readiness to occupy any part of North-West Europe in the event of German withdrawal or collapse' was not so easy as might have at first appeared. As GARBO succinctly commented when first reporting the matter to the Germans: 'It does not require a very wise man to deduce that should the way be left free they would not hesitate to take advantage of it.' However, he was able to give convincing proof of the existence of such plans by stealing from the office of his friend, J(3), at the Ministry of Information a document, prepared for issue after a German withdrawal from France, calling upon the population to co-operate with the Allied occupying troops.[1]

Let us remind ourselves of the methods suggested by BODY-GUARD for encouraging a belief in a later target date. Shortage of landing craft, a belittling of the strength of Allied forces in the United Kingdom and delayed long-term preparations were to create the illusion of unpreparedness. An exaggerated scale of assault was to make the necessary state of readiness appear to be more difficult of attainment than was in fact the case. The task of spreading these stories was shared between the double-cross agents and the diplomatic channels in the hands of the London Controlling Officer. Only a few cursory examples can be included here from the large and varied range of stories which were planted on the enemy in order to make him believe in a late summer invasion.

The method most favoured for indicating a shortage of landing craft was to play up the strikes in America. 'Labour troubles in the United States', said TATE on 20th January, 'have curtailed production of invasion barges to such an extent that the dates of future operations may be affected.'[2]

The backwardness of training was mainly associated with General Montgomery's recent assumption of command. 'There is an opinion held amongst us', said BRUTUS on 23rd January, 'that Montgomery will probably, as in Egypt, train all the troops over again.'[3]

The delay in long-term preparations was applied equally to real activities in the South and to invented ones in the South-East. For example, METEOR[4] on 2nd March wrote that work on widening

---

1. This forgery entitled 'Avis à la Population' was printed with a proper regard for correct detail and was sent to the Germans.
2. TATE 1815 MET 20th January, 1944.
3. BRUTUS 1435 GMT 23rd January, 1944.
4. One of the lesser double-cross agents.

and improving roads in the Portsmouth and Southampton area was continuing but 'without any signs of hurry', while TRICYCLE in his conversations with his masters in Lisbon was told to refer to such things as the proposed sinking of artesian wells at embarkation camps in Kent. Any attempt to convey to the enemy the impression that we intended to employ an augmented striking force for our late summer assault was necessarily deferred until more was known about the Pas de Calais operation. Before that time arrived, as will presently be seen, 'postponement' had been abandoned. In consequence this part of BODYGUARD was never put into effect.

A passing reference must be made to two other themes not so far mentioned because under the terms of BODYGUARD they remained the responsibility of the London Controlling Officer, but which had a direct bearing on 'postponement'. One of these sought to link the invasion date with the Russian summer offensive and suggested that the Western Allies would not attack until after the Russian offensive had been launched. The other carried 'postponement' as far as it could be carried by suggesting that the invasion would not take place at all since the Allies relied on bringing Germany to her knees by bombing alone.[5] Both stories were supported by the controlled agents as well as by diplomatic means. The Russian theme was never pursued with much vigour owing to the uncertainty that prevailed regarding the real Russian plans.

As the spring advanced, many good reasons were being adduced for dropping the 'postponement' policy, but what probably dealt it its death-blow was the decision to hold Exercise FABIUS, an invasion rehearsal, in the Channel early in May. We could hardly hope to conceal such a large-scale manœuvre from the enemy, since all the assault divisions and their associated naval forces were due to take part in it, while the Germans would be most unlikely to believe that we proposed to give our invasion forces a trial run over the course as much as ten weeks before the invasion was due to take place. After the beginning of March it will be found that these stories of a late summer invasion no longer find a place in the Special Means traffic.

---

5. This theme was generally referred to as POINTBLANK, the name of the real programme for bombing the interior of Germany.

Before leaving the subject of 'postponement', it will be convenient to refer to FOYNES, the plan initiated by the London
Controlling Officer to conceal the transfer of the eight battle-
trained divisions[6] from Italy to this country, a movement which
had been proceeding since November 1943, for this plan was
designed, not only to exaggerate our strength in the Mediterranean,
which Allied strategy then demanded, but also to belittle our
strength in the United Kingdom as part of the policy of 'postponement'. To achieve this end the formations concerned were
placed on wireless silence after their arrival in this country,[7] and
other normal security precautions were taken. At the same time
their mention was forbidden to the controlled agents. This involved
the latter in large-scale evasion, for by the New Year German suspicions were already aroused. Such well-known formations as the
50th British Infantry and 51st Highland Division had disappeared
from the Italian front. Fishing for information, they asked
BRUTUS on 11th January: 'What are the British divisions which
have been withdrawn from Italy and have come back to Britain?'[8]
The sudden outcrop of Africa Star medals which was to be
observed in all parts of the country led us to the conclusion that it
would be difficult to conceal from the enemy that a large number
of troops had, in fact, returned from the Mediterranean. Feeling
that it would be wise to meet trouble half-way, we accordingly
made the agents say that these were key-men, trained in battle, who
had been sent home to act as instructors for the invasion armies.
'English troops wearing the Africa Star have been seen and it is presumed that these have returned from the Mediterranean to help in
the training of the less experienced units.'[9] 'On New Year's Eve I
met some officers of the Eighth Army who were wearing the new
yellow-red ribbon of the African campaign. They said that they had

---

6. 1st United States Infantry Division, 9th United States Infantry Division, 2nd
   United States Armoured Division, 82nd United States Airborne Division,
   50th British Infantry Division, 51st Highland Division, 7th British Armoured
   Division and 1st British Airborne Division.
7. This ban was observed by the British formations until the invasion, but ceased
   to be observed by the American formations in February 1944.
8. BRUTUS Message received 1201 GMT 11th January, 1944.
9. MULLET and PUPPET Letter despatched 29th December, 1943.

been exchanged for officers from this country to lecture and teach the troops.'[10]

At the middle of March, since 'postponement' was being dropped and since the ban on the use of wireless was interfering with signals training, SHAEF proposed that the operation should be concluded. The Commander 'A' Force, however, was unwilling to do so, because it remained his task to exaggerate the Allied strength in the Mediterranean and for that purpose FOYNES was of value to him. A compromise was reached whereby the FOYNES divisions were released one by one from 1st April onwards. When the invasion took place the 7th British Armoured Division and the two airborne divisions alone remained subject to the ban.

This disposes of two out of the three demands which BODY-GUARD made upon SHAEF in respect of the 'overall' strategic programme. There remains the Norwegian threat to consider.

---

10. GELATINE Letter despatched 16th January, 1944.

VII

FORTITUDE NORTH

Let us recall what FORTITUDE said about the operations against Norway and the instructions which it gave for their execution. FORTITUDE provided for two landings on the Norwegian coast. One was to be made in the North by two divisions, which were subsequently to co-operate with Russian forces with the object of opening road and rail communication with Sweden. The other landing was to be made at Stavanger. An assault division, supported by commandos and parachute troops, was to capture the surrounding airfields to which long-range fighters were to be flown from the United Kingdom. This force was to be built up to a total of six divisions within three months, a part of the force being mountain trained. An advance to Oslo was to be made along the coast 'by a series of mutually-supporting land and amphibious operations'. Diplomatic pressure on Sweden having meanwhile secured to us the use of Swedish airfields, an assault was to be launched against Denmark as soon as the Allies were firmly established in Southern Norway, their Air Forces operating from there and from Southern Sweden.

In view of our limited resources and of the fact that Scotland's geographical position would make intensive reconnaissance by enemy aircraft difficult, it was agreed that elaborate visual misdirection, which was regarded as essential in the case of FORTITUDE SOUTH, would not here be necessary. Apart from one naval operation, the concentration of shipping in the Firth of Forth, and the display of a few dummy aircraft on Scottish airfields, FORTITUDE NORTH was executed by wireless and Special Means alone.

As is usual with plans of military deception, the foundation of FORTITUDE NORTH was provided by its Order of Battle. Before any real formation could be included one had to be satisfied that it was in the right place and that its location would continue to be suitable so long as the operation lasted. Before including imaginary formations one had to be sure that there were resources available to represent them on the air. An army was required to control both the operations; at least three army corps, one for the North and two for the South; and eight divisions, two for the North and six for the South, of which two had to be assault trained. In Scotland there were two British divisions, the 52nd Lowland Division near Dundee and the 3rd Infantry Division carrying out assault training in the Moray Firth in preparation for the real invasion. There was a large Polish force scattered over the Lowlands, a small Norwegian contingent at Brahan Castle near Dingwall, and a British Independent Brigade, the 113th, in the Orkneys. In addition there was the imaginary Fourth Army which had been created during the previous year to command the forces engaged in TINDALL. It was represented as an offshoot of Scottish Command having its headquarters a few miles from Edinburgh. It had ceased to operate, however, about November 1943. At that time, none of the real formations in Scotland, except the 3rd British Infantry Division, had been given any operational role connected with the invasion.

In Northern Ireland there was the 55th British Infantry Division (Lower Establishment) and an American Corps, the XV, with under command the 2nd, 5th and 8th United States Infantry Divisions. Although intended for ultimate employment in Normandy, the American force was not expected to leave until about three weeks after the invasion had started. The 55th British Infantry Division was performing garrison duties and might therefore be expected to remain in Ireland as long as we needed it. In Iceland there was the imaginary 55th United States Infantry Division which had been first reported about a year before by the British-controlled agents and had since been kept alive by COBWEB and BEETLE, the two double-cross agents who resided in that island. This division had never been represented on the air because it was held to be outside the normal range of the German intercept stations.

THE NORTHERN FORCE

Fourth Army

Currie near Edinburgh

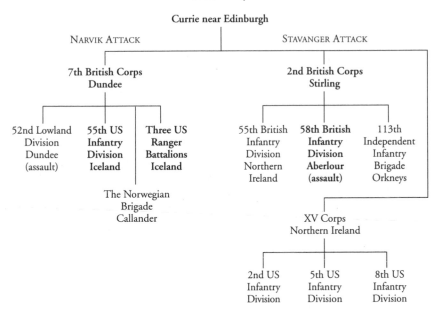

NARVIK ATTACK | STAVANGER ATTACK

7th British Corps
Dundee

2nd British Corps
Stirling

52nd Lowland
Division
Dundee
(assault)

55th US
Infantry
Division
Iceland

Three US
Ranger
Battalions
Iceland

55th British
Infantry
Division
Northern
Ireland

58th British
Infantry
Division
Aberlour
(assault)

113th
Independent
Infantry
Brigade
Orkneys

The Norwegian
Brigade
Callander

XV Corps
Northern Ireland

2nd US
Infantry
Division

5th US
Infantry
Division

8th US
Infantry
Division

Formations printed in heavy type were imaginary

With these forces, real and imaginary, at our disposal, the Order of Battle was built up in the following manner. The Fourth Army was to be brought to life again to command the entire force. For the Northern operation the 52nd Lowland Division was to be trained to carry out the assault and elaborate preparations were initiated to simulate assault training, first by brigades and then as a whole division, in the Clyde. For the follow-up formation the imaginary American division in Iceland was chosen, it being supposed that it would sail direct to Narvik immediately after the assault had been made. It was to be strengthened by three imaginary ranger battalions which would come from the United States to Iceland before the attack was launched. The Norwegian contingent in Scotland was also to be included in the force. No real corps being available to command the Northern force, an imaginary one was to be created. This came into being in March 1944 and was known as the 7th British Corps. Its wireless traffic was simulated by signallers of the recently disbanded 9th British Armoured Division. For the Southern assault the 3rd British Infantry Division, which had already been assault training in the Moray Firth for some time and whose activities we supposed must by now have become known to the Germans, was chosen, its follow-up division being the 55th British Infantry Division, stationed in Ireland. To command these two divisions, the 2nd British Corps was selected. This Corps, which had been stationed for some time at Scotch Corner in Yorkshire, was, in fact, in process of disbandment. Arrangements were therefore made to retain a small skeleton staff and a sufficient number of signallers to simulate its continued existence, and for its name to continue to appear unaltered in the War Office records. Under command of this, the assault corps, was also placed the 113th Independent Infantry Brigade in the Orkneys. The role of follow-up corps for the Southern operation was to be filled by the American XV Corps in Northern Ireland, with its three infantry divisions under command, the presumption being that they would sail direct from Belfast. This still left us one division short, for it will be remembered that FORTITUDE laid down six divisions for the Southern operation. However, with wireless resources strained and with no other real division available, it was decided to make do with a total of five. The Polish Divisions in Scotland could not be used; not only would their employment in an expedition involving Russian co-operation have been unrealistic from a political point of view, but there were security objections. Finally, a naval assault force capable of lifting one division was required for the Northern attack. The naval assault force for the Southern attack was already provided by the real 'S' Assault Force associated with the 3rd British Infantry Division in the Moray Firth.

This grouping of forces having been agreed as the result of consultations between SHAEF, GHQ, Home Forces, and Scottish Command, SHAEF on 10th March, 1944, issued instructions for assembling the necessary wireless resources.[1]

The first criticism of these proposals came from the Navy, who expressed the view that it would not be possible, taking into account the wireless silence periods which, of course, imaginary as well as real forces had to observe, to make the assault training of the 52nd Lowland Division seem realistic in the time allotted. The sailing

---

1. SHAEF/18216/1/Ops, dated 10th March, 1944.

date for the Northern operation was therefore postponed until 15th May. The sailing date for the Southern assault remained at 1st May as originally planned. Then a more serious difficulty arose. The Joint Commanders decided that it would be necessary to carry out a full dress rehearsal in the English Channel a month before the invasion was due to take place. This was the exercise FABIUS to which reference has already been made. The 3rd British Infantry Division being one of the real assault formations would, of course, have to take part in it. This would presumably be noted by the enemy and would prove to them that the division was not intended for an assault on Stavanger at the very moment when we wanted FORTITUDE NORTH to be exercising its strongest influence, for it will be remembered that, according to our calculation, it took a German division three weeks to travel from Norway to France. The proposal to employ the 3rd British Infantry Division in FORTITUDE NORTH had always been open to criticism. Before the rehearsal was contemplated, the intention had been to simulate its wireless traffic in the Moray Firth after it had left for the South, and so make the Germans go on believing that it was bound for Norway until it actually appeared on the Normandy beaches. Taking the long view this was a dangerous proposal, for it might have provided the Germans with conclusive evidence that the whole of FORTITUDE NORTH was deceptive on the very day of the invasion. Be that as it may, the decision to hold Exercise FABIUS forced the issue and so the 3rd British Infantry Division was dropped from the Order of Battle and an imaginary one substituted. This explains the otherwise unaccountable absence of assault training from the programme of the imaginary 58th British Infantry Division, which was created to take the place of the real assault formation. It was generally agreed that an attack over the open Stavanger beaches required a higher degree of training than that which the 52nd Lowland Division was called upon to undertake in its northern deep-water fjord. The training programme for the Northern force had now been perfected with the sailing date of 15th May. The Southern operation had relied upon the participation of 'S' Force and the 3rd Infantry Division. These were now suddenly withdrawn. So we find in the final programme that the 58th Infantry Division and its associated naval assault force have to content themselves with a mere embarkation and disembarkation exercise in preparation for an invasion against 'a very lightly defended part of Southern Norway'.[2]

The unexpected demand upon wireless resources caused by the creation of the 58th Infantry Division was met by 21 Army Group, who lent a detachment of 5 Wireless Group to represent it on the air. This newly formed division, which made its first appearance at Aberlour, south of Inverness, was supposed to have been recruited in the North and to have been built round a cadre of battle-trained officers and NCOs withdrawn from well-known Scottish regiments lately returned from the Mediterranean theatre. The formation sign, a pair of stag's antlers, was suggestive of the Highlands. It will be remembered that we were at this time trying to conceal from the Germans the return from the Mediterranean of certain formations, including the 50th British Infantry and 51st Highland Divisions.[3] There was always a danger of the enemy learning that troops belonging to these two formations had returned to the United Kingdom. In that event it was hoped that they might draw the conclusion for the time being at any rate, that these were merely drafts sent home to provide a cadre for the new division.

The Fourth Army wireless programme opened on 22nd March and by 6th April the whole network was active both in Scotland and in Northern Ireland.

Early in April two 'CLH' units, known respectively as Force 'V' and Force 'W', began their imitation of the naval assault forces in the Clyde. Force 'V' was to take part in the Northern operation and Force 'W' in the Southern.

From this point it will be easiest to follow the mounting of the two operations separately. Let us take the Southern assault first. Until 14th April the three brigades of the 58th Division were engaged in mountain training at Aviemore, Kincraig and Dufftown. On that date the whole Division moved south-west in the direction of Glasgow, conducting a series of mountain exercises as it went. On 23rd April it became associated on the air with its naval assault force. This association was confirmed on the 25th and 26th by the wireless

---

2. 'Naval Report Operation NEPTUNE, Radio Deception', Appendix 'B', dated 19th July, 1944, para. 4 (ii).
3. Plan FOYNES.

traffic of an exercise in embarkation and disembarkation at Greenock. At the beginning of May the division retired to the east of Glasgow, where it could be heard continuing its training. Throughout this period the 2nd British Corps at Stirling simulated a number of signals and administrative exercises of its own. Meanwhile in Northern Ireland, the 55th British Infantry Division, the follow-up formation for the Southern assault, and XV Corps, which was to provide the build-up, continued their normal training. In order to emphasise their operational connection, however, it was arranged that the British formation should take part in an exercise directed by the American Corps at the end of April.

Turning to the Northern assault force, any record of the 52nd Division's activities is complicated by the fact that it was a real formation, and its real movements did not always correspond with its fictitious ones.[4] For the purposes of FORTITUDE NORTH, it was required to show that the Division contained one assault and two follow-up brigades. It was decided to allot the latter role to the 155th and 156th Brigades, which were thus able, for the time being, to continue their real training without interruption. The 157th Brigade, on the other hand, which was allotted the assault role, was placed on wireless silence and represented by its signals as being in close association with the Combined Training Centre at Troon. By 12th April this brigade had established contact with Force 'V' in the Clyde, and on 24th April it was to be heard exercising in Loch Fyne. During a wireless silence period at the beginning of May the Division moved, in reality, from Angus to Kilmarnock. On 10th and 11th May a full-scale landing exercise with one assaulting brigade and two following-up brigades was simulated with Force 'V' in Loch Fyne. During this period the whole Division had to remain on wireless silence. Thereafter fiction and reality were able to coincide once more and the 52nd Division revealed itself with its Divisional Headquarters at Kilmarnock and its Brigades exercising in the neighbourhood.

The follow-up formation for the Northern attack, the 55th United States Division in Iceland, was, of course, imaginary. No link was

---

4. The following account is somewhat oversimplified, but does not involve any material distortion of fact.

established between it and 7th Corps Headquarters, but the volume of traffic on the United States link between ETOUSA and Iceland was increased. Like 2nd Corps, 7th Corps from the middle of April engaged in signals and administration exercises. During the wireless silence at the beginning of May, Headquarters 7th Corps moved from Dundee to Beith, a short distance south-west of Glasgow.

Thus, at the middle of May, we find all the land forces and all the naval assault forces destined for the two Norwegian operations assembled near the Clyde and ready to sail at short notice. The move of Fourth Army Headquarters from Edinburgh to Ayr, which it was hoped would complete this picture of imminent action, though already planned, had not yet taken place.

In addition to the assistance given by the two 'CLH' units in the Clyde, the Navy helped FORTITUDE NORTH in two other ways. First, on 26th April, C-in-C, Home Fleet, carried out a carrier-borne air reconnaissance operation off Narvik.[5] Second, it was arranged with the Ministry of War Transport that surplus shipping should be berthed at Methil in the Firth of Forth, with the result that the average number of ships anchored there rose from twenty-six in the first week of April to seventy-one in the second week of May. The concentration was supposed to represent part of the build-up force.

During the second half of April and first week of May, the Royal Air Force, by the display of dummy aircraft and the manipulation of wireless traffic, simulated the transfer of four medium bomber squadrons from airfields in Suffolk to others in Eastern Scotland. At the same time a flight of eight real Spitfires was stationed at Peterhead, to which eight dummy Spitfires were added. This was to provide protective cover for the medium bomber force.

It was the opinion of the operational staff at AEAF that if we were going to attack Scandinavia, we should not begin softening raids until about three days before the attack. For this reason no cover bombing was carried out. Similarly the existing scale of reconnaissance over Norway by carrier-borne aircraft was considered adequate and therefore, apart from the naval operation already mentioned, no additional measures were proposed.

---

5. Operation VERITAS.

VIII

FORTITUDE NORTH (Continued)

If FORTITUDE NORTH provided the largest wireless project hitherto undertaken, it also constituted the first attempt, at any rate in
the United Kingdom, to organise the controlled agents into a balanced and mutually-supporting team for the attainment of a
particular object and to plan their part in an operation just as one did
that of the forces engaged. For in order to be able to report to the
Germans those things which we wanted them to believe, it was as
important for the observer as for the things observed to be in the
right place at the right time.

The first task that lay before B1A and the Special Means Staff was
therefore to decide which agents were best fitted to tell the enemy
about each part of the operation and to see that their movements and
the circumstances of their lives were adjusted to meet the calls which
were now to be made upon them. It was in February 1944 that the
Directors of Intelligence lifted the ban which had until now prevented BRUTUS from being used for deception. He had a good
reason for visiting Scotland inasmuch as the majority of the Polish
troops were stationed there and he was recognised by the Germans as
a highly trained military observer. To BRUTUS, therefore, was given
the main responsibility for reporting on Scottish Order of Battle
and locations. For Northern Ireland FREAK was chosen. We had no
agent with Northern Irish connections, but as FREAK was a military
attaché, he seemed as likely as anyone to hear about this part of the
FORTITUDE NORTH Order of Battle. PANDORA in Dublin
was thought to be too unreliable. On account of his residence in
Glasgow, GARBO's agent Three was to cover the naval exercises in

the Clyde, while his sub-agent 3 (3), a seaman, was to be sent to Methil to watch the shipping concentrations there. Several of the lesser agents were to be made use of as the occasion offered.

Before FORTITUDE NORTH was set in motion, we had reason to suppose that the Germans already believed three things. First, that Fourth Army existed, or at any rate had existed in the autumn of 1943, as an offshoot of Scottish Command with its headquarters near Edinburgh. Second, that the 52nd Lowland Division was in the east of Scotland; they had had this both from our controlled agents and from their own Intercept Service. Third, that the 55th United States Division was in Iceland. They had been told this repeatedly by COBWEB and BEETLE.

Two days before the wireless net opened on 24th March, FREAK reported the arrival of the 2nd British Corps at Garter House, near Stirling, from Scotch Corner in Yorkshire.[1] A week later GARBO's agent, Three, said that he had seen in Dundee the 52nd Lowland Division as well as an unidentified formation with the sign of a shell on a dark background. Referring to the latter GARBO commented: 'This insignia is completely unknown to me.'[2] Two days later, on 30th March, FREAK ran into an officer from the American XV Corps in London, who told him that this formation was in Northern Ireland with the 2nd, 5th and 8th Infantry Divisions under command. His informant also mentioned that the 55th British Infantry Division was in Ulster.[3] Finally, he added the significant fact that he himself was stationed in Edinburgh and was attached to the staff of General Thorne, the Commander of Fourth Army, the reason being that XV Corps had been put under Fourth Army.[4]

Let us see what the Germans should have discovered by 1st April as a result of these reports. The location of Fourth Army at Edinburgh was confirmed. General Thorne was now its commander. It had under it the American XV Corps in Northern Ireland, which

---

1. FREAK 1413 GMT, 22nd March, 1944.
2. GARBO 1920 and 1924 GMT, 28th March 1944.
3. This division had previously been located in Sussex and had recently changed places with the 45th British Infantry Division. These movements were reported by PANDORA on 20th January to the German Minister in Dublin.
4. FREAK 1355 and 1403 GMT, 30th March, 1944.

comprised the 2nd, 5th and 8th United States Infantry Divisions. The 2nd British Corps had just moved to Stirling. It was, therefore, not unreasonable to suppose that it might be connected in some way with Fourth Army. The 55th British Infantry Division was in Northern Ireland and a strange insignia had been seen at Dundee. On this fragmentary intelligence the Germans might have been able to reconstruct the following grouping of forces:

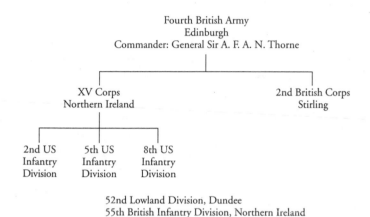

The most informative of these reports had been sent by FREAK. It was therefore only right that he should have received the highest commendation from his German masters. 'Your latest wires very satisfactory. Please continue. Congratulations. Wire as often as possible and watch out carefully in course of next few weeks. Please state exact numbers of divisions, &c., belonging to Fourth Army under General Thorne. Is anything pointing to intended landings in German Bay, Denmark, also Southern Sweden?'[5]

Let us follow the process a stage further. In a letter which was expected to reach the Germans about 6th April,[6] GELATINE told them how she had proposed herself to a friend in North Berwick for Easter, but had been put off on the ground that a 'visitors ban' was about to be imposed in the district. Her correspondent had gone on to say that her husband was working for General Thorne, who 'had

5. FREAK Message received 1204, 1212 and 1234 GMT, 12th April, 1944.
6. GELATINE Letter No. 5 in secret ink to Lisbon, dated 12th March, 1944.

been given command of some new army or other they are forming'.
The husband was to have an American for his deputy and was going
to ask the General if he could get 'Bud'. GELATINE then explained,
in the covering letter, that her friend in North Berwick was an
American married to an Englishman and that 'Bud' was her brother
and was stationed in Northern Ireland. This confirmed the connection between Fourth Army and XV Corps as well as the presence of
American officers at Fourth Army Headquarters.

Early in the month BRUTUS had told the Germans that he
would have to visit Scotland shortly for a conference with the Poles.[7]
Returning to London on 12th April he sent a series of messages
which filled in most of the remaining gaps.[8] Fourth Army, with its
headquarters at Edinburgh (insignia, a rectangle divided into stripes
of red, black, red horizontally with a design like the figure 8 in
yellow, the bottom part of the lower circle being missing)[9] was composed of 2nd British Corps with its headquarters at Stirling (insignia,
three wavy blue lines on a white rectangle and a red fish obliquely,
the head at the top)[10] and 7th Corps, headquarters in the Dundee
area (insignia, a sea-shell on a blue rectangle). This explained Agent
Three's observation in Dundee on 28th March. BRUTUS had heard
that the Fourth Army also included an American Corps, but he had
not been able to identify it. He had found the 58th Division
(insignia, a stag's head full face on a black square) in the district
south-east of Stirling, and the Norwegian Brigade at Callander.[11]
Many of the men of the 58th Division were wearing the Africa Star
medal. He had also seen the Lowland Division (insignia, an oblique
white cross on a blue shield with black outline) in the Perth–Dundee

---

7. BRUTUS 1733 GMT, 31st March, 1944.
8. BRUTUS 1203, 1210, 1216, 1221, 1227 and 1236 GMT, 15th April, and
   0907 and 0916 GMT, 16th April, 1944.
9. This imaginary insignia consisted of the medieval four placed upon the normal
   Army colours of red, black and red. Whether the enemy ever appreciated the
   significance of the hieroglyphic is not known. Like many others that we
   invented it appeared in due course among the instructional coloured plates of
   British formation insignia which were issued to the German troops.
10. This, of course, was the sign of the disbanded 2nd Corps which had fought at
    Dunkirk and was therefore well known to the Germans.
11. The Norwegian Brigade had in fact just moved from Brahan to Callander.

area and to the North. Finally, he mentioned that a British brigade stationed in the Orkney Islands was said to belong to this Army.

Four days later, on 20th April,[12] COBWEB reported from Iceland that he had heard from an American lieutenant that the 55th US Infantry Division was under the command of the 7th Corps, the latter being in Scotland. Thus, by the end of the month, Fourth Army had been confirmed beyond doubt at Edinburgh, with the 2nd and 7th British Corps under command as well as an American corps whose number was unknown to BRUTUS, but which FREAK had already identified as XV Corps. The composition of the 2nd British Corps had not yet been disclosed to the Germans, but they had been told that its headquarters were at Stirling and that the 58th British Infantry Division was in the immediate vicinity. COBWEB had told them that the 55th US Division was under the command of the 7th British Corps and they had learnt from BRUTUS that the 52nd Lowland Division also was near Dundee, where the 7th Corps Headquarters was situated. There was the Norwegian Brigade in Perthshire, and a British brigade in the Orkneys. The April budget of intelligence from the controlled agents might therefore have allowed the Germans to reach the following tentative conclusion:

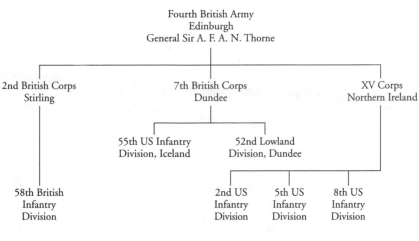

Fourth British Army
Edinburgh
General Sir A. F. A. N. Thorne

| 2nd British Corps | 7th British Corps | XV Corps |
| Stirling | Dundee | Northern Ireland |

55th US Infantry   52nd Lowland
Division, Iceland   Division, Dundee

58th British   2nd US   5th US   8th US
Infantry   Infantry   Infantry   Infantry
Division   Division   Division   Division

55th British Infantry Division, Northern Ireland
British Infantry Brigade, Orkneys
Norwegian Brigade, Callander

---

12. COBWEB 1220 GMT, 20th April, 1944.

With that Special Means felt that it had made as large a contribution to the FORTITUDE NORTH Order of Battle as it was safe to do. At the same time it must not be supposed that the controlled agents confined themselves to bare observation of troop movements in Scotland, refraining from any hint of Fourth Army's operational role, beyond that which the location and training of its formations might imply. These, indeed, could hardly fail to suggest Scandinavia as the objective and the agents did not hesitate to draw the obvious inference. BRUTUS's Scottish report concludes with a plain statement that an attack on Norway must be expected at the beginning of May.[13]

Naval developments were being watched at this time by GARBO's agents 3 and 3 (3) in the Clyde and on the Forth. The former followed with interest the movements of the naval assault forces off Greenock and sent an eye-witness account of the big exercise in Loch Fyne on 10th and 11th May.[14] He ended his report by expressing the belief that the manœuvre was a preliminary to an attack and, since the division concerned had been provided with arctic equipment, it was to be presumed that Norway was the objective. 3 (3), who arrived at Methil on 1st April and was to remain there for some six weeks, sent periodical reports on the shipping assembled there. He learned from sailors in the port that an operation was pending, that this concentration was for the transport of supplies and that the troops engaged would embark from other Scottish ports.[15] In order to provide corroboration from another quarter, TEAPOT, the triple-cross agent in Hamburg, was asked to send reports about the traffic on the Hamburg–Flensburg line and through the Baltic ports.[16]

It was to be hoped that the combined effect of the measures already enumerated would be enough to convince the Germans that Norway was the objective and May the target date. But FORTITUDE NORTH had more to tell than that. There were to be two attacks. There was to be Russian co-operation in the North. Diplomatic

---

13. BRUTUS 0923 and 0937 GMT, 16th April, 1944.
14. GARBO 2018, 2036, 2044, 2055, 2102, 2118, 2124 and 2140 GMT, 14th May, 1944, and 1902, 1914 and 1922 GMT, 15th May, 1944.
15. GARBO 1920 GMT, 27th April, 1944.
16. TEAPOT Message No. 9 sent 1630 BST, 9th April, 1944.

pressure was to be brought on Sweden in order to secure to us the use of Swedish airfields, and as soon as the Allies were firmly established in Southern Norway, an attack was to be launched against Denmark. Since calculated indiscretions on the wireless were not allowed, only Special Means could enlighten the Germans on these points.

The strongest evidence of an intention to attack in more than one place was provided by Plan PREMIUM. This ruse, which was used to help the threat to the Pas de Calais as well as the Norwegian operation, was entrusted to MULLET and PUPPET. At the beginning of February MULLET announced that he had accepted part-time employment at the Fire Office Committee.[17] This Committee has for many years provided a meeting ground for the leading British insurance companies where matters of common interest can be discussed, and has accumulated at its City office copious records about buildings and other insurable effects in all parts of the world. When the war came and communication with foreign and neutral countries practically ceased, these records proved to be of considerable value to the Service departments, a fact which was duly noted by MULLET, who, about a month after his appointment, drew the attention of the Germans to the numerous requests that were being made by 'Civil Affairs' Headquarters for inspection of documents in the Committee's possession.[18] He had the ingenuity to see that the places about which they required information might have an operational significance. For the time being, interest appeared to centre chiefly in Northern France and the Low Countries. 'They are requesting at the present moment urgent information on (1) flour mills, (2) bakeries, (3) cold storage plants, (4) printers.' Details of the places affected were then given.[19] Three days later there came a change of priorities and similar information was now required about Norway. 'Norway has been divided into two main sectors: one in the South and the second in the Narvik area. MULLET had details about Aalesund, Bergen, Oslo, Larvik,

---

17. MULLET and PUPPET Letter No. 54 in secret ink to Lisbon, dated 2nd February, 1944, to arrive 25th February.
18. MULLET and PUPPET Letter No. 64 in secret ink to Lisbon, dated 11th March, 1944, to arrive 2nd April.
19. *Ibid.*

Stavanger, Moss, Skien, Porsgrund, Kristiansand, Trondheim. I believe from the urgency of the requests that something is very definitely afoot in this direction, both because the strictest secrecy is imposed and because only trustworthy members of the Fire Office Committee have been informed about it, these being the people who will handle the work.'[20] About a month later MULLET was still working on the bakeries in Norway and, to lend colour to the story, he gave the names of some real bakers, 'Nordby and Olsen in Oslo, Kristensen in Kristiansand, Moller in Larvik'.[21] These names were, of course, extracted from the records of the Fire Office Committee, which we had borrowed. At the end of April MULLET was able to announce that he had finished his work on Norway and was back on Belgium and Northern France.[22]

The brief which TRICYCLE took with him to Lisbon at the beginning of March allowed him to speak of close Anglo-Russian military co-operation as a possible indication of an impending attack on Norway. But the only positive evidence of such collaboration was provided by BRUTUS on 4th May[23] when he stated that, according to his headquarters, a Russian military and naval mission had installed itself in Edinburgh.

It was the responsibility of the London Controlling Officer to bring diplomatic pressure to bear upon Sweden. With that end in view Plan GRAFFHAM[24] was devised. In March 1944 we really were making certain demands upon Sweden through diplomatic channels, the chief one being an attempt to prevent them from exporting ball-bearings to Germany. If to those demands which we genuinely wished the Swedes to concede could be added others, genuinely presented with the object of increasing enemy suspicion but to whose concession we did not attach any real importance, the threat to Norway might well be heightened. Accordingly, a number of such additional demands were framed. His Majesty's Minister, supported

---

20. MULLET and PUPPET Letter No. 66, dated 15th March, 1944, to arrive 5th April.
21. MULLET and PUPPET Letter No. 74, dated 14th April, 1944.
22. MULLET and PUPPET Letter No. 76, dated 25th April, 1944.
23. BRUTUS 2010 GMT, 4th May, 1944.
24. COS (44) 126 (O), 30th April, 1944.

by his United States and Soviet colleagues, was to present to the Swedish Government demands for the following facilities:

(1) Right of all civil aircraft to land at Swedish airfields, thus avoiding coming within the range of German fighters.
(2) Permission to send British transport experts to consult with the Swedish experts regarding transport of supplies to Sweden and Norway in the event of a German withdrawal.
(3) Permission for PRU aircraft to operate for survey and reconnaissance purposes over Sweden.

It happened that the Minister was in London during March. This made it possible for the London Controlling Officer to brief him personally. The very fact of his presence here could also be turned to our advantage. Thus TATE reported on 25th March: 'Mallet, British Ambassador in Stockholm, is in London for special conferences, according to a friend who knows him well. After intensive interviews he is going back there very soon. Said to be taking back extra staff. Friend believes that important negotiations with Sweden are being started.'[25] Other high officials and senior officers visited Stockholm shortly afterwards to add an air of reality to the negotiations.

The connection between the attack on Southern Norway and the subsequent capture of Denmark was not an easy thing to suggest to the enemy. It implied a knowledge of future plans which an enemy agent would seldom have the good fortune to acquire. BRONX did her best with the following: 'Commander, who is at the Admiralty, thinks that the logical place for invasion is Denmark and said that his Rear-Admiral was of the same opinion in spite of the difficulties of air support which would be resolved by the occupation of South Norway.'[26]

If some of the finer points in the story still remained unresolved, it was felt that this would do us no great harm. Indeed, so long as the German Commander in Norway believed that we were coming soon, lack of precise information as to where the attack was to be made would tend to make him stretch his forces, and that, after all, was what we wanted.

---

25. TATE 1834 MET, 25th March, 1944.
26. BRONX Letter dated 17th March, 1944, to arrive 31st March.

IX

The Camouflage Policy Reversed

The large scheme of visual misdirection inaugurated by COSSAC in the autumn of 1943 depended, on the one hand, upon the concealment or display of *real* warlike preparations and, on the other, upon additions to these preparations made for the sole purpose of deceiving German spies and reconnaissance aircraft. The policy of 'concealment and display' had been set in motion in September and was now being actively pursued by the Commands affected. Permission to embark on the 'false'[1] preparations had been given by the Chiefs of Staff at the end of November when they reviewed APPENDIX 'Y', and by the end of February 1944, when the Joint Commanders were entrusted with the detailed planning, some progress had been made. It was recognised at the outset that these 'false' preparations were bound to compete with the mounting of the real invasion in the demands that they made on manpower, materials and movement facilities. In October 1943, when APPENDIX 'Y' was still being written, the Director of Movements at the War Office had sounded a warning note: 'I must stress that this paper, as it stands, suggests the provision of additional shipping and movement activities which are impracticable.'[2] When the time came, however, for the Q (Ops) Committee at the War Office to

---

1. In this context 'false' preparations are intended to denote those preparations, real enough in the physical sense, which were undertaken solely for deceptive reasons, and which were not required for OVERLORD.
2. 120/General/1744. Q (M) 6/29/17, dated 21st October, 1943. Director of Movements, the War Office to G-3, COSSAC.

allocate the administrative resources available, their deliberations were characterised by efforts, not so much to settle rivalries between real and cover demands, as to discover what the cover demands were. These proved extraordinarily difficult to formulate. On 9th February SHAEF issued a guidance letter to the War Office[3] indicating the movement and administrative preparations required in the East and South-East *in addition* to those required for the embarkation of the OVERLORD forces. Constructional work undertaken for the purpose of deception was to continue 'as far as Command resources allowed', but until OVERLORD D minus 30, the main effort would be directed towards completing the real preparations. After that date the effort was to be transferred to the cover programme. This fitted in with the later target date for the Pas de Calais and avoided a direct conflict between the demands for real and 'false' preparations, since it was hoped that construction for the real operation would have been completed, or very nearly so, a month before the invasion date. The guidance letter of 9th February contained a number of miscellaneous provisions, some of them repeated from APPENDIX 'Y', which, it was felt, would add realism. Preparations were to be made for the reception of casualties and prisoners-of-war in South-Eastern Command. Military stores were to be displayed in the 'cover' areas. Members of the National Fire Service were to be moved in. Training units were to be evacuated.

The letter did not omit a reference to the conflict arising from our adherence to a postponed D Day, which affected this aspect of the plan just as it complicated every other. The story which would be told until the invasion took place was of an attack in July. From D Day onwards the Germans were to believe that the second assault might be launched at any moment. 'It will be seen that the two stories are in conflict as the first has a target date of NEPTUNE D plus 45, while the post D Day operation has a target date of, or just after, NEPTUNE D Day. Long-term preparations should therefore indicate the later target date while those final preparations, which take a comparatively short time to complete, should be delayed until the last possible moment compatible with apparent completion by D

3. SHAEF/1820/4/Ops, dated 9th February, 1944. SHAEF to the War Office (MO2).

Day.' This may be taken to mean that while such things as road-making and building should be proceeding apace during the month of May, such last-minute preparations as the appearance of convoys on the roads and the sweeping of shingle off the hards should be left as late as possible and, presumably, until after the real invasion had begun.

The letter also gave an indication of movement requirements. Until the invasion day it would be unnecessary to introduce real troops for deceptive reasons into the South-East of England for if they were not to embark until the middle of July, there would be no need for them to move into their concentration areas until June. Directly after the invasion date, however, when the story had changed, troops would be needed immediately and in strength. It was therefore proposed that as soon as operations in Normandy began, two real build-up divisions, one British and the other American, should move into the 'cover' area and 'spread themselves about' to make each camp look as if it were filling up.[4]

The directive of 26th February, relating to the command and control of FORTITUDE, informed the Joint Commanders that the guidance letter of 9th February 'had been issued to the War Office, which was interpreting this direction in detail to Commands through General Headquarters, Home Forces, Q (Ops) and Q (M) channels'. When 21 Army Group, together with the Naval and Air Commanders, took charge of the detailed planning, the fulfilment of many of its provisions still lay in the future and were, therefore, as yet no more than topics of active discussion at the Service Ministries, GHQ, Home Forces, and the Commands. On the other hand, some positive visual deception was already being practised on the ground. Thus, on 9th February, GOC in C, South-Eastern Command, reported to GHQ, Home Forces, as follows: 'The picture that I wish to convey to the Germans at this date is that although the camps are not being allowed to fall into disrepair, there is at present no sign of their being occupied by troops in the near future. This is being effected by small routine repair parties of Royal Engineers or Pioneers carrying out work in the camps, and also by some camps

---

4. S/00/355/6/G (O), dated 28th January, 1944. MGGS, GHQ, Home Forces, to BGS, South-Eastern Command.

being occupied from time to time for a few days by troops who may be training near them. As embarkation areas are for the most part in built-up areas, there is at present nothing for German reconnaissance to note and I am content that this should be so for the present. Some of the Hards have been covered with shingle washed up by the tides. The Navy has so far taken no steps to remove this shingle which should be a further pointer to the Germans that no immediate use of the Hards is contemplated. At some Hards, embarkation extension piers are being built and this will show up to any German air reconnaissance, and will give the correct impression that these Hards are to be used sometime in the future and are not being allowed to become derelict.'[5]

21 Army Group had never agreed with this extensive programme of physical deception. The presence of shipping in the ports rather than the construction of camps round these ports, they argued, would be looked for by the enemy as an indication of where the attacking forces would be coming from and of the scale of the attack. The enemy had made no inland air reconnaissance and even if he did, owing to the character of the British landscape, with its woods, towns and villages, he would be unlikely to discover much, providing that camouflage discipline was strictly enforced. So far as the enemy agent was concerned, they argued that the omission of preparations was less dangerous than the inclusion of those which the spy might recognise as deceptive. These costly measures would do little good and might do much harm.[6]

About the middle of February, when it had became clear that the Joint Commanders were to be entrusted with the detailed planning,

---

5. SE/00/3/BGS, dated 9th February, 1944. GOC in C, South-Eastern Command to GHQ, Home Forces.

6. As an example of the scale of effort involved, a statement by the MGA, South-Eastern Command, during a meeting held at the War Office on 3rd February, 1944, may be quoted: 'Accommodation could be provided to the full capacity of our ports,' he said, provided that (a) £80,000 worth of construction was carried out, (b) Wrotham Camp and Gravesend Barracks were made available for the Gravesend sector. Wrotham Camp and Gravesend Barracks, which were occupied respectively by 148 Training Brigade and 96 PTC, would have had to be evacuated.

21 Army Group decided to translate their views into action. At a meeting held on 23rd February the Chief of Staff, 21 Army Group, stated that the cover plan would now be governed by the following principles:

(i) There would be no camouflage policy of concealment in one area and display in another.

(ii) Concealment would be obtained by strict unit and formation camouflage.

(iii) Where possible new construction would be concealed, but not if it impaired the efficient working of camps or prevented their erection by the target date.

(iv) There would be no requirement for troops, camps or special preparations for cover purposes.

(v) the method of implementing the cover plan would be confined to –

The display of dummy craft.

The clearing of such hards as would not be employed in OVERLORD.[7]

On the following day 21 Army Group requested SHAEF to cancel any instructions which the latter had issued in connection with the camouflage, administration and movement preparations for the cover plan and to inform the War Office accordingly.[8] This meant the abolition of 'discreet display' in Eastern and South-Eastern Commands and the substitution of normal camouflage discipline, which was now to be practised in all areas. Maximum concealment was to give way only to operational necessity. The two divisions, one British and one American, and all the ancillary preparations which were to herald their arrival in the 'cover' area would no longer be required. Only the display of dummy craft and the clearing of hards were to remain.

---

7. Minutes of a meeting held at HQ, 21 Army Group, 1200 hours, 23rd February, Part 1 (c), issued under cover of 21 AGP/00/261/17G (R), dated 24th February, 1944.

8. 21 AGP/00/261/17/G (R) (1), dated 24th February, 1944. 21 Army Group to SHAEF G-3 Division.

Having considered 21 Army Group's request, SHAEF replied on 4th March.[9] In its view, the course proposed by 21 Army Group would expose us to unacceptable risks, both with regard to enemy air reconnaissance and to leakage through agents. Referring to air reconnaissance: 'Although there has been no extensive enemy overland air reconnaissance since 1941 either by day or night, the enemy is capable of obtaining photographic cover of a coastal belt of about fifteen to twenty miles deep, from the Wash to Land's End in about ten days of fine weather. Such cover would reveal the extent to which particular areas have been, and are being, developed for the movement and embarkation of troops. . . . If no preparations other than those required for NEPTUNE are made, it is considered that the enemy could deduce that no large-scale operation involving a high rate of build up was contemplated in the Pas de Calais.' With reference to enemy agents: 'The relative absence of preparations in Kent and East Sussex compared to the rest of the Channel coast is very obvious at the present time, and must be corrected. It is considered that information disclosing lack of essential preparations is more prejudicial than information suggesting that preparations are of a deceptive nature. The enemy will require confirmation, and if air reconnaissance discloses the presence of extensive preparations despite any reports he may have about their deceptive nature, he cannot afford to neglect the fact that these preparations have been made.' The letter concluded with the direction that the policy initiated on 22nd September, 1943, with regard to 'concealment and display' and that for the extension of movement and administrative preparations laid down in the letter of 9th February should be carried out. 'It is considered that failure to carry out any preparations essential to an operation in the Pas de Calais, when our resources allow such preparations, is an unacceptable breach of security, both from the point of view of enemy air reconnaissance and leakage.'

Under the FORTITUDE directive of 26th February 21 Army Group was entitled to deal directly with the War Office and GHQ, Home Forces. Doubt having been expressed[10] as to whether the

---

9. SHAEF/18209/Ops, dated 4th March, 1944. Chief of Staff SHAEF to Headquarters 21 Army Group.
10. SHAEF/18216/Ops, dated 16th March, 1944. DAC of S, to AC of S, G-3, Division, SHAEF.

latter were clear about this, SHAEF on 15th March wrote a letter for the guidance of those concerned. Having recited the policy letters of 22nd September, 1943, and 9th February, 1944, the FORTITUDE Directive of 26th February, 1944, and the letter of 4th March, 1944, upholding the existing policies, SHAEF concluded: '21 Army Group is therefore now empowered to arrange direct with the War Office and GHQ, Home Forces, for the continuation of the measures already initiated, adjusted as may be desirable and feasible with the resources and time available to support the detailed plan of the Joint Commanders, prepared under the directive given them and executed within the framework of the policies mentioned above.'[11] The only adjustment which seemed desirable and feasible to 21 Army Group was a return to the policy which had been put forward by them on 23rd February and rescinded by SHAEF on 4th March; in fact this paragraph was treated as an escape clause. Ten days later an instruction[12] issued to Commands through GHQ, Home Forces, gave effect to 21 Army Group's wishes.

This may seem a free interpretation of SHAEF's letter of 15th March. But the days were passing, the invasion was now little more than two months away, and the German spies and reconnaissance aircraft had not appeared. And so this reversal of camouflage policy was now found acceptable by all concerned.

---

11. SHAEF/18216/Ops, dated 15th March, 1944. SHAEF to 21 Army Group.
12. S/00/355/1/G (O), dated 26th March, 1944. GHQ, Home Forces, to South-Eastern, Southern, Eastern Commands and London District.

X

The Joint Commanders' Plan

As a result of the reversal of policy in the field of visual deception, which has been recorded in the last chapter, the fulfilment of the plan was now destined to rely basically on wireless and the controlled agents. Control of the latter having been reserved by SHAEF, the detailed plan of the Joint Commanders, in so far as it was concerned with a threat to the Pas de Calais, thus became in essence a programme of wireless deception.

As with FORTITUDE NORTH, the Order of Battle was to provide the foundation for the new plan. The Order of Battle for the Pas de Calais operation had exercised the minds of the Deception Staff at COSSAC since the previous summer, but in the early days it was difficult to know how far to go. It was always assumed that the Joint Commanders would be made responsible for detailed planning and it was realised that the sham Order of Battle was bound to depend largely on the real one, whose composition was not yet known. On the other hand, it was felt that both wireless and Special Means should have as long as possible to impress the false Order of Battle on the enemy. For that reason a start was made in September 1943. At that time the only available guide was to be found in the successive drafts of APPENDIX 'Y'. According to this plan, it will be remembered, the continuation of the threat after D Day was to be a mere diversion carried out by a force of six divisions; for the period antecedent to the invasion day no precise scale of assault was specified in the plan, but it could be assumed that the force would comprise the real invasion armies, together with the six divisions which had to be found for the post-assault phase. In the latter part of

1943, therefore, the deception requirement appeared to be for an army of two corps each containing three divisions, one of these divisions to be an assault division and another a follow-up division. This being so, it was decided to make GHQ, Home Forces, into the imaginary army, and on 19th September it was connected by two wireless links to 21 Army Group.[1]

During the ensuing months there were two arrangements which alternately seemed to find favour. These are given below:

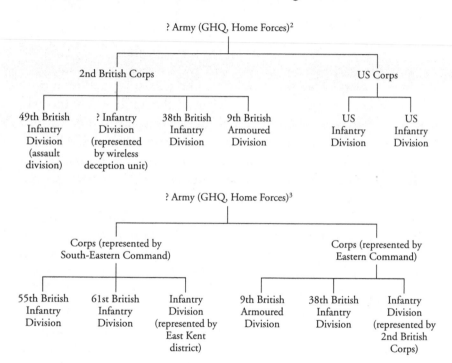

Both had GHQ, Home Forces, as the Army, but in one case 2nd British Corps and an unspecified United States Corps were to be employed, while in the other case Eastern and South-Eastern Commands were to represent two corps. Under the first arrangement, which was already taking shape in October, the 49th British

---

1. 21 Army Group Signal Instruction No. 1, dated 1st September, 1943, Appendix 'W'.

2. COSSAC/2356/Ops, dated 14th December, 1943.

3. SHAEF/18219/Ops, dated 29th January, 1944.

Infantry Division was to be used in the assault. The reader will remember this as being the reason for the recruitment of GARBO's contact 3 (2), who was reported to have said, in October 1943, that the 49th Division was the best in the country and would 'form the bridgehead' when the invasion came.[4] By December, however, views had changed, and on the 3rd of that month a wireless network on fixed lines was opened representing the second arrangement shown above.[5]

A decisive turn was given to deceptive planning, and one which was to have a profound influence on the Order of Battle, by General de Guingand's letter of 25th January, 1944, in which he proposed that, after the invasion had taken place, the Pas de Calais operation should be represented to the Germans as the *main* attack. This meant that the small imaginary force of six divisions required by APPENDIX 'Y' would be wholly inadequate. In order to provide the necessary increase in the striking force after D Day, SHAEF, on 3rd February, produced an amended false Order of Battle.[6] The imaginary army of six divisions under GHQ, Home Forces, was retained, its composition having reverted to arrangement number one, but with the omission of the 49th Division.[7] According to this proposal, we now had for the pre-invasion story, the GHQ Army for the assault east of the Dover Straits and for the attack west of the Straits, the real OVERLORD formations. The American V Corps and 1st British Corps were specifically earmarked for an assault south of Cap Gris Nez. After D Day, the GHQ Army, continuing its threat to the Channel coast east of the Straits, would 'operate with four additional assault divisions which will be mounted in the

---

4. GARBO Letter No. 252, dated 20th October, 1943, taken by the courier to Lisbon on 17th December.

5. According to the report on Army Wireless Deception for OVERLORD issued in July 1944 (32/Security/15/(Signals 9)), this fixed network continued to operate with minor modifications until the date of the invasion, although it bore no kind of relation to the FORTITUDE SOUTH Order of Battle as finally constituted.

6. SHAEF/18201/6/Ops, dated 3rd February, 1944.

7. It was no longer possible to make use of this division as its place in the invasion build up had been advanced and it was due to go overseas within a fortnight of the first landing.

Portsmouth area to assault south of Cap Gris Nez when the German
reserves have been committed'. But where were these four extra
assault divisions to be found after V Corps and 1st British Corps
had landed in Normandy? One could not start building them up
before the invasion because until then the story was to be that the
two real assault corps would attack south of Cap Gris Nez. Yet one
cannot produce four imaginary assault formations, ready to embark
at a moment's notice, by a wave of the hand. The weakness of the
proposal of 3rd February, a weakness derived from FORTITUDE
itself, lay in the fact that it did not take sufficient account of the
story that would have to be told after D Day. Another disadvantage
of this arrangement was that it put the imaginary 'GHQ' Army,
before the invasion date, under 21 Army Group. As 21 Army Group
clearly could not control the Normandy assault and a still bigger one
against the Pas de Calais, it would have meant detaching this Army
from 21 Army Group at the moment when the invasion occurred
and placing it under some other command. Such a change would no
doubt have been conceivable, but it would scarcely have helped to
strengthen the threat at the moment when strength was most
needed.

It was at this point that the Joint Commanders became responsible for detailed planning, and it fell to the lot of 21 Army Group to
determine finally the constitution of the FORTITUDE SOUTH
forces. 21 Army Group made two changes of fundamental importance. First, it decided to have two distinct Army Groups from the
start, one for Normandy and the other for the Pas de Calais. Second,
it decided to build the Order of Battle wholly from real operational
formations, that is to say, it dispensed with imaginary formations as
well as with those under the command of Home Forces and under
War Office control.

The creation of two independent forces was done in this way.
Although all the American formations in the United Kingdom were
at this time controlled and administered by ETOUSA, there was
already in existence, albeit in skeleton form, an American army group
which was destined ultimately to command the American forces in
the field, namely, the First United States Army Group.[8] All that was

---

8. Later renamed Twelfth Army Group.

required was to convince the Germans that the two army groups were in an equal state of readiness. Admittedly this course might have been held to militate against the policy of postponement, for it tended to show an increase rather than a decrease in the forces operationally available; but, as the reader knows, this policy in face of the difficulties to which it was giving rise, was already being set on one side.

It now became necessary to provide FUSAG with armies of its own. This was done on the one hand by fictitiously detaching the First Canadian Army from 21 Army Group and putting it under the Americans and, on the other, by representing Third United States Army, still in fact under ETOUSA, as being under the command of FUSAG. The next step was to give the FUSAG forces an eastern bias. The Canadians being already located in Kent and Sussex were ideally placed for their role. In order to complete the picture, it would be necessary to move the Third Army, then located in Cheshire, to the eastern counties. This was accordingly proposed, but an examination of the administrative implications showed that such a course would have placed an undue strain upon 21 Army Group's mounting programme.[9] A simple way out of the difficulty was found, however, in the expedient of representing the divisions of Third Army by wireless in East Anglia, at the same time placing the real divisions in the West on wireless silence.[10] Having accepted the risks attendant upon a general curtailment of the visual misdirection programme, that is to say, having decided that imaginary divisions need not be physically represented on the ground, this course was clearly justifiable. These arrangements automatically released the non-operational divisions from their role in the cover plan.

At a conference called by 21 Army Group on 30th March the final Order of Battle and location of forces was agreed upon. This Order of Battle provided a firm foundation for the operation, on which the wireless programme and the Special Means plan could now be built.

---

9. Information supplied verbally by GSOI G (R) 21 Army Group.
10. The effect of this decision may be studied on the map MC attached to the Special Means plan of 6th May at Appendix V.

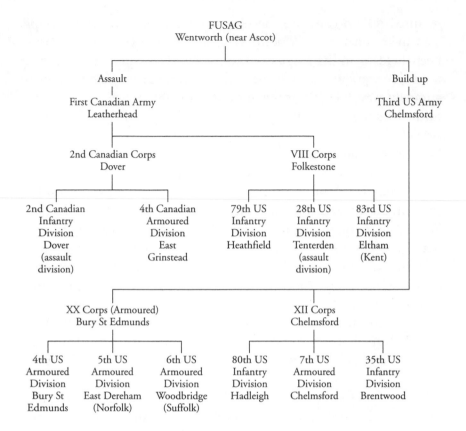

The Joint Commanders' Plan,[11] which gave the necessary instructions for all aspects of physical deception, and which gave the Special Means staff at SHAEF its marching orders so far as the controlled agents were concerned, did not receive the approval of the Chiefs of Staff until 18th May. Some weeks before that date, however, many of its provisions were already being carried out. At the end of March sites were chosen for the display of dummy landing craft. On 24th April the FUSAG wireless network became active[12]

---

11. NJC/00/261/33. Operation OVERLORD Cover and Diversionary Plans by C in C Allied Naval Expeditionary Force, C in C 21 Army Group and C in C Allied Expeditionary Air Force, dated 18th May, 1944. See Appendix IV.
12. The American links were supplied by 3103 Signals Service Battalion. Owing to the formidable size of the American force which had to be represented it was only possible to supply links down to the divisional level. The Canadian network, being real, required no artificial augmentation.

and at the same time the controlled agents began to report the move to concentration.

In an introductory paragraph, the Joint Commanders' Plan of 18th May recited the FORTITUDE story as outlined in the SHAEF plan of 23rd February. The body of the plan was divided into two parts. Part I related to the threat to the Pas de Calais. Part II was purely tactical in its scope and provided for a number of local feints and diversions in direct support of the Normandy landing. Parts I and II were sub-divided into serials to which the code name QUICKSILVER was given. Only the serials contained in Part I, of which there are five, need concern us here. QUICKSILVER I gave a much simplified version of the 'story'. The modifications which it effected in the SHAEF story will be considered later. QUICKSIL-VER II contained the wireless programme. QUICKSILVER III made provision for the display of dummy craft. QUICKSILVER IV laid down the bombing programme which was to be carried out against the Pas de Calais in support of FORTITUDE SOUTH. QUICKSILVER V gave instructions for the execution of certain limited measures of visual misdirection at Dover, including tunnelling operations in the cliff, and provided for night lighting at certain places on the Suffolk coast where dummy craft were to be moored.

XI

The Move to Concentration

When once the composition of FUSAG had been determined and locations fixed, the controlled agents could safely proceed with the task of building up the fictitious Order of Battle and of preparing for the false move to concentration. As with FORTITUDE NORTH, the disposition of the agents was the first consideration. It had for long been known that travel restrictions would be imposed in the embarkation areas. It was important that the movements of our observers should not be hampered by security measures, and it was to meet such a situation that Seven's sub-agents had been recruited in December 1943, the idea being that they should be sent to places on the south and south-east coasts early in the New Year and so acquire a resident's qualification before the visitors' ban was imposed. Thus on 18th February[1] GARBO informed the Germans that he was sending agent 7 (2) to Dover, 7 (4) to Brighton, 7 (5)[2] to Exeter and 7 (7) to Harwich.

On 3rd April, Madrid showed itself to be favourably impressed by the progress which Seven's new organisation was making: 'I have taken note with great interest of what you have told me in your letters about

---

1. Letter No. 16, dated 18th February, 1944, despatched to Lisbon on 19th February with eight other letters in a tin of curry powder.
2. Under the original arrangement agent 7 (5) was to have been placed in Southampton and agent 7 (6) in Exeter. On reflection we decided that it would be dangerous to put anyone in Southampton because he might see too much. That area could if necessary be covered by periodical visits. Under the revised arrangement 7 (6) was to remain in South Wales, his place in Exeter being taken by 7 (5).

the amplification of your network and the numerous messages which you have sent during the last few weeks have demonstrated to me that you have been absolutely right in your idea of nominating the old collaborators as sub-agents of their networks. In particular, the network of Seven appears to be the one which is giving the best results.'[3]

Meanwhile GARBO had been conducting tests upon the new recruits. Of 7 (2) he was able to report on 7th March: 'Dover. I was able to confirm last Sunday the accuracy of the recent report sent by 7 (2) from Dover. I am, therefore, able to classify him in future as a good reporter.'[4] Of 7 (4), in the same message: 'With regard to the military report, it is completely accurate so that we can catalogue this collaborator as being good.' Of 7 (7) on 13th April: 'I consider this first report of this collaborator fairly good as he tries to get details from which one is able to appreciate the interest he takes in explaining what he has seen.'[5]

Apart from the members of the World Aryan Order, it was only thought necessary to make one agent become resident in the prohibited zone. The decision to send TATE to Kent was not taken until after the visitors' ban had been imposed, but as the farmer for whom this agent worked in Hertfordshire had a friend, also a farmer, who lived near Ashford in Kent, and to whom TATE had been lent on several previous occasions, there was a good reason for exempting him from those restrictions on movement to which the general public were now bound to submit. Accordingly, on 25th May, TATE signalled: 'Farmer friend at Wye is being called upon to do practically full-time Home Guard duties as he is an officer. . . . Owing to this my chief has agreed to lend me to his friend to help him out,' and feeling, presumably, that exceptional times warranted exceptional risks, he added, 'I am going to refuse to go unless I can get lodgings where I know I can take my transmitter.'[6] Three days later: 'Have found first-class lodgings with elderly couple in Wye. So far as I can

---

3. GARBO Letter from Lisbon, dated 3rd April, 1944, received 22nd April.
4. GARBO 1806 and 1855 GMT, 7th March, 1944.
5. GARBO 1906 GMT, 13th April, 1944.
6. TATE 0634 MET, 25th May, 1944. TATE's transmissions from Wye provided a novel feature inasmuch as he did not go there at all. An aerial was erected in Kent and transmissions were made by remote control and the use of a GPO line.

see, ideal for radio purposes.'[7] On 1st June he was able to tell the Germans that he had moved in.[8] TATE's activities in Kent were, of course, greatly restricted by the fact that he was a farm worker, a limitation which the enemy did not seem fully to appreciate, for on 31st May they asked him to investigate concentrations, moves and preparations in the areas of London, Southampton, Plymouth, Bristol and Oxford.[9]

Apart from GARBO and BRUTUS, for whom special roles were being prepared, the other agents were to work as freelances travelling about and visiting their friends to suit our convenience. We had, however, to remember that with the exception of TREASURE, who had a wireless transmitting set, and of PUPPET, who had the use of the Ministry of Supply bag to Lisbon, the imposition of the air-mail ban would put all the lesser agents out of action altogether for a considerable time. During May TREASURE herself was to become involved in a domestic crisis which would debar her from taking any further part in deception.[10]

Let us now see what the moves to concentration, real and false, entailed. The dividing line between the true American and British concentration areas coincided with the Southern and South-Eastern Command boundary. The American assault and early build-up forces were already collected in the South-West of England. Here, therefore, there would be nothing more than a number of comparatively local movements. In the British zone, however, several early build-up divisions, notably the Guards Armoured and the 11th Armoured Divisions, were due to move from Yorkshire to the south coast at the end of April and the beginning of May. Apart from FORTITUDE, therefore, this would be the only unmistakable indication of a move to concentration.

---

7. TATE 0639 MET, 28th May, 1944.
8. TATE 2015 MET, 1st June, 1944.
9. TATE Message received 2120 MET, 31st May, 1944.
10. When TREASURE came to England, she brought her pet dog with her. Unfortunately the dog had died in quarantine and TREASURE held the British Security Service responsible for its death. In order to make the authorities atone for their alleged negligence, she threatened to disclose to the enemy, by means of a secret code word, that she was working under Allied control, a threat which she never carried out.

Let us next consider the false concentration. FUSAG would set up its headquarters at Wentworth near Ascot. There were to be two armies, one south and the other north of the Thames. The First Canadian Army, which was to command the forces in Kent and Sussex, was to remain in its real location at Leatherhead. Of its two corps, the 2nd Canadian Corps with its divisions under command was to move in reality during the second half of April from Sussex to Kent, while VIII Corps was to be falsely represented as transferring from Cheshire to Kent at the end of that month. Third Army, in command of the East Anglian forces, was to be shown as moving from Knutsford in Cheshire to Chelmsford, while of its two corps the XX, with three armoured divisions under command, in reality in Wiltshire, was to proceed fictitiously into Norfolk and Suffolk. Its other corps, the XII, which was to be shown in due course in Essex, with three divisions, two infantry and one armoured, under command, had not yet arrived from America.

Thus, two main false movements had to be shown, from Cheshire to Kent and from Wiltshire to East Anglia, to which must be added a smaller real movement of Canadian forces from Sussex to Kent. At the same time, we thought it inevitable that German Intercept would pick up the moves of British formations from Yorkshire to Hampshire and Sussex. We therefore decided that it would be unwise for the agents to remain completely silent about this, but in superimposing it upon the other two we hoped that the lesser transfer of forces from north to south would be eclipsed by the greater ones from north-west to south-east and from west to east. Over the activities of the Americans in the south-west a veil of silence was to be drawn.

The first step, so the Special Means Staff held, was to let the agents discover each formation in its existing location, for unless the Germans knew the points of departure as well as the places of arrival, the general direction of the move to concentration and the significance that we hoped they would attach to it would not be apparent.

In anticipation of this, TRICYCLE had already identified most of the formations in Yorkshire, having visited that county just before he left for Lisbon at the beginning of March. During the second week of April FREAK covered the ground a second time in order to fill in any gaps which had been left by his collaborator. By this time several

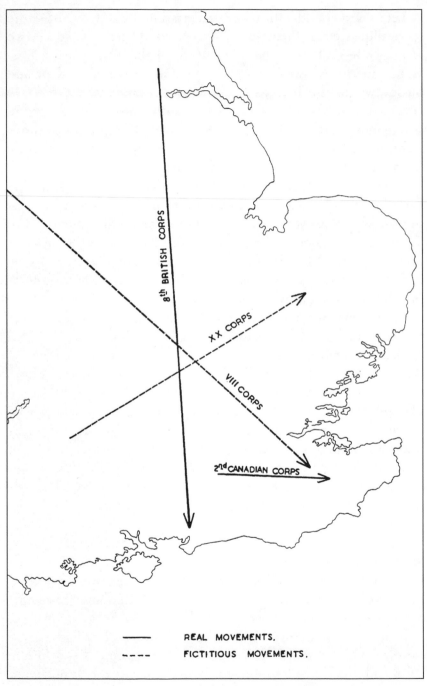

REAL MOVEMENTS.

FICTITIOUS MOVEMENTS.

A diagram indicating the principal Allied troop movements reported to the
enemy in May 1944

of the American formations included in FUSAG had arrived and were stationed in Cheshire. FREAK therefore extended his journey westwards and was rewarded by the discovery of the Third United States Army at Knutsford with the 79th and 83rd Infantry Divisions under command.[11] Meanwhile a visit by BRUTUS to Wiltshire revealed the presence of XX Corps and the 6th United States Armoured Division[12] in that region, while GARBO found the 28th United States Infantry Division,[13] which was to join VIII Corps in Kent when the latter came down from Cheshire, at Tenby in South Wales. Thus, by the time that the move was due to begin, the majority of the formations affected had been marked down in their old locations.

From this point the development of the operation, in so far as it concerned the double-cross agents, was governed by the Special Means plan of 6th May.[14] The main provisions of this plan had been worked out about a fortnight before that date, an unofficial draft of the Joint Commanders' Plan having been supplied to the Special Means Staff at SHAEF as early as 7th April. The Special Means Plan was therefore available for use before FUSAG's move to concentration began on the 24th of that month. Appendix D of this Plan, a 'Phased Programme for Identification and Grouping of Military Forces – 1st May to D Day', provided the controlled agents and their case officers with a working programme of release dates for disclosing the identity, as well as the location and grouping, real or false, of every operational formation in the United Kingdom. The movement of each formation was assumed to extend over a period of about a week. Troop trains and road convoys were routed in the usual way, all timings being linked to the wireless deception programme. Within this framework the movements of the agents could be so arranged as to give them the desired opportunities for observation. Thus the false pattern could be systematically elaborated, day by

---

11. FREAK 1125 GMT, 26th April, 1944.
12. BRUTUS 1634 GMT, 26th April, 1944.
13. GARBO 1910 GMT, 25th April, 1944. In reality, this division was to move to Chisledon in Wiltshire. FORTITUDE SOUTH extended its journey to Tenterden in Kent.
14. SHAEF/24132/4/SM/Ops, dated 6th May, 1944. See Appendix V.

day. Reports would flow in to the German Intelligence from agents stationed in all parts of the country, and each message would be found to confirm those that had gone before. And so at last the imaginary American Army Group in the South-East would gradually detach itself from the real British one in the South.

XII

Subsidiary Threats

With so many hands at work on such a broad canvas, it is very hard to say exactly when the strategic plan, whose aim it was to keep the enemy's reserves away from France, gave way to the tactical plan, which sought to reduce the rate of enemy reinforcement in the Normandy bridgehead. The change had certainly occurred before the Joint Commanders' Plan was approved on 18th May. There were at this time fifty-six German divisions in France and the Low Countries. Between the Seine and Den Helder, in the area of the Fifteenth Army, there were nineteen infantry divisions; in the Seventh Army area, between the Seine and the Loire, there were fourteen; in the South-West of France four, and on the Mediterranean coast nine. The Seventh and Fifteenth Armies were grouped together as Army Group 'B', of which Rommel was the Commander. The ten armoured divisions in France and Belgium were thought to be held as a centrally controlled mobile reserve, whose function would be to drive any invading force back into the sea before it had time to establish a lodgment. They were disposed as follows:

Area	Formation	Location
Fifteenth Army	1st SS Panzer Division	Turnhout (Belgium)
	2nd Panzer Division	Amiens
	116th Panzer Division[1]	Pontoise

---

1. This division was equal to little more than an armoured brigade in strength.

Area	Formation	Location
Seventh Army	21st Panzer Division	south of Caen
	12th SS Panzer Division	Dreux
	Panzer Lehr Division	south of Chartres
First Army	17th SS Panzer Grenadier	north-west of Poitiers
	11th Panzer Division[2]	east of Bordeaux
Nineteenth Army	2nd SS Panzer Division[3]	Toulouse
	9th Panzer Division	Avignon

Since the beginning of May the G-2 Division at SHAEF had been circulating periodical estimates of the enemy build-up against Operation OVERLORD. That of 3rd June, which differs little from its predecessors and which was the last to be issued before the invasion, forecast that within a week of the first landing all three Panzer divisions north of the Seine, namely the 2nd Panzer Division at Amiens, the 116th Panzer Division at Pontoise and the 1st SS Division at Turnhout, would have arrived in the bridgehead. The 116th Panzer Division was to be expected on D plus 1 and the other two between D plus 3 and D plus 7. Of the infantry divisions under command of the Fifteenth Army, it was estimated that the 84th, 85th and 331st Infantry Divisions, all field formations, would also arrive between D plus 3 and D plus 7. From the South and South-West it was supposed that the 2nd SS Panzer Division and the 11th Panzer Division would reach the bridgehead by the end of the first week.

To contain the forces north of the Seine, and in particular the three armoured divisions, was the task of FORTITUDE SOUTH. To this we shall return. In order to hold down the formations guarding the Mediterranean and Biscay coasts, two other plans were now put into operation, VENDETTA[4] for the South and IRONSIDE[5] for the West.

---

2. Until May 1944, this formation had been designated 273rd Panzer Division.
3. The location of this division would have allowed it to support the First or Nineteenth Army at short notice.
4. Approved by the Supreme Allied Commander, Mediterranean Theatre, 10th May, 1944.
5. SHAEF/18237/Ops (B). Approved by the Supreme Allied Commander, Western European Theatre, 4th June, 1944, but in operation from 23rd May.

ZEPPELIN, the Mediterranean counterpart of FORTITUDE, had, under the direction of the Commander 'A' Force, been in operation since the beginning of the year and included among its objects the prevention of reinforcements from reaching the German armies in France. Such an object, of course, precluded the exercise of any threat to the south coast of France. At the beginning of May, however, it was judged that the time had arrived when measures should be taken to contain the formations in that area. A subsidiary plan called VENDETTA was therefore introduced. This threatened an attack by a total force of about ten divisions on the French Mediterranean coast between Sete and Narbonne. The landing was to take place on 19th June, with the mission of seizing the Carcassonne Gap and exploiting to Toulouse and Bordeaux.

There still remained the problem of containing the formations in the South-West of France. It was impossible to associate an operation in that region with FORTITUDE SOUTH. The only reasonable story that suggested itself was that a long sea voyage operation should be launched from the west-coast ports in the United Kingdom against Bordeaux, with the object of capturing that place for the introduction of American forces sailing direct from the United States to France. The landing would be exploited along the Garonne Valley and would eventually link up with VENDETTA. This imaginary assault was given the name IRONSIDE. After several unsuccessful attempts had been made to mobilise physical resources such as air reconnaissance and minor naval operations in support of the plan, it was finally left to Special Means to perform the task.

Among the English-controlled agents the leading parts were played by BRONX and TATE. The story was such an improbable one that we were unwilling to embroil our best agents, although GARBO, through his very unreliable sub-agent 7 (6), did make a contribution.

In order to help BRONX to send urgent messages about the invasion with the necessary speed, the Germans had provided her with a code which she herself had subsequently elaborated to suit our requirements more exactly. The sectors of the European coast-line were given monetary equivalents: thus, £50 indicated the Bay of Biscay. The credibility of the information was denoted thus: 'for my dentist' meant that information on the place of the landings was certain, 'for my doctor' that it was almost certain and so on. 'Toute de suite' meant invasion in one week, 'urgent' meant in two weeks, 'vite' in about a month and 'si possible' that the date was vague. On 29th May, BRONX sent the following telegram: 'Send £50 immediately. I need it for my dentist.' This meant: 'I have definite news that a landing is to be made in the Bay of Biscay in one week.' One would have thought that the Germans might have felt a little uneasy about the reaction of the British censors when confronted with the news of this dental crisis, even though it was their own code. However, we later had reason to believe that no such anxiety disturbed their minds for, in March 1945, this agent was given a similar code relating to Norway, Denmark and North-West Germany.[6] In a letter ostensibly written at the same time that the telegram was despatched BRONX explained that she had picked up this valuable information at a night-club from a British officer who was under the influence of drink. 'After a cocktail party I stayed on at the Four Hundred Club with Captain X. After having a good deal to drink, he told me that I should hear some startling news on the wireless next day, as there was to be an airborne attack on the U-boat base at Bordeaux, preliminary to the invasion. Yesterday he came to see me, very much upset, and asked me to swear not to repeat anything as he had been drunk and now the attack had been postponed for a month, and if I repeated the conversation I would endanger thousands of lives. I am convinced that he spoke the truth and and have, therefore, decided to send you a telegram to warn you of this raid.[7]

TATE counted among his friends a number of naval officers, and of these no one had in the past supplied him with more useful 'high grade' naval gossip than a certain lady called Mary, who worked at

---

6. Letter No. 14 from Lisbon, dated 7th March, 1945, received 12th March.

7. When IRONSIDE failed to materialise, BRONX, in a letter despatched on 7th June, which may be presumed to have arrived about three weeks later, justified herself in the following way: 'Distraught by the news and convinced of the genuineness of the information given by Captain X. Dined with him last night but he did not respond to my teasing on the subject of his indiscretion, merely reminding me that I had promised never to speak of it again. Can only suppose that there has been a change of plan or else that this attack, also, will take place.'

the Admiralty. On 23rd May, TATE transmitted the following message to the Germans: 'Saw Mary for the first time for a long while. She was sent on a special mission to Washington. She says she worked on preparations for an independent expeditionary force which will leave United States for Europe. That is all I have found out so far.' And four days later: 'Saw Mary. Found out that the before mentioned expeditionary force consists of six divisions. Its commander is General Friedenhall.[8] The objective for this army, in Mary's opinion, is South France, but I believe that Mary herself does not know much on this point.'

On 5th June GARBO forwarded a second-hand report from 7 (6) which referred to the presence of an American assault division at Liverpool 'destined for an attack on the South Atlantic French coast in co-operaton with a large army which will come direct from America to the French coast'. GARBO viewed the report with scepticism and thus made it easy to dissociate himself from it should IRONSIDE turn out badly.

Thus, on the eve of the invasion, pressure was being exerted against both the southern and western seaboards. This brings us back to the Channel coast and to a further consideration of FORTITUDE SOUTH.

---

8. On the instructions of the War Department in Washington a press stop was placed upon the movements of this General, who was then in America. His real name was Friedendal, but TATE having described him wrongly in his first message felt obliged to persist in his error until the end of the war.

XIII

The ARTIST Crisis

If the conflicts inherent in BODYGUARD and FORTITUDE had given rise to problems in the field of physical deception, they bore even more hardly on Special Means. In the case of visual misdirection and wireless deception, a sudden alteration in the story could be attributed to human or mechanical error, to faulty air reconnaissance or to imperfect reception on the part of the intercept stations. Admittedly this would not tend to engender confidence in the channels, but it would not necessarily cause the later story to be disbelieved, nor would it offer prima facie evidence of an intent to deceive. The double-cross agents, on the other hand, did not enjoy this protection, and if the facts proved their stories to be wrong, it was often difficult for them to retreat. This was especially true when they spoke of Allied intentions as opposed to mere observation. The plan of 23rd February threatened to involve them in contradictions on two fundamental points. 'Invasion in July' meant committing them to a wrong target date, and 'invasion of the Pas de Calais' to a wrong initial objective. We already know how the story of invasion in July had been allowed to lapse. The Pas de Calais remained. During March and April the double-cross agents took various steps to direct the threat towards North-Eastern France and the Low Countries, but in a comparatively veiled manner and avoiding the suggestion that this was the only Allied objective. To this end Plan PREMIUM was formulated. Another example of an attempt to focus the attention of the enemy upon the cover target will be found in the 'airfield construction' plan, whose execution was entrusted to SNIPER, the Air Force sergeant employed at the Belgian Headquarters in London. SNIPER told the Germans[1] that he had been selected with others to attend a course of 'airfield construction' near St Albans. It appeared that the English and American units engaged in this work would, when they went abroad, have to depend to some extent on locally recruited labour and that national organisers, such as himself, would be attached to the various units. He gave a detailed account of these airfield construction companies, from which it could be inferred that in the initial stages of the assault the fighter aircraft would operate from airfields in this country. Thus, the two points were established: that an assault would be made on a part of the French coast that was within easy fighter range and that before long airfields would be required in Belgium.

The Joint Commanders' Plan, as has already been stated, began with an introduction which recited the SHAEF story, and then, in the body of the plan, under the title QUICKSILVER I, gave a modified version of its own. The latter, therefore, now became the operative one. The SHAEF story had, so to speak, been 'kept off the title'. According to QUICKSILVER I, the story before D Day was simply that the Supreme Commander had under command two army groups, 21 Army Group and First United States Army Group, the latter being located in South-East England. After D Day the story was to be that as soon as 21 Army Group had enticed the enemy reserves in the Pas de Calais towards Normandy, the Supreme Commander intended to attack the Pas de Calais with the American Army Group. This put the controlled agents on a much more satisfactory footing. Until the day of the invasion they would merely be required to build up the imaginary army group. After the assault had been made, they would be able to point to the fact that only 21 Army Group had been employed and draw the obvious inference that FUSAG was intended for an independent operation across the Dover Straits.

No one was quicker to appreciate the full implications of the new situation than GARBO's case officer. A memorandum dated 4th May, which outlines in detail the part to be played by the GARBO

---

1. Letters dated 27th March and 5th April, 1944.
[Note 2 is missing in the original.]

network during the coming weeks, concludes with the proposal that forty-eight hours after the invasion had begun, GARBO should state that since last communicating he had given careful consideration to all the developments of the last two months and that, after consulting with his agents, he had arrived at the conclusion that the present large-scale attack was only one prong of the Second Front to be carried out from this island. The strategic importance of the attack was that of drawing reserves to the assault area in order that the second assault force should be able to make a comparatively unopposed advance along their direct route to Berlin. 'GARBO will then proceed to compare the logic of this analysis with the build-up of reserve forces, as will have become apparent from his agents' reports to that date, laying particular stress on those divisions still in the FORTITUDE area. . . . He will end his message requesting that this report should be passed to Berlin together with his strong recommendation that they should guard against falling into this British trap by moving into the threatened area reserves which must be held available to hold and counter the second blow when delivered.'

Yet one cause for anxiety remained. It had been at 21 Army Group's request that SHAEF had included in the plan of 23rd February the proviso that when the real preparations indicated unequivocally that the assault was imminent, the threat to the Pas de Calais should be accelerated, so that what could in any event no longer be concealed might at least be wrongly interpreted. This proviso was repeated in the introduction to the Joint Commanders' Plan, where the original FORTITUDE story was recited, but here the remedial action was qualified and was specifically allotted to Special Means. Should the need arise, 'the imminence of the attack will be confirmed by Special Means, but the area of the attack will be the Pas de Calais'. Supposing that 21 Army Group judged that the security of OVERLORD demanded the exercise of such a threat by Special Means on the eve of the invasion, it would have been difficult for the Special Means Staff at SHAEF to plead that it formed no part of QUICKSILVER I, since the proviso was embodied in the SHAEF plan of 23rd February. Thus there was a danger that the double-cross agents might be forced once more into the position of having to say things that would be belied by events at a time when it was all important that their credit should stand high. Early in May the deus ex machina intervened, which was to remove this last potential source of embarrassment.

Although its full consequences were not realised at the time, the episode of ARTIST's arrest was of such importance to the ultimate success of the cover plan that a somewhat detailed account is given. When TRICYCLE had his first meeting with his German masters in Lisbon at the beginning of March, he received, according to his own account, a rather cold reception. On the following day, when the contents of his brief had been telegraphed to Berlin and their comments had been obtained, the atmosphere changed to one of trust and confidence. He gained the clear impression that his reports had been well received by the higher authorities. Some further light was thrown upon these events by an interview which took place on 28th April between ARTIST and the SIS representative in Lisbon. 'Abteilung III has announced that in their opinion TRICYCLE's material is not controlled by the British. This judgment is entirely on the basis of TRICYCLE's latest report, and Abteilung hold to their opinion that at one period of his career TRICYCLE was under Allied control. They explain the change as follows: The Allies provided poor material; ARTIST complained to TRICYCLE that he was not earning his keep; TRICYCLE then decided to collect material himself, and the result has been his last report – so good that Abteilung III is in entire agreement with the General Staff that it is inconceivable that the British should have deliberately fed it.' The SIS memorandum continues: 'From ARTIST's point of view, the outcome is a complete triumph, and he is sure that whatever happens, now, these two departments[3] – whose confidence it it hardest to win – will never reverse decisions so categorically expressed. To crown it all, ARTIST has been awarded the "Kriegsverdienstkreuz, 1st Class', an honour shared by no one in Lisbon; Schreiber in particular is envious.' To all appearances ARTIST's credit could hardly have stood higher. In reality, though neither he nor we knew it, disaster lay very near. Protracted negotiations had been going on for some time between Berlin and Lisbon regarding certain payments which were due to TRICYCLE. On 17th April Kuebart, the head of the Eins Heer in Berlin, instructed Schreiber and ARTIST, the former being

---

3. *i.e.* the OKW and Abteilung III.

head of the Abwehr in Lisbon, to meet Major von Bohlen, the financial administrator of the KO's, in Biarritz on 21st April to discuss the matter. Kuebart chose Schreiber and ARTIST because he thought they were the two who understood TRICYCLE's mentality best. ARTIST sensed danger and pleaded as an excuse for not going that it would spoil his cover vis-à-vis the British. Should not he appear to the British as being a discontented German 'skulking in the Peninsula' and surreptitiously helping Germany's enemies to arrange for the escape of Yugoslav airmen through the port of Lisbon? For he, like TRICYCLE, was concerned in the 'escape route'. On these grounds he declined the invitation and Schreiber went alone. On 29th April, under highly secret arrangements made between Berlin and Schreiber personally, ARTIST was kidnapped at his house in Lisbon. It is to be presumed that the award of the KVK was a hoax. On 2nd May Schreiber was able to inform Berlin that Plan DORA, as the kidnapping operation was called, had been completely successful, that ARTIST had arrived at Biarritz at 3 o'clock on 1st May, having been conveyed across the Franco-Spanish frontier in a Corps Diplomatique motor-car, and that he would be sent on to Berlin with all speed.

What precisely led to ARTIST's downfall has never been discovered. From fragmentary MSS data the following conjecture is made. ARTIST's inquisitive nature had led him to probe, perhaps unwisely, into the activities of one Brandes. Brandes was an uncontrolled agent employed by the Abwehr in Lisbon. Fearful that ARTIST's curiosity might show him up, there seems little doubt that Brandes sought to protect himself by taking the offensive against ARTIST. As will be readily appreciated, ARTIST's own position was even more vulnerable that of Brandes.

Apart from having incurred the displeasure of his masters through being engaged in certain dubious currency dealings, ARTIST was also known to have had periodical meetings with the English. He made no secret of these meetings, but explained that they were connected with the escape route. Nevertheless, Schreiber's office in Lisbon thought it necessary to send a telegram on 24th April to Schreiber in Madrid, then on his way back from Biarritz, to say that ARTIST 'was receiving at his urgent desire a visit from an Englishman from Madrid on 25th'.

Only a short time before the Abwehr had been severely shaken by the defection of one of their most important agents, Vermehren, in Turkey. ARTIST happened to be a friend of Vermehren. He also knew Vermehren's mother, who lived in Portugal but was recalled to Germany when her son went astray. The most likely explanation of the whole affair is that while Brandes had raised doubts as to ARTIST's reliability, the Germans could not, in fact, pin anything on him, but feared that he might at any moment follow in Vermehren's footsteps and thus deprive them of the valuable services of TRICY-CLE. For in spite of all this, German belief in TRICYCLE's veracity seems to have been quite unshaken.[4] That being so, it would be only prudent to place ARTIST in protective custody.[5]

The effect of ARTIST's arrest upon the cover plan will readily be seen. ARTIST knew that TRICYCLE was working under control and we had cause to believe that he had some knowledge of the GARBO case. Even if ARTIST had been arrested on a trumpery charge, there was every reason to fear that in the hands of the Gestapo inquisitors he might reveal the true state of affairs and so compromise the entire network of controlled agents in this country. From now onwards the Germans might, at any moment, tumble to the fact that all their spies in England were under Allied control. They would then conclude that the messages which they were receiving were the opposite of the truth. Moreover there could be no guarantee that we should be able to discover when ARTIST had revealed the true state of affairs. Now it was generally accepted that there could only be two reasonable objectives for the cross-Channel assault, namely, the Pas de Calais and Normandy. If the Germans perceived that we were trying to induce them to believe that we were coming to the Pas de Calais, the true

---

4. A message sent by FREAK on 15th May, recording the move of the 15th British Infantry Division from Yorkshire to Sussex, is recorded in Lagebericht West No. 1271 of 20th May, 1944.
5. Further news of ARTIST was awaited in vain. After the war TRICYCLE met Frau Vermehren, who told him that she and ARTIST were both confined in Oranienburg Prison and that he had disappeared when she was still there. She presumed that he had died in the camp. According to her he was being interrogated on financial matters. An SOE prisoner who escaped from Oranienburg confirmed that ARTIST was there and was still alive a short time before the war ended. All subsequent attempts to find him have failed.

objective would thus be automatically disclosed. So far no irreparable damage been done.[6] But for the future it was evident that no operational demand could justify a course of action which might reveal the OVERLORD objective. This, in effect, meant that reports of an imminent attack against the Pas de Calais by Special Means before D Day would no longer be permissible and that the energies of the controlled agents would now have to be confined to building up the Orders of Battle of the two independent army groups. The only remaining threat to the Pas de Calais so far as the controlled agents were concerned would be that which was implied by the location of the FUSAG forces. This development, it may be added, was viewed with comparative equanimity for, the invasion being now less than a month away, the opinion was gaining ground that German dispositions were made to meet all contingencies and however strongly they suspected that we were coming to Normandy, they would be unlikely to denude the Pas de Calais. Any intensification of the latter threat might, therefore, merely be seeking to secure certain dispositions of German forces which had, in fact, already been dictated by their own natural sense of caution.[7] Thus good came out of evil and the controlled agents, relieved of their last embarrassment, were now free to mobilise their full strength for a supreme deceptive effort in June after the invasion had been launched.

Towards the end of May, as the result of certain changes in the German dispositions in France,[8] 21 Army Group judged that the

---

6. As a security precaution an officer with no knowledge of the OVERLORD plan had already examined all the previous traffic, and although he had deduced from it a slight bias in favour of the Pas de Calais and a desire to suggest that the operation was by no means imminent, he found no clear indication of our intentions.

7. This view was soon to be supported by the Germans' own broadcast statements: 'Both at home and abroad landings at many points are predicted, some of which may seem almost unopposed until the High Command has identified the main thrust.' PWE Central Directive Part II, Guidance for Output for week beginning 1st June, 1944, para. 2.

8. Before 20th May, the 21st Panzer Division had moved from Rennes to an area immediately south of Caen, while the Panzer Lehr Division had been newly identified to the south of Chartres. Before 27th May, the 91st Infantry Division had moved from Redon near the mouth of the Loire to the Cherbourg Peninsula.

circumstances foreshadowed during the previous January had now come to pass and that the threat to the Pas de Calais should accordingly be intensified forthwith by Special Means. 'On account of various factors, in particular the concentration of photo recce flights in the NEPTUNE area, the enemy appear to have appreciated that area as the most likely point of attack. He has accordingly made troop dispositions unfavourable to the NEPTUNE assault.' The Seine bridges had just been destroyed by the Air Force, and it was proposed that the controlled agents should suggest that this had been done to prevent forces in Normandy from reaching the threatened area north of the Seine. In view of the ARTIST debacle it was now possible for SHAEF to resist this proposal on security grounds alone. Mention of the Pas de Calais might be treated by the enemy as Allied deception. The broader argument which lay behind this refusal is summarised in a memorandum submitted by the Special Means officer to the Chief of Ops (B) Sub-Section on 30th May, at the time when this proposal was made. 'Apart from the temporary crisis caused by ARTIST's arrest the reasons for not overplaying the threat against the Pas de Calais before D Day have been as follows: (*a*) There is no certain evidence that the target area has been compromised. But even if it was compromised . . . it is thought unlikely that they (*i.e.* the Germans) would alter their dispositions to any great extent before D Day. Their present dispositions represent the HCF of insurance against all possible risks. (*b*) In view of (*a*) it has been felt from the start that the object should be to keep German divisions away from the target area after D Day, rather than to attempt to influence their disposition before D Day. To attempt the latter would be unlikely to succeed and might prejudice our chances of action by Special Means after D Day. (*c*) The reason why an over-dose of the Pas de Calais before D Day is likely to prejudice the position after D Day is this. Once the NEPTUNE assault has gone in, it would be idle to try and keep up the story for any length of time, that it is a mere diversion. If we are to threaten the Pas de Calais after D Day, we can only do so by saying that the invasion comprises two major assaults. We cannot for security reasons talk about NEPTUNE before D Day. Yet it would be unreasonable for all our agents to find out everything about the Pas de Calais when they could find out *nothing* about the NEPTUNE assault. (*d*) We can so place them, and we *have* done so, that they get more *early* information about the Pas de Calais assault than about the NEPTUNE assault, and to that extent we can play up the Pas de Calais before D Day; but to that extent only. After D Day we can go absolutely all out.'

When the news of ARTIST's arrest first arrived, some held the view that it would be necessary to prohibit the double-cross agents from taking any further part in FORTITUDE. Although it was ultimately decided that so long as the precautions already described were strictly adhered to, such drastic action would be undesirable, it was agreed that the further employment of TRICYCLE and FREAK for deception would not be justified. It therefore became the policy of MI5 to allow the two cases to run on in a normal manner until the ARTIST crisis had receded a little into the background and then to find some excuse for closing them, if no clear evidence of the Germans' continued confidence in them could be obtained. No such evidence came, but a very convenient excuse for bringing their activities to an end did. It came to the knowledge of the British Security Service about the middle of May that an informer had made a report to Mihailovic's headquarters suggesting that FREAK might be working for the Germans. This report was intercepted by the enemy and caused some stir in Berlin. It being natural that such intelligence would sooner or later reach British ears, the Germans were allowed to know that this had, in fact, occurred. On 20th May TRICYCLE wrote: 'Yesterday I was called to the War Office for an interview. I was asked for a lot of information about FREAK's political views and why and how he had been brought to this country. I found out that the reason for this was a message from a British Intelligence officer in the Middle East, passing on some adverse report about FREAK which had, apparently, come from some Mihailovic circles in Yugoslavia. I do not know exactly what this report said but, from the questions put to me, it was clear that someone had suggested that FREAK had collaborated with the Germans. In view of FREAK's high position now, the British are not likely to take any strong steps against him unless they have definite proof but they may be making further investigations. That is the reason why FREAK and I decided to dismantle the radio set and hide it in a safe place for the time being in case the house is searched. So far as I can judge, no suspicion has fallen on me; on the contrary, the English seem to expect me to help them find out the truth about FREAK. I think this as I was asked not to mention the interview to FREAK. I think the British consider the source of the accusation a not very reliable one and very weak, as practically every third or fourth Yugoslav has, at some time, been accused by some Yugoslav source of being pro-German, so I do not see a very great danger in the accusation. FREAK expects that people in the highest positions will adopt a shocked attitude towards any accusation against him and will help to brush it aside. In the meantime please do not write to me in case my mail is being watched. Keep listening for the radio.'[9] The Germans continued to listen for more than two months. After a silence of six weeks FREAK, on 30th June, sent the following message: 'Had to stop for reasons given in TRICYCLE's letter 20th May. Have since had to travel with my master. Am just back but may be sent away on further unavoidable mission for him at short notice. Thanks to him, English doubts of me mostly overcome but some still exist.'[10] A petulant answer from the Germans on 4th July: 'Do not understand sudden and unnotified interruption of work in present critical times. Letter TRICYCLE 20th not received in view of postal restrictions',[11] brought the cases of TRICYCLE and FREAK to a close. All this helped to convince us that ARTIST had kept faith, that the two agents were still believed in and that, in consequence, this danger to the whole double-cross system had passed.

---

9. TRICYCLE Letter in secret ink, dated 20th May, 1944.
10. FREAK 1233 and 1248 GMT, 30th June, 1944.
11. FREAK Message received 1130 GMT, 4th July, 1944.

XIV

Physical Deception and the Invasion

Before tracing the further progress of physical deception as directed by the Joint Commanders' Plan, something must be said about Exercise FABIUS and its influence on the operation. This full dress rehearsal, in which four assault divisions and their associated naval forces were engaged, took place in the English Channel during the first week of May and was based on Southampton and the neighbouring ports. The total concealment of an exercise of such vast dimensions was too much to hope for. The wireless programme was therefore arranged, on the one hand, to preserve such well-guarded secrets as the hour of the assault and the landing of tanks before infantry, and on the other, to make the general pattern of the wireless traffic resemble as closely as possible that which would be audible at the time of the real attack, so that FABIUS could be presented as the first and OVERLORD as the second of a series of amphibious exercises.[1] In order to support this interpretation of events, the Prime Minister, at the request of General Eisenhower, had included in a speech which he broadcast on 27th March, the following passage: 'And here I must warn you that in order to deceive and baffle the enemy as well as to exercise the

---

1. For further particulars see (1) 'Reports on the Wireless Deception and Security Measures taken by the three Services in connection with Operation NEPTUNE, July 1944'. Naval Report (Appendix D) and Army Report (page 6, Effect of Exercise FABIUS). (2) History of G (R) 21 Army Group and HQ, R Force, April 1945. Part III, para. 3, Exercises.

forces, there will be many false alarms, many feints and many dress rehearsals.'

In certain respects the cover operation received some positive assistance from FABIUS. The invasion fleet was in fact divided into two task forces, the Eastern under British and the Western under American command. The wireless networks of these forces were dissociated in order to give the impression of two independent operations. Furthermore, certain wireless links controlled by the Admiralty were so arranged as to give a bias towards the East, these links continuing to operate after the exercise had ended.

At all times wireless provided the foundation for FORTITUDE SOUTH in its physical aspect. As recorded in a previous chapter, the network representing the land forces had already begun to operate on 24th April. To give further emphasis to the south-east coast, the wireless traffic of the Combined Headquarters at Dover and Chatham was increased in volume, and new links were introduced in order that these stations might resemble the Combined Headquarters at Portsmouth as closely as possible.

Arrangements now had to be made for the inclusion of amphibious training in the deceptive wireless programme. In this respect the Southern operation presented greater difficulties than had been experienced in Scotland. The danger of aerial reconnaissance over Loch Fyne had been comparatively remote, but this could not be said of the south or south-east coast of England. In order to give a reasonable time for assault training, it was necessary that the exercises should begin in April. But at that time none of the dummy craft was ready. For this reason it was decided to start by using a real naval assault force. Accordingly, at the middle of April, the 4th Infantry Brigade of the 2nd Canadian Division, one of FUSAG's assault formations, was represented as being at Studland training with Force 'G'. The reasons for choosing Force 'G' were, first, that it was newly formed and therefore not firmly linked with any particular military formation, and, second, that the division with which it had been training was British and therefore the addition of a Canadian brigade would be noticeable.

On 20th May the launching of the dummy craft began and by

12th June two hundred and fifty-five[2] were displayed at various points on the east and south-east coasts from Great Yarmouth to Folkestone.

At the same time, the CLH units provided suitable wireless traffic on an increasing scale until, by degrees, the semblance of a new assault force had been created. This became known as the Imaginary Force 'F'. Early in June the 28th United States Infantry Division left its fictitious location in Kent for a fortnight's training with Force 'F' at Felixstowe. In order to add realism, on 8th June the headquarters ship HMS *Lothian* was ordered to Harwich. The subsequent vicissitudes of Force 'F' will be considered later.

QUICKSILVER IV, which called for a deceptive bombing programme on the Pas de Calais, was not conducted as a separate operation. The real operations of the Allied air forces were, however, so adjusted as to focus attention on the false objective.[3] Before the invasion, for example, forty-nine airfields within a radius of 150 miles of Caen were attacked, of which eleven were in the Pas de Calais and four in the NEPTUNE area. During the same period nineteen railway junctions supplying the Pas de Calais were attacked, while no junction nearer to the assault beaches than Rouen was visited. A bombing programme was directed against the principal road and rail bridges over the rivers Seine, Oise, Meuse and the Albert Canal. This accorded with real invasion requirements, but again drew attention to the Pas de Calais by severing the communications which appeared to lead in that direction. When attacking coast defences and enemy radar installations a proportion of two in the cover to one in the assault area was maintained.

---

2. This number was made up as follows:

Great Yarmouth	49
Lowestoft	20
River Deben	59
River Orwell	63
Dover	46
Folkestone	18

3. Particulars given here are derived from Plan FORTITUDE, The Air Contribution, reference FEWB/JNA, Offices of the War Cabinet, dated 24th May, 1945.

Dummy landing
craft at anchor in
the River Orwell

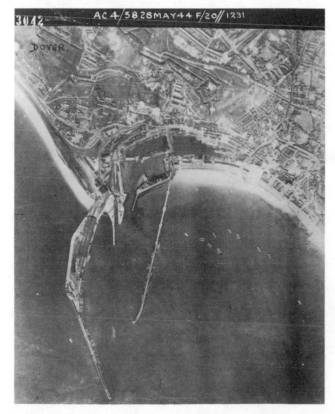

Dummy landing
craft at anchor in
Dover Harbour

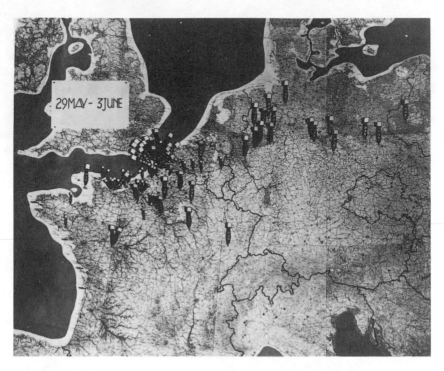

Allied bombing attacks on Northern France, the Netherlands and Northern
Germany during the periods 29th May to 3rd June, and 4th to 6th June, 1944

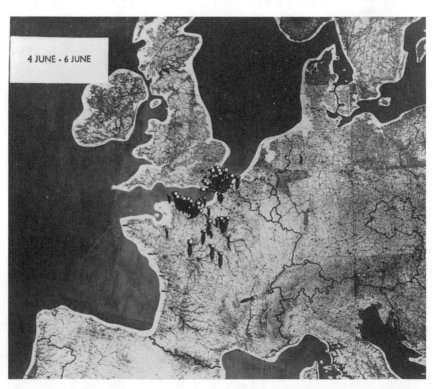

The significance which the enemy might attach to the location of short-range fighter aircraft bases in England had always been recognised. The British Second Tactical Air Force and the American IX Tactical Air Command which were to support the invasion were now located in Hampshire and in Kent; but the concentrations in the New Forest and at Tangmere in the former county were considerably greater than those at Lympne, Hawkinge and Manston. It is true that the distance from Southampton to the Pas de Calais was no greater than that to Normandy, yet it was felt that a preponderance of fighter aircraft in Hampshire might provide the enemy with a useful clue. It was impossible to conceal these concentrations because the aircraft were already operational. To counteract this unfavourable circumstance, a large-scale operation against the Pas de Calais was carried out by the Second TAF on 29th May, in which sixty-six squadrons took part. These squadrons were given advanced and rear bases, the former being in Kent, Surrey and Sussex, the latter their normal ones in Hampshire. They operated from the advanced bases and landed at the rear ones to refuel and re-arm. The purpose was to indicate to the enemy our intention of using fighter aircraft located in the Southampton area against targets in North-Western France, which would in the normal course of events have been too far from their bases, but which could be reached by the employment of an intermediate airfield. The exercise was observed by GARBO's sub-agent 7 (2), BRUTUS and TATE.[4]

The physical measures so far recorded were all designed to give an Eastern bias to the invasion preparations and to establish the false army group in South-Eastern England for future use. Other plans

---

4. BRUTUS 2010 GMT, 29th May, 1944, GARBO 1951 and 1956 GMT, 2nd June, 1944, and TATE 2nd June, 1944. As examples of the mishandling of controlled agents these three messages deserve study. Had the agents merely observed the aircraft in flight, no risk would have been run. But all three disclosed the fictitious object of the exercise. That this very singular item of operational intelligence should simultaneously have reached the ears of a Polish Staff Officer, a Welshman resident in Dover and a German prisoner-of-war working on a farm in Kent, all of them enemy agents, was indeed straining German credulity. Had the Germans analysed and compared the traffic of their agents at the time that it was received, their suspicions could hardly have failed to be aroused.

had been laid with the sole object of lowering German vigilance during the last critical days. The periods of wireless silence and of intense wireless activity which had been instituted at the end of 1943 were intended to prevent the enemy from discovering the date of the invasion through his reading of the wireless traffic. On reflection, however, it was felt that these measures, far from confusing the enemy, might be of direct assistance to him, since a period of wireless silence would denote a period of danger. If the networks to which the enemy had become accustomed could be simulated by artificial means at a time when the real formations were embarking under a wireless silence, the chances of putting the Germans off their guard would be greatly increased. During the month of May operators were accordingly infiltrated into the networks of all three Services in such a way that it was possible to simulate amphibious exercises in which the real assault divisions would appear to be engaged when they were, in fact, about to leave for France.[5] Although such exercises were prepared for Force 'S' with the 3rd British Division and Force 'J' with the 3rd Canadian Division and were designed to begin on the day preceding the invasion, it was felt when the time came, in view of the fact that there had been no recent enemy reconnaissance, that such exercises might encourage German air observation at the very moment when it was least wanted. The exercises were therefore cancelled. Instead, while the troops were on their way across the Channel 'the most "humdrum" of HF exercises between the more important ships were simulated and certain ship to shore waves were taken over by mobile stations ashore impersonating ships'.

A novel device for distracting the enemy's attention from affairs in this country on the eve of the invasion was provided by Plan COPPERHEAD. It was known that the Spaniards had an observation post overlooking the airfield at Gibraltar. This post was manned by a non-commissioned officer and ten men, and observation was continuous. Reports of all arrivals and departures were made immediately to the Spanish authorities, and these found their way ultimately to Berlin. At the beginning of April an actor called Clifton James, then serving in the Royal Pay Corps, was found who bore a

---

5. History of G (R) 21 Army Group and HQ, R Force, April 1943, page 11, Operation QUAKER.

Lieutenant Clifton James who visited Gibraltar on 27th May, 1944
disguised as Field Marshal Montgomery

close personal resemblance to Field-Marshal Montgomery. He was dressed in the Field-Marshal's clothes and, having accompanied him in the guise of a newspaper reporter for some weeks in order that he could study his characteristics, he set off on 27th May in a York aeroplane accompanied by a sham brigadier and ADC for North Africa. The ostensible purpose of the visit was a meeting with

General Wilson and General Patch to co-ordinate, with the French High Command, the operations against Southern France which were to precede the launching of OVERLORD.

It was arranged that the Field-Marshal and his party should break their journey for a few hours at Gibraltar and call on the Governor. Steps were taken to ensure that other Spaniards who would be likely to relate their experiences on the other side of the frontier should meet him. On arrival in North Africa Lieutenant James and his party dropped their disguise and after a few days in Cairo returned unostentatiously to London. COPPERHEAD was supported by the Mediterranean-controlled agents but not by those in the United Kingdom.

XV

BRUTUS Joins FUSAG

By the middle of May, the bulk of the reports concerning the move to concentration were in enemy hands. At this stage the Germans had, as it were, been given all the pieces belonging to the puzzle, but not the key which would explain how to fit them together. For the agents who had been posted to observe the recent troop movements, while they were well qualified to identify single formations and even to say what corps some division belonged to, were hardly of high enough standing to learn about the grouping of senior formations or to discover their operational tasks. For this someone with more exalted connections would be needed. In a certain degree GARBO's friends J (5) at the Ministry for War and 4 (3) at the American head-quarters in London had been able to fulfil such a role. On 10th May, for instance, GARBO gave the following account of a conversation he had had with his American sergeant friend: '4 (3) said that the Second Front would open as soon as the two Army Groups destined for operation were ready. One of these, the 21 Army Group, is under Montgomery. The other, the First Army Group, is provisionally under the orders of Bradley. The American troops which are expected here will enter the latter Army Group. He assured me that Eisenhower would give a very important task to the American Army Group.' But we now required a more continuous view of planning at the higher level.[1]

---

1. GARBO 2050 and 2102 GMT, 10th May, 1944.

FREAK, being a military attaché, would have been in a position to supply intelligence of this kind, and he had on 21st April informed the enemy that the Canadians in South-East England were to be grouped with Americans and not with British, and that an American corps would be brought under the Canadian Army,[2] but both he and TRICYCLE were now *hors de combat*. It was therefore decided to give BRUTUS an appointment at the headquarters of FUSAG, the imaginary army group. Here he would be able to weld together into a connected whole, the heterogeneous reports sent in by the 'ground observers'. In giving controlled agents highly confidential appointments one is always faced with the difficulty of withholding vital secrets which the agents, by virtue of their position, could hardly fail to discover. In order to be in a position to regulate the flow of intelligence reaching BRUTUS's ears, it was considered inadvisable to allow him to work at the main headquarters at Wentworth. The story was therefore evolved that a small section had been set up under FUSAG with the object of recruiting Poles who worked in the German-occupied territory which was likely to be overrun in the near future by the American Army Group.[3] This section was to be under the command of an American colonel and was to have Polish Army and Air Force officers attached to it. It was to be located at Staines. It would be necessary for the head of the section, accompanied by Polish Military and Air Force officers, to visit FUSAG formations before they went overseas in order to make the necessary arrangements. In such a position BRUTUS would be able, and yet not bound, to discover any kind of operational intelligence. There was a further advantage in placing him at Staines, inasmuch as it would separate him physically from his transmitter which CHOPIN had at Richmond. Thus any necessary delays could be explained by the difficulty which he experienced in maintaining contact with his assistant.

On 18th May BRUTUS announced his new appointment[4] and on the 25th reported that the posting was to take effect on the

---

2. FREAK 1338 GMT, 21st April, 1944.
3. As there were many Poles working in the neighbourhood of Lille, this incidentally provided an unobtrusive pointer to the false objective.
4. BRUTUS 1935 GMT, 18th May, 1944.

27th.[5] The Germans were delighted. 'All my congratulations on your post. It is a pity that you will not be able to stay in London.'[6] All the anticipated difficulties attaching to such an appointment were experienced by BRUTUS. On 10th June he complained: 'I have had to ask CHOPIN to come to Staines to collect the news. Difficult to leave this locality to come to London,'[7] and on the following day: 'With regard to FUSAG, it is difficult for me to penetrate the Operations Room because my personal relations are still weak and because security restrictions are very severe and in principle the Allied Liaison officers are kept apart. Nevertheless I am obliged to be there every day and each day I improve my relations.'[8] In spite of all these difficulties, he had, within a week of his arrival, begun the transmission of a series of messages which was to disclose to the enemy by the day of the invasion the entire chain of command of the shadow army group in South-East England.

At the end of May, all the FUSAG formations, with the exception of the 80th US Infantry Division and the 7th US Armoured Division, which were in fact only just disembarking in this country, had been discovered by the controlled agents in East and South-East England. The method by which BRUTUS drew all the loose threads together can best be explained diagrammatically. This extensive report was supplied in three instalments; the first from information gleaned at FUSAG, the second after a tour of Kent and the third after a visit to East Anglia.

If one compares this chart with the FUSAG Order of Battle laid down by 21 Army Group on 30th March, one will notice that two of the formations belonging to the First Canadian Army, namely, VIII Corps and the 79th US Infantry Division, have vanished, their places being taken by XII Corps and the 35th US Infantry Division, which were shown under the Third US Army in the original arrangement. A short time before the invasion, it was found necessary to advance the sailing dates of VIII Corps and the 79th US Infantry Division

---

5. BRUTUS 1833 GMT, 25th May, 1944.
6. BRUTUS Message received 2001 GMT, 29th May, 1944.
7. BRUTUS 2037 GMT, 10th June, 1944.
8. BRUTUS 2015 GMT, 11th June, 1944.

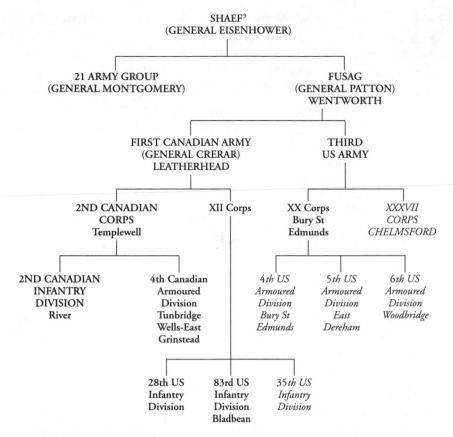

and send them to the bridgehead about a week after the first landing. This, of course, made it necessary to withdraw them immediately from the FUSAG Order of Battle. The gap in the First Canadian Army was filled by transferring the two formations referred to above from the Third Army. This in its turn left a gap in Third Army. The

9. Formations and groupings in large black type reported 31st May, 1944 (1605, 2051, 2056, 2108, 2112 and 2117 GMT), from information acquired at FUSAG.

   Formations and groupings in small black type reported 2nd June, 1944 (2003, 2007, 2101, 2105 and 2111 GMT), after Kentish tour.

   Formations and groupings in small italic type reported 6th and 7th June, 1944 (2005 and 2009 GMT 6th June, 1601, 1604 and 1609 GMT 7th June), after East Anglian tour.

   Formations and groupings in large italic type reported 14th June, 1944 (2006 GMT), from information acquired at FUSAG.

means employed for making good this loss will be considered in a later chapter.[10]

As the Germans were learning so much more about FUSAG than they were about 21 Army Group, it is not unnatural that they should have pressed their agents for further information regarding the latter. On 18th May FREAK was asked: 'Where do you locate 21 Army Group? Which armies and divisions belong to it?'[11] At the same time GARBO was addressed thus: 'With reference to the latest reports of 4 (3), I send the following *questionnaire*, the reply to which would be of much interest. Where is the headquarters of the 21 Army Group, English? The numbering of the armies within the said Army Group, and their headquarters. How many and which divisions are within each of the armies of the said Army Group, indicating, where possible, which divisions are armoured and which are infantry.'[12] On 4th June, while BRUTUS was making the final disclosures regarding the FUSAG Order of Battle, the answer came back: 'Give details of the composition of the 21 Army Group and of the location of the various headquarters.'[13] We had placed ourselves in a fairly strong position to meet questions of this kind. As a foreign

---

10. The fact that VIII Corps and the 79th US Infantry Division, which had just been falsely represented both by the controlled agents and by wireless as being in Kent and Sussex, were likely to come into contact with the enemy within a few days, led us to fear that American prisoners-of-war might reveal the fact that these formations had in reality come straight from Cheshire to their ports of embarkation. As an insurance against this danger, GARBO sent the following message on 5th June (2127, 2132 and 2140 GMT): 'I dined last night with 4 (3) – the majority of the American troops who have arrived in England have disembarked in the north-western ports of the Island. Formations and units first go to staging areas of Western Command. The majority in the area of Cheshire. They stay there until they have been brought up to strength and receive their equipment leaving for the concentration areas in the East and South of England. Therefore nearly all the camps in the North-West of England are those which receive American troops, manned by personnel of that nationality.' Thus any soldier who denied knowledge of the fictitious locations might be assumed to belong to a rear party which had been transferred directly from the staging camp to the port of embarkation.

11. FREAK Message received 1133 GMT, 18th May, 1944.

12. GARBO Message received 1955 GMT, 17th May, 1944.

13. BRUTUS Message received 0905 GMT, 4th June, 1944.

liaison officer attached to the staff of FUSAG, BRUTUS could hardly be expected to know very much about the other army group. GARBO's best source of information where matters affecting military organisation were concerned was an American. 'I questioned him', said GARBO on 27th May, referring to a conversation with 4 (3) on the 21 Army Group, but it seems that he does not know much about this formation. He was only able to say that there are a few American troops in it, but that the Americans are mainly in the First Army Group.'[14] Such information as we deemed it necessary to give about 21 Army Group in order to match the intelligence which we supposed was being supplied by their 'Y' Service, we put into the mouths of ground observers like 7 (2) and 7 (4). There was no need for them to give grouping,[15] also, as most of them worked in the Eastern and South-Eastern counties, such reports as they made placed emphasis where it was most needed.

---

14. GARBO 1906 GMT, 27th May, 1944.

15. In the matter of grouping, the only important disclosure affecting 21 Army Group was of the fact that First US Army was under General Montgomery's command (TREASURE 2010 GMT, 8th May, 1944). The reason for telling the Germans this was in order to induce them to accept the view that we were in the habit of mixing nationalities and so make them more ready to believe, when they saw TREASURE's statement was corroborated on the field of battle, that First Canadian Army was under FUSAG and VIII Corps under First Canadian Army. In fact the enemy had already learnt through its intercept service that First US Army was under 21 Army Group.

XVI

GARBO and the Invasion (I)

Form was already beginning to tell among the sub-agents of Seven's network. While 7 (2), 7 (4) and 7 (7) were improving their reputations daily, 7 (3), 7 (5) and 7 (6) were falling by the wayside. 7 (3), having finished her preliminary training at Mill Hill, had been sent about the middle of the month to a WRNS camp near Newbury, where she had already passed an examination in Hindustani. 'She thinks that she will be sent to India.'[1] The services of this imaginary sub-agent had already been offered to SEAC, and it was therefore thought best to leave her out of our calculations altogether. 7 (5) had never taken kindly to espionage. His nervous disposition unfitted him for the work. In his very first message, despatched on 19th April from Taunton, he confessed that he had found it impossible to establish himself in the protected zone. On 17th May he wrote from Exeter: 'I entered this prohibited area where vigilance is extremely strict. I do not see any possibility of remaining here owing to the continual demands for documentation which up to the moment I have been able to evade.'[2] On 2nd June he ran into trouble. A message reached GARBO through 7 (6) in Swansea, which revealed that 7 (5) had been arrested for being in Exeter without permission. No doubt his guilty looks had betrayed him. He had been sentenced to one month's imprisonment. 'Apparently there is no indication that any suspicion exists regarding the mission with which he was entrusted to me and that it was only a routine case for not having complied with

---

1. GARBO 2058 GMT, 19th May, 1944.
2. GARBO 2014 GMT, 17th May, 1944.

the present restrictions.'[3] With 7 (5)'s retirement from the scene we were relieved of the ungrateful task of having to send military reports from Devonshire.

For the sake of realism GARBO and his case officer thought that at least one of the sub-agents should prove to be a complete failure. This role was allotted to 7 (6), who resided in South Wales, an area upon which FORTITUDE was not dependent for reports. 'I received a long letter from 7 (6)', wrote GARBO on 28th April, 'with reports, the majority of which were stupid. We can therefore discount the ability of this agent as an informant in spite of the repeated instructions given. His usefulness to the Military Information Service is nil.'[4]

And now a word about GARBO himself. As with BRUTUS, it was felt that for an agent of his stature an appointment should be found which would enable him to penetrate more deeply into the inner councils of those who were directing the Allied war effort. It will be remembered that as early as February GARBO had stolen from the office of J (3) the specimen of a pamphlet which was to be dropped in France in the event of the Germans' voluntary withdrawal from that country. Describing this exploit as 'a master stroke', Madrid had added, 'very important facts can be obtained in that Ministry since they prepare all the propaganda for the countries in which they are interested for their projected offensive'.[5] An opening had already been made by the Germans themselves.

The head of the Spanish section at the Ministry of Information was, in fact, on a visit to Madrid at the beginning of May. Certain previous suggestions of GARBO had already led the enemy to suspect that this individual was no other than J (3). On 2nd May GARBO casually threw out the observation: 'J (3) has left England.'[6] It was fairly certain that the Germans would connect this remark with the Ministry official's visit to Spain. Meanwhile, the latter, at the instance of MI5, was requested to return to this country and arrived

---

3. GARBO 1915 and 1925 GMT, 2nd June, 1944.
4. GARBO 1804 GMT, 28th April, 1944.
5. GARBO Letter in microphotograph from Lisbon, dated 3rd April, received 22nd April, 1944.
6. GARBO 2115 GMT, 2nd May, 1944.

home at the middle of the month. On 22nd May GARBO reported: 'Result of interview today with J (3). He returned from Madrid for reasons connected with propaganda preparations for the Second Front. He proposed that I should help him, offering good remuneration for work which I could do at home. I accepted provisionally, telling him that I wished to consult my wife, in order to allow time to receive approval from you since it concerns work for the enemy which I would only accept as a sacrifice to be compensated by getting important information.'[7] Madrid was prompt in its reply. On the next day the following message was received: 'Have studied carefully the question of J (3). Am of the opinion that you should accept the offer, as apart from his being able to facilitate good information, this work assists your cover in every respect.'[8] The latter was an advantage which not even GARBO and his case officer had thought of. On 24th May GARBO was able to say that he had definitely accepted the proposition and had been made to sign the Official Secrets Act: 'I attach much importance to this because I learnt that only people who may get to learn details which may compromise secret plans are obliged to sign this.'[9]

The object of giving GARBO an appointment at the Ministry of Information was in order that he should gain access to the Allied propaganda directives. By reading these 'in reverse', he would learn the Allies' intentions. Thus supposing that, after the invasion had begun, these directives placed an emphatic veto on all speculation as to the possibility of a second Allied landing, it would be reasonable to suppose that such a landing was intended. The first few days were spent in studying the propaganda directives which had been prepared in connection with the African landing and the campaign in Italy. Speaking of the latter: 'What I was clearly able to get out of it and what I consider to be of the maximum importance is the intention to hide the facts in order to trick us.'[10] The same report contained a detailed and more or less accurate exposition of the functions of the Political Warfare Executive. 'It is the executive body

---

7. GARBO 2038 and 2044 GMT, 22nd May, 1944.
8. GARBO Message received 0110 GMT, 23rd May, 1944.
9. GARBO 1907 GMT, 24th May, 1944.
10. GARBO 2039 GMT, 29th May, 1944.

for all foreign propaganda and it co-ordinates directives issued which are based on policy recommendations of the Foreign Office, War Cabinet Office and Supreme Headquarters of Allied Expeditionary Forces. The latter is known by the initials "SHAEF". Thus PWE is the propaganda mouthpiece of Eisenhower, Eden and the British Chiefs of Staff. . . . In view of the fact that this department's work is secret it is very possible that Berlin is not aware of these important facts and I therefore recommend that steps should be taken to notify the competent chiefs in Berlin so that experts can evaluate and interpret the strategic plans behind the propaganda directives which are issued, hitherto unknown to us but which, through my present position, will be available to you in future. I am convinced that, knowing the intentions behind these directives, together with the reports from my agents, we will know the future intentions of the enemy.'[11]

GARBO's new appointment, and the greatly increased volume of traffic now passing between London and Madrid, made it essential for him to find personal assistants to relieve him of a part of the burden which he carried as head of the organisation. At the middle of May, therefore, the widow of Two, the agent who had died at Bootle in 1942, was called in to help with the enciphering, while GARBO's deputy, agent Three, was summoned from Scotland and assumed responsibility for collecting all messages and arranging for their despatch. When he took over, GARBO asked the Germans whether they would mind his sending the traffic in English. To this they readily agreed.

---

11. GARBO 2055, 2200, 2205 and 2212 GMT, 29th May, 1944.

XVII

GARBO and the Invasion (II)

GARBO had always insisted that, for the credit of the organisation, at least one of the agents should gain advance information of the invasion. We could not expect to be allowed to tell the enemy that the invading armies were on their way more than an hour or so before the landing took place, and it was arguable that a last-minute message of this kind might excite suspicion. In spite of this, however, the agent and his case officer held to their opinion. Agent Four, the Gibraltarian waiter in the NAAFI of the Chiselhurst caves was chosen for the task. The chain of events which will now be unfolded was designed with two objects in view. First to manœuvre Four into a position which would enable him to provide GARBO with news of the invasion when the Allied armies were still at sea. Second, to build up GARBO's connections with the ministries in London, as these were destined, ultimately, to provide the enemy with the key to Allied intentions. In order to trace the development of the plot, we must go back to FABIUS.

On 27th April GARBO received a message from Four to say that he was leaving the Chiselhurst caves for an unknown destination. He had already a few days before been requested to sign a 'security certificate' requiring NAAFI volunteers employed in the assembly areas to agree to meet no one outside the sealed area and to accept military censorship of mail. On 29th April he rang up GARBO and asked him to meet him at Winchester station on the following day. At this meeting Four explained that he had been posted to Hiltingbury Camp, situated in a wood a mile south-west of Otterbourne in Hampshire. This camp was, in fact, occupied by the 3rd Canadian Infantry Division, one of the real assault formations, and it would be from here that the Division would move to its port of embarkation at the beginning of June. The objection which we had previously had to sending observers into the Southampton area, where too many vital secrets would meet the eye, did not apply in this case, because he was in a sealed camp, and so his inability to communicate with GARBO could readily be explained. Indeed the problem now would be to find a way of putting him in touch with his chief when the time came for him to deliver his final message. At the end of March, when the repercussions of FABIUS upon the cover plan were being discussed, it had been agreed that it would be unreasonable to withhold all knowledge of the exercise from the agents. The policy was therefore established that a number of the agents should observe the preparations for the great rehearsal, but that there should be a realistic variety in the opinions which they expressed as to the purport of the activities observed. Some should be misled into believing that the great day had come; others should see the position in its true light. As the camps in the assembly areas were most rigorously guarded, it was clear that Four would not be able to make his report about the invasion without running the gauntlet in such a way as to jeopardise his future position in the network. After so hazardous an undertaking he would almost certainly have to go into retirement. Thus his ultimate reputation as an agent did not greatly matter. He could therefore act as the foil to other agents whose credit we wished to enhance.

At his meeting with GARBO on 30th April, Four accordingly told his master, referring of course to the embarkation for FABIUS, that 'all the 3rd Infantry Division are concentrated here ready to embark. There are other camps full of troops ready for attack. Have identified the 47th London Division[1] in a camp to the south of mine . . . it is extremely difficult to leave the camp. They are preparing cold rations for two days, also vomit bags, lifebelts[2] for troops' sea

---

1. The 47th and 61st British Infantry Divisions were, in fact, employed to provide 'hotel staffs' in the assembly areas. It could therefore be presumed that any district in which either of these formations was seen denoted a place of embarkation. This pointer was used subsequently to indicate preparations for embarkation in the East and South-East.
2. 'Vomit bags and lifebelts' became GARBO's 'leit motif' for imminent invasion. It may interest the reader to know that this message was scrutinised by Hitler himself.

voyage.'[3] GARBO added that Four was convinced that the invasion was imminent. On the other hand, on 2nd May, GARBO stated that J (5) at the Ministry for War had notified him that there was no possibility of immediate invasion, which drew from GARBO the comment: 'I am disconcerted by what Four said and cannot under any circumstances advise or give information.'[4] The Germans took the side of Four. 'I do not consider that you should attribute too much importance to the opinion of J (5) in the present situation, since it is very probable that the Ministerial personnel has received very severe orders with regard to the confidential handling of all military matters at the present moment. It is also possible that subordinates of Ministries are being falsely misled intentionally.'[5] The following day Four announced that the 3rd Canadian Division had just left in the Southampton direction with embarkation orders;[6] and on 5th May: 'Four communicates that orders have been given to clean and prepare the camp to receive troops once more. Agent supposes these will be second-line units. This proves J (5)'s lie because she suggested, naïvely, today that troops in the Southern area were on manœuvres, information which has been disproved, as in this case troops would have returned. My opinion is that, assuming they have not landed on the Channel coast, the troops which embark must at this moment be moving towards their far-off objective or to join the fleet, reported by Three in the Clyde.'[7] That was to give a little passing assistance to FORTITUDE NORTH.

Then came the anti-climax of 7th May. 'Four has displayed the ability of a simpleton. I am very disgusted with him, though I have not let him know this. He has, today, communicated that the troops he was awaiting, which he thought would be second-line troops, have arrived, but they are the same as had previously left, which is to say the 3rd Canadian Division. The troops at the other camps have likewise returned. Though too late, he tells me that they have been in one of the many rehearsals which Churchill announced would be

---

3. GARBO 1906, 1912, 1918 and 2130 GMT, 30th April, 1944.
4. GARBO 2115 GMT, 2nd May, 1944.
5. GARBO Message received 1905 GMT, 3rd May, 1944.
6. GARBO 2045 GMT, 4th May, 1944.
7. GARBO 1949 and 1954 GMT, 5th May, 1944.

carried out before the Second Front was opened. My last comments about J (5) should be disregarded. I see that her information was true and that the fault has been partly mine through being impressed by the agent. I see that I could get more accurate information through my Ministerial friends. Four, in excuse, says that his beliefs were confirmed by concrete military events, which I am unable to deny. In future he will make no further comments to influence me or my chiefs. I am afraid he is a little discouraged by his great stupidity.'[8] With engaging solicitude, Madrid replied: 'I do not consider that we should reproach Four at all since the troops and the majority of the officers left the camps convinced that it was to be the invasion and only a few high officers knew the real objectives. If Four is disillusioned through his mistake, which he could not avoid you should give him encouragement, as, if not, it might happen that when the real invasion is about to take place he will not notify this owing to over-precaution.'[9] Nevertheless the Germans were left with the realisation that where Allied intentions were concerned as opposed to mere observation, the people at the Ministries were likely to be better informed and that they were not 'being falsely misled intentionally'.

In reply to our request for permission to send an advance report of the landing in France the Supreme Commander gave instructions that a message might be sent three and a half hours before the first touchdown, that is to say at 0300 hours BST.[10] Unfortunately, under the transmission timetable which had come into operation at the beginning of May, Madrid closed down at 23.30 hours at night and did not listen again until 0700 hours. It was therefore necessary to find some means of bringing the Germans onto the air four hours sooner than the timetable demanded. Obviously one could not use the invasion itself as an excuse for keeping them on the alert. Some other inducement, therefore, had to be found. What better than a sudden revival of interest in FORTITUDE NORTH? Only on 22nd May Madrid had stated: 'I am particularly interested to know urgently whether the 52nd Division is still in the camps in the

---

8. GARBO 2035, 2046 and 2052 GMT, 7th May, 1944.
9. GARBO Message received 1959 GMT, 8th May, 1944.
10. In the ensuing narrative British summer time is referred to throughout.

Glasgow area after finishing the manœuvres[11] on the 11th in accordance with the message of Three. I should be grateful to have your reply as soon as possible. Please take every measure to ensure that you are notified of every movement of that division by the quickest possible means. I should be grateful if you would tell me how much time will be lost from the moment the division starts its embarkation operations until the news reaches you for the transmission to us by message.[12] In answer to this, GARBO on 26th May told Madrid that 3 (3), the only remaining agent in Scotland, had been called by telegram to London. 3 (3) had reported on his arrival that the invasion fleet was still in the Clyde and the 52nd Division in the Kilmarnock area. 'Since it was impossible for him to keep a check on the fleet and the 52nd Division at the same time, as they were no longer both in the same place, he was told that he should not lose contact with the fleet, as troops could not embark without ships, thus, while controlling one you control the other.'[13]

With these instructions 3 (3) had returned to Glasgow. On 3rd June GARBO informed the Germans that he had received a telegram from 3 (3) saying that he would be arriving in London at eleven o'clock on the same evening. 'Something must have happened which cannot be explained in the code which had been agreed between us for announcing the sailing of the Clyde fleet. Therefore you should be listening tomorrow morning at 0300 hours.'[14] 3 (3)'s explanation, of which the Germans were informed on the next day, showed that the sub-agent had lost his head. In order to understand what follows, we must, for a moment, anticipate our narrative of events in Scotland. At the beginning of June certain changes were made in the

---

11. These were the landing exercises in Loch Fyne to which reference has already been made.
12. We knew through Most Secret Sources that the question contained in the last sentence had emanated from Berlin. Madrid, anxious to supply Berlin with a prompt answer, had not waited for GARBO's reply but had stated that such information might be expected to reach Madrid within forty-eight hours. This expression of opinion having been duly noted by GARBO's case officer in London, GARBO on the following day informed Madrid that he could supply the required information in twelve hours. Madrid said no more.
13. GARBO 1952, 2022 and 2030 GMT, 26th May, 1944.
14. GARBO 2040 GMT, 3rd June, 1944.

constitution of Fourth Army. As part of this reorganisation, the 55th British Infantry Division had been transferred, on the 2nd of that month, from Northern Ireland to Dumfries, while the 2nd British Corps and the 58th British Infantry Division had received orders to move south. Having heard of the arrival of a large contingent of troops from Ireland, 3 (3) 'disregarded my instructions that he should not leave the Clyde. He discovered an entire division had, in fact, arrived and was encamped in the Dumfries–Lockerbie area. . . . He believes it is the 55th English Division. Returning to Glasgow, on arrival at Motherwell, he discovered that vehicles and men in full equipment in large numbers were assembling there . . . belonging to the stag's antlers division and the one with the sign of the fish in red on blue and white waves. . . . Becoming panicky and realising that his arrival in Glasgow would be delayed in view of the congestion, he decided to telegraph me and take the 1.22 train from Motherwell which was about to leave for London and, so, be able to notify me quicker. I am very disgusted as what he should have done was to have returned to keep a watch on the fleet. Therefore I am giving him strict instructions to return immediately to Glasgow giving him an password in order to telephone me to let me know whether the troops are embarking.'[15] Meanwhile the Germans should continue to listen by night so as to avoid any risk of delay when 3 (3)'s message came through.

We now return to agent Four, immured in Hiltingbury Camp. Since the end of FABIUS, GARBO had only met him once, namely on 22nd May, when he had been in London on twenty-four hours' leave.[16] This silence was not again broken until about midnight on 5th/6th June. Four's story may be told in GARBO's own words. 'Still no news from 3 (3) but, meanwhile, Four has hastened to London, having broken camp together with two American deserters who had arrived in the camp last Sunday. Discovering the plans of these two men, he decided to join them in view of the important news which he would otherwise have been unable to communicate in view of the complete sealing of the camps for the last week. *En route,* he tried to communicate by telephone, using the password prepared

---

15. GARBO 1956, 2002 and 2016 GMT, 4th June, 1944.
16. GARBO 2049 GMT, 23rd May, 1944.

in case of emergency, but found that only official calls were being accepted. He therefore continued his journey clandestinely to London in order to report to me personally. He arrived after a difficult journey created by the steps he took to slip through the local vigilance. He states that he wrote me three days ago, announcing anew the distribution of cold rations and vomit bags, &c., to the 3rd Canadian Division. This letter has not yet reached me due to the delay in the mails. Today he says that, after the 3rd Canadian Division had left, Americans came in, rumours having reached him that the 3rd Canadian Division had embarked. The American troops which are now in the camp belong to the First US Army. The two Americans who escaped with him through fear of embarking belonged to the 926 Signals Corps. The situation of this agent is very compromising for the service because his absence must have been noted owing to the many hours which have elapsed since he left the camp. In order to protect the service I have taken a decision which I think you will approve, which is to put him into hiding, taking advantage of the fact that Seven is here, who says that he can arrange this with absolute safety and without danger of compromise. Therefore, tomorrow, they will both leave for the South of Wales.'[17] According to the imaginary procedure, this message would have been enciphered by Three and the widow, and taken round by the latter to the operator, 4 (1), in time for him to transmit at 0300 hours.

Thus we may picture GARBO leaving for his office on the morning of 6th June, congratulating himself on having been able to give his masters advance information of the great landing in France.

We must now return for a short interval to the world of flesh and blood. On the evening of 5th June a small party consisting of GARBO, his case officer and wireless operator, the head of B1A Section and the Special Means Officer at SHAEF, repaired to a villa in the north of London, where GARBO's wireless transmitter was installed. The only messages received from Madrid that evening were concerned with technical matters affecting call signs[18] and the domestic affairs of agent Five in Canada.[19] Communication continued until

17. GARBO 0608, 0615, 0645 and 0651 GMT, 6th June, 1944.
18. GARBO 1929 hours GMT (2129 hours BST), 5th June, 1944.
19. GARBO 2004 hours GMT (2204 hours BST), 5th June, 1944.

shortly before midnight. The Germans showed no sign of uneasiness. By three o'clock in the morning the message containing the story of Four's escape was encoded, and the operator called Madrid. Madrid failed to reply. The call was repeated at intervals, but without result. At first this failure to attract the attention of the Germans caused some consternation. The invasion fleet was already approaching the French coast, and in a short time the landings would take place. It seemed as if we were to forego the benefits which would accrue from an advance report. On reflection, however, it seemed possible to turn the situation to our advantage, for since we now knew that the Germans would not receive the message until after the landing had occurred, we could strengthen the wording and still claim that GARBO had received it several hours before the troops landed. In fact the message did not go off until eight o'clock in the morning, by which time the imaginary GARBO was on his way to work at the Ministry of Information oblivious of Madrid's negligence.

GARBO's deception at the Ministry of Information was to be achieved by inverting fictitious PWE directives which warned the press not to speculate about future landings. On the day before the invasion took place the Special Means Staff had an opportunity of seeing the drafts of a number of the speeches that were to be made on the afternoon of the following day when the attack had been launched. Several of these speeches made veiled allusions to the possibility of further landings. This placed GARBO in a difficult position since the PWE directives about which he was telling the enemy forbade all reference to future assaults and diversions. In composing these imaginary directives we had worked on the assumption that no public mention would be made of a second landing. That seemed a reasonable assumption to make, for clearly no one would have been allowed to throw out hints about the real invasion before it occurred, and what held good for the first landing would presumably hold good for the second.[20]

----

20. It is only fair to add that the passages in the D Day speeches, which GARBO now found so embarrassing, had been included with the approval and indeed at the suggestion of SHAEF. In answer to a request for guidance, the Political Warfare Division had been specifically informed that public speakers might 'refer to OVERLORD as preliminary operations for the liberation of Europe.

Let us see how GARBO sought to find a way out of this new difficulty: 'After the crisis last night with agent Four I was summoned
early this morning to the Ministry of Information. I arrived to find
the department already in a complete state of chaos, everyone spec-
ulating as to the importance of the attack which had started this
morning against France. All the sections were handed copies of a
directive, distributed by PWE to the Ministry. I find it very significant and more still if compared with the speeches of the Allied
Chiefs. I transmit an exact copy of this directive.

'"*Special Directive on the Offensive against Northern France.*
'"*Political Warfare Executive. Central Directive.*
'"1. The offensive launched today by General Eisenhower forms
another important step in the Allied concentric attack on the
fortress of Europe.

They should say that, although the assault has not yet been made in any of their
countries, their hour of liberation is at hand' (SHAEF/18202/6/Ops, dated 1st
May, 1944). How this error of judgment occurred is of little consequence today.
But it is important to notice that the reply given to the Political Warfare Division
transgressed a principle of deception by allowing the cover story to emanate from
a source which the enemy could not fail to recognise as officially inspired, an
error which was not redeemed by the fact that in this particular case the
Germans were so obtuse as to take the speeches, for a time at least, at their face
value and argue that they provided evidence of 'further undertakings' having
been planned. (Appendix to OKH Lagebericht West No. 1288, dated 6th June,
1944.) Some three weeks later it became necessary to close the English Channel
to fishing boats. The Deception Staff recommended that the ban should include
the entire European coast from the Spanish frontier to the North Cape. After
some deliberation, the prohibition was confined to the coastlines of Holland,
Belgium and France, but in order, presumably, to show that an attack on
Norway was still to be reckoned with, SHAEF broadcast its instructions on 29th
June in the following terms: 'The Supreme Commander requires that no fishing
shall be carried on in the coastal waters between the French port of Bayonne,
near the Spanish frontier, to the West Frisian Islands until the 6th July at 9 p.m.
But the Supreme Commander warns fishermen in other coastal areas that fishing may become extremely dangerous at any time, and that it will not be possible
to issue special warnings immediately in advance of future operations.' A copy
of that message is to be found in the files of the OKW (OKW/WFS Papers, File
No. 605, teleprinter message dated 29th June, 1944). The second sentence has
been sidelined and the word 'deception' (Taeuschung!) has been added.

'"2. It is of the utmost importance that the enemy should be
kept in the dark as to our future intentions.

'"3. Care should be taken to avoid any reference to further
assaults and diversions.

'"4. Speculation regarding alternative assault areas must be
avoided.

'"5. The importance of the present assault and its decisive
influence on the course of the war should be clearly stated."

'Together with the directive J (3) handed me copies of the
speeches which had, at that moment, not been broadcast. After reading these documents I asked him for a further interview and told
him that, as a basis for propaganda, I considered that the directive
was in complete contradiction with the speeches as it was inevitable
that these speeches would be quoted and used as the basis of propaganda by the world press. I pointed out that these speeches gave a
latitude which is denied by the directive. For instance, in
Eisenhower's speech, which says: "A premature uprising of all
Frenchmen may prevent you from being a maximum help to your
country in the critical hour. Be patient. Prepare!" . . . And still more
important, the following: "This landing is but the opening phase of
the campaign in Western Europe. Great battles lie ahead." The
Belgian Prime Minister said: "Preliminary operations for the liberation of Europe have begun. The first assault is the certain signal for
your deliverance." And also "The moment of supreme combat has
not yet come." . . . J (3) told me, in confidence, that I had spotted
the one inevitable weakness in the policy which had been directed.
He explained that, in the first place, it was essential that Eisenhower
should keep the people from rising too early in areas which were yet
to be involved in operations but, at the same time, it was equally
necessary to try to hide all this information from the enemy. He said
he did not think the enemy would be able to draw any definite conclusions from these speeches but he thought that they, nevertheless,
constituted such a contradiction to the directives as to create a difficult situation internally. He went on to say that the Director-General
had himself raised my point. Nevertheless, he felt that, if the work
were done intelligently, he believed it possible to focus public attention on the present attack and thus detract from any other

suggestion of future plans, this being precisely the work with which he was entrusted.'[21]

On the following day GARBO told the enemy that, under pressure from the Ministry of Information, the PWE Directive had been amended so as to allow 'certain limited speculation in general terms as to future operations'.[22] Thus, the real speeches and the imaginary directive were brought into line, and it was to be hoped that the Germans would regard the veiled hints of 'more to come' as minor indiscretions, which had caused a momentary stir in the Ministries of Whitehall, rather than as evidence of organised deception. The amendment permitting limited speculation was, incidentally, a useful hedge against possible indiscretions in the press.

It was not possible, as it had been with the other speeches, to obtain in advance a draft of the Prime Minister's statement in the House of Commons. He went further than the other speakers and said: 'I have also to announce to the House that during the night and the early hours of this morning the first *of a series of landings in force* upon the European Continent has taken place.' This GARBO explained by saying: 'In spite of recommendations made to Churchill that his speech should contain every possible reserve, he based it on the consideration that he was obliged, on account of his political position, to avoid distorting the facts and would not permit that his speeches should be discredited by coming events.'[23]

On his return from the office, GARBO found the long-expected message from 3 (3) in Glasgow awaiting him. The fleet had not left the Clyde, nor had the troops embarked, but a state of alarm still existed.[24] After informing Madrid that he had as yet received no military reports from his sub-agents and that he had in consequence called them urgently to London, he continued: 'For the present I can only state a definite argument, based on the studies and appreciations which my work in the Ministry has facilitated and it is that the enemy are hiding their intentions behind this first

---

21. GARBO 2055, 2107, 2122, 2135, 2140, 2237, 2247, 2255 and 2300 GMT, 6th June, 1944.
22. GARBO 2158 GMT, 7th June, 1944.
23. GARBO 2152 GMT, 7th June, 1944.
24. GARBO 2040 GMT, 6th June, 1944.

action.'[25] His account of the day's events closed on a self-congratulatory note: 'Fortunately the first action was robbed of the surprise which they wished to create through the information from Four as, from the hour at which the assault is said to have started, I am able to prove, with satisfaction, that my message arrived in time to prevent the action coming as a surprise to our High Command. There is no doubt that Four has accomplished through his action a service which, though it will make it impossible to use his collaboration in the future, has justified a sacrifice by his last report. Four left this morning accompanied by Seven who will arrange for him to be hidden in a safe place. For myself, and counting on your approval, I intend to take care of this friend and give him every consideration in order to make him aware of our recognition.'[26] No sooner had this report been despatched than news reached him through the widow that Madrid had not been listening at 0300 hours that morning. 'On handing over today's messages, Almura[27] told the widow that he was not able to send the urgent messages until 0800 hours since you had not been listening. This makes me question your seriousness and your sense of responsibility. I therefore demand a clarification immediately as to what has occurred. If what I suspect is the case and Almura has failed in his duties, then I am absolutely decided in this event to abandon the radio service until I can find some other solution. I am very disgusted in this struggle for life or death, I cannot accept excuses or negligence. I cannot swallow the idea of endangering the service without any benefit. Were it not for my ideals and faith I would abandon this work as having proved myself a failure. I write these messages to send this very night though my tiredness and exhaustion, due to the excessive work I have had, has completely broken me.'[28] The German reply, which came back the same day, provides an interesting psychological study. 'I have read your last two messages of yesterday and I perfectly well understand your state of morale and feel moved to answer you the following. It would be difficult, if not

---

25. GARBO 2305 GMT, 6th June, 1944.
26. GARBO 2310 and 2322 GMT, 6th June, 1944.
27. German code name for agent 4 (1).
28. GARBO 2355 GMT, 6th June, and 0601 GMT, 7th June, 1944.

impossible, to find out who is to blame if a culprit really exists with regard to the delay in the transmission of the message of Four. After finishing on Monday at 2350 hours, having received your message, Centro was listening according to plan every hour up to 0300 hours and again from 0700 hours on Tuesday, getting the message of Four at 0800 hours. It is possible that, in spite of the staff having been listening properly, due to bad conditions having set in, there would have been no other calls from Almura during the night. Let us know at what time Almura tried to call us without success. But, even supposing the worst and Almura did not call, you must remember that Almura, according to what you have told us, is not aware of the true significance of your mission and it is possible that he, after his day's work and having been transmitting that night for nearly three hours, should have felt tired and, considering that he had fulfilled his duties, he could not imagine that the message was one of such importance that it could not be delayed for a few hours. I wish to stress in the clearest terms that your work over the last few weeks has made it possible for our Command to be completely forewarned and prepared and the message of Four would have influenced but little had it arrived three or four hours earlier. Thus I reiterate to you, as responsible chief of the service, and to all your collaborators, our total recognition of your perfect and cherished work and I beg of you to continue with us in the supreme and decisive hours of the struggle for the future of Europe.'[29] On 12th June GARBO replied: 'Almura communicated that on the night of the crisis he called at 0300 hours for half an hour and that he repeated his calls at 0700 hours without any result. With regard to the belief that Almura would not imagine the extreme urgency of the message handed to him, this I can dispel as whether or not he knew its contents is nothing to do with the fact that he had his instructions given to him by the widow, which were to tell him that it was of extreme urgency that that message should be sent that night. I cannot, therefore, accept negligence, even if he were tired from his long hours of transmission. I am also exhausted but I know how to fulfil my duties. Furthermore, the

---

29. GARBO Message received 2010, 2016, 2022, 2100 and 2108 GMT, 7th June, 1944.

payment he receives is the highest of the network and it would, therefore, be unwise for him to accept the possibility that the atmospheric conditions were bad but, on future occasions, I intend to take my security measures in urgent cases as in the one mentioned and will endeavour to see that the widow remains present at any important transmissions.'[30] Here the Germans thought it wise to let the matter drop.

The invasion took all the other agents by surprise. BRUTUS stated frankly: 'Unfortunately, by remaining without contact with 21 Army Group and through awaiting a state of alert at FUSAG, I was not able to give you details of the first landings.'[31] Similarly TATE confessed the date of the invasion had caught him unawares as in his district everything was apparently unchanged. No departures of troops had been observed; on the contrary more were coming daily.[33] Others reacted as best fitted their respective circumstances. One obscure double-cross agent, who does not otherwise figure in the invasion story, remarked fatalistically: 'It has arrived and I have not been able to let you know in time.'[33]

---

30. GARBO 2038, 2044 and 2050 GMT, 12th June, 1944.
31. BRUTUS 1816 GMT, 6th June, 1944.
32. TATE 1826 MET, 7th June, 1944.
33. SHEPHERD Letter to Lisbon, dated 7th June, 1944.

XVIII

FORTITUDE NORTH Continued and Ended

The time has come to turn our attention once more to Scotland and to follow the Northern operation to its conclusion. The reader will recall that, though the bulk of its forces were concentrated in the neighbourhood of Glasgow, the headquarters of Fourth Army were still near Edinburgh at the beginning of May. While it was important that we should sustain the Northern threat until the time of the invasion, and if possible beyond that date, certain factors militated against its continuance, at least on its present scale. The 2nd US Infantry Division had already been withdrawn from XV Corps and had moved from Northern Ireland to Tenby in South Wales, where it had replaced the 28th US Infantry Division. During May it would be necessary to transfer the naval deception units representing assault forces 'V' and 'W' for employment in the South. Finally the withdrawal of shipping from Northern ports would compel us to admit a reduction in the scale of the assault. With these considerations in mind, the position was reviewed at the middle of April.[1] It was expected at that time that the 2nd Canadian Corps, which then formed part of the imaginary FUSAG, would be going overseas about eight days after the invasion began. Since shipping space and assault craft would now be inadequate for the requirements of Fourth Army as then constituted, it was suggested that a part of the Scottish force might be moved to the South-East of England to

---

1. SHAEF/18216/1/Ops, dated 18th April, 1944. Notes for meeting regarding programme for forces engaged in Plan FORTITUDE (Scandinavia) for period Y minus 15 to Y plus 28.

take the place of the Canadian formations in the FORTITUDE
SOUTH Order of Battle. Not every formation in Fourth Army
could, however, be used in a false role, in South-East England. XV
Corps with the 5th and 8th US Infantry Divisions was due to move
from Northern Ireland to the Midland counties at the middle of
May, but its early transfer to Normandy precluded its employment
in FORTITUDE SOUTH. The 52nd Lowland Division was prevented by its training programme from leaving Scotland and the
employment of the imaginary 55th US Division in Iceland was
considered impracticable. The 7th British Corps could have been
used, but since its two divisions were tied down, it seemed better to
leave it where it was. This left the 2nd British Corps with its two
divisions, the real 55th British Infantry Division in Northern
Ireland and the sham 58th British Infantry Division in Scotland.
There was no difficulty about the 2nd British Corps and 58th
British Infantry Division, as they were both imaginary and were provided with adequate deceptive wireless resources, but it was not so
easy to make the real British division in Ireland available. After
some negotiation with the War Office, it was agreed that the signals
of this formation should be formed into an advance party and transferred to Scotland, where they could represent it on the air, the
remainder being instructed to use low-powered sets in the division's
old location. It was accordingly arranged that the 2nd British Corps
with its two divisions should be earmarked to fill the gap caused by
the departing Canadians. It was proposed that this force should
stage for a time near the Humber whence it could assist both the
Northern and the Southern threats. It was thought wise to leave
Fourth Army in Scotland for the present, as a senior headquarters
was needed to command the 7th British and XV Corps so long as
they were able to fulfil their present cover role in the North.
Although XV Corps was about to move to England, it would be
possible by placing these American formations on wireless silence
and by representing them as being in their old locations, to include
them in Fourth Army for some time after the date of their departure. During the week following 21st May a detachment of 3103
Signals Service Battalion was sent to Northern Ireland to give effect
to this, and in that manner XV Corps remained ostensibly a part of
Fourth Army until the end of June. A plan to give effect to these

proposals was issued on 4th May.[2] In accordance with this plan, the Scottish formations awaiting embarkation would continue to carry out exercises in the neighbourhood of Glasgow. Towards the end of the month Fourth Army Headquarters would move from Edinburgh to Ayr. At the same time the wireless nets of the 55th British Infantry Division would open at Dumfries. On 2nd June a large-scale Army exercise lasting some four days would take place, and on the 5th this exercise was to be interrupted by the order for the 2nd Corps and its two divisions to move to Lincolnshire. Throughout May this programme was adhered to, but as a result of a request from 21 Army Group that the transfer of the 2nd Corps should be advanced by three days, that formation and the two divisions under its command left on 2nd June, and accordingly the exercise did not take place. On 5th June 2nd Corps, still netted to Fourth Army, came on the air at Louth with the 55th British Infantry Division at Skegness and the 58th at Horncastle,[3] and on the 6th a link was opened between 2nd Corps and FUSAG. We will leave its subsequent movements to a later chapter dealing with the Southern operation.

Meanwhile in the North the 113th Independent Infantry Brigade in the Orkneys, which had formed part of 2nd Corps, was brought under 7th Corps, while a link was opened between 7th Corps and the 55th US Infantry Division in Iceland. With this reduced force, it could not be pretended that the Scandinavian assault was still contemplated on the original scale. From now onwards, therefore, the operation was only to be undertaken in the event of a considerable weakening of German forces or of a total withdrawal.

---

2. SHAEF/18216/1/Ops, dated 4th May, 1944.

3. Scottish Command expressed some concern over the speed at which this move was carried out. It was suggested that the employment of operators in Lincolnshire who had been transmitting only twenty-four hours earlier in Scotland was unrealistic. It was also contended that if it had been necessary to route the 55th Infantry Division through Scotland instead of sending it direct from Northern Ireland to Skegness, it would have been more reasonable if it had maintained wireless silence while it was in Dumfriesshire. (SCCR MS 4/43878/2/Ops, dated 6th June, 1944 – Scottish Command to SHAEF.)

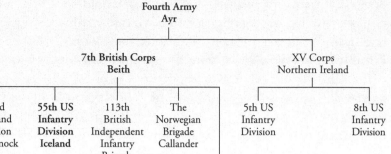

THE NORTHERN FORCE AS RECONSTITUTED AT THE BEGINNING OF JUNE 1944

Fourth Army
Ayr

7th British Corps
Beith

XV Corps
Northern Ireland

| 52nd Lowland Division Kilmarnock | **55th US Infantry Division Iceland** | 113th British Independent Infantry Brigade Orkneys | The Norwegian Brigade Callander | 5th US Infantry Division | 8th US Infantry Division |

Three US Ranger Battalions Iceland

TRANSFERRED TO FUSAG

2nd British Corps

| 55th British Infantry Division | **58th British Infantry Division** |

Formations printed in heavy type were imaginary

When June came, it was in any case obvious that the force of FOR-
TITUDE NORTH was spent. The battles in Normandy were already
monopolising the attention of the enemy and presently the few
remaining formations which had survived the regrouping of early
June were to be withdrawn. On 30th June, since XV Corps was about
to land in the beach-head, the detachment of 3103 Signals Service
Battalion closed down in Northern Ireland. On 2nd July the 52nd
Lowland Division was released from its fictitious role.[4] At the middle
of July Fourth Army and 7th British Corps were required to command forces in the reconstituted FORTITUDE SOUTH Order of
Battle, and proceeded to England.[5] A plan for keeping alive a very
slender threat against Scandinavia which would have involved the

---

4. It moved to Buckinghamshire in August, where it was observed by BRUTUS
   (1707 GMT, 21st August, and 1750 GMT, 24th August, 1944) and in the following month was transferred to Belgium.
5. See Chapter 27: The New Plan.

transfer of the 55th US Infantry Division to Scotland was drafted, but never came into operation.[6]

Among the controlled agents, since Three had now left for London to help GARBO, the main burden fell, during the latter days of FORTITUDE NORTH, upon GARBO's agent 3 (3). The Germans had regarded Three's departure as a somewhat dangerous exposure of the flank: 'If you consider it advisable to call Three to help you, please ask him to consider carefully if in this event the North will be well covered by 3 (3), since it is very possible that some action will start up also from those ports.'[7] Nevertheless it was a risk which had to be accepted and by the middle of the month 3 (3) had moved to Glasgow, as being a more central position.

On his arrival in London Three had expressed the view that the *initial* attack of the European invasion would be against Norway. In this he was supported by 3 (3). GARBO, with his wider outlook, had been disinclined to accept their view, which he evidently regarded as somewhat parochial, though he had felt bound to add: 'Nevertheless I take notice of this opinion since Three is in a better position than I am to assess this question due to what he has been able to see in his recent stay in the North.'[8]

3 (3)'s erratic behaviour during the next two or three weeks, while it succeeded in provoking a number of German questions which showed that they had not yet lost interest in the Clyde, was really part of the rather intricate plot connected with the invasion in the South, which has already been described in the last chapter. The only other Scottish news was provided by BRUTUS. On two occasions, once before and once after the invasion he confirmed that Fourth Army retained its independent role.[9] He also told the enemy about the move South of 2nd British Corps and the consequent reorganisation of forces in the

---

6. A force of three divisions comprising the 55th US Infantry Division, the real 48th British Infantry Division at Lincoln and a new imaginary division were to be held in readiness to occupy Southern Norway immediately there was any indication of a German withdrawal. (SHAEF/18252/Ops (B), dated 27th July, 1944.)

7. GARBO Message received 2045 GMT, 15th May, 1944.

8. GARBO 1950 GMT, 20th May, 1944.

9. BRUTUS 1707 GMT, 17th May, and 2113 GMT, 11th June, 1944.

North.[10] Thereafter apart from a first-hand account by 3 (3) of a Fourth Army exercise in Ayrshire,[11] nothing more was heard from Scotland until the final dispersal of forces occurred in July, when GARBO made this appreciation: 'There is something important which I wish to stress. If I recall correctly, the Fourth British Army was in Scotland with the concentration observed by 3 (3) in Motherwell, that is to say, together with 2nd Corps, the 55th and 58th Divisions. If, therefore, the British Army moves down, the only division left to effect the proposed attack against Norway will be 52nd Division. I therefore consider that an attack against Norway is impossible for the moment. My present observation goes to show how right I was when I expressed the opinion against the views of Three and 3 (3) that this operation would not then come off at that time of the year. I therefore consider that a state of alarm in Norway need no longer be maintained.'[12]

FORTITUDE NORTH did not end officially until 30th September, when the Combined Chiefs of Staff considered that owing to lack of German reserves one could no longer hope to contain enemy forces in non-active sectors such as Scandinavia, and that, in consequence, the cost of maintaining such threats would no longer justify the effort required.[13] The 55th US Infantry Division and the three Ranger Battalions, the only surviving formations in the FORTITUDE NORTH Order of Battle,[14] remained in Iceland until March 1945, when a report from BEETLE that the Americans were withdrawing may allow us to conclude that they left at that time for some unknown destination.[15]

---

10. BRUTUS 1629 and 1634 GMT, 14th June, 1944.
11. GARBO 1948, 1958, 2006 and 2014 GMT, 22nd June, 1944.
12. GARBO Letter No. 22, dated 20th July, 1944.
13. Teleprinter message WX39193, dated 30th September, 1944. AGWAR from Combined Chiefs of Staff to SHAEF and other addressees. This instruction also brought BODYGUARD as a whole to an end: 'In view of present rapidly changing situation, it has been decided to cancel Plan BODYGUARD, and you should therefore prepare a short-term deception plan to cover your respective operational requirements, these plans to be co-ordinated through London Controlling Section. The Russians have agreed to cancellation of Plan BODYGUARD.'
14. The 113th Independent Infantry Brigade and the Norwegian Brigade dropped out in July, 1944, when Fourth Army went South.
15. BEETLE Message No. 251, sent 5th March, 1945.

XIX

Reactions to BODYGUARD and FORTITUDE NORTH

In writing a history of this kind, it is hard to choose the right moment to lift the curtain and let the reader into the enemy's thoughts. If one does so too soon, one tends, by revealing much that was hidden from us at the time, to obscure and overlay the true causes of contemporary action. If on the other hand one waits too long, one makes it very difficult for the reader of a story of such length and complexity to relate each allied action to its corresponding enemy reaction.

The somewhat arbitrary course has therefore been taken of selecting the invasion as the most suitable date for a full disclosure. On the one hand the bulk of the planning now lay behind us; on the other the fulfilment of our plans was already giving us an insight into the working of the German mind. From this point therefore it becomes possible, without the fear of serious historical distortion, to follow the story from both sides. Henceforward we will carry the Germans with us.

Before going any further we must look back and try to assess the results of our efforts during the previous six months. Let us take the plans in chronological order. BODYGUARD had made SHAEF responsible for telling the Germans that we were ready to reoccupy any part of Western Europe in the event of an enemy withdrawal, that the cross-Channel assault would not be undertaken until the late summer and that we intended to attack Norway in the spring.

No evidence of a reaction to the 'occupation' story has come to light. This is hardly surprising, for, as GARBO observed at the time, the enemy would naturally assume that arrangements must exist for entering any part of the Continent which the enemy vacated. Hence there would be little purpose in alluding to such plans in any contemporary German appreciation.

The story of postponement in all its guises found its way to the enemy through practically every Special Means channel. Diplomatic circles in Stockholm, Berne and Lisbon, as well as Abwehr agents, are quoted. The effect of these numerous reports was by no means what had been hoped for. Contrary to our belief, the Germans imagined that a cross-Channel invasion in the winter or early spring was perfectly possible. At the same time the uncontrolled agents, afraid of appearing to have been caught unawares, found safety by prophesying imminent invasion continuously from the New Year onwards. Having become convinced, as early as February, that our preparations were already far advanced, the suggestion of a greatly postponed invasion did not ring true to the Germans. 'Occasional statements', says OKH Intelligence Summary of 24th February, 'from various sources about current reorganisation, and the strong emphasis on "safety first" (especially by Montgomery) encourage the idea of a (perhaps only trifling) postponement. . . . However, the greatest caution must be exercised when reflecting on this consideration, since enemy diplomatic sources seem to be systematically spreading information about the postponement of the invasion.'[1] Some three weeks later a telegram[2] from the German Embassy in Lisbon informed Berlin that 'Portuguese and Spaniards coming from London confirm the view, which prevails there, that England will not undertake any large-scale invasion, but will continue to try by means of air attacks and possibly small landings to tie down Germans in the West, to weaken the German arms industry and in this manner to support the military successes of Russia.' Berlin's evaluation can scarcely be said to

---

1. Appendix to Lagebericht West No. 1185, dated 24th February, 1944. A complete series of daily OKH Legeberichte for the whole of 1944 and the early part of 1945 was discovered by the United States Seventh Army in a cave in Thuringia during the last days of the war. It provides by far the most valuable evidence of the progress of FORTITUDE, stating in nearly all cases the source of intelligence upon which each entry is based.
2. OKW/WFSt papers, file 603. Note by OKW/WFSt, dated 17th March, 1944, initialled by Keitel, Jodl, Warlimont and Krummacher.

have advanced the interests of Allied strategic deception. 'Numerous reports of an alleged postponement of the invasion or of its complete abandonment in favour of an intensification of the air war or of smaller local landing operations are, in the opinion of this Abteilung, to be regarded as systematic concealment of the actual plan.'[3]

As has been explained in a previous chapter, no attempt, apart from FOYNES, the plan to conceal the divisions returning from the Mediterranean, was made during the earlier phase of FORTITUDE, before the Joint Commanders' Plan came into operation, to vary the numerical strength of Allied forces in this country. Had we attempted during the spring of 1944 to reduce that strength as was recommended in BODYGUARD, it is unlikely that we should have made any significant impression, for there is conclusive evidence to show that at the end of 1943 the Germans exaggerated our strength by about 50 per cent, a miscalculation which persisted until the end of the war. As the real total increased, so the German estimate rose in like proportion.

As to FOYNES, the Germans, before the end of 1943, were already beginning to notice that these eight divisions had disappeared from the Italian front. That they might have returned to the United Kingdom occurred not only to the Germans but also to the uncontrolled agents as the most likely explanation. The latter, therefore, having been asked by the Germans to locate the missing divisions, thought England as good a guess as any other, and so we read: 'Independent reports about the transfer of parts of the Eighth British Army from the Mediterranean to England continue. The possibility must, therefore, be considered that individual formations which have not appeared in Italy or North Africa for some considerable time have been transferred wholly or in part to the British Isles.'[4] These suspicions were confirmed by occasional disclosures arising from the interrogation of prisoners-of-war and from captured mail. In February a letter from a British soldier stationed in the United Kingdom, which fell into German hands, told them that 'the Scottish division which came from Italy will presumably take part in the great events due to

---

3. Appendix to Lagebericht West No. 1210, dated 20th March, 1944.
4. Appendix to Lagebericht West No. 1151, dated 21st January, 1944.

take place'.[5] The enemy had no difficulty in elucidating the fact that the writer intended to imply that the 51st Highland Division had returned to England and was to take part in the invasion.

In spite of these and other indications of a more general nature such as the transfer of landing craft from the Mediterranean to England,[6] the Germans tended to regard the evidence as inconclusive and preferred to hold the FOYNES divisions in the base area of the armies on the Italian front, that is to say in Central or Southern Italy, or even in North Africa. On 7th March, the transfer of the 7th British Armoured Division to England was held to be probable, 'but the inadequacy of available data compels us to await confirmations'.[7]

With one minor exception, the controlled agents made no reference to any of the FOYNES divisions until the second half of April.[8]

---

5. AOM No. 2717, dated 16th February, 1944, reflected in Appendix to Lagebericht West No. 1178 of 17th February, 1944.
6. 'The transfer, which has recently again been recognised, of landing craft from the Mediterranean to England, though small in extent (20–22 LCT), does, however, fit in with our existing view regarding the formation of a Schwerpunkt in England.' (Appendix to Lagebericht West No. 1170, dated 9th February, 1944.) This was probably based on observation at Gibraltar.
7. Appendix to Lagebericht West No. 1197, dated 7th March, 1944.
8. In a letter dated 16th February, GARBO, in giving an account of his visit to the South-West of England, was allowed by an oversight to say: 'In Portland harbour I saw some American soldiers with the number one in red on khaki ground in the neighbourhood of the town. I learned that the insignia belongs to the 1st American Division.' It so happened that the Commander of 'A' Force, a closely interested party, was in London at the time. He took the view that the wording of the message suggested troops on leave rather than the return of a whole formation. The accuracy of this diagnosis may be gauged by the following quotations: 'The reported appearance of traces of the 1st American Infantry Division, hitherto assumed to be in the Western Mediterranean, still lacks confirmation' (Appendix to Lagebericht West No. 1189 of 28th February, 1944), and 'a well regarded source reports the appearance of *weak forces of the 1st American Infantry Division in Great Britain*. This division was hitherto assumed to be in the Western Mediterranean. It *may* be that these are remnants since the 1st Infantry Division was in Great Britain before being sent to the Mediterranean. Since there is no further reliable evidence for the transfer of this division from the Mediterranean to Great Britain, we must, for the present, accept it in an unknown location.' (Ueberblick USA No. 22 for 2nd March, 1944.)

The 51st Highland Division was the first to be released.[9] This was followed by the 9th US Infantry Division and the 50th British Infantry Division at the beginning of May.[10] During May these three divisions were constantly alluded to in the controlled traffic and their presence in the United Kingdom accepted by the Germans without reserve. One brief mention was made of the 2nd US Armoured Division on 17th May.[11] The remaining three divisions[12] were not referred to at all by the controlled agents before the invasion and continued to be shown as 'unlocated' in the German records.

To sum up, it would appear that, although the Germans suspected the return of these divisions from the New Year onwards, they did not accept any movement as an accomplished fact until it had been notified by one of the controlled agents. It is of interest to note that whereas the United States formations were allowed normal signals facilities from February onwards, while the British formations remained on wireless silence[13] until D Day, no significant leakage through intercept is reported in the OKH Intelligence Summary either from the British or from the Americans. It is true that the German Intelligence Summary for 15th January alludes to 'suggestions from a sure source that parts of the 82nd Airborne Division have been transferred to England',[14] but that was a month before the division had been allowed to resume normal wireless activity. Moreover the Intelligence Summary remarks a fortnight later: 'The suspected transfer of parts of the 82nd American Airborne Division does not seem to be substantiated. The bulk of the division must henceforward to assumed to be in Italy.'[15]

*

---

9. FREAK 1213 GMT, 24th April, 1944.
10. GARBO 1755 and 1803 GMT, 1st May, 1944.
11. TREASURE 1053 GMT, 17th May, 1944.
12. 7th British Armoured Division, 1st British Airborne Division and 82nd US Airborne Division.
13. The order to the British formations provided that they might operate divisional wireless nets but they were forbidden to establish rear links to corps. High-powered 22 sets were not to be used. No officers with RT peculiarities were to speak on RT and WT operators were to be changed.
14. Appendix to Lagebericht West No. 1145, dated 15th January, 1944.
15. Appendix to Lagebericht West No. 1160, dated 30th January, 1944.

Let us now examine the effect of FORTITUDE NORTH upon the enemy. TINDALL, the threat which had been made against Norway in 1943 as part of COCKADE, came to an end in November of that year. The uncontrolled agents continued unceasingly to speak of large assemblies of shipping in the Scottish ports. The Germans, however, were more inclined to fall in with a view, more than once expressed by GARBO, that an attack across the North Sea during the winter was highly improbable. 'Norway has fallen more and more into the background during the last months.'[16] The forebodings of the alarmists continued, but the Germans refused to be stampeded. 'Reports of the movement of shipping into the harbours of Eastern Scotland may show preparedness for a later move down to the invasion ports in South-East England. On the other hand this measure cannot be taken as pointing to the planning of large-scale operations from Scotland, since the present distribution of forces does not offer the necessary conditions for this.'[17] There is evidence to show that these uncontrolled reports were doing us some harm at this time. 'As regards the alleged enemy troop movements and preparation of shipping in Scotland, the impression is growing stronger that such information is consciously intended to direct German attention to this region. An operation of *limited* scope from Scotland does not seem out of the question, but forces are inadequate for a *large-scale* operation from this sea.'[18]

FORTITUDE NORTH came into operation during the third week of March 1944. Only a short time before the enemy had made a fairly detailed appreciation of Norway as a likely Allied objective. This is worth quoting because it shows the German frame of mind just before Allied deception was brought into play.

Reports from otherwise proven Abwehr sources about enemy troop movements and shipping preparations in the *Scotland area* amount to the following:

The available information consists exclusively of news at third or fourth hand. It in no way provides, therefore, a sure

---

16. Appendix to Lagebericht West No. 1149, dated 19th January, 1944.
17. Appendix to Lagebericht West No. 1189, dated 28th February, 1944.
18. Appendix to Lagebericht West No. 1199, dated 9th March, 1944.

foundation. Other reconnaissance means have lately failed to produce further data from the Scottish area. . . . We must reckon with four to six active divisions in this area. The shipping reported in East Scottish waters corresponds approximately to the tonnage which would be necessary to transport this force. Troops and shipping available to the enemy command would therefore allow the latter to embark forces in Scotland to a strength of four to five divisions. One or two American divisions from Iceland might be added to this number.

It is thus abundantly clear that if the enemy carries out an undertaking from Scottish ports this *will not be a large-scale operation which will seek to be decisive.* (Keine entscheidungssuchende Operation grossen Ausmasses.)

The *Norwegian coast* might be the target of this undertaking. This Abteilung holds that it would be absolutely improbable for Russian agreement to be obtained to a Petsamo–Murmansk undertaking. . . . An operation by part of the enemy's forces against Jutland is only to be expected immediately prior to the great all-out attack against France, as otherwise the Anglo-Saxon forces on Jutland would run the risk of annihilation by free German reserves. Since the course of the weather and certain other factors in the Channel area point away from the imminence of a large landing, the Jutland undertaking seems scarcely likely and Norway the most conceivable target.

Since the operations of the enemy command in the present stage of the war all mean the tying up of German forces on subsidiary fronts, or alternatively their removal from the decisive Atlantic front to subsidiary fronts, and as the enemy has already been successful in this sense in Italy, it seems thoroughly *possible* that he has come to a like decision in the Scandinavian area. The hitherto inadequate data do not allow us to call this certain or even probable.

It seems nevertheless that henceforward enhanced preparedness on the Norwegian coast and *above all an intensification of air reconnaissance over the whole of the North Sea area are indispensable.* This measure appears to constitute the only means, which has any prospect of success, of avoiding surprises such as those of the Sicily and Nettuno landings. The pressing home of

port reconnaissance in the North Scottish area and the employment of naval forces (U-boats) with exclusively reconnaissance
and observation tasks in the direction of Scotland must be
regarded as an important additional measure.[19]

BODYGUARD had miscalculated in two particulars. First in the
German appraisement of inter-Allied relations. The enemy saw us as
rivals, rather than as partners, in the extreme north. Second in the
German belief that Denmark could be attacked without the previous conquest of Norway. This, however, did not materially affect the
issue. Taken as a whole, the threat was well aimed. The Germans
were predisposed to believe in an attack on Scandinavia 'to tie down
forces on subsidiary fronts', and already, without assistance from us
they thought that four or five British divisions with shipping to
transport them might be available in Scotland, to which might be
added one or two American divisions in Iceland. It will thus be
seen that FORTITUDE NORTH began its career under favourable
auspices.

The confession that all sources of intelligence other than Abwehr
agents had failed to produce information from Scotland and that the
latter had only been able to give third- or fourth-hand reports shows
that we owed our flying start chiefly to German preconceptions, but
partly also to the uncontrolled agents, even if the latter had on occasion somewhat overplayed their hand.

An appreciation of 3rd April gives us the German view after FOR-
TITUDE NORTH had been in operation for a little over a week.
'Information about the concentration and preparedness for invasion
of the *Scottish group of forces* in the region of Edinburgh continue.
Their strength is still to be regarded as five to seven divisions.[20]
There is no concrete evidence as to their target. It therefore remains
undetermined whether reports about their proposed employment
against Norway or Denmark are correct. The essential fact remains
that in either case theirs could only be a diversionary undertaking.'[21]

---

19. Appendix to Lagebericht West No. 1194, dated 4th March, 1944.
20. In spite of the world 'still', it will be noted that the number of divisions has
    increased since 3rd March when an estimate of four to six divisions was given.
21. Appendix to Lagebericht West No. 1224, dated 3rd April, 1944.

It is not possible to deduce from that brief statement how much was due to FORTITUDE NORTH. Things, however, seemed to be moving in the right direction.

With the arrival of BRUTUS's series of messages[22] which were sent between 13th and 16th April after his fictitious visit to Scotland, one is left in no doubt as to whether FORTITUDE NORTH had struck its mark. 'An Abwehr source, which has hitherto reported accurately, has been able to provide a clarification of the distribution of forces in Scotland.'[23] Although no attempt at grouping was made, nearly all the elements of which the force was composed were now accepted by the enemy, those at least to which Scottish locations had been given. The 2nd and the 7th British Corps were included, also the 52nd Highland Division and the 58th British Infantry Division. 'The 7th English Army Corps', says the German Intelligence report, 'whose location was hitherto unknown, is in the Dundee area.'[24] We had only just invented the 7th British Corps and this was the first time that we had told the Germans about it, but they never liked to admit that any item of military intelligence was entirely new to them. It will be remembered that when christening the 58th British Infantry Division we chose that number because we knew from Most Secret Sources that the Germans believed such a formation to be located in the area of Windsor. It was therefore gratifying to read: 'In the same area (*i.e.* between Edinburgh and Stirling) is the 58th English Infantry Division which was hitherto assumed to be West of London in the Southern Command. Since there has, for a considerable time, been no confirmation of the presence of the division in the latter area, its transfer to Scottish Command at the beginning of this year must be presumed.'[25] Unaccountably the 50th British Infantry Division was also included and was located between Edinburgh and Stirling.

It will thus be seen that on the British side the FORTITUDE NORTH Order of Battle, thanks mainly to BRUTUS, had been

---

22. BRUTUS 2043 GMT, 13th April, 1105, 1117, 1124, 1814 and 1820 GMT, 14th April, 1203, 1210, 1216, 1221, 1227 and 1236 GMT, 15th April, 0907, 0916, 0923, 0937, 0944, 0949, 0935 and 0959, 16th April, 2944.
23. Lagebericht West No. 1244, dated 23rd April, 1944.
24. Appendix to Lagebericht West No. 1244, dated 23rd April, 1944.
25. Appendix to Lagebericht West No. 1244, dated 23rd April, 1944.

accepted almost in its entirety. The American part of it, however, had not gone so well. The reader may recall that the main report on XV Corps and its three divisions had been sent by FREAK on 30th March. The fact that he had been congratulated on his message made us assume that it too had borne fruit. By some mischance, however, it evidently went astray with the result that BRUTUS's veiled and confirmatory reference to the fact that the Fourth Army also included an American army corps 'not identified by him' became linked in the German mind with an uncontrolled report of American forces in North-Eastern Scotland. Thus we find in the appendix which analyses BRUTUS's Scottish report the statement: 'In addition American troops in unknown strength were reported, and these are probably the American Infantry Division of unknown number, assumed to be in the county of Aberdeen.'

BRUTUS's reports must have been greatly welcomed by the German Intelligence Staff. If one looks at the Fremde Heere West map of 31st December, 1943, one will find no fewer than three British infantry divisions in Scotland without number. These numbers could now be provided, so long as one insisted that there had been no substantial increase in the total of forces located in the North. Hence their statement that from BRUTUS's report there 'emerges the fact that the *total number* of Anglo-American formations hitherto believed by this department to be in that area has increased by one division. As the source in question has supplied a comprehensive explanation, the presence of additional formations is held to be unlikely.' Hence also the entirely unwarranted assertion that 'since these changes go back to the beginning of the year, our erstwhile appreciation of enemy intentions from this area remains unaffected'.[26]

In spite of the efforts of COBWEB,[27] we never succeeded in persuading the Germans of the presence of the 55th US Division in Iceland. By the beginning of May they had accepted it as part of the Northern force, but they preferred to locate it in Scotland.[28]

The accompanying map, published by the General Staff Fremde

26. Lagebericht West No. 1245, dated 24th April, 1944.
27. The 55th Division was identified by COBWEB on 5th March and again on 20th April, 1944.
28. Map published by Fremde Heere West on 15th May, 1944.

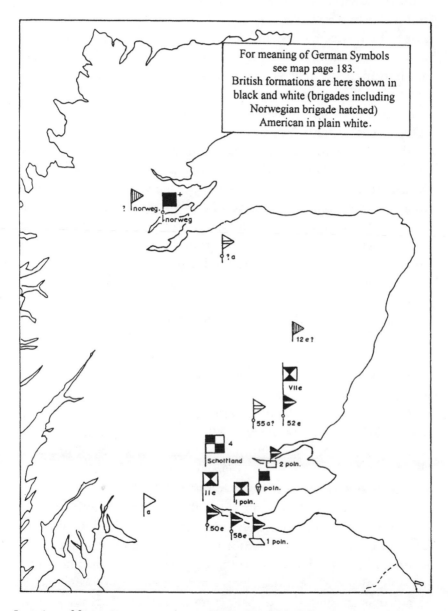

For meaning of German Symbols
see map page 183.
British formations are here shown in
black and white (brigades including
Norwegian brigade hatched)
American in plain white.

Location of formations engaged in FORTITUDE NORTH given on the Fremde
Heere West map of 15th May, 1944 (Northern Ireland omitted).

Heere West on 15th May, 1944, provides the best measure available of the success achieved by FORTITUDE NORTH, at least so far as Order of Battle is concerned. In Scotland the position shown leaves little to be desired. Northern Ireland, on the other hand, largely, no doubt, as a result of the failure of FREAK's message, is held to contain nothing more than an American brigade of unknown number and a miscellaneous collection of low-grade American troops with a total strength of about twenty thousand.

Of the ancillary measures taken to support FORTITUDE NORTH, pride of place must be given to GRAFFHAM. That the story reached its mark is proved by the report of a leakage from the British Embassy in Stockholm. This leakage was, of course, intentional and the ambassador's remarks were designed for German ears. 'From a reliable diplomatic course (Stockholm) 11th April, 1944: The English Ambassador, Mallet, who was in England for some time, gave on his return a talk to the Embassy staff which, according to an agent's statement, contained the following passage . . . We have always had good relations with our Swedish friends and hope that these will remain so. We must, however, reckon with the possibility that this good relationship will be put to the test. We can no longer calmly look on while neutral countries deliver goods to our enemies, which do us harm. We will therefore make representations to the Swedish Government to stop these deliveries or at least to reduce them. We must approach this delicate task with tact. In particular, deliveries of iron ore and ball-bearings benefit Germany and harm us. That must not continue in the future. We must find suitable ways to prevent it. *Other problems, too, are of greater significance politically and may come between us and Sweden.*'[29]

That GRAFFHAM not only reached the most influential quarters but caused a favourable reaction is shown by the following quotation from the OKH Intelligence Summary: 'Reliably reported soundings by high-ranking English Air Force officers in Sweden which aimed at the handing over of Swedish air bases for invasion purposes, may be regarded as an indication of the planning of a *small operation* in the Scandinavian area (Sweden, Norway and Denmark). The employment

---

29. OKW/WFSt Papers, File 603. Note initialled by Keitel and Warlimont and shown to Hitler by Jodl.

of a stronger group of forces in this direction with an operational target is still held to be unlikely.'[30]

No evidence has so far been found to show that wireless deception or visual misdirection made any contribution to FORTITUDE NORTH. On the contrary, so far as the latter is concerned, the OKH Intelligence Summary complains on more than one occasion about the lack of air reconnaissance over Scotland. Solitary flights are recorded from time to time, but as the Germans themselves admitted, 'these single results do not give a clear picture of the shipping situation in Northern English ports'.[31]

Inasmuch as FORTITUDE NORTH aimed at convincing the Germans that certain forces were located in Scotland for a certain purpose when in fact those forces either were not there at all or at least were not there for the purpose stated, the plan, through the operation of Special Means, will be seen to have succeeded. The Germans accepted the danger of a diversionary attack against Scandinavia. They also accepted the presence of most of the formations which we had created or appropriated for the purpose of exercising that threat. To what extent did FORTITUDE NORTH succeed in tying down additional forces in Norway and Denmark? We have it from Jodl[32] that Hitler had always been obsessed by the fear of an Allied attack on Scandinavia. It would not have required more than 100,000 troops to garrison the two countries and keep the native population in subjection. In fact the average number of occupational troops had been in the region of 250,000 even since Norway was first occupied. The balance of 150,000 was to be regarded as an insurance against invasion. In these circumstances any minor troop movement that may have occurred in the spring of 1944 (and it is true that the garrison was increased at that time by one formation, the 89th Infantry Division) loses its significance, and one is thus forced to the conclusion, if one accept's Jodl's view, that FORTITUDE NORTH, though successful as a deceptive operation, had no influence upon the course of the war. It was, in fact, a case of the fly on the axle-tree.

---

30. Appendix to Lagebericht West No. 1279, dated 28th May, 1944, Short Appreciation for the West.
31. Appendix to Lagebericht West No. 1197, dated 7th March, 1944.
32. Statement made under interrogation.

XX

The German View, Spring 1944

Before attempting to trace the influence of FORTITUDE SOUTH upon the Germans it will be well to acquaint ourselves with the enemy's views before the deception plan was set in motion.

The interrogation of those who held positions of responsibility under Hitler has made it clear that the choice of the Pas de Calais as the cover objective was well placed. Long before deception began to exert its influence, the enemy had reached the conclusion that an analysis of relevant military factors weighted the scales in favour of an attack across the Straits of Dover. General Blumentritt has lately expressed the view that a successful landing there followed by a rapid advance into Germany would have cut off all their forces in France, and has stated that this is what they thought would be attempted. That the Fuehrer himself shared the opinion of his experts is shown by an order which he issued in November 1943: 'I can no longer be responsible for further weakening of the West in favour of the other theatres. I have, therefore decided to strengthen its defences, especially in the place from where we shall begin the long-range fight against England. For there the enemy must and will attack, and there will – unless everything deceives – the decisive landing blow be struck.'[1] The 'long-range fight' refers to the V weapons which were to come into operation during the following summer. As these were chiefly concentrated to the north of the Seine, it is fair to suppose that this is the area to which Hitler was referring.

---

1. Fuehrer's Order No. 51, dated 3rd November, 1943.

At the beginning of 1944 the Germans seem to have held no positive views about the date of the invasion. As has been explained they were constantly being alerted by the uncontrolled agents. Nor had they realised how impossible a winter landing would be. At the middle of January 1944 they thought that the 'expected attack in the West' might come in about a month's time, adding, 'experience shows that a sufficiently long fine weather period suitable for landing operations may be expected at this time'.[2] Three weeks later we read: 'To sum up, the continuation of invasion preparations of every kind is to be seen, which, according to present opinion, points for the first time to the second half of February as a critical period.'[3] These constant alarms continued with hardly a break until, at the beginning of April, the German Intelligence found itself compelled to state: 'There is a complete absence of information, apart from worthless gossip, regarding the date of the assault. The only protection against surprise is, therefore, to be found in intensively organised sea reconnaissance by air and naval forces (for example U-boats).'[4] While soon afterwards the C in C West was to complain of the abundance of new dates for the invasion, 'some of which are already past'.

As already stated, the Germans greatly over-estimated Allied forces in the United Kingdom at the New Year. They gave us fifty-five divisions when we had in fact only thirty-seven. Let us examine their beliefs in somewhat greater detail.[5] Unaccountably, GHQ, Home Forces, remained at Leicester.[6] Armies were identified with Commands, which, of course, were known to the Germans before the war. Thus Northern Command was also described as Third Army, Eastern Command as Sixth Army, a legacy from COCKADE, South-Eastern Command, described as Fifth Army, was divided in two to make room for the First Canadian Army at Leatherhead, the boundary running through London, Tunbridge Wells and Hastings, with the

---

2. Appendix to Lagebericht West No. 1149, dated 19th January, 1944.
3. Appendix to Lagebericht West No. 1173, dated 12th February, 1944.
4. Appendix to Lagebericht West No. 1224, dated 3rd April, 1944.
5. The following assessment of German views is derived from examination of the Fremde Heere West maps and of the Ueberblick des Britischen Reiches, also compiled by Fremde Heere West, both of which were published monthly.
6. It was shown in this location in Das Britische Kriegsheer issued 10th April, 1942.

Canadians to the West and the British to the East; Southern Command was also designated Second Army. With the exception of Sixth Army, it is impossible to say where the Germans got these British Army numbers from. Scottish Command was shown as an Army Headquarters, but the number 'Four' does not appear on the Fremde Heere West map of 31st December. It must, therefore, be assumed that, in spite of what had been done during the previous year, Fourth Army was not yet firmly established in the German mind. At this date no American Army was shown. Of the fifty-five divisions believed to be in the country, twenty-two were correctly named and of these, ten were correctly located. The balance was made up of real divisions in fact abroad, non-existent formations or mere flags on the map without number or designation.[7] No particular significance attaches to the German grouping of Allied formations within the Commands. These were spread fairly thinly and fairly evenly along the whole length of the east coast from the North of Scotland to the Thames and more thickly along the south coast from Kent to Devonshire.[8] Practically nothing was placed on the west coast, and only two divisions in Northern Ireland. The grouping of formations within these so-called armies seems to have depended upon their location, each army being given all the forces that lay within the Command boundary. Thus a division located in East Anglia would automatically be under the command of the Sixth Army at Luton.

Almost every bay and inlet of the British coastline was shown to contain concentrations of landing craft, the only notable exceptions being the west coast of Scotland, including the Clyde, and Northern Ireland.

At this time and during the ensuing months there was a tendency to speak of three groups of forces, a Northern, a Central and a Southern. The Northern group developed naturally into the Fourth Army of FORTITUDE NORTH, while the Southern group became the FUSAG of latter days. Aided by reports from the uncontrolled agents the Germans sustained their belief in the Central group of

---

7. Among other things the Germans still believed in the existence of the 'County Divisions' which had of course long since been disbanded.

8. A note on the map of 31st December states that many of the unlocated divisions were probably in the South or South-West.

forces throughout the spring. It was only under the pressure of the invasion itself and the arguments put forward in support of FOR-TITUDE SOUTH that they were ultimately willing to admit that it had been dispersed. 'In view of Abwehr reports of shipping concentrations in the North of Scotland, we must emphasise the possibility that these may be held ready for the group of forces known for some time to be in central England',[9] and again: 'The troop movements in England have mainly been completed since the assembly areas seem to have been reached. The movements have above all led to the concentration of the central English group of forces, which has hitherto been spread over a wide area compared with the main group in the South of England. It has reached a total strength of some twenty divisions by the addition of one or two American formations. It also includes strong parachute units.'[10] Yet another example of this firmly held belief may be given. On 14th April BRUTUS, anxious to dissociate the 1st Polish Armoured Division in Scotland from the Fourth Army, stated that it formed part of the Army Group under General Montgomery. Six days later we read: 'According to a trustworthy message the 1st Polish Armoured Division is under the command of the group of forces in central England.'[11] From this it appears that the Germans had done the central group of forces the honour of giving it Montgomery as its commander.

What has just been said may be described as the geographical solution. Another line of investigation pursued by the Germans, which provided more successful results, was an analysis of the Allied Air Forces. On 15th November, 1943, the Second TAF, which was ultimately to provide the air support for 21 Army Group, was formed from units of Fighter Command and came under AEAF. On 19th December following, the Ninth TAC, providing the air support for the American army group, was placed under the same command. By some means, which have not been brought to light, the Germans must have learnt something of these arrangements, for on 28th January, 1944, they made the following appreciation: 'According to Luftwaffe Command/Ic. the British *close combat* formations are being

9. Appendix to Lagebericht West No. 1197, dated 7th March, 1944.
10. Appendix to Lagebericht West No. 1224, dated 3rd April, 1944.
11. Appendix to Lagebericht West No. 1241, dated 20th April, 1944.

taken away from the organisation of Fighter Command and organised into two close combat corps. This reorganisation is a further sign that they are reforming in accordance with the organisation tried out in the Mediterranean and accords with credible reports about parallel measures within the American Air Force in England.'[12] It may be assumed that the two British close combat corps referred to were the 83rd and 84th Groups. The significance of the Mediterranean parallel is revealed in the ensuing sentence: 'If existing suppositions are confirmed, we must reckon with the employment of two British and two American close combat corps and, following experience in the Mediterranean, also with two British and two American armies.' In the meantime they had established by wireless intercept the presence of the First American Army Group and the First American Army in the United Kingdom.[13] On 17th January a Reuter message had given General Bradley as commander of the US forces in Europe under General Eisenhower.[14]

About the middle of March wireless intercept disclosed the presence of another American army, the Ninth, in this country. 'The support given by a sure source to the presence of the Ninth American Army in England confirms the supposition that for the coming operations two American armies (the First and the Ninth?) will be employed in addition to two British armies. This fits in with the organisation of close support formations. It is possible that General Patton, hitherto commander of the Seventh Army in the Mediterranean, will command one of the American armies.'[15]

They still could not place the Canadians. 'It is not yet possible to determine whether they will come under Montgomery's Army Group or will be employed independently.'[16] By 20th April they had found

---

12. Appendix to Lagebericht West No. 1158, dated 28th January, 1944.
13. 'Furthermore, the appearance of higher American Command Staffs seems to be of significance (according to a sure source possibly American First Army Group and American First Army).' (Appendix to Lagebericht West No. 1145, dated 15th January, 1944.) 'The First US Army has been confirmed in Southern England from a sure source.' (Appendix to Lagebericht West No. 1152, dated 22nd January, 1944.)
14. Appendix to Lagebericht West No. 1147, dated 17th January, 1944.
15. Appendix to Lagebericht West No. 1210, dated 20th March, 1944.
16. Appendix to Lagebericht West No. 1212, dated 22nd March, 1944.

a niche for them, and so the picture was more or less complete. 'The assembly of two English close combat corps in the sector Southampton–Dover leads to the conclusion that two British armies (the Fifth English?[17] and First Canadian) will be launched, while further West we have to reckon with two American armies, the First and the Ninth.'[18] With the further information that 'according to an official English source there is in Great Britain a *21st English Army Group*; this is, presumably, the English army group under the command of General Sir Bernard L. Montgomery, of which the number was hitherto unknown',[19] we now have the following arrangement of forces:

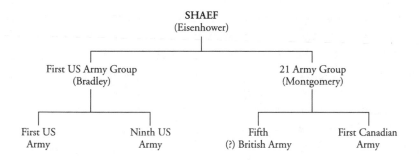

This is what the Germans believed the Southern group of armies to be when on 24th April FORTITUDE SOUTH was set in motion.

---

17. Identified with South-Eastern Command.
18. Appendix to Lagebericht West No. 1241, dated 20th April, 1944.
19. Ueberblick des Britischen Reiches No. 28, dated 29th April, 1944.

XXI

The Influence of FORTITUDE SOUTH

The brief which was given to TRICYCLE at the end of February before his departure for Lisbon may be taken as the foundation of the FORTITUDE SOUTH Order of Battle. As already stated the main objects of that brief were first, to dispel the clouds which had been raised by the uncontrolled agents and give the Germans a clear-cut picture of our version of the state of Allied forces in this country,[1] and second, to fix the positions of certain 21 Army Group formations which we knew would later move to concentration areas not unfavourable to FORTITUDE SOUTH in order that these moves might be noticed and their significance be appreciated. Everyone at the time, TRICYCLE included, felt some doubt about the value which the German General Staff would place on the Lisbon report. In fact that deception far exceeded our hopes. A very full account of it is given in the Intelligence Summary for 9th march, which opens with these words: 'A V-man message which reached the Abteilung on 7th March, 1944, brought particularly valuable information about the British formations in Great Britain. The reliability of the report could be checked. It contains information about three armies, three army corps and twenty-three divisions, among which the displacement of only one formation must be regarded as questionable. The

---

1. Many true reports of troop locations in the British Isles had been given by the controlled agents during the previous twelve months, mainly with the object of building up their reputations. All the correct information appearing on the Fremde Heere West map, dated 31st December, 1943, had been supplied by them.

report confirmed our own overall operational picture.'[2] Knowing as one does today that this report filled in a good many gaps on their operational map, the reference to confirmation of the overall operational picture and still more to the doubtful location of one single formation provides an interesting sidelight on German intelligence methods.

This brings us to 24th April, the real starting point for FORTITUDE SOUTH. Let us now focus our attention more directly on the Channel coast and see what the Germans thought about our dispositions in the South. While they never doubted the existence of the 'southern group of armies', they changed their minds very frequently as to its main point of concentration. Sometimes it was in the South-West, sometimes in the South-East and sometimes in both. At the end of April the pendulum seemed, from our point of view, to be swinging in the wrong direction. This may have been due to the fact that such limited aerial reconnaissance as they had been able to carry out had shown concentrations of landing craft in the South and South-West. 'Increased air reconnaissance of the south coast of England has revealed that two Schwerpunkte are showing themselves in this area at the present time, namely in the Portsmouth and the Dartmouth/Saltcombe [sic] areas.'[3] As they hardly reconnoitred the coast east of Portsmouth at all, presumably because it was too strongly defended, it will be agreed that this appreciation was misleading to say the least and provides yet another example of that persistent tendency to distort the evidence rather than admit that information on any particular was lacking.

It will be remembered that the first thing which the agents had to do was to discover the FUSAG formations in their old locations before they moved to concentration. This meant showing the Third US Army and its subordinate formations in Cheshire, and XX Corps in Wiltshire with its armoured divisions under command. A message from BRUTUS[4] giving XX Corps at Marlborough and the 6th Armoured Division in the northern part of Gloucestershire reached Berlin about nine days later in a somewhat garbled form. 'According

2. Appendix to Lagebericht West No. 1199, dated 9th March, 1944.
3. Ueberblick des Britischen Reiches No. 28, dated 29th April, 1944.
4. BRUTUS 1634 GMT, 26th April, 1944.

to an unconfirmed Abwehr message the American armoured division hitherto accepted in an unknown location is in the Worcester area. This may possibly be the 6th American Armoured Division.'[5] On 26th April FREAK[6] gave the Third US Army as being located near Knutsford in Cheshire with the 79th and 83rd Infantry Divisions under command. This resulted in the following rather surprising entry: 'The two American formations assumed to be in Yorkshire and Norfolk may, according to a good Abwehr message, be the 79th and 83rd American Infantry Divisions. Confirmation of this must be awaited.'[7] The connection between FREAK's message and this passage is beyond dispute. Neither of these divisions had been referred to by the Germans for many months and even then they had never been spoken of together. What clearly happened was this. For reasons best known to themselves the Germans had previously located one American division in Yorkshire and another in Norfolk without giving their numbers. FREAK provided them with the opportunity of filling in the blanks on their map. Such slipshod evaluation robbed the message of all its value from our point of view.

After this halting start, an unbroken spell of good fortune attended our efforts. A glimpse of the 6th Armoured Division by GARBO's agent 7 (7) at Ipswich[8] at the beginning of May caused the enemy to place it on record that: 'The 6th American Armoured Division, hitherto believed to be in the county of Worcester (see Lagebericht West No. 1255) is, according to an as yet unconfirmed Abwehr message, said to be in the East of England in the Ipswich area.'[9] Similarly a report by 7 (2)[10] that the 28th US Infantry Division had turned up at Tenterden in Kent and another from 7 (7)[10] to say that the same formation had left South Wales find their counterpart in the summary three days later: 'The 28th American Infantry Division was, according to a further Abwehr message, moved from its previous area round Swansea (South Wales) to the

---

5. Lagebericht West No. 1255, dated 4th May, 1944.
6. FREAK 1125 GMT, 26th April, 1944.
7. Lagebericht West No. 1255, dated 4th May, 1944.
8. GARBO 1955 GMT, 2nd May, 1944.
9. Lagebericht West No. 1256, dated 5th May, 1944.
10. GARBO 1840 GMT, 1st May, 1944.

Folkestone area in South-East England.'[11] It is not necessary to remind the reader that both these moves were false. In reality the 28th US Infantry Division left Swansea but only moved as far as Chisledon in Wiltshire. The 6th US Infantry Division did not move at all. This information, together with a chance message from BRUTUS,[12] in which he reported that while on his way to Torquay he had seen troops of the American VII Corps in Salisbury, led to this somewhat premature appreciation. 'The advance reported by good sources of the 6th American Armoured Division to Ipswich, of the 28th American Division to Folkestone (south-west of Dover) and of the VII Army Corps into the Torquay area points to the already known main concentration areas and further rounds off the picture of completed concentrations.'[13]

Day by day the plot now began to unfold itself. The discovery of VIII Corps in Folkestone by 7 (2)[14] brought us another step forward. 'The observation by a useful source of the VIII American Army Corps in South-East England (probably in the Folkestone area) makes it seem probable that in that area there are, in addition to the 28th American Infantry Division already reported there, one or two further American formations hitherto not exactly located. The general picture therefore emerges that besides the strong Anglo-American group of forces in South-West England, we must reckon with the employment of single American divisions from all the remaining jumping-off areas.'[15] This passage rather suggests that while the Germans still regarded the South-West as the base for the main attack, they thought that a number of small diversionary operations by single American divisions would be launched from the South-East. During the next forty-eight hours further messages from the controlled agents came to be evaluated. The majority of these related to factual movements of 21 Army Group divisions to the South of England. A message from BRUTUS,[16] however, despatched

---

11. Lagebericht West No. 1256, dated 5th May, 1944.
12. BRUTUS 1206 GMT, 29th April, 1944.
13. Appendix to Lagebericht West No. 1256, dated 5th May, 1944.
14. GARBO 1840 GMT, 1st May, 1944.
15. Appendix to Lagebericht West No. 1623, dated 12th May, 1944.
16. BRUTUS 1730 and 1735 GMT, 9th May, 1944.

on 9th May, strengthened the American position in the Eastern counties. 'In East Anglia, in the Bury St Edmunds area (some 50 Km. south-west of Norwich) are situated, according to a well-regarded Abwehr source, the XX Corps as well as the 4th Armoured Division.'[17] This intelligence was not without its influence and by 15th May we find that German opinion had moved a little further in the required direction. 'The main enemy concentration is showing itself ever more clearly to be in the South and South-East of the Island. This is supported by the transfer of two English divisions into the Portsmouth area and the recently observed introduction of American formations into the English group of forces in South-East England (so far observed one corps and one infantry division). The launching of single American infantry divisions from the other invasion areas has also to be reckoned with,'[18] A subtle change had occurred since 12th May inasmuch as the South and South-East of the Island were now the main invasion bases. The minor and perhaps diversionary operations by single American infantry divisions were relegated to 'other invasion areas', presumably the eastern and western fringes of this main concentration in the South and South-East.

Information, real and false, continued to flow in from the controlled agents for the rest of the month. Each item found its place in the German Intelligence summary after an interval of a few days. The position on 31st May is summarised in the Ueberblick des Britischen Reiches No. 30 issued by Fremde Heere West. It will now be useful to examine the contents of that document.

At this time, while most of the FUSAG formations had been given to the enemy, practically nothing had been said about grouping. This was about to be disclosed by BRUTUS in his series of messages sent between 31st May and 2nd June. It is therefore natural to find that the Germans, although they had accepted all that we had to say about the Allied formations and their locations, were obliged to fall back largely on their old preconceived ideas when it came to grouping. Thus the Commands still provided armies as they had done six months before, the only change here being the finding of a space for the First US Army in the western half of

---

17. Ueberblick des Britischen Reiches No. 29, dated 15th May, 1944.
18. *Ibid.*

Southern Command.[19] The total of divisions in the country was still greatly overestimated. In fact it had now risen to fifty-two, including non-operational formations. The Germans put the figure at seventy-nine.[20] Of the FUSAG divisions to which reference has already been made, the 4th and 6th US Armoured Divisions were accepted as being in Eastern Command (Sixth Army), while the 28th and 83rd US Infantry Divisions were put under South-Eastern Command (Fifth Army). The Guards Armoured Division and the 11th Armoured Division, whose move from Yorkshire to Sussex had been reported to them by BRUTUS on 25th and 26th May,[21] were placed under the command of First Canadian Army, presumably on geographical grounds. There was, as always, a generous sprinkling of non-existent divisions. FORTITUDE NORTH was rather unfairly weakened by the reported moves of the 3rd and 50th British Infantry Divisions from Scotland to the South. The 3rd British Infantry Division we had for long been at pains to exclude from the FORTITUDE NORTH Order of Battle. As for the 50th British Infantry Division, the Germans had only put it in Scotland by a misreading of BRUTUS's messages sent during the first half of April. Now, rather than admit to any mistake, they preferred to base their view on the assumption that the division really had gone to Scotland first. The central group of armies, having lost the Guards and the 11th British Armoured Divisions as well as the 15th and 47th British Infantry Divisions, was also sensibly weakened. Referring to the move of the armoured divisions, the Germans said: 'The group of forces in the centre of England has thereby suffered a fresh weakening, a fact which again allows us to conclude that the forces employed from this area will only be given a limited objective.'[22]

For information regarding concentrations of landing craft and shipping the Germans appear to have relied almost entirely on aerial reconnaissance. Estimates of shipping capacity were consistently too

---

19. The Ninth Army is not mentioned at all though it is shown on the Fremde Heere West map of 15th May located near Didcot.
20. In arriving at this total they made no distinction between higher and lower establishment divisions.
21. BRUTUS 1836 GMT, 25th May, and 1605 GMT, 26th May, 1944.
22. Appendix to Lagebericht West No. 1280, dated 29th May, 1944.

high. By 25th April they had calculated that between Portsmouth and Falmouth landing craft and shipping space would be enough to lift thirteen and a half landing divisions and even this they regarded as an under-estimate. 'We must suppose that without doubt a considerable proportion, particularly of landing craft, have remained unobserved, since these are, as we know from experience, well camouflaged and are hidden, withdrawn from sight into the numerous bays and waterways along the south coast. We must therefore reckon with a considerably higher landing tonnage.'[23] Air observation, however, was exceedingly scanty. The C in C West's appreciation for 15th–21st May records that 'air observation was not carried out during the time covered by the report'. The Ueberblick des Britischen Reiches of 31st May gives a total lift for fifteen and three-quarter divisions.

It has been the aim of the writer to complete the story in every particular up to the day of the invasion before proceeding further. In analysing the German conception of the Allied invasion force it will, however, be more convenient to make an exception and pursue our enquiry as far as the middle of June. This course, which can be undertaken without upsetting the sequence of our narrative as a whole, will enable us to study the effect of BRUTUS's reports on grouping and so bring the first phase in the development of the false Order of Battle to a proper conclusion.

On 6th June, the day of the invasion, the Germans, as a result of information supplied by BRUTUS, made the following appreciation: 'According to a reliable Abwehr message of 2nd June, the forces at present in the South of England are organised into two army groups (21 English and First American). It seems from this report that the American First Army Group contains the First Canadian Army (approximately thirteen divisions), known to be in Southern Command, as well as the Third American Army, between the Thames and the Wash (approximately twelve divisions). It is not yet clear whether they are under the command of General Bradley or General Patton. 21 Army Group commanded by General Montgomery seems to contain the formations at present in the South and South-West of England which are probably organised in three

23. Appendix to Lagebericht West No. 1256, dated 5th May, 1944.

armies. All the formations which have so far appeared in the landing areas come from this group of forces which is to the west of the line Brighton/Oxford, while at the same time official English pronouncements confirm Montgomery's command of the landing troops.'[24]

Something must be said here about the command of FUSAG. At the end of May growing faith in the staying power of FORTITUDE SOUTH led us to fear that Bradley might be revealed as commander of the American forces in France at a time when the deceptive threat to the Pas de Calais was still holding down divisions in that area. It was therefore decided to substitute General Patton, the latter being at that time in command of Third Army, which was not due to go to France until July. BRUTUS told the Germans that Patton was in command on 31st May.[25] As it had been officially announced in January that Bradley was in command of the United States forces in Europe and as it had been stated by GARBO[26] on 10th May that he was the commander of the First US Army Group, it is not surprising that the enemy accepted BRUTUS's statement with reserve. A few days later, however, GARBO was able to resolve this doubt. 'I attempted to find out from 4 (3) where the headquarters of General Bradley are to be found, but as he is at present under Montgomery's orders in 21 Army Group, 4 (3) had been unable to say where this headquarters might be. I asked him who, then, was now in charge of FUSAG, to which he replied that it was General Patton who had taken over the command which had temporarily been held by Bradley during the first phase of its formation. In the conversation held, I was able to find out that the headquarters of General Patton, that is to say of FUSAG . . . is situated near Ascot.'[27]

A comparison of the Ueberblick des Britischen Reiches for 31st May with the subsequent issue of 15th June reveals some interesting developments. Eastern and South-Eastern Command were now combined under the heading of First American Army Group. Southern Command had become 21 Army Group. FUSAG had

---

24. Appendix to Lagebericht West No. 1288, dated 6th June, 1944.
25. BRUTUS 1605 GMT, 31st May, 1944.
26. GARBO 2050 GMT, 10th May, 1944.
27. GARBO 2055, 2101 and 2108 GMT, 12th June, 1944.

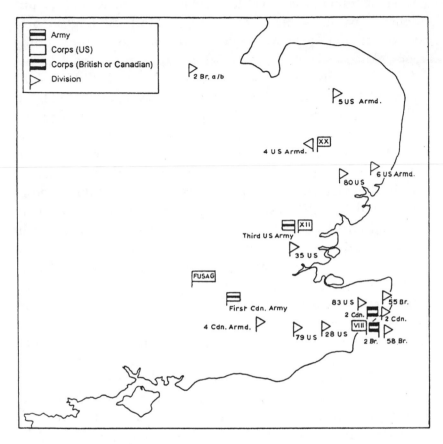

Location of FUSAG formations according to the Joint Commanders' Plan of 18th May, 1944, with the addition of 2nd British Corps and 55th and 58th British Infantry Divisions, transferred from Scotland at the beginning of June.

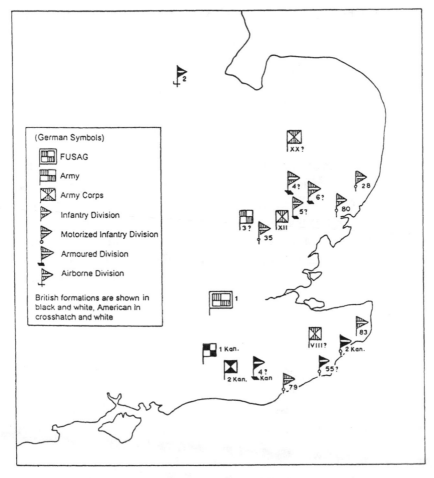

Location of FUSAG formations given on the OKH map of 19th June, 1944.

Notes

1. Formations included by the Germans in FUSAG without our authority are omitted.
2. By this date, VIII Corps and 79th US Infantry Division had already been withdrawn from First Canadian Army and had been replaced by XII Corps and the 35th US Infantry Division. This information, however, had only just reached the Germans.
3. Although the 58th British Infantry Division is not shown on this map, it was accepted as being in Kent in the Lagebericht of 24th June, 1944.
4. The 28th US Infantry Division is shown in Suffolk and not in Kent, because we had reported it carrying out assault training at Harwich at the beginning of June.

achieved the imposing total of twenty-six divisions, exclusive of airborne divisions. With the single exception of the 7th US Armoured Division, whose presence we had not yet disclosed,[28] all those formations that we intended them to accept now found a place in the FUSAG Order of Battle, making a total of ten[29] divisions. To these must be added four divisions which in reality belonged to 21 Army Group, but which had presumably been included because they had located them in South-Eastern Command,[30] six lower establishment divisions, which had been included on similar grounds,[31] and six purely imaginary ones,[32] some of them being followed by question marks. Our airborne strength was very considerably over-rated. The newly formed fictitious 2nd British Airborne Division, which had been reported by BRUTUS on 7th June as being in the region of Grantham, was given under FUSAG. 21 Army Group was shown to have under its command in the United Kingdom no fewer than three wholly imaginary British airborne divisions, the 3rd, 5th and 7th, while another American formation, the 11th Airborne Division, was also put in England, but in an unknown location. The 1st British Airborne Division, in fact still in England, was believed to be in Normandy.

Having now established the fact that the Germans had, by the middle of June, accepted the entire FUSAG Order of Battle, discarding the more accurate estimate which they had previously formed without our assistance, we may pause for a moment in order to consider more precisely what made them change their opinions.

---

28. This division was first reported to the Germans by BRUTUS on 24th June, 1944.
29. 28th, 35th, 79th, 80th and 83rd US Infantry Divisions, 4th, 5th and 6th US Armoured Divisions, 2nd Canadian Infantry Division and 4th Canadian Armoured Division.
30. 43rd, 53rd and 59th British Infantry Divisions and 11th British Armoured Division.
31. 45th, 47th, 55th, 61st and 76th British Infantry Divisions and 9th British Armoured Division.
32. Essex County Division, 14th British Armoured Division, 6th and 7th Canadian Infantry Divisions, one British and one Canadian division of unknown number.

Wireless intercept had given them one or two useful isolated facts such as the appearance of the First and Ninth US Armies. It had occasionally revealed the presence of a lower formation. It had twice attempted the grouping of formations, but in neither case had it succeeded in giving a wholly accurate report.[33] Locations had been attributed to intercept on three occasions only and then only when the location had already been given by a controlled agent.[34] Lastly and most significantly from our point of view there had been no single instance of the German intercept service having picked up any one of the deceptive FUSAG nets.[35]

---

33. (1) 'The 4th American Infantry Division as well as possibly the III American Army Corps have been identified in Great Britain by a sure source. They are under command of the American First Army.' (Lagebericht West No. 1235, dated 14th April, 1944). III Corps was not in the United Kingdom.

(2) 'According to a sure source the 10th Light American Division as well as the 30th Infantry Division may be under the command of XIX American Army Corps.' (Lagebericht West No. 1259, dated 8th May, 1944). There was no 10th Light American Division in the United Kingdom.

Otherwise the information given on both these occasions was correct.

34. (1) 'The English 6th Airborne Division has been confirmed in Great Britain through a captured document. Reports from the Abwehr and from a sure source agree that the division is no longer in the area south of Hull (Northern Command) but in the neighbourhood of Salisbury (Southern Command).' (Lagebericht West No. 1215, dated 25th March, 1944.) This information had already been given by BRUTUS on 21st February and again on 8th March.

(2) 'According to a useful piece of information, the 28th Infantry Division hitherto in the Swansea area has been moved to the Folkestone area. The move from the original area around Swansea could be confirmed by a sure source.' (Ueberblick des Britischen Reiches No. 29 for 15th May, 1944). This was confirmation of GARBO's message of 1st May.

(3) 'According to trustworthy Abwehr messages which have been confirmed by "Y", the 50th English Infantry Division (Mot.) hitherto accepted in the Scottish Command, has been identified in the area north of Southampton (Southern Command).' (Lagebericht West No. 1273, dated 22nd May, 1944.) This had been reported by TREASURE on 17th May.

35. Unless we count the move of the 28th US Infantry Division. This, however, is a very doubtful claim as apart from the fact that the move had already been reported by the Abwehr, the division really did move at that time from Tenby to Chisledon in Wiltshire, and in these circumstances one cannot be certain that a breach of signals security on the part of the real division might not have caused the leakage.

Let us next examine the claims of air observation. The inadequacy of air reconnaissance was a constant cause of complaint by the German Intelligence Staff. 'The southern English ports are not able to be checked owing to the present lack of adequate air reconnaissance',[36] and two months later, 'air reconnaissances during the last weeks covering some of the southern English ports (Falmouth, Cowes, Hamble Estuary) show a considerable increase in landing craft as compared with previous results; nevertheless, the defective reconnaissance results do not permit any deductions to be made as regards the distribution of landing craft'.[37] The rather scanty observations of the south coast between Portsmouth and Land's End that they were able to make during April and May had led them to the conclusion that we had nearly twice as many landing craft as was in fact the case. Overland reconnaissance had nothing placed to its credit at all.

Finally, there was the Abwehr. No matter how much the German General Staff despised the Abwehr as an organisation, they had, owing to the failure of intercept and air reconnaissance, little else to guide them, and were compelled in consequence to base their appreciations on Abwehr reports. Moreover, as the Germans had no effective spy system in the United Kingdom, these reports were supplied exclusively by the British-controlled agents in the United Kingdom and by the uncontrolled agents abroad. The latter, who held the field until the month of April, being denied all knowledge of the Allies' true intentions, were obliged to content themselves and their masters with evasive and conflicting statements, which kept the enemy in the dark as much as they were themselves. It is therefore not surprising to find that the British-controlled agents, as soon as they had a positive story to tell, rapidly outstripped the freelances. It will thus be seen that the Allied double-cross team opened their campaign practically without a competitor.

Of the British-controlled agents, it is evident that GARBO, BRUTUS and TRICYCLE enjoyed reputations of a high order throughout the whole period of FORTITUDE deception. This came as a surprise to us. We never doubted GARBO's position. We knew

---

36. Appendix to Lagebericht West No. 1144, dated 14th January, 1944.
37. Appendix to Lagebericht West No. 1199, dated 9th March, 1944.

that BRUTUS had attained something at least approaching GARBO's stature by midsummer, but we had supposed that he had risen during the spring from comparative obscurity. Although we believed that TRICYCLE and FREAK stood in the front rank until the time of ARTIST's arrest, we feared that they might both have been discredited by that event.

That BRUTUS enjoyed the full confidence of the Germans at the beginning of the year, before we had been allowed to use him for deception at all, is proved by a contemporary German report which states: 'He is very well regarded and up till now has produced much accurate information on South-East England (formerly Polish General Staff Officer sent to England by us in 1939).'[38] Reasons for believing that TRICYCLE's reputation had not been compromised by the ARTIST affair have already been given. It is now clear that we could have continued to use him and FREAK for deception during the summer of 1944, but there was no way of telling this at the time.

If we under-estimated BRUTUS and TRICYCLE, we certainly over-estimated the capacity of TATE. We realised that TATE was in rather low water when we started to use him for deception in the spring, but we supposed that a sustained diet of high-grade deceptive intelligence would restore to him his position in the front rank. We could not, as was the case with the other agents, observe his progress through a reading of Most Secret Sources, since his control in Hamburg communicated with RSHA Headquarters by land line only. In fact, by the date of the invasion, not one of the messages which we sent through him had found a place in the OKW Intelligence Summary. TATE, both before and for the few weeks succeeding the invasion, was to be a source of weakness, for we were giving him essential parts of the plan to tell the enemy and they were not being told.

Except for the occasional identification of a formation by TREASURE and a few very doubtful scores by MULLET and PUPPET, information from the other controlled agents appeared to have made no impression at all.

---

38. Report dated 25th January, 1944. OKW/WFSt Papers, File No. 605. 1939 is clearly a misprint for 1940.

According to the available evidence, therefore, the enemy's belief in the imaginary FUSAG, upon which the successful prosecution of FORTITUDE SOUTH now depended, resulted solely from the messages of the three British-controlled agents, GARBO, BRUTUS and TRICYCLE, the contribution of the last-named being restricted by the fact that he ceased to be employed for deception some three weeks before the date of the invasion.

The reader will recall that after the arrest of ARTIST, the controlled agents were debarred from making any direct allusion to the false objective and date of assault.[39] It must not be supposed, however, that all measures calculated to draw the enemy's attention to the Pas de Calais or to mislead him as to the date of the attack were suspended in consequence. The Air Force bombing programme with its intense concentration on targets in the north-western departments of France only began in May. Its influence is very apparent in contemporary German appreciations. 'The concentration of enemy air action against the coastal defences between Dunkirk and Dieppe and on the Seine–Oise bridges as well as the neutralising of the south flank between Rouen and Paris might be held to indicate the North-West of France as the objective.'[40]

Such measures as were taken during May in respect of the timing of the operation were designed rather to conceal the true date of the attack than to mislead the enemy by suggesting a false one. In that regard, the wireless silence periods had, of course, been in operation since the beginning of the year. Their purport had not been lost on the enemy. 'The wireless silence which was observed for several hours on 24th January was several times noticed in the Mediterranean in the same form and during periods of large-scale undertakings. The silence presumably serves purposes of training primarily, but is also intended to deceive and to lower German vigilance.'[41] Nevertheless

---

39. There is nothing to show that such isolated attempts to draw the attention of the enemy to the Pas de Calais as Plan PREMIUM and SNIPER's 'airfield construction' plan, which were made before the new policy took effect, produced any useful result.
40. OKW War Diary.
41. Appendix to Lagebericht West No. 1154, dated 24th January, 1944.

the Germans had soon resigned themselves to the view that the observation of wireless traffic would be of little assistance to them in estimating the invasion date. 'The wireless silences which are noticed from time to time in the various English wireless networks (armed services, railways, &c.) are to be regarded as exercises designed to ensure the smooth working of the wireless silence during the invasion. From these silences we must conclude that the invasion will in all probability not be revealed by the wireless network.'[42] After the inception of FORTITUDE SOUTH, our chief concern had been to counteract the effect of FABIUS. The Germans claimed that this exercise had been observed both by wireless intercept and by the Abwehr. The Abwehr reports had been supplied by us and were therefore of little assistance to them. Nor do they appear to have learned anything useful from intercept, except our intention to land at low water, information which might have, but apparently did not, enable them to determine the hour of the assault and to modify their coastal defences to our disadvantage. 'In the area from the Isle of Wight to approximately Brighton there took place from 4th to 6th May a large landing exercise by all three Services during which the recognition and removal of off-shore obstacles at low water seems to have played on important part.'[43] This was confirmed by subsequent observations on 23rd May. 'A landing exercise on the south coast of England at *low* water on 23rd May, identified by a sure source, may point to a decision to effect the landing on the ebb tide on account of the danger of German under-water obstacles.'[44]

It will be remembered that when the invasion drew near a final attempt was made to put the Germans off their guard by impersonating Field-Marshal Montgomery at Gibraltar. The numerous questions as to Montgomery's whereabouts which were received by controlled agents both in this country and in the Mediterranean showed that COPPERHEAD had caused a considerable stir in the lower levels of the German Intelligence Service. There is no evidence, however, that it reached the ears of those for whom it was

---

42. Appendix to Lagebericht West No. 1192, dated 2nd March, 1944.
43. Ueberblick des Britischen Reiches No. 29, dated 15th May, 1944.
44. Appendix to Lagebericht West No. 1283, dated 1st June, 1944.

intended. A possible explanation may lie in the fact that only a few days before, JOSEPHINE, an uncontrolled agent operating in Stockholm, had played exactly the same game. A signal dated 19th May and headed 'Staff Talks at Gibraltar' had reported that Tedder, Leigh-Mallory, Bedell-Smith, Maitland-Wilson and other senior officers of the latter's staff had met in Gibraltar on 14th and 15th May. 'According to information emanating from the War Office', they were supposed to have examined the state of preparedness of the large reserves in North Africa as well as the question of a combined operation against France, while the placing of these formations under Eisenhower had been confirmed. That message was seen by Hitler.'[45] Supposing that the Germans had accepted JOSEPHINE's story at its face value, it would seem extraordinary that Montgomery should not have seized the opportunity of meeting Maitland-Wilson at Gibraltar on 15th May and so have saved himself the trouble of going all the way to North Africa ten days later. In fact the evidence goes to show that they did not believe it for it bears the marginal note: 'Irrefuehrung?' (deception) and in Colonel Krummacher's[46] handwriting the arch comment, written in English, 'Who knows?' It is therefore likely that any COPPERHEAD reports reaching the OKW at all were rejected before they even reached Krummacher's table.[47]

---

45. OKW/WFSt Papers, File 605, Invasion West.
46. Head of the OKW Intelligence branch, and described in greater detail in chapter 23 *seq.*
47. Further evidence that COPPERHEAD had not reached the desired quarter was provided by the interrogation of Colonel Meyer-Detring, formerly Ia, at Field-Marshal Rundstedt's headquarters. At the end of the interview, the Colonel took up a copy of the *Sunday Express* and, drawing the attention of his interrogator to an article by Lieutenant James recounting his wartime exploit at Gibraltar, commented on the ingenuity of the idea, clearly indicating by his remarks that this was the first that he had heard of it.

XXII

German Opinion in May

We have recorded in some detail the immediate impression made by FORTITUDE SOUTH upon the enemy's intelligence service from the day on which it was put into operation until the time of the invasion. Let us now consider the effect which this false intelligence had upon their military appreciations and how it influenced their actions during the weeks which preceded the Normandy assault. We have already seen that until the second half of April they had made their appreciations without any assistance from us. During May a growing belief in the imaginary FUSAG combined with the bombing programme of the Air Force undoubtedly tended to 'shift the centre of gravity' from west to east. But Allied deception could not yet claim to exercise a decisive influence on the enemy's opinion as to our aims, nor was it intended that it should.

We will first consider the enemy's latest opinions as to invasion objectives. Hitler could always be relied upon to hold a view about Allied intentions. But, like so many other gamblers, he was apt to pursue the unprofitable system of backing every chance. We already know of his predilection for the Pas de Calais. In April he began to hedge extensively. 'In the Fuehrer's opinion', says the OKW War Diary, 'the targets aimed at by the enemy were the Peninsula of Cotentin and Brittany with the ports of Cherbourg and Brest.' About the same time we read: 'Contrary to the opinion that had cropped up from time to time that it had recently been a question of bluff, the Fuehrer maintained the same standpoint as that held by the Chief of the Wehrmachtsfuehrungsstab that at any time an attack had to be reckoned with on the Atlantic coast and also against the South of

France.' We are told that C in C West submitted a strategic plan and proposed distribution of forces to meet the possibility of the enemy attacking in the Bay of Biscay and the south coast of France only, and that a memorandum was prepared by the Wehrmachtfuehrungsstab to provide for simultaneous landings in the Channel and on the south coast. During May the belief in an impending attack on the south coast of France was maintained, though it was expected that it would be in the nature of a holding operation. On the other hand 'action against the southern part of the Bay of Biscay might have to be regarded as cover operations of small calibre'.[1] From this it will be seen that FERDINAND had a better start than IRONSIDE.

As to the date of the invasion, the Germans remained entirely in the dark until the very hour of the assault. 'The enemy command continues to attempt, by every method of nerve warfare, to obscure its invasion plans. Rumours of political differences which compel a postponement of the invasion alternate with announcements of imminent attack. The object of these machinations is the gradual blunting of German watchfulness designed to bring about the conditions necessary for successful surprise.'[2] The uncontrolled agents must be allowed their share of the credit for producing this atmosphere of frustration and bewilderment.

The OKW War Diary contains a general survey of the situation as seen during these later weeks which is of unusual interest and provides as full an exposition of the FORTITUDE story, so far as it had yet been revealed, as one could reasonably hope for. On 27th April Fremde Heere West established that there was a concentration of American troops noticeable in Southern England. In the Midlands of England it was the same case with British formations. Forces having apparently been augmented in Scotland and Iceland, there seemed to be an increasing possibility of a thrust against Norway, in which an attack against Central and Southern Norway appeared to be more likely than against the North. The first half of May was mentioned latterly as the date which seemed probable judging by various indications. Operations to be expected in Southern France as well as the fighting in Italy would be, it was thought, of a holding nature. The

---

1. Appendix to Lagebericht West No. 1265, dated 14th May, 1944.
2. Appendix to Lagebericht West No. 1287, dated 5th June, 1944.

weather now no longer furnished any decisive reason for delaying the offensive, and the setting up of the second front was demanded by the Soviet press; time, however, went on and nothing happened. By mid-May the Scottish force, owing to withdrawals to the South, had become so weakened that it was now only capable of operations of a restricted nature; the risk of a landing in the northern area became again correspondingly less likely. On 21st May C in C West's estimate of the situation was as follows: 'Schwerpunkte of the enemy invasion concentration lie in the South and South-East of England. The area round the Isle of Wight (Portsmouth, Southampton) is a main gate of preparation. The Channel front between the Scheldt and Normandy, together with the northern part of Brittany including Brest remains *unequivocally*[3] the threatened main front.' Seventy to eighty formations were assumed to be on our opponents' side, a fairly clear idea having been formed of their organisation and employment.

By the end of May, although the main story was still held back and was not to be told until after the invasion had begun, enough clues had been given to enable an intelligent observer to make a fairly shrewd guess as to what was coming. Hitler's renowned intuition was equal to the task. A conversation between him and the Japanese Ambassador shows that by 28th May he had acquired a thorough grasp of the FORTITUDE SOUTH plot, thus anticipating by more than a week the systematic programme of disclosure which the Allied deception staff had set for the performance of the game. 'Speaking of the Second Front, Hitler said that he, himself, thought that sooner or later operations for the invasion of Europe would be undertaken. He thought that about eighty divisions had already been assembled in England (of these divisions about eight had had actual experience of fighting and were very good troops). I accordingly asked the Fuehrer if he thought that these British and American troops had completed their preparations for landing operations and he replied in the affirmative. I then asked him in what form he thought the Second Front would materialise, and he told me that at the moment what he himself thought was most probable was that after having carried out diversionary operations in Norway, Denmark and the southern part

---

3. The italics are the writer's.

of the west coast of France and the French Mediterranean coast, they would establish a bridgehead in Normandy or Brittany, and after seeing how things went would them embark upon the establishment of a real second front in the Channel. Germany would like nothing better, he said, than to be given an opportunity of coming to blows with large forces of the enemy as soon as possible. But if the enemy adopted these methods his numerical strength would be dispersed and he (Hitler) intended to watch for this. . . .'[4] Irresistibly the parable of the mote and the beam springs to mind.

An appreciation[5] issued by Von Rundstedt on 5th June shows that the enemy remained wholly ignorant of the Allied objective

---

4. Obtained from Most Secret Sources (BJ 508, dated 28th May, 1944). Before the invasion Most Secret Sources told us very little of what the enemy believed our dispositions and intentions to be. The reason for this is now clear. Until FORTITUDE SOUTH had been in operation for about a month, they had no definite opinions about the invasion for us to discover. This conversation provided one of the rare instances where we obtained, before D Day, a really valuable insight into the enemy's thoughts. It gave us the first definite assurance that the Germans greatly over-estimated our strength and thus emboldened us to confirm the error in GARBO's culminating message of 8th–9th June (of which more will be said later), greatly to the advantage of FORTITUDE SOUTH. It is hardly necessary to add that Hitler's prognostications as to objectives and sequence of attacks were most encouraging to us, though the reference to Normandy gave ground for some uneasiness.

5. This appreciation, which is contained in a teleprinter message despatched 2150 hours on 5th June, 1944, states: 'C in C West estimates situation as follows: The systematic pursuit and appreciable increase of enemy air attacks indicate that preparations for an assault are well advanced. As previously supposed, the place chosen for the attack will probably lie between the Scheldt and Normandy, while an extension of the northern front to Brittany, including Brest, is not to be ruled out. Where, within this entire sector the enemy will attempt a landing is still problematic. The concentration of enemy air attacks on the coastal defences between Dunkirk and Dieppe and on the Seine–Oise bridges, in conjunction with the paralysing of the south flank, with its supply routes, between Rouen and Paris (inclusive), may indicate the Schwerpunkt of a projected landing on a large scale. The elimination of the Seine crossings would, however, have the same effect on troop movements in the event of an enemy attack on a sector to the west of the Seine bay, Normandy or Brittany. That the invasion is actually imminent does not seem to be indicated as yet.'

and of the date of the attack, even after the invasion fleet had put to sea, and is a notable tribute to the work of the Allied Security Services. When one finds that the same commander, who knew so little about the invasion when the Allied forces were already approaching the coast of France, was able to state that during the third week of May '244,385 British Mines were laid at sea',[6] one is forced to the conclusion that the Germans could not see the wood for the trees.

We are now familiar with the main trends of opinion which influenced the German Command during the first half of 1944. Let us consider the effect of these opinions upon the disposition of their forces in France and in particular upon the struggle which took place for the control of the mobile reserve.[7] Early in the year Rommel, the Commander of Army Group B, pointing out that every possible means should be employed to intercept and repulse the enemy on the beaches, argued that the resources not only of C in C West but also of the OKW should be placed under his control. Von Rundstedt did not agree. 'His main idea was to hold his strategical reserves in readiness, so as to be able, in case of need, to meet the enemy in pitched battle.' In other words, since the Allied objective was not known, the reserves must remain in a central position. Rommel then seems to have gone straight to Hitler. 'Field-Marshal Rommel had been urging that his powers should be extended and had asked the Fuehrer, on the occasion of his visit to Klessheim[8] (middle of March), even then to place the armoured formations, the mechanised troops and army artillery under his orders, in order to make all the preparations for the defence.' He had also 'claimed it as his right to exert his influence on the First and Nineteenth Armies'.[9] After discussion, Von Rundstedt appears to have gone some way towards meeting Rommel's demands, but not far enough to satisfy

---

6. C in C West's Appreciation for 15th–21st May, 1944.
7. The account which follows is derived principally from the OKW War Diary.
8. Presumably a misprint for Klesheim near Salzburg, frequently occupied by Hitler during the war.
9. The German First Army occupied South-West France and the Nineteenth the South of France and the Mediterranean coast.

the Commander of Army Group B. C in C West, so we are informed, 'established the powers of Army Group B on a fresh basis. But Field-Marshal Rommel's wishes were not in this way fulfilled. C in C West declining to meet them any further it was necessary to obtain a decision from the Supreme Command, more especially in regard to the highly mobile formations and their command.' On the advice of the Wehrmachtfuehrungsstab, Hitler gave his decision in favour of Von Rundstedt. Rommel obtained control neither of the mobile reserves nor of the First and Nineteenth Armies. The War Diary goes on to point out, however, that as Army Group B's orders then stood Rommel was responsible for meeting an enemy landing wherever it came, even, for example, if the attack was made on the south coast of France. In consequence, 'it still remained possible for him to bring his influence to bear on them (*i.e.* the First and Nineteenth Armies) within the scope of his orders. Overlapping of orders was thus unavoidable.'

At the beginning of May Rommel adopted new tactics. 'On 4th May C in C West sent a report from Field-Marshal Rommel on his impressions of his visits of inspection to the coast. According to this report no men could be spared either from the right or from the left for Normandy. The Field-Marshal proposed therefore to move formation of OKW reserve. C in C West demurred at this on the grounds that reserves would thus already be pinned down before the fighting had started.' Rommel had been beaten last time on the ground that the enemy's objective was not known and that in consequence the mobile reserve could not be committed to advance. Rommel now, however, offered the objective. The interesting thing to note is that he chose Normandy.

Meanwhile Von Rundstedt had foiled Rommel's efforts to obtain control of the First and Nineteenth Armies by the formation of Army Group G in the South. He justified his action on the ground that had Army Group B been called upon to meet an attack in the South of France and had this been followed by a second attack on the Channel coast, there would have been no one left but himself to conduct the operations.

About this time the following allocation of the mobile reserve was made by the OKW:

Army Group B	Army Group G	OKW Reserve
2nd Panzer Division	9th Panzer Division	1st SS Panzer Division
21st Panzer Division	11th Panzer Division	12th SS Panzer Division
116th Panzer Division	2nd SS Panzer Division	17th SS Panzer Grenadier Division
		Panzer Lehr Division

Rommel still did not give up hope of getting more of the reserve under his control. It will be remembered that the Fuehrer had more than once expressed the view that the Cotentin Peninsula of Brittany would be the first point of attack. Already the 3rd and 5th Parachute Divisions had been sent to Brittany as a direct result of Hitler's fear. A rather obscure passage in the War Diary suggests that in the face of opposition from C in C West he was seeking to play on Hitler's fears with regard to the Cherbourg Peninsula in order to get his way. 'The OKW Operational Staff, in a telephone message at 1900 hours on 6th May, drew the attention of the Chief of the General Staff of the Western Command to the fact that the Cotentin Peninsula would be the first target of the enemy. The OKW reserves, however, would not be released to reinforce it; other forces would have to be drawn upon.' As a concession to Rommel, however, the 243rd Infantry Division was sent to the Peninsula and a little later the 91st Infantry Division, which Von Rundstedt had preferred to hold near Rennes.[10] At the same time the Pas de Calais was reinforced in the latter half of May by sending the 19th Panzer Division to Holland.

All this time the fixed coastal defences were being improved. In April we read of a shortage of cement and in May of transport difficulties. Finally the OKW War Diary tells us that 'in addition, ready for service, a second position was consolidated, which, by the end of May, was already constructed almost as a continuous line along the Channel coast or was already in the course of construction'. It may be claimed that the second object of FORTITUDE, that of inducing the enemy 'to expand his available effort on fortifications in areas other than the target area' had at any rate in part been achieved.

---

10. This was the movement which led 21 Army Group to suggest drawing attention to the cover objective by Special Means on the eve of the invasion.

XXIII

The Invasion through Enemy Eyes

We now enter the post-assault phase, and we will start by visiting Von Rundstedt's headquarters on the morning of the invasion. The interrogation of a clerk who was then employed in the Ic section of OB West provides an interesting, if not very high level, first-hand account of the effect which the first news of the invasion had at his headquarters.[1] 'D Day at OB West was marked by a "let's not get excited" attitude. I was aroused at 0130 by an Ia officer with orders to take down reports from Army Group B. For the time being I was not to awaken anyone else, Major Doeternbach stood by at the telephone for important messages, Rommel and the Ia, Colonel Meyer-Detring, were in Berlin. The first reports from Vierville, Grandcamp, Ste Honorine, Port en Bessin and Courseulles mentioned both sea and airborne landings. However, as the excitement of Dieppe was on everybody's mind, this was regarded as just another feint. Further feints and landings were expected. The situation map of England showed only a few units along the S.W. shore, but heavy concentration in the S.E.'[2]

---

1. This man was employed as a clerk in the Ic section at OB West from June 1942 until November 1944. He was described as 'an intelligent man whose knowledge about matters of strategy is necessarily limited to the talk current among the enlisted staff personnel, although he appears to have enjoyed the confidence of several staff officers'.
2. Twelfth Army Group. PW Intelligence Bulletin No. 1/51, dated 24th March, 1945.

The OKH Intelligence Summary for 6th June tells us: 'The enemy landing on the Normandy coast represents a large-scale undertaking; but the forces already engaged represent a comparatively small part of the total available. Of the approximately sixty divisions at present in the South of England, it is likely that at the most ten to twelve divisions are at present taking part, including airborne troops. The main objective of the undertaking must be regarded as the capture of the port of Cherbourg, and the simultaneous closing of the Cotentin Peninsula to the south. . . . Within the framework of his group of forces Montgomery still has over twenty divisions available to reinforce his operations, which allows us to expect further air and sea landing attempts in the area of the Cotentin Peninsula, to force the capture of his objective. Attacks against the Channel Islands, coupled with attacks against the west coast of Normandy, seem possible here, as well as surprise thrusts against Brest. The entire group of forces which make up the American First Army Group, comprising about twenty-five divisions north and south of the Thames, has not yet been employed. The same applies to the ten to twelve active divisions held ready in the Midlands[3] and in Scotland. The conclusion is, therefore, that the enemy command plans a further large-scale undertaking in the Channel area which may well be directed against a coastal sector in the central Channel area.'[4]

With the departure of 21 Army Group for Normandy, BRUTUS lost no time in underlining the independence of FUSAG and the sense of imminent action which pervaded his headquarters. 'Received, this morning, news of the beginning of the invasion. Extremely surprised because our FUSAG remains unmoved. It is clear that the landing was made only by units of the 21 Army Group. I do not yet know whether all units of the 21 Army Group are

---

3. This of course refers to the central group of armies which they were still unwilling to abandon altogether.

4. Appendix to Lagebericht West No. 1288, dated 6th June, 1944. This appreciation also refers for the first time to a theory which was held by the Germans for several weeks after the invasion that we had retained the bulk of the Allied Air Forces in the United Kingdom. This suited us well enough as it provided additional air support for the second landing. 'As part of this undertaking we may expect the employment of large parts of the Anglo-Saxon Air Forces which have been held back.'

taking part. Am returning to Wentworth and will seek the details. Am surprised that the army groups, although independent, are attacking separately. The general opinion at Wentworth was that it should arrive simultaneously. FUSAG, as I reported, was ready for an attack which is capable of being released at any moment, but it is now evident that it will be an independent action.'[5]

On 8th June the belief that Montgomery might put in an attack against Brittany seemed to be losing ground. The opinion was also expressed that the Seine might form the dividing line between Montgomery and Patton. 'Since for reasons of concentration of forces as well as for tactical reasons of command, the employment of other of Montgomery's forces at any *far distant* place seems unlikely, it is conceivable that the *dividing line* between the 21 Army Group and the American Army Group standing ready in South-East England (Patton?) will be roughly along the Seine. Within the framework of the operations *so far* carried out, we must, therefore, reckon with the rapid arrival of further Montgomery formations in the *Normandy area*, and here *new landings*, especially on the west coast of Cotentin, seem possible. The employment of *strong forces* against Brittany or against the Atlantic front seems *at the moment not very* probable, on account of the Anglo-Saxon concentration and of the fact that *both* the enemy *armies* held ready in South-West England have been used against *Normandy*. . . . The fact that still *no formations* of the *forces held ready in South-East and Eastern England* have so far been identified in the landing operations, strengthens the view that the strong Anglo-American forces still available in that area are being held together for *further designs in other areas*.'[6]

By the 10th it had become clear to the Germans that Montgomery was concentrating his whole effort on the Normandy bridgehead. 'Of the *English* 21 *Army Group* concentrated in South-West England, approximately *sixteen* divisions have so far been in action in Northern France, while a *further nineteen divisions* of this group of forces are available and uncommitted in England. Reinforcement to the extent of three further divisions from the West of England and the West of

---

5. BRUTUS 1805, 1807 and 1810 GMT, 6th June, 1944.
6. Appendix to Lagebericht West No. 1290, dated 8th June, 1944.

Scotland[7] is possible. Since nearly half of all Montgomery's formations are employed in Normandy it is to be expected that his
remaining formations will also be used here. The *group of forces in
South-East England,* which has not yet been touched, comprises at the
moment about *twenty-seven divisions,* and could possibly be joined by
a further five divisions from the centre of England and three more
from Scotland.'[8]

In the South of France VENDETTA was holding well. 'The opening of the invasion against the north coast of France makes it
probable that the approximately twelve divisions available in French
North Africa will be used in operations against the south coast of
France, since the enemy command will presumably try by every
means to prevent the German troops stationed in the latter place
from being transferred to the main front.'[9] The only reference to an
attack on the west coast of France, for which IRONSIDE could
scarcely claim the credit, occurred on 9th June. 'The enemy convoys
seen off Southern Ireland and west of Brest on 8th June, among
which was a troop transport convoy, may possibly indicate small and
insignificant diversionary undertakings in the Biscay area.'[10]

What was the effect of these opinions on the reinforcement of the
bridgehead during the first few days of the invasion? On 6th June

---

7. This rather strange passage is explained in the OKH Situation Report for 8th
   June, 1944. 'In this connection it is noteworthy that two English divisions are
   getting ready for embarkation in the Firth of Clyde area (West Scotland).
   These are the 52nd and 58th English Infantry Divisions which a short time
   ago were standing by on the east coast of Scotland. It follows that these divisions will not be included in any operation against the Norwegian area. It can
   thus be seen that the enemy will have recourse to forces in the Scottish area to
   extend his operations in France.' In planning FORTITUDE NORTH we had
   originally chosen embarkation ports on the east coast of Scotland, reviving the
   plan which had been adopted for TINDALL during the previous autumn. At
   the instance of the Administrative Staff at COSSAC these arrangements were
   changed on the ground that the capacity of the eastern Scottish ports was inadequate. The expedition was consequently made to embark in the Clyde. This
   was the result!

8. Appendix to Lagebericht West No. 1292, dated 10th June, 1944.

9. Appendix to Lagebericht West No. 1228, dated 6th June, 1944.

10. OKH Situation Report, a.m. 9th June, 1944. Enemy Situation West and
    North.

Von Rundstedt requested the unconditional release of the OKW Armoured Reserve.[11] This request was only satisfied in part. The 1st SS Panzer Corps, comprising the 12th SS Panzer Division, the 17th SS Panzer Grenadier Division and the Panzer Lehr Division, were made available at once. The 2nd and 21st Panzer Divisions, being already under the control of Rommel, were also ordered to the bridgehead immediately.[12] On the other hand a situation report sent by Von Rundstedt to Jodl on 7th June tells us that 'C. in C. West refuses to consider any weakening of the south coast of France. Army Group B must try to arrange from its own resources any redistribution of forces that may be necessary.' So far, then, the only armoured formation ordered away from the area of Fifteenth Army was the 2nd Panzer Division.

On 8th June, in view of the growing Allied strength in the bridgehead, the remainder of the OKW armoured reserve was released, and at half-past ten on that evening an order was issued by C in C West stating that the 1st SS Panzer Division, the Panzer Regiment Grossdeutschland of the 116th Panzer Division, and certain other troops would with immediate effect come under command of Army Group B. Further, the Commander of Army Group B was to earmark two infantry divisions in the Pas de Calais for employment in the Normandy bridgehead. The Daily Situation Report for 9th June from the Commander of Army Group B stated that the 1st SS Panzer Division was now 'moving out of its present are in the district east north-east of Bruges'.

At half-past seven on the morning of the following day, 10th June, C in C West issued an order which reads as follows: 'As a consequence of certain information, C in C West has declared "a state of alarm II" for Fifteenth Army in Belgium and Northern France (for Netherlands Command if Army Group B thinks fit). The move of the 1st SS Panzer Division will therefore be halted and it will go into the area previously occupied by the 19th Luftwaffe Division.' The 1st SS Panzer, together with the 116th Panzer Division, both of which

---

11. Signal from C in C West to OKH, dated 6th June, 1944.
12. From what happened now it would seem that the 116th Panzer Division was under OKW control at this time although the War Diary states that it was placed under Army Group B at the beginning of May.

had already started for Normandy, now converged on the Pas de Calais, while the whole of Fifteenth Army area as well as Belgium and Holland were ordered to adopt the second or highest degree of alert.[13] On the following day Rommel reported: 'In the Netherlands Command and in the fifteenth Army area every German soldier and man is standing by night and day for defence.'

Speaking of these early and critical days the OKW War Diary says: 'That it actually was the long-anticipated D Day emerged from an order of Eisenhower broadcast in the morning hours and followed by speeches of the enemy Prime Ministers. It was, however, not yet clear whether it was the case of an initial attack to pin down our own forces or really the main operation. . . . It seemed possible that the enemy first wanted to cut off the Contentin Peninsula and thus get Cherbourg into their own hands in order, simultaneously or subsequently, to attack the Fifteenth Army with the forces waiting in South-East England. . . . Reinforcements from the West and from the Reich were brought up to the aid of our main forces, but it presently became evident that these forces were not sufficient to hurl the enemy back again into the sea. Therefore the Fuehrer gave orders on 9th June, in accordance with a report of the Chief of Armed Forces Operational Staff, that more forces should be sent in.' The divisions selected to provide the reinforcements are then listed. The War Diary goes on to say: 'As a report had come to hand according to which the enemy was planning a landing in Belgium, the 1st SS Armoured Division was transferred as reserves to the rear of the 48th Division, that area having been left exposed owing to the withdrawal of the 19th GAF Assault Detachment.' This was rather an understatement when one remembers that the movements of at least four divisions, and perhaps six, were effected by the counter order.

What was this report which caused such a drastic change in the plan and on whose initiative had the change been made? As the order was issued by Von Rundstedt it seemed right, after the Allied

---

13. According to a recent statement by General Blumentritt, the moves of two other divisions, the 85th Infantry Division and the 16th GAF Division, from locations north of the Seine to Normandy were cancelled at this time on OKW instructions. The recall of the 85th Infantry Division was known to us at the time from Most Secret Sources.

victory had brought him within our reach, to ask him to give his own explanation.[14] Both he and his Chief of Staff, Blumentritt, who were interrogated together, had no hesitation in saying that the counter-manding order was given as the result of a personal telephone call from Keitel. Von Rundstedt complained strongly that the battle on the beaches had been lost because the OKW would not release their reserves soon enough. When the release of the 1st SS Division and the armoured elements of the 116th Panzer Division was given on the evening of 8th June it was already too late. This does not quite fit in with the situation report sent by him to the OKW on 7th June in which he said: 'Having regard to the strength and resources used by the enemy against Normandy it is to be anticipated that a landing operation at least as strong, if not stronger, will shortly take place at another part of the coast.' Be that as it may, he held firmly to the statement that he wished to send all available resources to the bridge-head from the time of the first landing and refused to accept any responsibility for the countermanding order. It therefore became necessary to interrogate Keitel and Jodl. They both agreed that the initiative had come from the OKW. What had occurred between 10.30 p.m. on 8th June and 7.30 a.m. on 10th June to cause such a complete reversal of plan? It is clear that Hitler and his entourage were in a highly undecided frame of mind from the moment that the first landing took place and that their fear of a second landing was based chiefly on their belief in the First American Army Group in South-Eastern England. Under pressure from C in C West they had on 8th June agreed to release armoured formations from the Fifteenth Army area. Then some report had reached them which had made them change their minds.

Before going any further a word must be said about how these Abwehr reports reached the High Command. In the early part of the war when the Germans thought they were winning, Hitler had not thought it necessary for the OKW to have an intelligence branch at all. Reverses in the Russian campaign, however, led him to revise that

---

14. Interrogations of senior German commanders and staff officers for the pur-poses of this report were carried out by Mr F. C. B. F. Hesketh (Holcombe Court, Holcombe Rogus, Wellington, Somerset), who can amplify, if required, the record of interviews given in these pages.

opinion. Such a branch was accordingly formed and at its head was placed a certain Colonel Krummacher, who had hitherto acted as a kind of liaison officer between the Abwehr and the OKW. Krummacher was essentially an Abwehr man. Feeling himself more at home with agents' reports than with other forms of intelligence, he seems to have concentrated his attention mainly on these, which of course was a great help to us.[15] All Abwehr reports went direct to the RSHA Headquarters, who would circulate by teleprinter summarised versions to the OKW and other interested headquarters. C in C West was usually included. If Krummacher thought a message was of sufficient importance he would show it to Jodl and perhaps to Warlimont, who initialled it. If Jodl in his turn thought that the Fuehrer should see it, he put a different kind of mark on it and added, if Hitler had seen it, either 'erl.' (erledigt) or 'hat K.' (hat Kenntnis).[16]

Having discovered this procedure, the next step was to see what messages had passed through Krummacher's hands during these critical hours which might have influenced the German High Command. There are three competitors for the distinction. The first came in at 1335 hours on 9th June. It concerned an intercepted wireless message from London to an Allied sabotage organisation in Brussels of which the Germans had gained control. The message contained two code phrases: 'Message pour la petite Berte' and 'Salomon a sauté ses grands sabots.' The first code phrase was alleged by the German Intelligence Service to mean that a landing would take place 'the day after tomorrow at the latest' and the second that the invasion fleet had already started. The Abwehr Stelle forwarding the message commented that the Allies must have known that this network was under German control and that in consequence it was probably deceptive, but the senior headquarters through which the message passed expressed the view that the Allies had not had time to discover that their organisation had been penetrated and that it must in consequence be taken at its face value. It is referred to in the OKW Intelligence Summary. 'There is still no concrete evidence

---

15. Admiral Buerckner, his former chief at the Abwehr, described him as 'bone lazy' (stink faul).
16. Information supplied by Jodl.

regarding the beginning of the attack or the objective of this group of forces. Observations from wireless interplay with the enemy Intelligence Service again point to the area of Belgium and to an early commencement of the attack.'[17] On the other hand Krummacher did not think it of sufficient importance to show to Jodl. It has been found impossible to discover the origin of this message. Deliberate deception at no time formed a part of the SOE policy, though admittedly they did at times continue to run organisations which were known to be under enemy control, mainly to give their agents a chance of escaping. It is possible that the construction placed by the Germans upon this message may have resulted from a misinterpretation of the code phrases. In passing one may point out that this provides a good example of the dangers which attend any attempt to use an espionage network of our own which has fallen into enemy hands for deception by the triple-cross method.

The second message came in on 9th June at 1810 hours. As this was the work of an uncontrolled agent it will be necessary to explain very shortly a new development in their technique which was becoming evident at this time and was causing us a good deal of embarrassment. The evidence of Most Secret Sources was beginning to make the conclusion almost irresistible that the uncontrolled agents, or at any rate the two most highly regarded ones, OSTRO[18] in Lisbon and JOSEPHINE[19] in Stockholm, had acquired some knowledge of the FORTITUDE story. It is true that a second attack on the Pas de Calais following after the Normandy invasion might

---

17. Appendix to Lagebericht West No. 1291, dated 9th June, 1944.
18. OSTRO, a German of Czech origin named Paul Fidrmuc, was a businessman in Lisbon who sent regular reports to the Abwehr in Germany for which he was very highly paid. These he collected from imaginary networks of agents in France, Britain, the United States and the Middle East.
19. JOSEPHINE and HECTOR, the two most prolific German spies operating in Sweden, were 'run' by a certain Dr Kraemer, a German journalist residing in Stockholm. Both agents were, of course, 'uncontrolled'; indeed, it is not clear that they really existed at all. It seems that Dr Kraemer's motives were pecuniary and he used these channels alternately to convey spurious intelligence in exchange for money payments. Most important operational messages went to JOSEPHINE, who in consequence enjoyed the higher reputation.

have been guessed at by any intelligent but uniformed person as the likely sequence of future events, but there were too many similarities of detail to allow us to attribute this development to chance. We now know that Dr Kraemer had in fact access to German Intelligence documents. This is also very probably true in the case of OSTRO, though the point has not been proved. It was in these documents that Dr Kraemer read successive instalments of the FORTITUDE story and handed them to the Germans a second time with his own embellishments. The effect, mainly unfortunate, of this practice upon our own efforts to deceive will be considered in greater detail in a later chapter. All that need be said here is that if this particular message of JOSEPHINE contributed in any way to the issue of the countermanding order we may perhaps be allowed to claim a part of the credit since he was taking his cue from us and basing his appreciation on the assumed presence of FUSAG in the South-East of England, a force which he himself had done nothing to establish in the German mind. JOSEPHINE's message runs as follows: 'Very reliable V-man[20] reports regarding invasion situation early on 9th June (time of report the night of 8th June): General opinion, according to statements of War Office spokesman to English and American journalists afternoon of 8th June (conference takes place thrice daily), is that conditions for Allied landing troops have improved. Impression shared in authoritative British military circles. According to statements by Harrison,[21] an absolutely clear picture on the British side cannot yet be given as the critical period for the invading troops is only just beginning. Strength so far employed is also described by him as considerable, greater than was originally intended. In his opinion and according to information from other sources a second main attack across the Channel directed against the Pas de Calais is to be expected. . . . British public very optimistic. But views in political circles more cautious. In Conservative circles the danger of too heavy losses is

---

20. By arrangement JOSEPHINE was always referred to as 'sehr zuverlaessiger V-Mann'.

21. Harrison was a fictitious air marshal to whom JOSEPHINE attributed much of his most sensational intelligence. It is possible that he was thinking of Air Marshal Harris, but mistook the name.

continually emphasised, whereas the Labour Party and other Left-wing movements are very satisfied with the beginning of the invasion.' It is marked 'sofort' in Krummacher's handwriting and was seen by Jodl and the Fuehrer.

The third and last message arrived at 2220 hours on 9th June. It came from GARBO. As soon as GARBO had learned from Agent Four that the invasion had started, he called his three trusted sub-agents, 7 (2), 7 (4) and 7 (7), to a meeting in London. At half-past seven on the evening of 8th June he informed Madrid: 'I have had an extremely agitated day today, but I have the satisfaction of being able to give you the most important reports of my work. As I have not got all the messages ready, I hope you will be listening tonight at 10 GMT.'[22] At seven minutes past midnight on 9th June GARBO began to send his great message, the transmission continuing without a break until nine minutes past two in the morning. Having announced that agents 7 (2), 7 (4) and 7 (7) had arrived in London and delivered their reports, GARBO proceeded to give a full list of all major formations, real and fictitious, in Sussex, Kent and East Anglia. This, in effect, was a summary and a recapitulation of the reports of the previous days.[23] He also referred for the first time to landing craft on the rivers Deben and Orwell.[24] Following

---

22. GARBO 1928 GMT, 8th June, 1944.

23. As vehicles of nearly all the formations going to Normandy, including the assault divisions, were embarked at Tilbury and the London Docks, it was possible to report their insignia in those districts without any departure from truth. This tended to increase the apparent size of the Eastern concentration.

24. Permission to refer to the dummy landing craft was given on 8th June. In order to provoke an air reconnaissance, GARBO told the Germans that 7 (7) had received this information through a new and untried source. He therefore requested them to check these statements by aerial observation in order that he might assess the value of the agent. No such flight was undertaken, but on 17th June GARBO was informed: 'With reference to the report of the friend of 7 (7) about barges, you may consider this as confirmed.' The Abwehr were evidently not anxious to advertise their inability to have their demands met by the German Air Force. It may be noted here that where it is necessary for controlled agents to refer to dummy equipment of any kind, it is usual for them to attribute the observation to a third party. This is an obvious precaution against the danger of the enemy discovering that the display in question is a false one.

closely on the lines recommended by GARBO's case officer a month previously the message concluded thus: 'From the reports mentioned it is perfectly clear that the present attack is a large-scale operation but diversionary in character for the purpose of establishing a strong bridgehead in order to draw the maximum of our reserves to the area of operation and to retain them there so as to be able to strike a blow somewhere else with ensured success. I never like to give my opinion unless I have strong reasons to justify my assurances, but the fact that these concentrations which are in the East and South-East of the Island are now inactive means that they must be held in reserve to be employed in the other large-scale operations. The constant aerial bombardment which the area of the Pas de Calais has suffered and the strategic disposition of these forces give reason to suspect an attack in that region of France which, at the same time, offers the shortest route for the final objective of their illusions, which is to say Berlin. This advance could be covered by a constant hammering from the air since the bases would be near the field of battle and they would come in behind our forces which are fighting at the present moment with the enemy disembarked in the West of France. From J (5) I learnt yesterday that there were seventy-five divisions in this country before the present assault commenced. Supposing they should use a maximum of twenty to twenty-five divisions, they would be left with some fifty divisions with which to attempt a second blow. I trust you will submit urgently all these reports and studies to our High Command since moments may be decisive in these times and before taking a false step, through lack of knowledge of the necessary facts, they should have in their possession all the present information which I transmit with my opinion which is based on the belief that the whole of the present attack is set as a trap for the enemy to make us move all our reserves in a hurried strategical disposition which we would later regret.'[25]

GARBO's message reached Krummacher in the following abbreviated form: 'After personal consultation on 8th June in London with my agents, Jonny,[26] Dick and Dorick, whose reports were sent

25. GARBO 0144, 0149, 0155, 0204 and 0209 GMT, 9th June, 1944.
26. Misprint for Donny.

today, I am of the opinion, in view of the strong troop concentrations in South-East and Eastern England which are not taking part in the present operations, that these operations are a diversionary manœuvre designed to draw off enemy reserves in order then to make a decisive attack in another place. In view of the continued air attacks on the concentration area mentioned, which is a strategically favourable position for this, it may very probably take place in the Pas de Calais area, particularly since in such an attack the proximity of air bases will facilitate the operation by providing continued strong air support.'[27] Krummacher underlined the words 'diversionary manœuvre designed to draw off enemy reserves in order then to make a decisive attack in another place', and added at the end: 'confirms the view already held by us that a further attack is to be expected in another place (Belgium?)'. This message was seen by Jodl, who underlined the words 'in South-East and Eastern England' and took it to the Fuehrer.

Berlin acknowledged GARBO's report in the following terms: 'The report is credible. The reports received in the last week from the ARABAL (GARBO) undertaking have been confirmed almost without exception and are to be described as especially valuable. The main line of investigation in future is to be the enemy group of forces in South-Eastern and Eastern England.'[28]

Attempts to find out from Keitel and Jodl which of these was the message referred to in Von Rundstedt's order and in the War Diary were not altogether satisfactory because it was evident that they could not clearly remember the individual reports which they had received at that busy time. Professor Percy Schramm, who had the specific task of keeping the diary, stated that he would not have seen the document in question. When confronted with the text of GARBO's message, Keitel replied: 'There you have your answer. If I were writing a history I would say, with ninety-nine per cent certainly, that that message provided the reason for the change of plan.' Later when the other two messages came to light these too were put before Keitel and Jodl. They both dismissed the message containing the code phrases to the sabotage organisation in Brussels as being of

27. The frontispiece [page xxiii] contains a facsimile reproduction of this message.
28. Berlin to Madrid, 11th June, 1944.

little importance. Jodl did so largely on the ground that the hiero-glyphics proved that Krummacher had not thought it of sufficient importance to show to himself. They both thought that the other two must have had a decisive influence. Jodl gave slight preference to JOSEPHINE. Keitel on the other hand held to his original view. 'I am personally still of the opinion that message A played the decisive role, B had the second place in importance and C the last in the forming of the decision.'[29] Whatever the relative importance of the three messages, they both agreed that GARBO's message as it came last of the three must have tipped the balance.[30] There is, however, yet one more pointer in GARBO's favour. It will be remembered that his messages came through Madrid, while those of JOSEPHINE came from Stockholm. Attached to the OKW War Diary were a number of appendices, one of which contained copies of important documents relating to the Normandy invasion which were received from day to day at the OKW. On Jodl's instructions the OKW War Diary was preserved with a view to its probable value to historians in the future, but unfortunately, according to Professor Schramm, the appendices were destroyed, so that we only have the bare headings. Of the four 'invasion' documents included for 10th June one is entitled 'News from Madrid' (Nachricht aus Madrid). There is no corresponding heading entitled 'News from Stockholm'. It is natural to suppose that any message which altered the course of a campaign should have been thought worthy of inclusion in an appendix to the War Diary.

Taking the evidence as a whole, the reader will probably agree that GARBO's report decided the issue. But whatever view one may take it must always be remembered that no message would have spurred the Germans to action on the morning of 10th June had they not already been convinced of the presence of FUSAG beyond the Straits of Dover. And the establishment of that force on either side of

29. A – GARBO; B – JOSEPHINE; C – Belgian sabotage organisation.
30. Both Jodl's and Krummacher's signatures on GARBO's message are fol-lowed by the date 10th June. All were agreed that this merely implied that the signatures had been put on after midnight on the night of the 9–10th. This would be natural as the message only came into the office at 2220 hours.

the Thames Estuary had been the combined achievement of GARBO and BRUTUS.[31]

Of the four 'invasion' documents appended to the War Dairy on 10th June there is another which claims our attention for it bears the title 'Enemy Propaganda Directive' (Richtlinien der feindlichen Propaganda). A copy of GARBO's 'inverted' PWE Directive is to be found in Krummacher's file. This entry in the War Diary therefore provides fairly circumstantial evidence that this plot also worked successfully and that GARBO's activities at the Ministry of Information played a decisive part in influencing German plans at this vital period.

The reader may wonder why the transmission of GARBO's message was delayed for more than forty-eight hours after the first landing in Normandy had been made. It was, of course, necessary to give Donny, Dick and Dorick time to get from Harwich, Dover and Brighton to London, but to find the main reason we must look back to a memorandum written by GARBO's case officer on 4th May, more than a month before. 'With the approach of D Day and even after, until the nature and full significance of NEPTUNE is discovered, there will almost inevitably be a certain divergence of opinion as to Allied intentions even in the German High Command. There will, we hope, be among the leaders of Germany some who will draw the conclusions we are trying to inspire through FORTITUDE. If we can continue through GARBO and the Abwehr to supply those Germans who are already inclined to believe in our cover plan with further ammunition for their arguments . . . it may well be that we shall be helping those elements in Germany to influence plans in our favour during the few critical days of the post-assault period.' It may be thought that the message went a few hours too late, but it was not late enough to matter. Perhaps this was an advantage, for people who have changed their minds once seldom care to do so again.

---

31. This view of the matter is supported by a remark made by Von Rundstedt to Captain B. H. Liddell Hart, and quoted by the latter in his book *The Other Side of the Hill* (Cassell, 1948), at page 251: 'The scale of the invading forces was not a surprise – in fact, we had imagined that they would be larger, because we had received exaggerated reports of the number of American divisions present in England. But that over-estimate had an indirect effect of important consequence, by making us the more inclined to expect a second landing, in the Calais area.'

XXIV

Removal of Security Restrictions

During the weeks immediately preceding the invasion, it was found necessary to introduce a number of special security measures in order to obviate as far as possible the danger of leakage at that critical time. At the end of March the air-mail service between this country and Lisbon was discontinued. 1st April witnessed the imposition of military censorship, of the ban on travel to Ireland and of the visitors' ban, which prohibited all but residents from visiting certain specified parts of the coast. On 6th April Service leave was stopped; on the 18th travel to and from the United Kingdom was disallowed; finally, on the 24th, a censorship was imposed on all diplomatic mail. While these regulations were being drawn up, the Ops (B) staff had been consulted, so that the needs of deception could be met. At their suggestion the area affected by the visitors' ban had been extended to satisfy the requirements of the cover operations then in force, and other adjustments had been made. In these preliminary discussions, however, insufficient attention was paid to the desirability of continuing such measures, in support of FORTITUDE, after the invasion had been launched. It was not until 17th May that this aspect of the matter was brought to the forefront, when, at a meeting of the Home Defence Executive, the Deception Staff suggested that the diplomatic ban should be continued at least until D plus 30. This request revealed a deep cleavage of opinion and drew an immediate retort from the Foreign Office representative: 'He would object very strongly to any suggestion that the diplomatic ban should continue in force after D Day; he would, in fact, never have agreed to the ban except on the understanding that it would cease when OVERLORD had been launched. The Foreign Office were quite certain that, once it was common knowledge that we had landed on the Continent, they would be quite unable to hold the position with either the Allies or the neutrals and, if the proposal was pressed, it would have to go to the Cabinet.'

The matter was referred to the Chiefs of Staff who had already received a note from the Foreign Secretary on the subject. The latter had expressed the view that it would not be possible to continue the diplomatic ban for any length of time after D Day. He had, therefore, suggested that the ban should be lifted not later than D plus two, but that practical obstacles should be imposed whereby diplomatic travellers and uncensored diplomatic communications would not be able in fact to leave the country before D plus seven. This suggestion was accepted by the Chiefs of Staff, and on 30th May another meeting of the Home Defence Executive was called to consider the effect of the withdrawal of the diplomatic ban on other security measures. It had been argued at the previous meeting that its removal would undermine the value of many of these and while this was generally agreed a plea was put forward by the London Controlling Officer that the other restrictions should not be withdrawn *en bloc* but that their removal should be staggered. The removal of the diplomatic ban would undoubtedly harm FORTITUDE SOUTH, but that was unavoidable. The simultaneous removal of all important restrictions would be disastrous. The meeting recommended that all special security restrictions should be reviewed together on or about D plus twelve.

The decision to withdraw the diplomatic ban put us in an awkward position. If this unprecedented measure had been necessary for the invasion of Normandy it would indeed be hard to understand why it was any less necessary for the equally or perhaps more important attack on the Pas de Calais. We at least had the advantage, however, of knowing that the ban was to be removed in little more than a week and this gave us time to think of an explanation. To meet the difficulty, GARBO, soon after the invasion had been launched, informed Berlin of a dilemma which faced two British Departments of State. The neutrals had accepted the imposition of the ban with reluctance. The impending attack on the Pas de Calais demanded that the restriction should be continued, but this the Foreign Office declared would be impossible unless we gave our reason for wishing to do so: namely that we intended to undertake a second assault. Rather than disclose our operational intentions to neutral diplomatists, the War Office preferred to dispense with the ban and so the Foreign Office was to have its way. That seemed to us at the time a neat way out of the impasse, and it was with a feeling bordering on mortification that we found our message in Krummacher's file with the comment 'of no general interest' (keine allgemeine interesse). However, as no one else in the OKW appears to have seen anything odd in a full restoration of diplomatic privileges just before the second assault was to be launched, Krummacher's failure to rise to the occasion did not really matter.

In the event the diplomatic ban was continued, through the personal intervention of the Supreme Commander, until 21st June. On 19th June GARBO gave advance information of its removal and amplified his previous report regarding the differences of opinion which had arisen between the two Departments of State.

When asking for an extension of the diplomatic ban the Supreme Commander also requested that all other restrictions, which had been specially imposed for the invasion, should continue until 1st July. To this the War Cabinet agreed on 13th June. It also agreed to the retention of any particular restriction after the end of the month if good cause could be shown. A meeting of the Home Defence Executive was held on 23rd June to consider the matter. Of the numerous security measures which came under review only two were of such special significance as to concern us here, the withdrawal of the visitors' ban and the restoration of Service leave. The Home Office was naturally anxious to get rid of the visitors' ban altogether as it caused hardship to the public. SHAEF was willing to agree to its removal west of Southampton. The Chairman of the Home Defence Executive, in his report to the Chiefs of Staff, laid some emphasis on the apparent success which had already been achieved by the cover plan and this carried the necessary weight with the Cabinet, which decided on 7th July to continue the ban between the Wash and Southampton at least until 1st August. It was in fact extended for another month after that and it was not until 6th September that BRUTUS reported to the Germans that it had been lifted altogether.

The restoration of Service leave was also discussed at the Home Defence Executive meeting of 23rd June. The suggestion that leave should be restored to non-operational troops was resisted by SHAEF on the ground that the Germans would not be able to distinguish the type of troops affected and that any report of the resumption of leave would be damaging to FORTITUDE. This view was upheld by the War Cabinet. At the beginning of August, as a result of strong representations from the Service Ministries, SHAEF finally agreed to the full restoration of leave on 15th August. During July an important change took place in the FORTITUDE Order of Battle inasmuch as the real formations were replaced in almost every instance by imaginary ones. Thus it was possible to say without fear of contradiction when 15th August arrived that although leave had been restored to non-operational troops the ban still remained on all FUSAG formations, since these formations did not really exist. 'It is expected', reported BRUTUS on 11th August, 'that seven days' leave will shortly be restored. These orders do not apply to the forces in FUSAG.'[1]

The lesser restrictions which had been introduced to safeguard the invasion were removed one by one during the months of July and August. At the end of July the normal airmail service was restored. This made it possible once more to enlist the services of the letter-writing agents for deception.

---

1. BRUTUS 1705 GMT, 11th August, 1944.

XXV

TWEEZER

FORTITUDE required that the threat of a second landing should be kept alive for three weeks after the invasion had begun. As the illusory army group was composed solely of real formations, it was essential that none of its component parts should appear in France while the plan was still in operation. We have already seen how it had become necessary, for that reason, to omit VII Corps and the 79th US Infantry Division. We were now confronted with the possibility of losing the two corps comprised in the First Canadian Army, that is to say the 2nd Canadian Corps and the XII Corps, before the end of the month. 21 Army Group therefore thought it wise to withdraw them, too, without delay from the false Order of Battle. The proposed withdrawal of 2nd Canadian Corps came as no surprise for, as the reader will recall, we had counted, some time previously, on losing it as early as D plus 8 and it was to meet such an eventuality that the 2nd British Corps had been started on its journey to the South. Thus it was now available to fill, at least in part, the gap left by the two retiring corps. The plan which gave effect to this change was known as TWEEZER,[1] and was issued on 8th June, two days after the invasion had started. The 2nd British Corps, so the new story ran, had recently been detached from the Scottish force with a view to its ultimate employment in France. At first it had only been brought as far as Lincolnshire as it was thought that it might be required to revert at short notice to Fourth Army, which was still available for a Norwegian operation. After D Day it had appeared to

---

1. 21 AGP/00/261/33/IG (R), dated 8th June, 1944.

the Supreme Commander that the Normandy assault was likely to proceed too slowly and would require a reinforcement of two further corps. He had therefore decided to allot the 2nd Canadian Corps and XII Corps to 21 Army Group as from 14th June and to move in the 2nd British Corps to take their place.

Adjustments were made in the deceptive wireless programme to indicate this regrouping. The First Canadian Army and its subordinate formations were to observe wireless silence from 14th June. On 16th June the wireless links of the 2nd British Corps were to close in Lincolnshire and simultaneously to open in the vicinity of Dover, that corps having already established wireless communication with FUSAG on 4th June.

It will be convenient at this point to complete the story of the 2nd British Corps' move to the South. The reader may remember that we left it at Louth on 6th June with its two divisions at Skegness and Horncastle.

Agent 3 (3)'s encounter on the platform of Motherwell station on the eve of the invasion had already persuaded the Germans that the 2nd British Corps and the 58th British Infantry Division were on the move and heading for England.[2] A subsequent message from BRUTUS,[3] who had included a visit to Doncaster at the end of his East Anglian tour, found its place in the Lagebericht for 11th June. 'The same source, whose reports about the location of the English 2nd Army Corps' Headquarters and the 58th English Infantry Division in Scotland have so far been confirmed, reports these on 7th June in the Doncaster area (30 kms. north-east of Sheffield).'[4] By the middle of the month GARBO's sub-agent 7 (2)

---

2. The Germans slightly garbled 3 (3)'s story which was transmitted to them at 1956 hours GMT on 4th June. 3 (3), having heard of the arrival of a large contingent of troops from Ireland, disregarded GARBO's instructions that he should not leave the Clyde and went to investigate in the Dumfries–Lockerbie area, where he found the 55th British Infantry Division. Returning to Glasgow he found troops of the 2nd British Corps and the 58th British Infantry Division at Motherwell also on the move. The Germans reported the 2nd British Corps and the 58th British Infantry Division as having gone to Dumfries and said nothing about the 55th Division at all.

3. BRUTUS 1625 GMT, 7th June, 1944.

4. Lagebericht West No. 1293 of 11th June, 1944.

was identifying troops in Kent with the 2nd Corps and 58th Division insignia, GARBO being prompted to add: 'I attach the greatest importance to the reference by this agent to these insignia as it is an indication that all the troop concentrations seen by 3 (3) in Motherwell have been moved south.'[5] Three days later the Lagebericht duly recorded: 'From England there are further signs that the FUSAG formations are closing up towards the south-east coast. The hitherto unconfirmed transfer of the English 2nd Corps' formations accepted in Central England to Kent fits in with this south-eastern concentration.'[6] No mention had been made, on our side, of the 55th British Infantry Division since 3 (3) had found it at Dumfries, an observation which the Germans had ignored. When during the previous January PANDORA had disclosed to the German Minister in Dublin the fact that the 45th and 55th British Infantry Divisions, hitherto stationed respectively in Northern Ireland and in Sussex, had changed places, they had accepted the move of the 45th Division from Northern Ireland, but had apparently left the 55th where it was. 'A good source reports that the 45th English Infantry Division is stationed in South-Eastern Command and has relieved the 55th English Infantry Division employed on the coast. The 55th English Infantry Division is still on the south coast.'[7] FREAK's message about the troops in Northern Ireland sent in support of FORTITUDE NORTH would have disabused their minds on this point, but it had gone astray. Perhaps this explains why they could not believe that the 55th Division had turned up in Dumfries. At any rate, when on 20th June 7 (2) reported the division as being in his area,[8] the Germans recorded the fact in the following terms: 'The 55th English Infantry Division, hitherto accepted doubtfully north of Dungeness, has been confirmed by the same source. This formation is seemingly subordinate to the 2nd English Army Corps.'[9] In other words it looks as if the 55th Division, both in reality and according

---

5. GARBO 2201 GMT, 16th June, 1944.
6. Appendix to Lagebericht West No. 1301, dated 19th June, 1944.
7. Lagebericht West No. 1179, dated 18th February, 1944.
8. GARBO 2110 and 2120 GMT, 20th June, 1944.
9. Lagebericht West, dated 24th June, 1944.

to our cover story, went to Ireland for six months, but remained all the time, according to German opinion, 'doubtfully north of Dungeness'.[10] Be that as it may, the Germans now had the 2nd British Corps and its two divisions where we wanted them to be, namely, in Kent.

Certain other minor changes in the FUSAG Order of Battle which occurred during the first half of June must be recorded here. Shortly before the invasion, as has already been stated, VIII Corps and the 79th US Infantry Division had been withdrawn from First Canadian Army and had been replaced by XII Corps and the 35th US Infantry Division,[11] both these formations being transferred from Third Army. A gap had thus been left in the latter army. We now had to ask ourselves the question, should we continue to use misplaced real divisions or should we fall back on wholly imaginary ones? For reasons which will be examined later, the latter course was decided upon. Accordingly XXXVII Corps and the 59th US Infantry Division were brought into being[12] and introduced to the Germans in the following way: at the end of May the 28th US Infantry Division had moved from its imaginary location in Kent to carry out fictitious training with the sham naval assault force 'F' at Felixstowe. 'According to a reliable message the American 28th Infantry Division, hitherto accepted in the Dover area, has been transferred to

---

10. At this moment the true position was that an advance party of the 55th Division, specially constituted for wireless deception, had now arrived in Sussex, having travelled via Dumfries and Lincolnshire, while the main body was about to join it from Northern Ireland.

11. Following an observation of GARBO's agent 7 (4) transmitted at 2146 hours GMT on 16th June, 1944, the Lagebericht West No. 1300 of 18th June, 1944, records: 'According to a credible report the 35th American Infantry Division has been moved from the area south-west of Ipswich to the area north of Brighton.'

12. The numbers of fictitious Allied formations were supplied by the London Controlling Section who allotted blocks to each theatre of war upon which the latter could draw at will. The London Controlling Section in turn received British numbers from the War Office and American from the War Department in Washington. So far as the North-West European theatre was concerned, fictitious British insignia were designed by the Special Means Staff of Ops (B) Sub-Section and American were supplied by the War Department through the London Controlling Section.

the Harwich area.'[13] Its training having been completed by 7th June, the division was made to return in due course to its previous location. 'According to credible reports the 28th American Infantry Division has been moved back to Kent from the Ipswich area, where it is said to have been carrying out landing exercises.'[14] The proposal was to make the new division, the 59th, which was supposed to be assault trained, take the place of the 28th and continue its amphibious training with Force 'F'. In the message reporting the departure of the 28th US Division from Harwich GARBO therefore announced the arrival of the new one, so that the Lagebericht quoted above continues: 'In the place of the 28th American Infantry Division there is said to be a new infantry division in the Ipswich area, which is said to have arrived recently in England.'[15]

Shortly afterwards the XXXVII Corps was discovered to have taken XII Corps' place in Third Army. 'According to an unconfirmed agent's report the American XXXVII Army Corps is in the area around and south-west of Harwich and has under command the American 7th Armoured Division (Chelmsford area) and the American 59th Infantry Division (Harwich area).'[16] The 7th Armoured Division, a misplaced real formation and part of the original FUSAG, had only just arrived from America, yet the OKH Intelligence Summary saw fit to add: 'The 7th Armoured Division may be the armoured division of unknown number which on previous evidence was hitherto believed to be in the South-West of England,'[16] and of the newly created and wholly fictitious 59th Infantry Division: 'The 59th Infantry Division is probably the American infantry division of unknown number which hitherto, for want of further information, was believed to be in Scotland, but which had not been confirmed there for a long time.'[16]

Other additions to the Order of Battle included the imaginary 2nd Airborne Division which was brought into existence at Skegness in

13. Lagebericht West No. 1292, dated 10th June, 1944, based on BRUTUS 2005 GMT, 6th June, 1944.
14. Lagebericht West No. 1301, dated 19th June, 1944, based on GARBO 1910 and 2110 GMT, 17th June, 1944.
15. Lagebericht West No. 1301, dated 19th June, 1944.
16. Lagebericht West dated 25th June, 1944, based on BRUTUS 1846 and 1852 GMT, 24th June, 1944.

Lincolnshire as the result of a 21 Army Group instruction of 11th June, and which opened a wireless link with the 2nd British Corps in Kent on 17th June. This division had already been reported by BRUTUS as being in the Grantham area on 7th June, and in the Lagebericht for the 11th we read: 'According to an Abwehr source which has reported accurately for a long time, the 2nd English Airborne Division, hitherto thought to be in the Western Mediterranean, location unknown, is now in the Grantham area (30 kms. east of Nottingham).'[17] Finally on 6th June arrangements were made for the inclusion of the Nineteenth Tactical Air Force in the FUSAG Order of Battle. This was to correct a mistake which had resulted from an oversight in the signals arrangements. The Nineteenth Tactical Air Force in reality provided the air support for the Third US Army. When the latter was moved fictitiously to Chelmsford at the end of April from its real location at Knutsford in Cheshire, the wireless links of the Air Force with which it was associated continued to operate in their true location in Cheshire. This was not noticed until the beginning of June, when steps were immediately taken to remedy the situation. In fact the Nineteenth Tactical Air Force moved during June to Biggin Hill in Kent, an admirable location for the support of FORTITUDE SOUTH.

At the middle of June, therefore, the FUSAG grouping of forces was theoretically as follows:

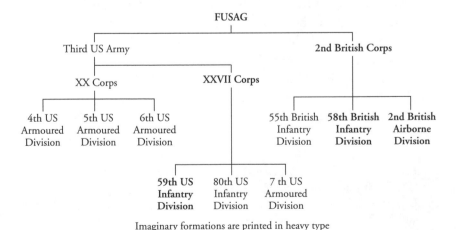

Imaginary formations are printed in heavy type

---

17. Lagebericht West No. 1293 of 11th June, 1944.

It was not necessary, of course, for the controlled agents to tell the enemy that the 2nd Canadian Corps and XII Corps had been transferred to 21 Army Group until these formations really went to France. Consequently, since wireless deception was telling them nothing, the Germans were for the time being merely left with the impression that FUSAG had been reinforced by the 2nd British Corps.

TWEEZER provided that the whole of the FUSAG wireless network should go off the air on 26th June and, in a final attempt to hold such formations of the German Fifteenth Army as still remained in the North-West of France, the impression of imminent embarkation was to be given. Thereafter the forces engaged in deception would disperse. The 2nd British Corps and the 58th British Infantry Division with their supporting wireless would return to Scotland. The party representing the 55th British Infantry Division would rejoin its main body on the latter's arrival from Ireland. The other formations engaged in FORTITUDE SOUTH would duly appear in Normandy, while No. 5 Wireless Group and 3103 Signals Service Battalion would become available for service overseas.

Before the invasion was many days old, indications were not lacking of the enemy's belief in our intention to effect a second landing north of the Seine. On 3rd June the Allied Intelligence Staff had forecast that by the 13th three armoured and three infantry divisions would have left the Fifteenth army's area for the bridgehead. As it was, only one, the 2nd Armoured Division, had crossed the Seine. On 12th June Sertorius, the German commentator, announced: 'Of the German reserves, only a fraction have taken an active part in the battle, while the remainder are still being held in their reserve positions. Consequently there can so far be no talk of a major German counter-offensive against the Allied armies on the Cotentin and Calvados shores. This temporary holding back and sparing of German forces arises from the consideration that the Anglo-US attack on the Normandy sector is only the first part of the invasion action, and that equally strong, if not stronger, actions will certainly follow on other sectors of Europe's Western flank. The place and time of these coming actions cannot exactly be foreseen, but obviously a new major landing will not be started before the situation on the

Normandy shore has been so far stabilised that further assistance from the bulk of the enemy's air and sea forces can be dispensed with.' Most significantly of all, Most Secret Sources had revealed the order for the transfer of the 85th German Infantry Division to the bridgehead and the subsequent rescinding of that order.

At the middle of the month it was possible to take either a short-term or a long-term view. If we completed the operation with a show of embarkation at the end of June we should probably be more certain of pinning down German forces in the immediate future, but by doing so we should be spoiling our chance of keeping the threat alive in July. Once we had persuaded the enemy that the expedition was about to sail, subsequent inaction would cause them to wonder why we did not come and thus begin to sow seeds of doubt.

While it was agreed by this time that a new story designed to continue FORTITUDE SOUTH into July would probably be needed, 21 Army Group still thought that some advantage could be gained by bringing the original plan near to 'culmination'. Providing that matters were not pressed too far it was felt that this could be done without damage to any future story. Thus, on 2nd June, Force 'F', having been joined by its headquarters ship, HMS *Lothian*, moved to its battle station at Sheerness, decoy lighting was increased at the hards and finally, as already stated, wireless silence was imposed on 26th June, this being intended to suggest the movement of the forces to their ports of embarkation.

The Special Means Staff at SHAEF was invited by 21 Army Group to support the move to embarkation. Knowing that measures were already being considered which would require the controlled agents to tell a story altogether at variance with any suggestion of imminent attack, the Special Means Staff found itself in a somewhat difficult position. A solution was attempted in the 'Southern Railway Plan', also known as Plan MERCURY. If we could suggest a movement of the FUSAG formations from their existing locations to the ports without actually specifying any dates, we should still have a line of retreat when invasion of the Pas de Calais at the end of June did not materialise. It was therefore decided to let one of our agents come into possession of a Southern Railway movement table based on an undisclosed D Day. This could hardly excite the suspicion of

the Germans, for to omit dates from such a document would be a
normal security precaution. With the assistance of the Traffic
Manager of the Southern Railway, tables were accordingly prepared
showing the movement of all the FUSAG formations from their
concentration areas to the ports of Tilbury, Gravesend, Dover,
Folkestone and Newhaven. As GARBO and BRUTUS were both
fully occupied at that time, it was decided to employ TATE for this
particular task. TATE had removed to Kent at the end of May and
was working on the farm of his employer's friend. On 8th and 9th
June he sent the following message: 'The Special Trains Section of the
Southern Railway has opened an advance control office at Ashford
Junction. This section is a part of the London East Division of the
Southern Railway . . . and all important troop movements are dealt
with by it. A friendly clerk in the Ashford office billeted here tells me
that the advance control office has been opened to cope with
increased troop movements in that area.'[18] The idea now was to
throw a fly over the Germans by letting out a few details of this
movement plan in the hope that their interest would be aroused and
that they would ask for more particulars so that eventually we could
give them the complete story. On 14th June TATE therefore followed
his first message with this: 'Railway clerk friend has been very busy
working out adjustments to timetables. Was able to see at his place a
railway notice called "Special Working Arrangements in Connection
with Movements of Troops". Unfortunately no dates given. Dates
also unknown to friend. On the cover were several instructions. The
first page dealt with twenty-three trains to Tilbury from Tenterden on
a date described as "J minus 11". . . . Thirteen of them were for
tracked vehicles and the rest were passenger trains, each with about
500 seats for men and thirty or so for officers. There were about six
pages in all but had not much time get much detail of the others.
They covered a period from J minus five or six. The places of departure include Heathfield, Ashford, Elham.[19] The destinations were
mainly Gravesend, Tilbury and Dover. Every timetable carried a list
of trains to carry tracked vehicles. . . . One included eight trains of

---

18. TATE 1802 MET, 8th June, 1944, and 0602 MET, 9th June, 1944.
19. These, of course, were the places where our imaginary formations were
    located.

ten "warflats", which I was told were for tanks and other big vehicles. There were only twelve trains in this timetable. There were frequent references to connections with the LMSR line. On the last page of the timetable there was a list of hospital trains destined for Birmingham but no times for the movement were shown.'[20] The Germans did not rise. On 21st June TATE was told: 'Do everything possible to investigate troop formations which pass through your place or are in the district. If there are no troops there try to get information about concentration areas and reserve areas either from your own travels or from a third party. Especially now such messages are of colossal importance.'[21] But nothing was asked about the friendly clerk in the advance control office at Ashford Junction.[22]

---

20. TATE 1802, 0606 and 1814 MET, 14th June, 1944.
21. TATE Message received 0614 MET, 21st June, 1944.
22. Had this plan been put through GARBO or BRUTUS the results would almost certainly have been different. We did not know that at this time and indeed for several months to come TATE's messages were having no apparent influence on the Germans. The enthusiasm of TATE's control in Hamburg led us to suppose that he was thought well of and we had not the advantage of an MSS check because the retransmission of messages from Hamburg was done by land-line and not by wireless.

XXVI

German Reactions in June

Before proceeding further with our account of Allied deception, it will be convenient once more to look behind the curtain and examine the state of German opinion during the weeks immediately succeeding the invasion. Even before the fateful countermanding order had been issued on the morning of 10th June, the enemy had been impressed by the fact that none of the FUSAG formations had yet appeared in Normandy, and had drawn the desired inference.

'The fact that not one of the formations still standing by in the South-East and East of England has been identified strengthens the supposition that the strong Anglo-American forces which are still available are being held back for further plans.'[1] The enemy Intelligence reckoned the FUSAG forces to be much larger than we had ever suggested. This was due to the fact that they included all formations in Eastern and South-Eastern Command, although many of these, both in fact and in imagination, should have been placed in 21 Army Group. This was to prove both a strength and a weakness to us as will be seen hereafter. For the time being this over-estimate operated wholly in our favour for it gave us an unexpected accretion of strength in the South-East. At the same time the Germans were so firmly convinced of the independence of the two army groups that on the few occasions when a formation which was not included by us in FUSAG, and whose movements we therefore omitted to explain, went to Normandy from the Eastern counties, they themselves found some good reason for avoiding the conclusion that

---

1. Appendix to Lagebericht West No. 1290, dated 8th June, 1944.

Patton was being made to reinforce Montgomery. 'The arrival of the 51st English Infantry Division (hitherto believed to be the Cambridge area) in the English Second Army area is *not* to be regarded as an encroachment on the group of forces in South-Eastern England; it is rather to be assumed that this division was already transferred to the sphere of Montgomery's army group *before* the start of the invasion.'[2] A few days later: 'From the appearance of the 49th English Infantry Division and the 9th English Armoured Division in the bridgehead which were last observed in the South-East of England, we cannot conclude yet that an encroachment has been made on the American Army Group, since both these divisions were last observed presumably on the *march to the south* and have clearly not remained (long) in the last named places.'[3] And even at the end of the month: 'The employment in the Normandy bridge-head of the 76th English Division, hitherto accepted in the area north of Norwich, cannot be regarded as an encroachment on Patton's formations, since the fact that this division was last identi-fied in that area six weeks ago is not necessarily a proof that it formed part of the American army group.'[4]

At the middle of June, although the Germans realised that limi-tation of shipping space might involve staggering the FUSAG attack behind the Normandy invasion, they were nevertheless inclined to regard the operation as imminent. 'To sum up, despite the absence of any concrete information about the enemy's actual intentions it can only be said that there is no serious evidence against the early employment of the American Army Group and that our own meas-ures must therefore take this possibility into account.'[5] Two days

---

2. Appendix to Lagebericht West No. 1291, dated 9th June, 1944.
3. Appendix to Lagebericht West, dated 15th June, 1944. The 49th British Infantry Division had been reported on several occasions by the controlled agents as being in the Eastern counties. The 9th British Armoured Division having just been disbanded, the designation had been allotted to 21 Army Group for cover operations in France.
4. Appendix to Lagebericht West, dated 28th June, 1944. Like the 9th British Armoured Division, the 76th British Infantry Division, hitherto stationed at Norwich, had just been disbanded, and was now being used for deception by 21 Army Group.
5. Appendix to Lagebericht West, dated 15th June, 1944.

earlier the flying bomb attacks had started and the opinion was evidently expressed in some quarters that this might make the Allies attack sooner in order to capture the sites. The German Intelligence staff, however, took a contrary view. 'Enemy reports show that the V weapon seems so far to have had considerable moral effects. The present impression is that *for the moment* a determined and short-term destruction by the English Command of the form of attack is not expected.'[6] And two days later: 'There is still no information regarding the time of the attack. Neither is there any evidence that the German rocket attack is having the effect of advancing the FUSAG attack.'[7]

The large scale of General Montgomery's operations in Normandy was daily becoming more apparent to the enemy. 'The consolidation of the Anglo-Saxon bridgehead area is emphasised by the reported transfer of Montgomery's headquarters thither and by the construction of usable air strips.'[8] One gains the impression that even at the middle of the month the Germans did not exclude the possibility of Montgomery using a part of his reserves for another landing. 'In spite of the appearance of twenty recognised formations in the bridgehead, Montgomery still disposes of considerable reserves (fifteen to seventeen divisions) which may be assumed to be standing ready in the invasion harbours in the South of England.'[9] As more of his forces came to France and his reserves became weakened both in quantity and quality this opinion began to lose favour. Montgomery's reserve was further weakened by the fact that the Germans had, without encouragement from us, placed some non-existent airborne divisions in the South-West of England and now transferred them to General Patton. 'Of Montgomery's Army Group twenty-two to twenty-four divisions have so far been identified in the bridgehead. We must take into consideration the fact that these include almost all the battle-tried divisions from England, and will therefore contain a somewhat higher proportion of soldiers with experience of battle than will the remaining formations. Since moreover we must

---

6. Appendix to Lagebericht West, dated 17th June, 1944.
7. Appendix to Lagebericht West, No. 1301, dated 19th June, 1944.
8. Appendix to Lagebericht West No. 1293, dated 11th June, 1944.
9. Appendix to Lagebericht West, dated 15th June, 1944.

reckon with the fact that the mass of the airborne divisions accepted in South-Western England will only be used in a new landing operation and so presumably as part of the American Army Group, we can determine that the mass of Montgomery's Army Group is in action in Normandy and can *for certain* only fall back on a reserve of ten to twelve formations.'[10] Although the belief in subsidiary landing operations by 21 Army Group had decreased and the Channel Isles had already been ruled out, the enemy still seemed to have a lingering fear about Brittany. 'Mining from the air of the harbours in the Channel Islands, Guernsey and Jersey, shows that the enemy does not contemplate landings against these islands at present. On the other hand observations in the West Brittany area deserve attention. Besides the already reported attack on a German locating apparatus in this area, much shipping movement has been noticed during the last days north of the coastal area Morlaix-Brest as well as increased air reconnaissance. Since also the coastal mining shows considerable forbearance in the Brest area, a sudden stroke again at Brest does not seem to be excluded. This might have as its object, besides the capture of the harbour, after it was known that German troops had withdrawn, the tying up and diverting of forces. On the other hand the employment of the still available army group Patton in this area continues to be regarded as unlikely.'[11]

So far as General Montgomery's left flank was concerned, the mere belief in the existence of FUSAG made the Seine into the most likely boundary. On 28th June the Germans were able to find confirmation for this view. 'In connection with the objective of the American Army Group, further captured documents (map issues) from the English Army Group are noteworthy since it can be seen from them that an operation by Montgomery on the north bank of the Seine does not seem to be intended.'[12]

As Montgomery's reserve diminished and with it the probability of a secondary landing by 21 Army Group, so the real operation gained in importance while Cherbourg became more clearly recognised as

---

10. Appendix to Lagebericht West, dated 22nd June, 1944.
11. Appendix to Lagebericht West, dated 22nd June, 1944.
12. Appendix to Lagebericht West, dated 28th June, 1944.

the immediate objective. 'The early capture of the port of Cherbourg for disembarking operational reserves from the USA may therefore be likely to assume correspondingly greater importance for the enemy command.'[13]

As to Patton's Army Group: 'The American First Army Group remains in East and South-East England in a strength of approximately twenty-eight divisions available and uncommitted to which must be added three to four airborne divisions in the West of England, so that the total strength of the Army Group corresponds fairly exactly to that of Montgomery.'[14] In support of the view that this Army Group was ready to attack at any moment, agent 7 (7)'s report of landing craft in the Harwich–Yarmouth district is quoted as well as a claim by the Luftwaffe Command Ic that on 19th June they had identified 'indications of definite and completed preparations for air landing and parachute operations'.[15]

It mattered little to us where exactly the Germans expected the second landing, so long as it dissuaded them from sending the Fifteenth Army to Normandy. Anywhere between Dunkirk and Le Havre would serve the purpose equally well. It was never necessary, therefore, for the controlled agents to specify a precise objective.[16] Nevertheless the enemy soon formed his own opinions on the subject. As early as 11th June the imaginative Luftwaffe Command Ic had expressed the opinion that 'the concentration and retention of strong Anglo-Saxon close-combat formations speaks against the intention to support a *Belgian* undertaking. The concentration is regarded as rather directed against the southern Channel coast. If

---

13. Appendix to Lagebericht West, dated 22nd June, 1944.
14. Appendix to Lagebericht West, dated 22nd June, 1944.
15. Appendix to Lagebericht West, dated 22nd June, 1944. This was imagination. The Lagebericht contains many contributions from the Luftwaffe Command Ic which have no foundation in fact.
16. The original FORTITUDE SOUTH plan had stated simply that the assault would be made in the Pas de Calais. Its successor, FORTITUDE SOUTH II, which is described in a later chapter, defined the objective in greater detail. The assault was to be made by three infantry and three airborne divisions on the beaches exclusive River Somme to inclusive Boulogne. For the reason given above, however, these particulars were never communicated to the enemy by Special Means.

this were correct it would be an important pointer to the intended use of the Eastern Anglo-Saxon group of forces (American First Army Group). Since the Normandy Peninsula is already assumed to be the concentration area for Montgomery's entire Army Group (approximately thirty to thirty-five divisions) and is the disembarkation area for the strong reserves to be transported to Cherbourg from the USA, another landing sector lying in the vicinity must (in the opinion of the Luftwaffe Command Ic Foreign Armies West) be assumed for the American First Army Group. On reflection, the sector between the Somme and the Seine seems to be indicated in the first place, because it corresponds to the Anglo-Saxon Air Force concentration and may be expected to afford the possibility of early co-operation between the two Anglo-Saxon Army Groups, roughly towards the line Paris/St Quentin.' The more cautious OKH added: 'It is emphasised that apart from this appreciation by Luftwaffe Command no concrete evidence is available in support of these reflections from captured documents, from a sure source or from the Abwehr.'[17] The uncontrolled agents could be guaranteed to provide support for any prophecy that the German Intelligence cared to make. Thus it is not surprising to read in the summary issued two days later: 'Concrete evidence which would indicate the target of these forces is still lacking. It seems, nevertheless, worthy of attention that the view is held at a headquarters of the Central English Command that the operations which have opened are the preliminary to a later thrust to the east on both sides of the Seine; plans based on the Le Havre area are expressly mentioned.'[18] And three days after that: 'The current reinforcement of the beach-head continues; it must, however, not be forgotten that at present only twenty-five per cent of the divisions available in England have been employed here. Worthy of note is an Abwehr message which, though it arrived after the landing, nevertheless forecast accurately the landing so far carried out, and in which a second landing in the area between the Somme and the Seine is foretold with the final object of launching a thrust in the direction of Paris on both sides of the Seine from the two beach-

17. Appendix to Lagebericht West No. 1293, dated 11th June, 1944.
18. Appendix to Lagebericht West No. 1295, dated 13th June, 1944.

heads thus formed.'[19] At the middle of June therefore Belgium was ruled out and the Seine–Somme sector was regarded as the most likely place for Patton's attack.

On 24th June further evidence that the Allies intended to attack immediately east of the Seine was adduced. 'The air reconnaissance tasks given by Montgomery's Army Group (rivers Toucques and Risles) show that this Army Group may in the foreseeable future be directed eastwards against Paris. The direction of this thrust again points to a corresponding attack by Patton's Army Group in the Seine–Somme area with a view to affording operational support.'[20] By this date BRUTUS had completed his series of messages on the grouping and location of FUSAG forces in Kent and East Anglia. These reports were also advanced in support of an assault west of the Straits of Dover, though the reasoning employed is curious. 'Recent troop identifications have shown even more clearly the strong concentration of forces in the south-eastern part of England. The forces under First Canadian Army consist mainly of English and Canadian troops, the Third American Army concentrated north-east of

19. Appendix to Lagebericht West No. 1298, dated 16th June, 1944. References to a message purporting to have been written two days before the invasion, which prophesied the Normandy landing and a subsequent assault further to the east, appear in several of the OKH Intelligence Summaries during the few days succeeding 6th June. In the Appendix of Lagebericht West No. 1289 of 7th June, we find the following entry: 'As regards the group of forces in the East of England (American First Army Group), there exists an Abwehr message from *before* the beginning of the invasion (4th June, arrived 7th June) containing relevant information about the start of the invasion, and stating that a further and larger operation is planned against Belgium.' It will be noted that although the message is reported to date from 4th June, it did not arrive until the 7th. It does not appear in Krummacher's personal file (OKW Papers, File 605) until 1500 hours on 10th June, when it was initialled by him and by Jodl, but did not go to the Fuehrer. It cannot therefore be considered as a proximate cause for the revocation of the order to move the armoured divisions from the Pas de Calais to Normandy. The quotation from the Intelligence Summary of 16th June given above appears to be a blend of this somewhat doubtful message of 4th June, which gave Belgium as the objective of the second assault, and the subsequent uncontrolled message of 13th June, which specified the Seine-Somme sector.

20. Appendix to Lagebericht West, dated 24th June, 1944.

London mainly of American formations. The composition of both armies points to their employment in the central Channel area[21] inasmuch as the army standing nearer to the Continent is made up of the more highly valued British formations.'[22] In other words the mere proximity of troop locations in England to the supposed objective, without any apparent regard for embarkation or landing facilities, seems to have counted as an argument with the enemy. It will be observed that in favouring the Seine–Somme sector as the objective of our second assault no reference was made to the natural features of this coastline which would have placed almost insurmountable difficulties in the way of any attacking force and which had ruled out this stretch of coast from Allied deliberations at an early stage of planning.

So far as the other threats were concerned, the Intelligence Summaries made several references to the possibility of an attack on the south coast of France during June; an appreciation made on the 24th of that month may be regarded as typical. 'Though the numerical prerequisites for a large-scale landing from North Africa are there, there is no sign of adequate preparations for moving these forces. We are still of the opinion that they are intended to tie down German forces in the South of France and the enemy Command would no doubt not refrain from using them to occupy areas vacated by German troops in the event of the latter being withdrawn from extensive areas of the Southern French coast.'[23] No fresh news came from Bordeaux; Norway had receded well into the background. 'The weak state of the forces in Central England and Scotland speaks now as hitherto against any plans worth mentioning against Jutland or Scandinavia.'[24]

Such were the opinions of the Germans during the month of June. Let us see how they affected the disposition of their forces. The

---

21. Although there is some confusion in the use of the term 'central Channel area' or 'central Channel zone', it seems usually to refer to the Seine–Somme sector and is assumed to do so in the present context.
22. Appendix to Lagebericht West, dated 26th June, 1944.
23. Appendix to Lagebericht West, dated 24th June, 1944.
24. Appendix to Lagebericht West, dated 28th June, 1944.

SHAEF G-2 Intelligence Summary, it will be recalled, had forecast that by 13th June three Panzer and three field infantry divisions would have gone to Normandy from the Fifteenth Army's zone, two Panzer divisions from South-West France and one Panzer division from the Mediterranean coast. In fact two Panzer divisions only had moved, namely, the 2nd Panzer Division from Amiens and the 17th Panzer Grenadier Division from south of the Loire. The longest forecast made by the G-2 Division before the invasion was for 1st July. It was estimated that by that date a total of ten divisions, three Panzer, three field and four limited employment divisions would have gone to the bridgehead from north of the Seine, that a total of two Panzer and one field division would have been sent from South-West France and from the Mediterranean coast two Panzer divisions and two field divisions.

When the invasion took place there were fifteen infantry divisions in the Seventh Army area, of which seven were field divisions. Of the armoured reserve there were three Panzer divisions between the Seine and the Loire, the 21st Panzer Division south of Caen, the 12th SS Panzer Division at Dreux and the Panzer Lehr Division south of Chartres. A month later there were eighteen[25] infantry divisions in the Seventh Army's zone, many of them mere remnants, of which eleven were field divisions. The armour had increased during the same period from three to nine[26] divisions. While the strength of the armour had thus increased, that of the infantry, taking into account

---

25. There had been six arrivals and three departures.
     Arrivals (placed in order of arrival)—
        16th GAF Division and 346th Limited Employment Division from Fifteenth Army area; 276th Field Division from Hendaye (S.W. France); 272nd and 277th Field Divisions from Sete-Narbonne (Mediterranean coast); 2nd Parachute Division to Brest area, place of origin not known.
     Departures—
        245th Limited Employment Division to Dieppe; 709th Limited Employment Division captured at Cherbourg; 716th Limited Employment Division to Perpignan (Mediterranean coast) replacing 272nd Field Division.
26. This increase was due to the arrival of six divisions: 17th SS Panzer Grenadier Division from south of the Loire, 2nd Panzer Division from Amiens, 2nd SS Panzer Division from Toulouse, 1st SS Panzer Division from Ghent, 9th and 10th SS Panzer Divisions from Germany.

the heavy casualties which had been suffered, had most certainly declined.

After the 2nd Panzer Division had gone into the battle the armoured reserve north of the Seine still comprised two divisions, the 116th and 1st SS. These, it will be remembered, had converged towards the Pas de Calais on 10th June. Before the end of the month the 1st SS Panzer Division went to Normandy but was replaced by the arrival from Germany of the 19th Panzer Division in Holland. Of the formations belonging to Fifteenth Army, the 346th Limited Employment Division left Le Havre before 18th June to join the 81st Corps in the bridgehead, while the 16th GAF Division went from Haarlem to join the 86th Corps before 25th June. The strength of the Fifteenth Army was further reduced by the departure of the 19th GAF Division from the neighbourhood of Bruges just after the invasion took place.[27] On the other hand, the 245th Limited Employment Division appears to have been withdrawn from the battle zone and sent to Dieppe at the beginning of July, while the Fifteenth Army received five other field divisions from Germany and from other theatres of war as reinforcements.[28] Thus whereas immediately before the invasion took place there were nineteen infantry and parachute divisions in Fifteenth Army's area, of which six were field divisions, on 8th July there were twenty-two, of which eleven were field divisions. Before the invasion there had been three armoured divisions north of the Seine, now there were two. In fact the forces in the Fifteenth Army area were stronger at the beginning of July than they had been at the beginning of June.

---

27. It is not clear what became of this division.

28.

Formation	New Location	Date of Arrival
6th Parachute Division	Abbeville	Before 18th June
363rd Field Division	Bruges–Ghent area	Before 18th June
89th Field Division	Havre–Rouen area	Before 25th June
70th Field Division	Ghent–Antwerp area	Before 8th July
271st Field Division	Beauvais (from Montpelier in the South of France)	Before 8th July

During the month succeeding the invasion, seven field and three armoured divisions were sent to France as reinforcements – of these, five field and one armoured division went to Fifteenth Army, one field and two armoured to Seventh Army and one field to the South of France.

By the end of the first week in July the South-West of France had lost, in addition to the 17th SS Panzer Grenadier Division which had crossed the Loire before 10th June, one field division, the 276th, this formation having gone to Normandy before 25th June. The Mediterranean coast lost three field divisions at the beginning of July; the 272nd and the 277th went to the bridgehead, the 271st to Fifteenth Army. On the other hand, the 198th Field Division had arrived at Narbonne during June, and it was shortly to receive the 716th Limited Employment Division from Normandy in place of the 272nd Field Division. Responsibility for the loss of the 2nd SS Panzer Division, which had been stationed at Toulouse and which went to Normandy before 18th June, may be shared between IRON-SIDE and VENDETTA.

In order to prove that a deception plan has achieved its purpose, it is not enough to show that it reached the enemy Intelligence and was accepted by them as true. It is also necessary to establish the fact that it influenced the actions of the commander and so changed the course of battle. It would be difficult to avoid the conclusion that the German appreciations and troop movements which have been sum-marised above were not closely related. Lest any doubt should remain on that score, that doubt can be dispelled by the testimony of Field-Marshal Jodl himself. Speaking at a conference in Berlin on 3rd July about the situation in Northern France, he said: 'The main enemy force used in the landings in this area was Montgomery's Army Group. This group now has in England no more than four or five infantry divisions and two armoured divisions. On the other hand, it is obvious that Patton's Army Group (eighteen infantry divisions, six armoured divisions, five airborne divisions) is being made ready in London and in Southern England for the next landing. It is also evi-dent, from the operational sectors of the two enemy army groups and the state of preparations, and from the fact that it would be difficult for the port of Cherbourg alone to supply two army groups, that the landing area will be the Channel region facing the German Fifteenth Army. We conclude that the enemy will plan operations with both army groups on both sides of the Seine, heading towards Paris. Reports of preparations for large enemy landings on the Mediterranean coast of Southern France appear to be largely delib-erate propaganda reports by the enemy. We are prepared for landings

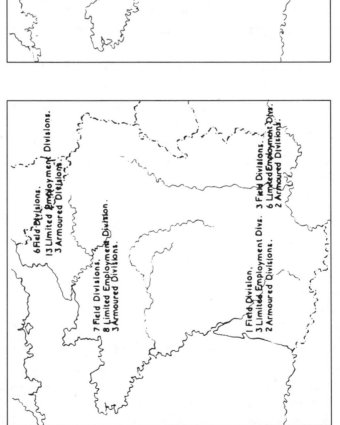

Location of German armoured divisions on the eve of the invasion

1 S.S.Pz.

2 Pz.

16 Pz.

Pz. Lehr.

12 S.S.Pz.

21 Pz.

17 S.S.P.G.

9 Pz.

II Pz.

2 S.S.Pz.

---

6 Field Divisions.
13 Limited Employment Divisions.
3 Armoured Divisions.

7 Field Divisions.
8 Limited Employment Division.
3 Armoured Divisions.

3 Field Divisions.
6 Limited Employment Divs.
2 Armoured Divisions.

1 Field Division.
3 Limited Employment Divs.
2 Armoured Divisions.

Disposition of German Forces at 6th June, 1944
(319 Infantry Division in the Channel Islands is omitted)

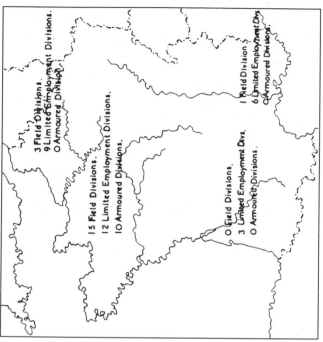

G-2 Intelligence Forecast of German dispositions at 1st July, 1944, made before the invasion

(The total of fifty-seven divisions in France on 6th June is increased to fifty-nine by the anticipated arrival of two infantry divisions from Scandinavia or Denmark.)

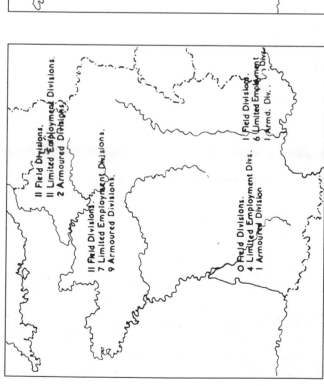

Disposition of German Forces at 8th July, 1944

in the vicinity of Bordeaux and on the coast of Belgium and the Netherlands, although there is little probability of such landings; it is believed at present there is almost no probability of landings in Denmark and Norway. *The defences on the front of the German Fifteenth Army are extremely strong; moreover, our troops are disposed with an equal number of coastal defence divisions and of rear groups (nine or ten divisions) directly behind them.* Nearly all of the enemy's seasoned troops with experience in the African and Italian fighting have been expended in the present landings; there are not more than two divisions acknowledged to be seasoned troops in Patton's Army Group which is to carry out the next landing. *Moreover, since this Army Group intends to land in the face of strong German defences, we have every confidence of defeating them.'*[29]

---

29. This passage is extracted from the exposition by General Jodl of matters referred to in German Despatch No. 776. The exposition is quoted by Admiral Abe, the Japanese Naval Attaché in Berlin, in his despatches to Tokyo. The italics are the writer's.

XXVII

The New Plan

The original FORTITUDE story, no matter how firmly believed on 3rd July, was now being overtaken rapidly by events. The real formations which had been used to build up the false FUSAG were about to leave for Normandy. Had nothing more been done their appearance in the bridgehead could hardly have failed to open the eyes of the enemy to the truth. In consequence the pressure which we had hitherto been exerting on the Pas de Calais might have been removed altogether within the space of a few hours, thus releasing the whole of the Fifteenth Army for service in Normandy where the enemy was suffering so acutely from a shortage of infantry divisions.

More than three weeks before this time, however, steps were being taken to meet such a situation. The new plan, known as FORTITUDE SOUTH II, had been initiated, partly because the indications which we had observed during the days immediately following the invasion had convinced us that there was a chance of prolonging the threat beyond the period originally stipulated, partly to protect our deceptive machine by preparing a satisfactory explanation which could be offered when events belied our previous statements.

What were the requirements of the plan? An explanation had to be found for the appearance of all the FUSAG formations in France, a reason had to be given for Patton's decline from army group to army commander, a new commander had to be found to take his place and finally East and South-East England had to be replenished with forces to continue the threat.

After several variations had been proposed the following story was agreed upon[1]: General Eisenhower, having been obliged to reinforce the present bridgehead with formations immediately available, namely, the formations under command of FUSAG, had decided that it was necessary to form another American army group. For reasons of ease of command and administration General Bradley, who had more than proved himself in the previous few weeks, had been promoted to the position of army group commander and had been instructed to form an army group headquarters to be known as Twelfth US Army Group. He had been authorised to call upon the existing FUSAG for officers. Meanwhile General Patton, the Commander of FUSAG, had objected strongly to being deprived of so many formations under his command. A sharp difference of opinion had arisen between him and General Eisenhower with the result that the former was deprived of his command and placed in command of Third Army. In the meantime new formations, British and American, were to be introduced into East and South-East England and placed under the command of the old FUSAG staff to carry out the attack on the Pas de Calais at a later date. For this purpose the British Fourth Army would be moved from Scotland to take the place of the First Canadian Army in Kent, and a newly landed American army, the Fourteenth, would replace Third Army in East Anglia. These two armies would provide the assaulting force, while the Ninth Army[2] at Bristol would also be included in the Order of Battle and would supply build-up formations only. A high-ranking general would be sent from America to take command of the reconstituted FUSAG.

---

1. The main features of this story were proposed by 21 Army Group at a meeting held by Supreme Headquarters at Main 21 Army Group Headquarters on 26th June. The story agreed at that meeting, however, made FUSAG the headquarters of the American forces in Normandy and proposed creating a new army group headquarters to continue the FORTITUDE story. A subsequent proposal by 21 Army Group (21 AGP/00/272/2/G (R), dated 2nd July, 1944) recommended the redesignation of the real FUSAG so as to leave the imaginary FUSAG in command of the deception forces in South-East England with its name unchanged. This amendment was adopted.
2. This, of course, was a real army, destined ultimately to go overseas.

In the true course of events the First American Army Group which had existed in skeleton form in the United Kingdom since the beginning of the year was to go abroad at the beginning of July and take command of the American forces in Normandy. In accordance with the new deception requirements this army group was now redesignated the Twelfth, a title which it retained until the end of the war. Until after the invasion started Bradley, it will be remembered, had held the dual command of the real American Army Group and of the First US Army. At the end of June he relinquished the latter command to General Hodges. Here therefore no further explanation was required, and he thus appeared in Normandy with a single function, that of Commander of Twelfth Army Group.

In making up the new Order of Battle a continuation of the system of misplacing real divisions in the South-East of England was considered, but the proposal was abandoned, the objection being that the formations available for the purpose would for the most part be American divisions staging here for a few weeks only on their way to France, so that FUSAG would soon appear to be nothing more than a holding organisation. It seemed essential that at least the spearhead of the assault should not change. The necessary quality of permanence could only be achieved by creating imaginary forces over which deception could claim an undivided control. On the British side, the Scandinavian threat having run its course, we had the Fourth Army ready to hand. Some of its formations had already gone to Kent, and so it merely meant bringing down such of the remainder as could be moved south. For the American part in the assault a new and wholly imaginary army had to be created. It was considered, on the other hand, that frequent changes in the composition of the reserve would in no way detract from the realism of the picture. This was held to justify the inclusion of the real Ninth Army to command the later build-up formations. With these considerations in mind the new FUSAG was constituted in the following way:

The names of departing FUSAG formations are shown in italic, in cases where the same locations were chosen.

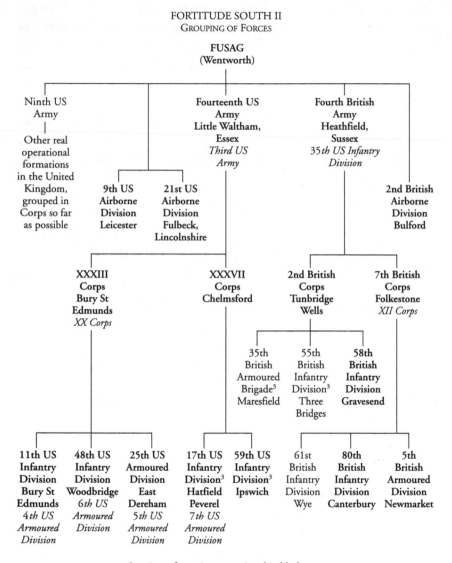

FORTITUDE SOUTH II
GROUPING OF FORCES

FUSAG
(Wentworth)

Ninth US Army

Other real operational formations in the United Kingdom, grouped in Corps so far as possible

Fourteenth US Army
Little Waltham, Essex
Third US Army

9th US Airborne Division
Leicester

21st US Airborne Division
Fulbeck, Lincolnshire

Fourth British Army
Heathfield, Sussex
35th US Infantry Division

2nd British Airborne Division
Bulford

XXXIII Corps
Bury St Edmunds
XX Corps

XXXVII Corps
Chelmsford

2nd British Corps
Tunbridge Wells

7th British Corps
Folkestone
XII Corps

35th British Armoured Brigade[3]
Maresfield

55th British Infantry Division[3]
Three Bridges

58th British Infantry Division
Gravesend

11th US Infantry Division
Bury St Edmunds
4th US Armoured Division

48th US Infantry Division
Woodbridge
6th US Armoured Division

25th US Armoured Division
East Dereham
5th US Armoured Division

17th US Infantry Division[3]
Hatfield Peverel
7th US Armoured Division

59th US Infantry Division[3]
Ipswich

61st British Infantry Division
Wye

80th British Infantry Division
Canterbury

5th British Armoured Division
Newmarket

Imaginary formations are printed in black type.

---

3. Assault formations.

Let us analyse the constituent parts of this Order of Battle in greater detail. We will first examine Fourth Army. The composition of 2nd British Corps was to remain as it had been when it came south at the beginning of June. In view of its previous training in Scotland, this corps was chosen to carry out the British assault, the 35th British Armoured Brigade, a real formation then stationed in England, being added to provide the DD element. The only other point to note here is that the 55th British Infantry Division had now in fact returned from Northern Ireland so that its imaginary location in Sussex also became its real one. On the other hand, as has already been explained the two divisions comprised in the 7th British Corps, namely the 52nd Lowland Division and the 55th US Infantry Division, could not be used. The former was a real formation and had to remain in Scotland to complete its training, the latter was supposedly in Iceland and it was thought inadvisable to move it from there. So the 7th British Corps came alone and was given command of three divisions not hitherto included in Fourth Army, the 61st and 80th British Infantry Divisions and the 5th British Armoured Division. A few words of explanation must be given to show how these became available. The brigades of the real 61st Infantry Division had in fact been employed both in Suffolk and in Kent as 'hotel staffs' to assist in the embarkation of troops leaving for Normandy. All that was necessary here was to give the division a higher establishment and represent it as concentrating in Kent.[4] The controlled agents had already thrown out several hints that it might be upgraded in the near future. The 5th British Armoured Division was purely imaginary and had no previous history. The 80th British Infantry Division rose from the ashes of the disbanded 80th Reserve Division in the following circumstances. In the summer of 1944 the War Office decided to disband three Lower Establishment Infantry Divisions, the 38th, the 45th and the 47th. As they had been well-known territorial formations before the war whose numbers were familiar to the public and were therefore of recruiting value, it was decided to renumber three surviving home service divisions, namely the 76th and 80th Reserve Divisions and

---

4. In July this formation was in fact reunited as a Training Division at Wye in Kent.

the 77th Holding Division, as the 47th, 38th and 45th respectively, so as to keep alive the familiar designations. The Deception Staff had already made considerable play of the 38th, 45th and 47th Infantry Divisions. Thus if the proposed renumbering could have been avoided the three better known numbers would have been available for deception purposes. The War Office was asked if it would be willing to allow the 76th, 80th and 77th Divisions to retain their original designations so that the other three might be included in the new FUSAG, but held to the view that the renumbering would be necessary for the reason given. Special Means therefore fell back on the story that as the war was now nearing its end the 38th, 45th and 47th Infantry Divisions were reverting to their peacetime territorial function in order to prepare for recruiting after the war and that the resources and equipment so released were to be given to the 76th, 77th and 80th Divisions which would now receive a higher establishment in order to fit them for operations overseas. This gave us three imaginary infantry divisions, though admittedly not the three we should have liked best. Of these, the 76th Infantry Division was given to 21 Army Group for employment overseas, the 77th was held in reserve and the 80th[5] now went to the Fourth British Army.

Let us now turn our attention to the new American Fourteenth Army. The only formations which will be recognised here are XXXVII Corps and the 59th US Infantry Division which had been introduced during June to fill gaps in the old FUSAG. All the others had to be drawn from our reserve list of imaginary formations. Washington supplied a detailed record of the imaginary previous activities of each division, which proved to be of great value to the controlled agents but which need not be repeated here.

The three airborne divisions included in the force were placed directly under command of the Army Group. Of these the 2nd British Airborne Division is already familiar to the reader; the two American formations were newly created.

---

5. As its predecessor in title, the 80th British Reserve Division, had been located at St Annes, in Lancashire, it would in due course be represented as moving from that place to its new location in Kent.

The Fourth British Army was to move from Scotland to South-Eastern Command between 11th and 21st July. The Fourteenth US Army, which was supposed to have landed at Liverpool in May and June, was to move to East Anglia during the same period. Ninth Army, a real formation, was to remain at Bristol both in fact and in fiction. The new nets were to be fully established by 26th July. 3103 Signals Service Battalion was to provide the wireless links for FUSAG and the Fourteenth Army, whilst the improvised force[6] which had executed the FORTITUDE NORTH wireless programme would continue to supply most of those required by Fourth Army. The 55th and 61st British Infantry Divisions, however, being real formations, could be made responsible for producing their own traffic. The wireless representation of the 5th British Armoured Division and the 35th British Armoured Brigade was to be provided by the following rather confusing arrangement. The 5th British Armoured Division was a new and fictitious formation. The 35th British Armoured Brigade was a real formation under command of GHQ, Home Forces. The latter formation would go to Newmarket to represent the 5th Armoured Division, while the Yorkshire Hussars, the Armoured Car Regiment belonging to the 61st Division, would go to Hailsham to represent the 35th Armoured Brigade. Thus the 35th Armoured Brigade would be in one place representing the armoured division while the armoured car regiment would be in another place representing it.

The Navy also had its part to play. Force 'F', it will be remembered, was already in being and had become associated with the 59th US Infantry Division at Harwich. With the release of the CLH units from the Clyde it now became possible to create two more imaginary assault forces. These were named Forces 'M' and 'N'. It was arranged that the former should train at Portsmouth and Newhaven with the 55th British Infantry Division now reconstituted as an assault formation, and that the latter should train in the Southampton and Studland area with the 17th US Infantry Division. Assault exercises were to take place on the brigade level during the latter part of July and on a divisional scale at the beginning of August. The whole force would be ready to sail on 5th August.

---

6. In July this miscellaneous collection of signals units was given an establishment and designated the Twelfth Reserve Unit.

The Allied Air Forces agreed to lend their support by continuing to bomb targets in the Pas de Calais while Special Means was to suggest that a part of the fighter force attached to the Eighth US Air Force in the Eastern counties would be available to support the attack.

While the Supreme Commander retained overall control of the execution of the plan, responsibility for giving effect to the bulk of the wireless arrangements was allotted to ETOUSA.

Finally a suitable commander was required. On 6th July the Supreme Commander sent General Marshall the following telegram: 'OVERLORD cover and deception plan (FORTITUDE) has proved remarkably effective. Reliable intelligence indicates that enemy is preparing for decisive Allied effort by First US Army Group in Pas de Calais area under the command of Patton.

'Since under existing plans the enemy will unquestionably soon learn of the presence in the Lodgement area of First US Army Group and Patton with his Third Army, it has been necessary to devise a new and plausible plan for continuing the cover threat. The new cover plan involves retention First Army Group nominally in United Kingdom, redesignation of First Army Group in France under Bradley's command as Twelfth Army Group, downgrading Patton from his fictitious status as Commander of First Army Group to actual command Third Army, and naming suitable well-known commander of high reputation as the commander of the proposed fictitious First Army Group comprising assumed United States and British divisions in the United Kingdom. The designation of "Twelfth Army Group" has been selected for Bradley's Army Group to obviate confusion in mail and other communications resulting if a number identical with one of the armies in this theatre were to be selected.

'All arrangements to implement the new cover plan can be made here except that a suitable notional commander for the First Army Group is not available in this area. Desire therefore to suggest for your consideration that some well-known officer such as McNair, de Witt, or another of corresponding reputation be ordered to this theatre without delay. He would be required here for a considerable period, probably at least three months, the exact period being determined by the length of time the new cover plan remains effective.

During his stay the officer would be usefully employed, and he would have unusual opportunities for observation.

'The names I have given you are suggested because they have been fairly well advertised throughout the world. While I had thought of using Simpson[7] for this purpose, I feel that his name will not be of sufficient significance to the enemy. If you find it impossible to comply, I will have to start immediately to build up Simpson as well as I can.

'I would be most grateful for a radio reply as time is pressing and I cannot overemphasise the great importance of maintaining as long as humanly possible the Allied threat to the Pas de Calais area, which has already paid enormous dividends and, with care, will continue to do so.'[8] On 9th July General Marshall replied that Lieutenant-General L. J. McNair, Commander in Chief of the Land Forces in the United States, would leave the United States in three days' time to take command of FUSAG.

Lest it should ever be suspected that the Deception Staff were taking liberties with the reputations of distinguished American generals and particularly with the name of Patton, whose role in the FORTITUDE story was such an unhappy one, the following memorandum of 10th July to General Bedell Smith, the Chief of Staff, written and personally initialled by General Eisenhower, is quoted in full. 'I have just received a telegram to the effect that General McNair is soon to be here. You will note from the telegram that General Marshall intends to say in Washington that McNair has left to take an important command in the field. Please send a short wire to General Marshall saying that I fully concur with his idea in making such an announcement. Through a "leak", I think we should let out something about as follows:

'(*a*) Certain information which we are sure the enemy can check up on as authentic, thus giving an atmosphere of plausibility. I suggest something like identification of certain units in France.

---

7. Commander of Ninth US Army.
8. SHAEF Outgoing Message 'BIGOT' to AGWAR for Marshall from Eisenhower No. S-55125, dated 6th July, 1944.

'(b) A story that Patton has lost his high command because of displeasure at some of his indiscretions, and that he is reduced to Army command.

'(c) That the most capable and most experienced senior American commander has been brought in to take over Patton's Army Group.

'(d) That due to damages to landing craft inflicted by the storm some weeks ago, the next expedition has been slightly delayed and it is now estimated that it will take a certain length of time to launch it. (This time should not be so long as to make the enemy believe he could bring divisions into the NEPTUNE area and get them back to the threatened point, but should be long enough to help assist in carrying on the deception.)

'(e) The location of McNair's headquarters should probably be given and he should be directed to make a tremendous show of activity.'

FORTITUDE SOUTH II was not approved until 19th July,[9] but it was necessarily in operation before that date, for the planting of a story by means of controlled agents is bound to be a gradual process. Thus it fell to the lot of the Special Means Staff to anticipate these future requirements. The establishment of Fourteenth Army was begun before the invasion had been launched. When agent Seven visited Liverpool at the beginning of June to investigate agent 7 (6)'s unsubstantiated report of an impending attack on Bordeaux,[10] though he had found nothing to confirm these rumours, he had noticed much activity in the district and ample evidence of the continuous arrival of American troops in the port. This information was sent on by GARBO[11] on 15th June, and on the 17th we read: 'Further evidence of the arrival of a new American formation over and above the number already mentioned is at present lacking. Nevertheless reports of the arrival of fresh American transports

9. SHAEF/18250/Ops (B), dated 19th July, 1944. See Appendix VI. The Special Means plan of 20th July is given at Appendix VII.
10. 7 (6)'s report in support of IRONSIDE I is here referred to.
11. GARBO 2106, 2112, 2122 GMT, 15th June, 1944.

deserve attention. We must therefore reckon with an early increase in the number of American divisions in England.'[12] On 17th June BRUTUS reported: 'I have heard that a new American army is in process of being formed in the West of England and is coming under the command of FUSAG. I am looking for details.'[13] Three days later GARBO carried the story a little further. 'In conversation with 4 (3) I today learned some very important news. I casually asked him in which division his uncle was. He replied in the 48th US Division. To my question as to whether this division belonged to the First US Army Group, he replied that it did not, nor did it belong to 21 Army Group, thereby drawing the conclusion that there are many American troops here who belong to other large units. As is natural, I will investigate this matter as much as possible,'[14] and on 2nd July: 'Today I lunched with 4 (3) and brought the conversation round to the subject which interested me, which is to say about the American units which have recently arrived in England. He told me that FUSAG will undertake a more important task and that in order to be able to accomplish it, four American divisions have recently arrived in this country under the command of another American army. These divisions are stationed in the Liverpool area. He insinuated that the war was about to enter a new and decisive phase. In view of this interesting news, I intend to send Seven immediately to investigate what is going on in the Western area, which I am not controlling at the moment. I intend to clarify this matter and will invite 4 (3) out frequently.'[15] By 10th July BRUTUS had most of the facts. 'I have obtained details about the American Army in the region of Liverpool. It is the Fourteenth Army; there is also, in the West, another army, already reported, namely, the Ninth American Army, Commander-in-Chief General Simpson; both under the command of FUSAG. No details about the Ninth. The Fourteenth Army, headquarters at

12. Appendix to Lagebericht West, dated 17th June, 1944.
13. BRUTUS 2010 GMT, 17th June, 1944.
14. GARBO 1950 and 2110 GMT, 20th June, 1944.
15. GARBO 2036 and 2045 GMT, 2nd July, 1944, reflected in Appendix to Lagebericht West No. 1316, dated 4th July, 1944. 'According to a report as yet unconfirmed, an American army headquarters (Ninth?) is in Liverpool. If this is correct, then it may be an army which is destined to take over command of formations arriving later from the USA.'

Mobberly in Cheshire; composition XXXIII Corps and another, number unknown. I hear that it is due to move to the East or South-East of England in the near future. The XXXIII Corps at Marbury in Cheshire; composition 11th and 48th US Divisions and an American armoured division. The 11th and 48th Divisions arrived during the month of June, well trained.'[16] A short time before this BRUTUS had been able to offer some additional air support for the operation. 'I have learnt that FUSAG will receive during the assault, very strong support from the Eighth and Ninth Air Forces, composed of heavy bombers. This last appears to indicate an attack against a strong position and the possibility of an attack across the Channel is discussed.'[17]

---

16. BRUTUS 2019, 2036 and 2041 GMT, 10th July, 1944.
17. BRUTUS 1015 GMT, 18th June, 1944, reflected in Appendix to Lagebericht West No. 1301, dated 19th June, 1944. 'Attention is deserved by a report from a particularly trustworthy source according to which FUSAG will be supported in action by strong portions of the heavy bomber force, which points to its employment against strong fortifications and so fits in with our existing appreciation (Middle Channel coast).'

XXVIII

The Departing Formations

Before tracing the growth of the new army group any further, we must turn aside for a moment to consider the problem of the departing formations. Naturally 21 Army Group wanted to appear to the Germans to be as weak as possible in the Normandy bridgehead so as not to draw fresh forces against them. From that point of view it was therefore clearly undesirable to say that any of the old FUSAG formations had gone to Normandy. Even to admit that they had left their old locations might lead the Germans to suppose that they had gone overseas as reinforcements. On the other hand, if agents were believed to be living in a particular district and had reported every troop movement in that district for months past, a sudden failure to do so would be almost certain to excite suspicion. The problem was one of timing.

As a rough basis of calculation it was agreed that a formation would be likely to be identified in battle a week after its advanced elements had landed in France. It was also agreed that before such identification took place a ground spotting agent should at least be allowed to say that the formation in question had left his neighbourhood even if he could say nothing as to its destination. Although this concession provided adequate protection for the lesser agents, it still left GARBO, and to a lesser extent BRUTUS, in a difficult position, for it obliged them to keep silence about many of the old FUSAG formations whose activities they had hitherto kept under almost continuous observation. It was clear that it would simplify our problems enormously if both these agents could temporarily be put off the air altogether.

There was another reason which made it very desirable to put GARBO out of communication with the Germans. He was being asked some very awkward questions about the new secret weapon V. 1 with which the Germans had started to bombard London on 13th June. To explain how this arose we must go back six months. In December 1943 the Germans set up a new organisation at Arras known as the 68th Corps to control the bombardment of this country by means of flying bombs. The local Abwehrstelle had helped the 68th Corps to organise its signals communications. In doing so it had made arrangements whereby GARBO's messages from Madrid could go direct to Arras without having to be re-enciphered in Berlin. These facts became known to us through Most Secret Sources, so that it was already apparent before the New Year that the Germans intended to use GARBO as an 'observation post' for the secret weapon. This was confirmed by a message which GARBO had received on 15th December, 1943. 'Circumstances dictate that you should carry out your proposition with regard to setting up your home outside the capital. This warning is strictly confidential for you and, in taking the necessary measures, the collaborators must on no account suspect your reasons. Should the threatened action commence, in making your preparations, leaving to your judgment their execution, you must ensure that your collaborators maintain their contact with you.'[1] GARBO did not lose the opportunity that this gave him of trying to find out more about the secret weapon, and during the spring he sent a number of fishing questions. On 22nd February, for instance, announcing that agent Four's lodging had been bombed in a recent air raid, he added: 'I should be grateful if you would let me know immediately that these are the preliminaries of other, more intense attacks so that I can take immediately protective measures for the Service. Let me know immediately, therefore, whether one is to expect other, graver developments such as, for example, the rocket, as if this were so I would remove the present radio apparatus to a safer place, taking the precaution to make it appear as if the present bombardments were the motive for my doing so, thus avoiding comment by the agents and, at the same time without alarming them, being able to make them change their

---

1. GARBO Message received 2120 to 2154 GMT, 15th December, 1943.

residences.'[2] When, four months later, the storm broke GARBO did not receive the promised warning for as his German masters explained: 'We had not been informed by headquarters about this project, owing no doubt to the fact that all attention has been absorbed in the operations in France.'[3] However, they went on to tell GARBO that it was of the utmost importance that he should inform them of the effects of the bombardments.

Without some direction from those in authority it was impossible for GARBO to know what to answer, and such direction was not forthcoming. He could not deny the fact that V. 1s were dropping in London; equally, he could not send accurate reports. He might, by a systematic programme of false reports, succeed in deflecting the mean point of impact from one part of London to another, but clearly he could not make himself personally responsible for sparing, let us say, Westminster at the expense of Paddington or Southwark. Here therefore was another strong argument for removing GARBO temporarily from the scene.

As the Germans had told him to report flying bomb damage, the idea suggested itself to his case officer that he should be arrested while carrying out their instructions. Not only would this have the desired effect of putting him out of the way, but it might even make his masters realise how dangerous this type of work was and so induce them to tell him to confine himself to military reports in future.

For some unexplained reason the enemy told GARBO to use a

---

2. GARBO 1847 to 1905 GMT, 22nd February, 1944, and 1807 GMT, 23rd February, 1944.
3. GARBO Message received 1950 GMT, 16th June, 1944. GARBO expressed annoyance. 'It has upset me very much to have to learn the news of this arm having been used from our very enemies when I had hoped to have heard about it in advance from you in order to be able to leave the city.' (2054 and 2102 GMT, 16th June.) Madrid answered with apparent sincerity: 'Today Headquarters has notified us that it has been impossible for them to warn us in advance as to the date on which the new arm would be employed since they themselves were not informed on account of an order from the High Command that the secret should only be disclosed to those people who had to be told in order to put it into operation.' (GARBO Message received 2121 GMT, 17th June, 1944.)

map of London published by Pharus of Berlin for plotting the falls of the flying bombs. The only map which could be found to answer that description was one published in 1906 and the only known copy in London was in the British Museum. This gave GARBO an excellent opportunity of playing for time. Meanwhile he had sent agent Three to collect information, though he remarked rather discouragingly: 'The area affected is so extensive that it embraces a semi-circle from Harwich to Portsmouth.' As Three did not take very kindly to the work, GARBO saw that he would have to undertake it himself. 'As Three is a little timid I am going to do this work myself and make the observations starting from tomorrow.'[4] Meanwhile the Germans had evidently realised that there was some danger of GARBO's military reporting suffering in consequence. 'I wish to repeat again that news about troop movements, units, locations, &c., continues to be your principal mission and you should add information about the objectives hit only to the extent that circumstances permit.'[5] But GARBO was not now to be deterred. On 5th July agent Three reported: 'GARBO did not turn up yesterday; he also has not appeared for daily meeting today . . . to avoid delay am sending reports which have not yet been sent by him.'[6] The next day matters looked serious; his wife had no news of him. 'I fear that any investigations of the Police or Civil Defence might turn out disastrous as knowing his methods it is quite likely that he has gone off on some new track which has taken him to a prohibited area from where he cannot communicate.'[7] Madrid replied on the 7th: 'I am very much puzzled indeed about what you told me about GARBO. Of course it might be possible that he left London on a special mission, although it appears rather strange that in this case he should not have informed either you or his family.'[8] Then rather unhelpfully: 'It is very difficult for me to advise you as there are a lot of details which I ignore as regards the inner construction of the Service. I think the first condition is to keep calm and quiet and to

---

4. GARBO 2115 GMT, 30th June, 1944.
5. GARBO Message received 2200 GMT, 30th June, 1944.
6. GARBO 2044 GMT, 5th July, 1944.
7. GARBO 2012 GMT, 6th July, 1944.
8. GARBO Message received 1939 GMT, 7th July, 1944.

give anything you may undertake the fullest consideration. If the worst has happened and GARBO has been arrested Three must do what he can to save the Service and take all measures to protect its members and prevent clues of any kind from falling into the hands of the Police.'[9] This message crossed with one from Three containing the fateful news: 'Widow reports alarming news just learnt from wife of GARBO. Police went to Taplow today to investigate and collect Red documentation.[10] GARBO was arrested on Tuesday. No details known. Consider situation critical. Am immediately breaking communications to and from all agents.'[11] There we will leave GARBO for the moment.

The case of BRUTUS was not so difficult because he had no sub-agents like 7 (4), 7 (2) and 7 (7) living among the old FUSAG formations. Even so we thought it prudent to send him on a week's visit to Scotland after he had sent his message about the Fourteenth Army on 10th July.

We must now go back a week or two in order to examine in greater detail the manner in which the news of the departing formations was handled. With the knowledge that the two principal actors were to retire from the scene, the one on 4th July and the other on the 10th, our problem was greatly simplified. The first formation to go was the 83rd US Infantry Division, hitherto represented as being stationed at Wye in Kent and forming part of XII Corps. Permission having been obtained to announce its departure, TATE reported on 23rd June: 'Convoy of the 83rd US Infantry Division passed through Wye in a westerly direction. A driver said that they had come from Elham and many had gone ahead of him.'[12] This was confirmed by agent 7 (2) on 28th June.[13] By now the 28th Division had left Tenterden and the 2nd Canadian Infantry Division at Dover was about to move. Furthermore the 43rd, 53rd and 59th British Infantry Divisions, which were all stationed in 7 (2)'s area but which

---

9. GARBO Message received 2015 and 2036 GMT, 7th July, 1944.
10. These false Spanish credentials had been supplied to him by the Germans some time previously for use in an emergency.
11. GARBO 1920 GMT, 7th July, 1944.
12. TATE 0603 MET, 23rd June, 1944.
13. GARBO 2044 GMT, 28th June, 1944.

belonged both in fact and in fiction to 21 Army Group, were already departing for the bridgehead. 21 Army Group, however, rightly insisted that none of these should be alluded to in any way. On 30th June GARBO had reported that his agent 7 (2) had tried to visit Tenterden, where the 28th US Division and the 43rd British Division were stationed, but was unfortunately turned back at the station as he was not in possession of the correct pass.[14] On 5th July GARBO had been allowed to send a message from 7 (2) with the news that: 'Many troops of the 2nd Canadian Division have been leaving the area. Have seen large convoys of this division moving North on the London road. The 28th US Division is said to be leaving Tenterden.'[15] The idea behind this message, apart from protecting the agent, was to suggest that the formations might be about to embark in the Thames Estuary. The Germans did not react quite in the way that they were intended to. They thought that these two divisions must have gone to join the Third American Army north of the Thames and suggested that 'this transfer of forces may be a result of the V. 1 attacks and may be a way of dispersing forces in the area under fire'.[16] After that GARBO's sub-agents were saved from any further trouble by the arrest of their master. The information which they continued to collect was not despatched until the beginning of August, by which time it was wholly innocuous.

GARBO was involved in this difficulty solely by virtue of the fact that he had sub-agents in the coastal areas. He was therefore able to protect himself merely by reporting the movements of individual formations. BRUTUS on the other hand could hardly fail to know something about a major regrouping of forces under the command of the army group to which he was attached. On 6th July he had told the Germans that the 83rd US Division, recently reported by him at Elham, had been removed from the FUSAG Order of Battle,[17] and on the 11th he stated ambiguously: 'The 2nd Canadian Corps moved from FUSAG but the 2nd British Corps remains in FUSAG in the region of Kent. Will try to discover the reason for the move;

---

14. GARBO 2055 and 2106 GMT, 30th June, 1944.
15. GARBO 2055 GMT, 5th July, 1944.
16. Appendix to Lagebericht West No. 1320, dated 8th July, 1944.
17. BRUTUS 1908 GMT, 6th July, 1944.

probably connected with the movement reported of the Fourteenth Army.'[18] Four days later, having sent his report on Fourteenth Army to which reference has already been made, he went to Scotland.

The advantage which we had derived during June from the German over-estimate of forces in South-East England has already been pointed out. At the beginning of July, however, we began to pay the penalty. The 15th, 43rd and 53rd Divisions, which had been located in Sussex and Kent, were identified in the bridgehead, and this was taken, for reasons already given, to imply a reinforcement from Patton's group of armies. The Germans, however, were still unwilling to accept the fact that any actual reduction in the latter's forces had been made and they preferred to believe that Patton's numbers had been made up from Montgomery's reserve. They also concluded that this reinforcement from the 21 Army Group reserve was going to the Third US Army in East Anglia rather than to the First Canadian Army in Kent and Sussex. This led them to modify their opinion as to Patton's objective. 'There are no concrete indications of an alteration in the grouping of forces in Great Britain. The fact that individual formations of the First Canadian Army have appeared in the bridgehead (15th, 43rd and 53rd English Infantry Divisions) can be accounted for by other divisions hitherto assumed to be in Montgomery's Army Group (*e.g.* 38th and 54th Divisions) having been put under the command of Patton's Army Group. In all, we must therefore continue to reckon that the latter army group comprises some thirty to thirty-two divisions including the airborne divisions destined for its use. The recognised great strength of the formations in the area between the Thames and the Wash (some sixty divisions)[19] is remarkable. It causes one to wonder whether the enemy command may actually be disposed to carry the bulk of these forces through the Straits of Dover as part of an undertaking against the Somme and Seine gap. The considerable risk which is unquestionably bound up with this suggests the possibility that part of this force might perhaps be used as part of a diversionary operation in the area between Dunkirk and Calais. Such a decision may

---

18. BRUTUS 1615 GMT, 11th July, 1944.
19. A gross overestimate and almost certainly a misprint.

doubtless have been encouraged by the thoroughly disturbing effect of the V. 1.'[20] Three days later this newborn expectation of a 'diversion' between Dunkirk and Calais had grown to the fear of an 'operation' in that region. 'On the basis of evidence received up to now the American Third Army probably disposes of at least seventeen divisions. The view already expressed that an operation against the central Channel area (Dunkirk–Calais)[21] may also have been planned from the area north of the Thames is again emphasised by the foregoing evidence, because the shipment of this strong group of force in its entirety through the Straits of Dover is regarded as particularly risky.'[22] It will be remembered that it was at this time that we made our first reports of the departure of Canadian formations from their locations in Kent, the Germans suggesting on their own initiative that they had gone to Third Army to escape from the flying-bombs. Here was yet another argument in support of Calais–Dunkirk, for the strength of the forces north of the Thames was thereby still further increased and that to the south correspondingly weakened. Although belief in a landing near Dieppe was never abandoned, the possibility of a second one further to the east now seemed greater. 'Particularly striking is, however, the continued reinforcement of Third American Army which seems even to have received some formations from the First Canadian Army (28th American?, 2nd Canadian?) which has led to the American Army being practically double the size of the Canadian. This transfer of forces may be a result of the V. 1 attacks and may be a way of dispersing the forces in the area under fire. In this case the measure would point away from an early beginning of the second landing operation. It can, however, also denote a change in the operation plans in connection with the V. 1 attack and create the necessary conditions for a special undertaking against the V. 1 sites. In any case the area Dunkirk–Boulogne deserves increased attention in view of the existing picture. The view of this department that the enemy command would hardly decide to ship a force of seventeen to twenty

---

20. Appendix to Lagebericht West No. 1316, dated 4th July, 1944.
21. In most other contexts Dunkirk–Calais is referred to as the 'Eastern Channel Area'.
22. Appendix to Lagebericht West No. 1318, dated 6th July, 1944.

divisions through the Straits of Dover without striking a blow against the German coast is maintained.'[23]

This state of affairs, however, did not last long. Although 'the greatly increased enemy strength in the Normandy beach-head (about thirty divisions) must not be allowed to deceive us into forgetting that the enemy still has at hand all that is required for carrying out a new landing operation', there could be no denying that Patton's group of armies had been sensibly weakened and even if he were receiving some reinforcement from the 21 Army Group reserve, he would scarcely be in a position to launch two attacks. So we find that the Calais–Dunkirk assault loses favour and Dieppe is accepted once more as the single objective. The Intelligence Summary for 10th July gives a clear impression of the views held at that time.

'The distribution of forces in England shows broadly the following picture:

'(*a*) In the rearward area of Montgomery's Army Group there are at the most a further ten to eleven divisions. This does not include the airborne divisions in this area; they are included in Patton's Army Group because they will presumably be employed in co-operation with it. Furthermore, the possibility must be reckoned with that a few divisions which on the map are still in the rearward area of Montgomery's Army Group have been actually transferred unbeknown into Patton's area. Briefly, therefore, we can say that Montgomery's Army Group probably no longer disposes of large-scale reserves in its rearward area. Also the recourse which has several times been had of late to Patton's formations to strengthen the beach-head points in the same direction and underlines, moreover, that the operations in Normandy could not be carried to success with the forces originally envisaged in the time intended.

'(*b*) Patton's Army Group disposes of about thirty divisions between Brighton and the Humber if we include four airborne divisions, and these forces have to an increasing

---

23. Appendix to Lagebericht West No. 1320, dated 8th July, 1944.

extent their main concentration north of the Thames. Their strength might be increased by a few divisions if such were transferred unbeknown from the South-West of England. It is, however, particularly important to remember that this army group is undoubtedly inferior in quality to that of Montgomery.

'(c) The mass of Montgomery's Army Group engaged in the beach-head consists at present of at least thirty-two divisions and also represents from the point of view of strength, and above all of quality, the strongest concentration of force which the Anglo-Saxon Command possesses, hence the entrusting to this army group of the main task, the thrust towards Paris.

'(d) The remaining groups of forces in Central and Northern England do not exceed three to four divisions each and, therefore, possess compared with the groups mentioned in (b) and (c) above no great significance. The massed concentration of Montgomery's Army Group and its reinforcements from Patton's Army Group suggests that the latter army group has not been given the decisive role, which again leads to the conclusion that it is intended to employ it with the idea of early co-operation with Montgomery's Army Group and, therefore within the latter's operational sphere.

'The area hitherto suggested in the Central Channel zone retains therefore its validity.'[24]

No Allied deceiver could have taken exception to that appreciation, but we were drawing perilously near to the danger line. Reinforcement of the bridgehead from the South-Eastern counties was already suggesting that Patton's Army Group had not been given the decisive role. During the next ten days the greater part of FUSAG, as the enemy then knew it, would be on its way to France. Furthermore, the uncontrolled agents, the loose horses in the race, constituted an added risk. Thus OSTRO reported from Lisbon on 6th July: 'All indications point to the fact that trans-shipment to

---

24. Appendix to Lagebericht West No. 1322, dated 10th July, 1944.

Normandy of divisions already assembled will proceed, other landings having been abandoned. Large-scale movements to South-East England have taken place, as transports by day however, so that they were obviously intended as deception manœuvres, especially as some of these troops have already been transported back to embarkation points area Bognor Regis–Weymouth.'[25] On 19th July the same agent declared that 'General Patton's Headquarters was transferred to Dorchester, King's Arms Hotel, on 11th July. Simultaneously, United States troops have moved from South-Eastern to Southern England. Patton's Army has, since the beginning of July, been regularly supplying troops to the First US Army in Normandy.'[26]

25. OSTRO Message, dated 6th July, 1944.
26. OSTRO Message, dated 19th July, 1944.

XXIX

FORTITUDE SOUTH II Executed

As the day was fast approaching when the release of the new FOR-
TITUDE story would become imperative, we now thought that the
time had arrived for GARBO to leave his prison cell, bearing in
mind that it would take some time to restore him fully to life and
action. On 12th July Madrid received the news from agent Three:
'Widow just reported surprising news that GARBO was released on
the 10th and is back at his hotel. . . . My instructions from him are
to give agent 4 (1) ten days' holiday and return immediately to
Glasgow and await orders there.'[1] On 4th July, as a result of a conversation which he had heard in a public house about some bombs
which had fallen at Bethnal Green during the previous night,
GARBO had gone to investigate. He had casually questioned a man
in the crowd, who unluckily for him had turned out to be a plain-
clothes policeman. The latter's suspicions had been further aroused
by GARBO swallowing a piece of paper on which he had previously
made some notes. In his zeal the police officer who had made the
arrest had detained GARBO at the Police Station for a longer period
than he was legally entitled to do without a warrant, a fact that was
pointed out to GARBO by one of his fellow prisoners. On the latter's
advice he had written a letter to the Home Secretary stating his
grievance to which reference has already been made. This action had
resulted in a marked change in the attitude of the Police. In an interview with the Chief of the Station GARBO had explained that he
had had a conversation several days before with J (3) in which he had

---

1. GARBO 2005 and 2015 GMT, 12th July 1944.

questioned the efficacy of the defence measures used against the new weapon. In order to prove his point he had decided to make some personal observations and this had led to his ultimate arrest. J (3) was of course able to corroborate the conversation and so GARBO had been able to leave the prison without a stain on his character. In taking leave of the Chief of the Station, the latter admitted that the Police had been over-zealous in the fulfilment of their duties and GARBO ended his account of the interview with the remark: 'As I did not understand half of what he was saying, I reacted to his amiability by thanking him for having had me in the prison, which, when I look back now, I see how ridiculous my words must have been.'[2]

The effect of GARBO's arrest was precisely that hoped for. Nearly all the other agents had been asked to report bomb damage. On 12th July BRUTUS was told: 'Discontinue from now on, all reports of damage caused by flying bombs and send us only information about location of troops, &c., &c., in accordance with instructions given.'[3] As soon as the Germans had received details of GARBO's arrest and subsequent release, they adjured him to 'cease all investigation of the new weapon'.[4] Similarly TATE was informed that messages about troops were of more interest than those about flying bombs.[5]

By the middle of the month the time had arrived when we could no longer with safety withhold the full story. Before 9th July, one division from each of the army corps[6] in the fictitious FUSAG had sailed. Allowing one day for the sea passage we were bound to assume that all these divisions would be identified in France by 16th July. It

---

2. GARBO Letter No. 21, dated 14th July, 1944.
3. BRUTUS Message received 1705 GMT, 12th July, 1944.
4. GARBO Message received 2049 and 2106 GMT, 23rd July, 1944.
5. TATE Message received 1833 MET, 31st July, 1944.
6. 83rd US Infantry Division (XII Corps) sailed 20th June; 2nd Canadian Infantry Division (2nd Canadian Corps) sailed 3rd July; 35th US Infantry Division (XII Corps) sailed 6th July; 4th US Armoured Division (XX Corps) sailed 8th July. The only other corps was the XXXVII, but as both it and its subordinate formations were imaginary they could not of course have been identified by the enemy even if they had been ordered to France, which was not the case.

had by now become very difficult to maintain the press stop on General Patton and the Ministry of Information thought it would be impossible to hold it beyond 20th July. The FORTITUDE SOUTH II wireless links were due to open on 21st July. Finally GARBO and BRUTUS had both come to life again, the latter having returned from Scotland on the 15th.

These points having been put to 21 Army Group, it was agreed that the release of FORTITUDE SOUTH II might begin on 18th July. It was arranged that BRUTUS should deliver the story in a series of messages sent between the 18th and 21st of the month, while GARBO, who was still out of touch with his transmitter, would meet his friend 4 (3) and give his own version in a letter which would reach the Germans at the end of the month and would corroborate what they had already heard from BRUTUS.

BRUTUS's report ran as follows: 'I learnt at Wentworth that FUSAG has undergone important changes owing to the necessity for sending immediate reinforcements to Normandy. So far as I know, the Supreme Commander, namely Eisenhower, decided that it was necessary to send urgently a part of the forces under FUSAG, who would pass under the command of a new army group. These forces will be replaced in FUSAG by new units arriving from America and by British reserves. No exact details but I can confirm that FUSAG will include the Ninth American Army, the Fourteenth American Army and the Fourth British Army. FUSAG, changes in the Command: I suppose that Eisenhower and Patton were not in agreement over the change in the Order of Battle because Patton has been replaced by General McNair as Commander-in-Chief of FUSAG. I have discussed, with my colonel, the latest changes which have caused a good deal of bother at our headquarters. He tells me that Montgomery demanded immediate reinforcements in Normandy in such a fashion that it was necessary to send units from FUSAG which were already in the South of England, notably the First Canadian Army and a large part of the Third American Army. The fresh units in FUSAG will take up the duties of the units which have been despatched. The staff command of FUSAG remains unchanged. The Fourteenth American Army has already removed towards East Anglia, to the area formerly occupied by the Third Army. The headquarters are at Little Waltham. The Fourth British

Army is also in the South. My colonel considers that the fresh units in FUSAG will be ready to take the offensive towards the beginning of August.'[7] Before the transmission of BRUTUS's message had been completed, the *Pariser Zeitung*, the German newspaper printed in Paris during the occupation, published the following article: 'Patton's Army in the Bridgehead. In the Normandy peninsula it is noteworthy that amongst the enemy reinforcements which have been employed in the last few days are divisions which apparently no longer form part of Montgomery's Army Group but are already under Eisenhower's other Army Group, which is under the command of the American Patton. Whereas the enemy army group which has so far been fighting in the bridgehead was called the "South-Western invasion army" because it was located in the South-West of England, these new divisions probably belong to the "South-Eastern invasion army" and their employment shows to what extent the German defence in Normandy is depleting the enemy forces.' No higher tribute could have been paid to the success of FORTITUDE than that the Germans should have used Patton's Army Group to support their own propaganda. But the passage also shows that BRUTUS's message had not gone too soon. A clearer proof that the release of FORTITUDE SOUTH II was accurately timed is to be found in the OKH Intelligence Summary for 27th July, which states that 'according to captured documents confirmed by credible Abwehr reports' the American Third Army had now transferred to France.[8]

Jodl stated under interrogation on 11th December, 1945, that he considered the Pas de Calais (FUSAG) threat to be over by the middle of July when formations of Third US Army began to appear in Normandy. He admitted, reluctantly, as his loyalty to Hitler remained unshaken, that the continued retention of a large part of the Fifteenth Army in the Pas de Calais after that date was due to the Fuehrer's own persistent belief in the imminence of a second landing. It would probably be unfair to put the whole blame on Hitler, for the Intelligence Summary of 27th July, after drawing attention to the

---

7. BRUTUS 1725, 1731 and 1737 GMT, 19th July, 1944, 2019, 2024 and 2144 GMT, 20th July, and 1709 GMT, 21st July.
8. Lagebericht West No. 1339, dated 27th July, 1944.

large scale on which Normandy was now being reinforced, went on to say: 'Patton's Army Group is thus gradually losing its potential strength for large-scale operations and it is therefore unlikely that it will be committed against a strongly fortified and defended sector of the coast in the near future. More probably it will be subjected to further weakening in favour of the Normandy operations and will be held ready to attack a sector of the Channel coast when such a sector has definitely been laid bare. Patton's Army Group represents therefore, in the opinion of this Department, no acute danger. It must, however, be remembered it can gradually be rehabilitated by shipments from America and made ready for large-scale operations. It will then probably consist of two armies, presumably the Fourth English in the South-East of England, and the Ninth or Fourteenth American in the area between the Thames and the Wash.'[9] This is the first recorded reaction to BRUTUS's report.[10] Two days later we read that although 'an early launching of FUSAG (still in the South-East of England) in a new landing operation is still held to be unlikely in view of the recent evidence . . . the presence which has recently been reported by several proven sources of two American armies (Ninth and Fourteenth) within the framework of this army group and the subordination to it of the English Fourth Army brought down from Scotland underline the significance which must be attached to FUSAG if the gaps made by its relinquishment of forces sent to Normandy have been made good.'[11] The reference to 'several proven sources' would suggest that GARBO's confirmatory letter, which was posted in Lisbon on 22nd July, had also reached Berlin.

In accordance with the new plan the wireless network of the reconstituted FUSAG opened in Kent, Sussex and the Eastern counties between 21st and 26th July, each formation being represented in its concentration area as shown in the chart on page 244.

---

9. Appendix to Lagebericht West No. 1339, dated 27th July, 1944.
10. Unless we count the *Pariser Zeitung*, but this seems doubtful. BRUTUS's transmissions were made on the evenings of the 19th to the 21st inclusive. The newspaper article appeared on the morning of the 21st.
11. Appendix to Lagebericht West No. 1341, dated 29th July, 1944.

Simultaneously the CLH units embarked on their programme of assault training. Operational commitments prevented the Allied air forces from giving full effect to the bombing programme in support of FORTITUDE II to which they had agreed in June.[12] By the time that the apparatus for physical deception was set in motion, the controlled agents had already acquainted the enemy with the main features of the new Order of Battle. During the last days of July, reports from BRUTUS and TATE disclosed the concentration of these forces in the East and South-East of England and these, in due course, found their way into the German Intelligence Summaries.

About this time there occurred an unexpected disaster, to which reference must now be made. A few days after his arrival in England General McNair decided to pay a short visit to France to observe the progress of operations. While there he was killed during an air attack. There was little chance of concealing his death from the enemy. It was therefore of the greatest importance that no time should be lost in providing the new army group with another commander. General McNair's death was reported to the Germans on 26th July. 'I have learnt that General McNair has been killed in Normandy where he had gone for a short visit to consult with General Montgomery and to inspect the coastal defences. This loss is considered here as very serious. It is thought that a successor will be appointed immediately to command the FUSAG operations.'[13] Two days later the news was released to the press. As there seemed little chance of getting another general of McNair's standing, but as something had to be done at once, it was decided to fall back once more on Simpson. At the same time the Supreme Commander felt that it would be worth asking General Marshall if he could help a second time. 'As continuation of the threat to the Pas de Calais area depended to a considerable extent

---

12. 'The programme of FORTITUDE air operations . . . has not to date progressed to an extent sufficient to create any significant pattern in the mind of enemy Intelligence.' (SHAEF/18250/Ops (B), dated 8th August, 1944. General W. B. Smith, Chief of Staff, to C-in-C Allied Expeditionary Air Force.)
13. BRUTUS Message No. 921, 26th July, 1944.

on the reputation of McNair, and particularly as his appointment as Commanding General First US Army Group has already been passed to the enemy, it would be desirable to assign another general officer from the United States with a reputation comparable to McNair's to replace him as First US Army Group Commander. I appreciate that it may not be possible to make a suitable replacement available in time to be effective. Consequently, Simpson is being designated, for cover purposes, acting Commander of First United States Army Group, while at the same time retaining his present actual command of the Ninth US Army.'[14] General Marshall very promptly rose to the occasion. General de Witt would be immediately available to take command of the First United States Army Group. General de Witt was at that time Director of the Army and Navy Staff College at Washington, an appointment which he had held for about two years. He had previously commanded 9th Service Command and Fourth Army at San Francisco, and while there had dealt with the Japanese problem in the Western United States after Pearl Harbor. It was therefore likely that the Germans would regard him as a suitable successor to McNair.

Meanwhile the first half of the story had reached its goal. 'According to reliable reports Lieut.-General L. J. McNair, until recently Commander-in-Chief of the Land Forces in the United States, who has since been killed while on a visit to the front, was destined to succeed Lieut.-General Patton as Commander-in-Chief of the American First Army Group (England). It seems that Lieut.-General Patton has now assumed command of the Third American Army in Normandy. No information is available about the new commander of the American First Army Group in Great Britain.'[15]

General de Witt arrived on 6th August. So as not to put too much on to the controlled agents it was thought better on this occasion to allow the first announcement to appear in the press. On 9th August *The Times* printed the following short notice: 'US Army Appointment–Lieut.-General John de Witt is now in the United Kingdom to fill the assignment previously held by General Lesley

---

14. SHAEF/Fwd/12466, dated 26th July, 1944. General Eisenhower to General Marshall.
15. OKH Situation Report, dated 4th August, 1944.

McNair. It was announced in *The Times* on 28th July that General McNair was killed in action in Normandy. Until recently he was in command of the US Army Ground Forces.' Two days previously a similar announcement had been made in the United States, which the Germans had recorded in the following terms: 'According to an official American announcement Lieut.-General John L. de Witt has been appointed successor to Lieut.-General L. J. McNair, killed in action. General de Witt was, until 1st September, 1943, Commander-in-Chief of the Fourth American Army in the United States and subsequently Commandant of the Academy for Higher Command in the Army and Navy (Army and Navy Staff College). He is said to be a particularly capable organiser. Lieut.-General de Witt has presumably assumed command of the First American Army Group (FUSAG) in Great Britain.'[16]

While these events were in progress, GARBO had been taking steps to extricate himself from the dangerous position in which his arrest had placed him. The rather grudging letter of apology which he succeeded in extracting from the Home Secretary he immediately sent to Madrid[17] and on 23rd July received the following answer: 'In my possession all your documents announced. Shocked by the story of your detention. We send cordial congratulations for your liberation. The security of yourself and of the Service requires a prolongation of the period of complete inactivity on your part, without any contact with collaborators. . . . For urgent and important military information Three should be able to take charge of communicating with us.'[18] GARBO, however, was not one to remain idle for long. Before 20th July, as we have already seen, he had met 4 (3) and given a detailed report about the reorganisation of FUSAG. On 28th July he was able to tell Madrid that he had had a meeting with Three and Seven and had reorganised his entire network to suit the changed conditions.

Before examining these new arrangements some reference must

---

16. Lagebericht West No. 1351, dated 8th August, 1944.
17. The letter was subsequently returned to him as it was thought that it might be found useful on another occasion.
18. GARBO Message received 2049 and 2106 GMT, 23rd July, 1944.

Any communication on the
subject of this letter should be
addressed to—

THE UNDER SECRETARY OF STATE,
HOME OFFICE,
LONDON, S.W.I.

and the following number quoted:—

P. 17829.

HOME OFFICE,
WHITEHALL.

10th July, 1944.

Sir,

  I am directed to acknowledge the receipt of your letter dated 7th July, 1944.

  The Secretary of State has caused inquiries to be made into the incident to which you refer and is satisfied that your conduct on the afternoon of the fourth instant at Old Ford Road was of such a nature that you have only yourself to blame for your arrest. The detective officer concerned was doing no less than his duty in detaining for the purpose of inquiries an alien who appeared to him to be a visitor in the district and to display an undue inquisitiveness into the extent and circumstances of damage caused by enemy action. In making the arrest this officer was acting fully within the powers conferred upon him as a police constable by the Defence Regulations.

  In view of the explanation of your conduct and of your presence in the Bethnal Green area which you made to the police shortly after your arrival at Bow Police Station, it is regretted that steps were not immediately taken to verify your story with the Ministry of Information. On receipt of your letter this Department at once made inquiries of the Ministry of Information as a result of which the Secretary of State directed your immediate release. Further inquiries are being pursued into this aspect of the matter.

/OVER

Facsimile reproduction of forged letter purporting to have been written by the Home Secretary to GARBO and forwarded by him to Madrid, July 1944.

It has been brought to the notice of the Secretary of State that the police officer who executed the Order authorising your detention beyond the usual statutory period of 48 hours was a Chief Inspector who was at the time deputising for the Superintendent of the Division. This department does not support the view that a Chief Inspector of Police or indeed any police officer other than the Commissioner of Police or a Chief Constable is entitled under the Defence Regulations to make such an Order and the Secretary of State.is satisfied that in purporting so to do the Chief Inspector acted in excess of his authority.

I am accordingly instructed to tender to you the sincere apologies of the Secretary of State for the inconvenience caused to you by the mistaken and excessive zeal of the police in the exercise of their duties and to inform you that the incident is being referred to the Commissioner of Police of the Metropolis to consider whether disciplinary action should not be taken against the officers concerned or against any of them.

I am, Sir,

Your obedient servant,

be made to an incident well calculated to restore the confidence of this agent after his recent unfortunate experiences. 'With great happiness and satisfaction', said Madrid on 29th July, 'I am able to advise you today that the Fuehrer has conceded the Iron Cross to you for your extraordinary merits, a decoration which, without exception, is granted only to first-line combatants. For this reason we all send you our most sincere and cordial congratulations.'[19] GARBO replied: 'I cannot at this moment, when emotion overcomes me, express in words my gratitude for the decoration conceded by our Fuehrer, to whom humbly and with every respect I express my gratitude for the high distinction which he has bestowed on me, for which I feel myself unworthy as I have never done more than what I have considered to be the fulfilment of my duty. Furthermore I must state that this prize has been won not only by me but also by Carlos and the other comrades who, through their advice and directives, have made possible my work here and so the congratulations are mutual. My desire is to fight with greater ardour to be worthy of this medal which has only been conceded to those heroes, my companions in honour, who fight on the battle front.'[20] Not unnaturally GARBO and his case officer were anxious to get possession of this interesting token of German esteem and on 12th August the agent wrote: 'I want also today to amplify my message with regard to the Iron Cross which I have been conceded. From the time of knowing this, I have carried the series of reverses which I have suffered with greater resignation and, I can now say, with greater courage than previously. My fervent desire is to possess this and to hold it in my very hands. I know that this desire is difficult to fulfil as I cannot glorify myself with it when I have it. But for my personal satisfaction, I should certainly like to have it by me, even though it be hidden underground until I am able to wear it on my chest, the day when this plague which surrounds us is wiped off the face of the earth. Can you possibly send it camouflaged, via the courier?'[21] It never came.

GARBO saw the wisdom of leaving the whole organisation in the

---

19. GARBO Message received 2050 GMT, 29th July, 1944.
20. GARBO 1906 and 1922 GMT, 31st July, 1944.
21. GARBO Letter No. 25, dated 12th August, 1944.

hands of Three. As Three himself suggested, the Police might have set him free in order to keep a check on him and have him followed. It was therefore only prudent that for the time being at any rate he should sever all contact with his comrades. Agent Four had already dropped out as a result of his adventures at Hiltingbury Camp and had been in hiding in South Wales for nearly two months. GARBO described him as being in despair owing to his inactivity and afraid that sooner or later he would be found and tried as a deserter. Seven, too, was beginning to lose his nerve. He was worried by the detention both of 7 (5) and of GARBO within such a short space of time and he thought that the third arrest might be unlucky. He was thinking of returning to the Merchant Service. GARBO therefore asked him if he would at least help him to get Four out of the country and this he agreed to do. The proposal was to send him to Canada where Five could look after him. Of the rest, 7 (5) and 7 (6) had already been proved failures. GARBO therefore proposed to release them both. This, however, still left him with the best sub-agents, notably Donny, Dick and Dorick. Under the new scheme Three would be at the head, 7 (2) would be called in to act as a free-lance, taking the place of Seven in that respect. The territory of 7 (4) would be enlarged to include Kent as well as Sussex, thus filling the gap caused by 7 (2)'s departure. 7 (7) and 3 (3) would continue as before, the former in the Eastern counties and the latter in Scotland.

During the three weeks that GARBO had been out of touch with his organisation the sub-agents had continued to make observations and compile reports. By now, of course, some of these were a little out of date. Nevertheless GARBO felt that it was worth sending them on if only to show that they had not been idle. From 7 (2) came full details of the departure of the First Canadian Army at the beginning of July, now indeed a matter of history but confirming the story of FORTITUDE and confirmed by identifications in the bridgehead. His later reports spoke of the arrival of the Fourth Army which had already been observed by BRUTUS. From agent Seven came another old report dating back nearly a month. It will be remembered that he had been sent by GARBO at that time to carry out investigations in Western Command. Here he had found all the newly arrived formations of the Fourteenth Army, again confirming and amplyfying what BRUTUS had already told the Germans. From 7 (7) came the news of the departing Third Army followed by the arrival of the American forces from Cheshire, the most notable feature of this change being the substitution of infantry for armour in the Eastern counties.[22]

---

22. 'Norwich/Ipswich: There has been a reduction in armoured divisions in this area (despatched to France) and an increase in American infantry divisions.' OKH Report dated 10th August, 1944, based on GARBO's message of 7th August, 1944, sent at 2126 GMT.

XXX

Developments in August

By 4th August the Germans appear to have held the view that the danger of a second landing had fallen a little further into the background. 'Particularly strong landings in the Seine Bay during the past two days (on 2nd August alone seventy-nine freighters of approximately 1.8 million BRT) lead us to suppose that considerable reinforcements have been brought into the Normandy area which will have resulted in a further weakening of the First American Army Group (Southern England) and again makes it seem unlikely that early new landing plans of extensive scope are envisaged.'[1]

A pointer to which the German Intelligence paid great attention in trying to assess our intentions was the organisation of the higher command. After it had become evident that a second army group was engaged in the bridgehead they were anxious to know who was in charge of the operation as a whole. On 29th July GARBO was asked: 'Could you find out if the Twelfth US Army Group, recently constituted, is under the supreme command of Montgomery or who is the supreme chief in Normandy of the two army groups which are now there.'[2] BRUTUS was asked a similar question on the same day and on 1st and 2nd August replied: 'All American forces destined for the Normandy operation, namely, the First and the Third American Armies, are included in the Twelfth Army Group, of which the head is General Bradley. There is also in Normandy the 21 Army Group, composed of the First Canadian Army and the Second

---

1. Appendix to Lagebericht West No. 1347, dated 4th August, 1944.
2. GARBO Message received 2056 GMT, 29th July, 1944.

British Army. The chief is General Montgomery. Both Army Groups come directly under SHAEF, of which the supreme head is General Eisenhower. It is possible that, in practice, Montgomery commands both Army Groups on the battlefield.'[3] In the OKH Situation Report of 4th August we read: 'It is thought that Lt. General Bradley has taken command of the American Twelfth Army Group in Normandy. General Montgomery retains his overall command of the operations in Normandy and remains Commander-in-Chief of the English 21 Army Group.'[4]

If the belief was to be sustained that the second landing would be on a scale comparable with that of the Normandy invasion, it was important that the Germans should continue to imagine that Supreme Headquarters were still located in England, for it would obviously be inconvenient to direct the second assault from France. At the beginning of August General Eisenhower established a small command post in France and it was unfortunate that the newspapers announced the Supreme Commander's removal to the Continent on 10th August. On that day the *Daily Telegraph* reported: '*Eisenhower Moves Across—HQ now in France.* It was revealed last night that General Eisenhower, Allied Supreme C-in-C, had established HQ on the Continent to maintain the closest possible contact with the fast-rolling offensive against the German forces. His HQ unit was moved to Normandy by air in the past few days. Officers and enlisted personnel, including WACs, are living in tents in a camouflaged area under constant patrol by heavily armed military police. The general himself lives in a trailer under a 24-hours' guard, during which a military policeman sits in a dug-out behind a machine-gun. Immediate telephone communication with Supreme HQ in London is available from the trailer. General Eisenhower's quarters are near an airfield from which he makes speedy trips daily for personal conferences with General Montgomery and General Bradley. On Tuesday he saw his British and American field commanders. On Bank Holiday he conferred with Mr Churchill.' The significance of this press release was not lost on the Germans. 'For the rest we must count on the enemy command bringing over sufficient forces from

3. BRUTUS 2033 GMT, 1st August, and 1741 GMT, 2nd August, 1944.

4. OKH Situation Report, dated 4th August, 1944.

Great Britain to ensure the full exploitation of his present success as the transfer of General Eisenhower's Headquarters from Great Britain to France has also emphasised the decisive character of the operations in the later stages.'[5] To compensate for this, however, the new FUSAG was gaining in strength and the appreciation continues: 'The accelerated reinforcement of the FUSAG formations still in England from the United States seems to have started.' At the same time GARBO did what he could to correct the impression which had been created by the report of the Supreme Commander's departure. '4 (3) told me that, in view of the possibility of the immediate collapse of the German Army, the Allied Chiefs of Staff want Eisenhower to maintain the closest contact with Montgomery at the present time. For this reason a section of Supreme Headquarters has been transferred to the Normandy front with the category of Advanced Headquarters for those two Army Groups, but the structure of Supreme Headquarters remains here. He said that it was merely a question of establishing closer liaison between the headquarters of Montgomery and Supreme Headquarters. Also learned the following from him: the Commander-in-Chief of the two Army Groups fighting in France is Montgomery.'[6] A few days later, the Germans, having stated that at the moment there was no evidence of any new landing operations in the Channel area, appreciated: 'It must, however, be pointed out that the neutralisation of strong German forces in Normandy as well as the weakening of Northern France both in the forward and rear areas which is already known accurately by the enemy creates the conditions necessary to enable the enemy command quickly to put into operation again plans which have hitherto been postponed. In this connection the continued retention in Great Britain of strong airborne forces is noteworthy, formations whose employment is only envisaged within the framework of a new operational phase.'[7] The 'strong airborne forces' referred to the new First Allied Airborne Army, whose formation had been officially announced on 10th August and about which more will be said later.

---

5. Appendix to Lagebericht West No. 1354, dated 11th August, 1944.
6. GARBO 1907 and 1925 GMT, 12th August, 1944.
7. Appendix to Lagebericht West No. 1358, dated 15th August, 1944.

On 15th August through some misunderstanding between the Censorship Departments, it was announced that General Eisenhower was directing operations in the Argentan–Falaise sector. This was immediately contradicted by the SHAEF official spokesman. 'General Montgomery still commands the 21 Army Group, under which is the Twelfth Army Group. This means that General Montgomery is over General Bradley, but both are under General Eisenhower as Supreme C-in-C, which always was the case. An announcement by General Eisenhower apparently caused the erroneous belief that General Montgomery had been removed from active command of all Allied ground forces in Western France. This is not the situation. It simply is not true.'[8] The whole business caused a considerable stir. On 17th August the *Daily Mirror* contained a strongly worded leading article demanding that an apology should be offered to General Montgomery and a cartoon suggesting indecision in high quarters. From the point of view of deception the contradiction was really worse than the announcement because it made it look as if we were trying to conceal something. This time, however, the incident appears to have escaped the enemy's notice for it provoked no fresh comment.

Bearing in mind the importance which the enemy attached to our choice of commanders, we now felt it incumbent upon us to select commanders for the two fictitious armies comprised in the new FUSAG. For Fourteenth Army General Lucas was chosen. General Lucas was in the United States at the time. A press stop was placed on his movements and it was hoped that his true whereabouts would not become known to the Germans. For the Fourth Army the best that the Military Secretary could offer was General Morgan, the GOC-in-C of Southern Command. This choice was not altogether to our liking since Home Commands are not normally subject to the severe security restrictions which apply in the case of commanders of operational troops. There was always the danger that the activities of a General holding such an appointment might be reported in the press and so spoil our story. Fortunately there were at that time several Generals Morgan. We therefore hoped that it might be possible to keep the Germans in doubt as to which one it was. On 26th July

---

8. Extract from the *Daily Telegraph* of 16th August, 1944.

BRUTUS had been asked: 'Who is CO Fourth Army?'[9] On 18th August, after his visit to the headquarters of the Fourth Army at Heathfield, he was able to tell them that General Morgan held that appointment.[10] On 26th August the Germans asked GARBO: 'Did you ever hear about a General named Morgan? If yes, what post does he occupy and which is his christian name?'[11] And to BRUTUS on 13th September: 'What are the christian names of the British General Morgan, Commander-in-Chief Fourth Army.'[12] Both agents took a long time in answering. On 29th September BRUTUS came back with us: 'With regard to General Morgan, I have twice, without result, tried to fall in with my FUSAG friends in London. Can you not verify it with the British Army List?'[13] On 1st October GARBO explained: 'There are the following Generals Morgan listed in *Who's Who*: Major-General, temporary Lieutenant-General, Frederick Edgworth Morgan, born 1894; temporary Major-General Harold de Riemer Morgan, born 1888; Brigadier-General John Hartman Morgan, born 1876; Lieutenant-General Reginald Hallward Morgan, born 1871; Brigadier-General Rosslewyn Westropp Morgan, born 1879; temporary Lieutenant-General William Duthie Morgan, date of birth not given; General Llewellyn Isaac Gethin Morgan Owen, born 1879. The first of these was given a lot of press publicity recently as the chief planner of the invasion.'[14] Doggedly the Germans came back to GARBO on 6th October: 'Would like to know christian names of General Morgan Fourth British Army.'[15] But neither GARBO nor BRUTUS had anything more to say on the subject.

Throughout the month of August the planting of the new Order of Battle proceeded most expeditiously. It will not be necessary here to record the whole process in detail. By an examination of the

---

9. BRUTUS Message received 1708 GMT, 26th July, 1944.
10. BRUTUS 2019 GMT, 18th August, 1944.
11. GARBO Message received 2112 GMT, 26th August, 1944.
12. BRUTUS Message received 1738 GMT, 13th September, 1944.
13. BRUTUS 1820 GMT, 29th September, 1944. By this time BRUTUS had given up his appointment at FUSAG and had returned to the Polish Headquarters in London.
14. GARBO 1933 and 1950 GMT, 1st October, 1944.
15. GARBO Message received 1819 GMT, 6th October, 1944.

relevant documents the progress of each formation can, however, be traced first in the agent's message, then in the German Intelligence Summary and finally on the Fremde Heere West Location Map. The map of 29th August reveals practically the whole of the new FUSAG with all the locations, if not correct, erring by a few miles only.[16] There are only two formations missing altogether, namely the 25th United States Armoured Division and the 35th British Armoured Brigade, but the former is accepted in the Intelligence Summary for 31st August, so that out of a total of one army group, three armies, four army corps, two armoured divisions, eight infantry divisions, three airborne divisions and one armoured brigade, all sham except for one army and two infantry divisions, only the armoured brigade is missing.

There is no evidence to show that all of this intelligence was not supplied by the two agents, GARBO and BRUTUS, possibly with some assistance from TATE. Yet it is interesting to note how very far we were from realising this at the time. At the beginning of August, when manpower shortage was becoming a matter of serious concern, an investigation was made with a view to reducing military establishments whose strength exceeded their needs. In defending the continued employment of the special units that were employed on wireless deception, the two battalions which were manning the dummy craft and a small party of about 200 men, who were still 'lighting fires in woods, hanging out washing, &c.', to animate the

---

16. This statement requires one qualification. The Ninth Army was in fact at all times at Bristol. A deceptive wireless link operated between FUSAG at Wentworth and Ninth Army at Bristol from 26th July until 17th August. The controlled agents had not yet said where the Army was. The reader will remember the Germans' doubts as to whether it was the Ninth or the Fourteenth Army which would replace the Third Army in East Anglia. The map of 29th August shows both the Ninth and the Fourteenth Armies as being in the Eastern counties. During August, however, both BRUTUS and GARBO gave its true location and accordingly we find in the German appreciation for 31st August the following entry: 'The American Ninth Army, which hitherto was thought to be in the South-East of England in the immediate neighbourhood of FUSAG, is now, according to credible information, in the Bristol area.' (Lagebericht West No. 1374, dated 31st August, 1944, based on BRUTUS 1810 GMT, 10th August, 1944, and GARBO 2055 GMT, 16th August, 1944.)

embarkation camps of South-Eastern Command, a letter from Ops (B) Sub-section concludes with the remark: 'It is interesting to note from the foregoing that, after subtracting the personnel who are engaged on FORTITUDE on a "part-time" basis, the Fifteenth German Army, consisting of twenty-two divisions, is being "held" by a force of approximately 1,500 all ranks.'[17]

When we last examined the state of the German forces in France, we found that at the beginning of July there were twenty-two[18] divisions north of the Seine. That was still the position at the middle of the month. During the following two weeks this total was reduced by two only. By 18th July the 326th Limited Employment Infantry Division had gone to Normandy and before the end of the month the 19th Panzer Division had left for Russia. It was not until the beginning of August that the landslide really began. It will probably be agreed that this was the result of *force majeure* rather than from any feeling that the danger of a second landing had been removed. By 6th August the 84th and 89th Field Divisions stationed between Le Havre and Rouen as well as the 116th Panzer Division had left for the bridgehead. There still remained seventeen divisions. During the next few days no fewer than five[19] divisions were transferred to Normandy, leaving on 13th August a total of twelve. The SHAEF Intelligence Summary for 12th August tells us: 'Fifteenth Army is now sending infantry divisions to West Normandy as fast as the railways, or more often bicycles and legs, can carry them. They seem to be arriving more or less in order of nearness: 84th and 89th Infantry Divisions, pocket divisions from across the Seine, arrived first, one on either wing, and the next batch, just arriving, all from the Pas de Calais, are 85th, 331st and, apparently, 344th Infantry Divisions, elements of all of which have been contacted. Moreover, the training divisions still remaining in the N.E. (182nd and 165th) are contributing generous drafts. The quality and morale of these latest

---

17. SHAEF/18250/Ops (B), dated 4th August, 1944, Chief Ops (B) Sub-Section to Chief Ops Section.
18. Two Panzer, nine field and eleven limited employment divisions.
19. 49th, 85th and 331st Field Divisions, 6th Parachute Division and 344th Limited Employment Division.

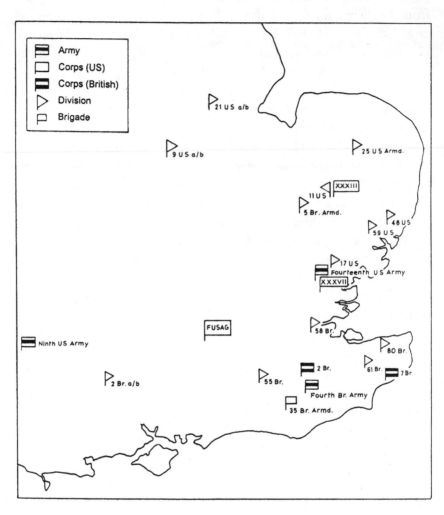

Locations of FUSAG formations according to FORTITUDE II.

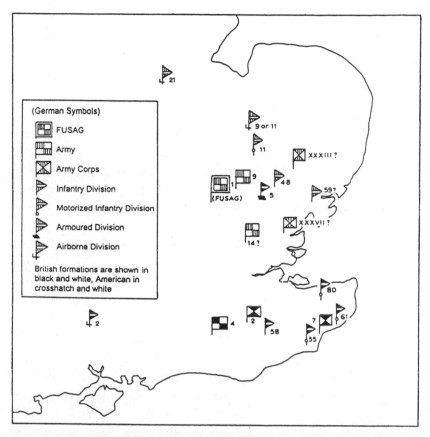

Location of FUSAG formations given on the OKH map of 29th August, 1944.

Notes

1. Formations included by the Germans in FUSAG without our authority are omitted.
2. The reason for the incorrect location of Ninth US Army is considered in the text. This mistake was rectified in the Lagebericht of 31st August and, no doubt, subsequent issues of the OKH map were amended accordingly.
3. The 17th US Infantry Division though omitted from this map was accepted as being in the Eastern Counties in the Lagebericht of the same date.

arrivals are deplorable.'[20] By 14th August the 48th Field Division had gone and by the 27th there remained north of the Somme an odd lot of one field and six limited employment divisions, two of the latter having just arrived from Germany as reinforcements.

On 7th August a Berlin broadcast stated: 'Large-scale landing operations by the Allies need no longer be reckoned with, a German military spokesman declared today. Since the Allies are employing four armies in the invasion territory, Eisenhower has now concentrated his main forces in that area. The intentions of the Allies are now quite clear, and that is an advantage to the Germans. It is always easier to plan counter-measures when the opponent's objective is apparent.'[21] The German propagandist refrained from adding that it would have been easier still to plan counter-measures if the opponent's objective had become apparent two months sooner.

Before recording the movements of German troops in South and South-West France during this period, something must be said about the threats which were now being directed against these parts of the French coast. It had been decided that the Seventh United States Army should invade the South of France on 15th August. To cover the landing a plan known as FERDINAND was put into operation on 7th July. The aim of FERDINAND was to convince the Germans that no invasion of the south coast of France would take place by finding alternative employment for the forces which had been assembled for the attack. Included among the several measures which were adopted in pursuance of that object was the threat of an amphibious assault by an American corps on the Gulf of Genoa in August. The Germans were also to be persuaded that one of the two French corps, which were in fact to take part in the landing, was under orders to proceed to England with two infantry divisions under command. On arrival it would also take command of the 2nd French Armoured Division which was in fact already in this country and about to go to France. The suggestion was to be made that the use of this French corps in Normandy would go some way to satisfy French opinion

---

20. SHAEF G-2 Weekly Intelligence Summary No. 21 for week ending 12th August, 1944.
21. IP (1) Daily Digest of World Wireless Propaganda, 7th–8th August, 1944.

which would otherwise be disappointed by the cancellation of the Southern attack. This plan was operated from the Mediterranean. At the request of the Commander of 'A' Force TATE sent two messages at the beginning of August confirming the arrival of the French Corps in England.[22] There is a satisfactory reflection by FERDINAND in the German Intelligence Summary for 4th August.[23]

On 5th July General Maitland Wilson[24] requested SHAEF to simulate preparations for an attack against the Biscay coast, the threat to exercise its greatest effect immediately before 15th August with a view to holding German troops in South-West France, which might otherwise be sent to reinforce the Mediterranean coast.[25] On the following day SHAEF replied that the request was being urgently examined.[26] SHAEF was against doing anything of this nature. The possibility of making the threat convincing was felt to be remote and it was thought that the plan would be prejudicial to FORTITUDE SOUTH. A triangular correspondence between London, Washington and the Mediterranean ensued. On 25th July the Combined Chiefs of Staff informed the Supreme Allied Commander, Mediterranean Theatre, that they approved General Eisenhower's recommendation that the 'existent latent threat only to the Biscay coast be maintained'. It was not until 8th August that a plan, IRONSIDE II, was approved. The story was that operations by the Maquis in the South of France had proved more effective than had originally been expected. Generals Eisenhower and Wilson, in consultation with General de Gaulle, had therefore decided to exploit this by increasing the supply of arms and trained organisers to the Maquis in the Bordeaux–Bayonne area to an extent which would enable the whole organisation to take control of this area unsupported by large-scale amphibious operations. As soon as the ports of Bordeaux and Bayonne became untenable as a result of these operations the seaborne forces would be despatched from the United States to open

---

22. TATE 1840 MET, 3rd August, 1944, 1602 MET, 8th August, 1944, and 0620 MET, 9th August, 1944.
23. Appendix to Lagebericht West No. 1347, dated 4th August, 1944.
24. Now Field-Marshal Sir H. Maitland Wilson.
25. FX.68506, dated 5th July, 1944, from AFHQ to SHAEF.
26. S.55127 SHAEF to AFHQ, dated 6th July, 1944.

these ports as bases for supplying the Maquis with heavy equipment. The target date was to be 14th August. The plan was to be put into operation by Special and Diplomatic Means.

In the early part of July there remained in the South of France one Panzer, one field and five limited employment divisions, and in the South-West of France one Panzer and four limited employment divisions. By 16th July the 716th Limited Employment Division, originally in the Normandy bridgehead, had gone to reinforce the south coast. Before 6th August the 9th Panzer Division, which had been in the South of France, was transferred to Normandy and its place was taken by the 11th Panzer Division which had been at Bordeaux. At the same time the 189th Limited Employment Division moved from the Hautes Pyrenees to Sete on the south coast of France. By that date therefore the south-west coast was reduced to two limited employment divisions and the forces on the south coast had risen to nine divisions, one Panzer, one field and seven for limited employment. That was the position when the landing took place.

Whether IRONSIDE II would have achieved anything even if it had been given a longer run may be doubted, but it is certain that when Special Means received its instructions on 8th August, any chance that there might have been of rendering assistance had already passed, since the only formation of any real value, the 11th Panzer Division, had already left for the south coast of France.

XXXI

FORTITUDE Ended

After the defeat of the German Seventh Army in Normandy at the beginning of August it was supposed that the enemy would take up a defensive position on the Seine and that the Allies would have to regroup for a new attack. It was believed that deception might assist the operation and it was proposed that part of FUSAG should be transferred to France for that purpose. This suited the position in England well enough. By the middle of August the Pas de Calais was rapidly being denuded of troops. If nothing were done to meet this change in the situation the Germans would soon begin to wonder why we did not attack. The transfer of one of the FUSAG armies to Normandy would help to solve the problem. The choice between the Fourth British and the Fourteenth US Armies was decided by the nature of the wireless organisations by which they were represented. 3103 Signals Service Battalion was trained and equipped for operations overseas. 12th Reserve Unit included a large number of low category men who could not serve abroad. So it was the American army which was chosen for the battle of the Seine.[1]

---

1. SHAEF/24183/3/SM/Ops, dated 18th August, 1944. 'Special Means Interim Plan for the Movement of Fourteenth Army from East Anglia to the South Coast.' When this plan was being written it was hard to know exactly when the remaining German forces would be withdrawn from the Pas de Calais. As one did not wish to run any risk of relieving the pressure too soon, the plan provided that the move of the Fourteenth Army could, temporarily, be interpreted as the 'culmination' of FORTITUDE II. Advantage was never taken of this provision since, by the time that the plan came into operation, practically all the enemy's troops had left. See Appendix VIII.

At this time events were moving fast and the defeat of the Germans was becoming more complete than had been anticipated. The Seine was crossed without a battle and before the end of the month British and Canadian forces were approaching the Pas de Calais. Thus the two arguments which had made the reorganisation of FUSAG necessary earlier in the month, now ceased to apply. There was no need to reinforce the attack on the Seine line because the Seine had already been crossed. There was no need to relieve pressure on the Pas de Calais from the United Kingdom because we were now approaching it overland and that was obviously a more economical way of capturing the North-West of France than an amphibious operation. However there appeared to be other good reasons for continuing with the proposed reorganisation.

One is apt to forget the general optimism which prevailed during the month of August 1944. The Germans were retreating on every front. Their armies in France had suffered a defeat from which it seemed unlikely that they would be able to recover. The recent attempt on Hitler's life made it appear as if his authority was being undermined at home. It will be agreed that Mr Churchill as Prime Minister and Minister of Defence was never given to over-statement, yet in *The Times* of 3rd August we read: 'Mr Churchill, in a long and heartening review in the House of Commons today of the war situation, declared that, although he greatly feared to raise false hopes, he "no longer felt bound to deny" that victory would perhaps come soon.' In these circumstances what better role could deception perform than to convince the enemy by an overwhelming show of force of the hopelessness of resistance? This in fact became the new deception policy which was ultimately embodied in the directive of 8th September which formally brought FORTITUDE SOUTH II to an end. The situation is there described in these words: 'The enemy is in retreat in the West in face of superior Allied forces. He is being compelled on all sectors to conform to the Allied manœuvres. It is considered that he is unlikely to react to any large-scale deceptive operations on the Allied front in the West, though he may be susceptible to making faulty dispositions elsewhere, and is in a position where disintegration of control may take place at any time.' In order to create the desired state of alarm in the mind of the German Command they were to be told that the armies in France were being reinforced by two additional armies, the Ninth and the Fourteenth; the former, a real formation, would be going overseas in September in any case. At the same time their rear and right flank was to be threatened by a large-scale combined seaborne and airborne assault launched from the United Kingdom.

In reporting the impending move of the Fourteenth Army to France GARBO did not lose the opportunity of promoting the new terror campaign by hinting at frightfulness to come. Having explained that the Fourteenth Army had originally been intended for Japan, 4 (3) had told GARBO 'a lot of curious things about the basis of the composition of this Fourteenth US Army; amongst them he said that in their ranks there were many convicts who were released from prisons in the United States to be enrolled in a foreign legion of the French or Spanish type. It can almost be said that there are brigades composed of gangsters and bloodthirsty men, specially selected to fight against the Japanese, men who were not supposed to take prisoners, but, instead, to administer a cruel justice at their own hands.'[2]

In mounting the threat across the North Sea the task of deception was assisted by the formation of the First Allied Airborne Army at the beginning of August. This reorganisation of the Allied airborne forces had been begun in June. General Eisenhower had pointed out that there was no suitable agency available to the High Command for assuming responsibility for joint planning between the troop carrier command and airborne forces. 'My idea in setting the Airborne Commander directly under this Headquarters is to give him this responsibility . . . he would not command troops actually fighting on the ground, but would be responsible for providing them all with logistical support until normal lines of communication could be established. Assuming that an airborne attack by two or three divisions took place within a single area, a temporary corps commander would be designated to conduct the fighting on the ground. He would operate under directives issued by this Headquarters until his force could join up with the nearest army, whereupon he would be taken over by the army commander both operationally and logistically.'[3]

---

2. GARBO Letter No. 26, dated 24th August, 1944.
3. S.55194, dated 8th July, 1944. SHAEF Personal from Eisenhower to AGWAR to General Marshall.

The formation of the new airborne army was announced on 10th August, and on the same day we read in the OKH Situation Report: 'According to an official British announcement all British and American airborne forces, including the Anglo-American gliders and transport formations, are being combined to form a new airborne army. The commander of this army is an American, Lieutenant-General Louis H. Brereton (hitherto Commander of the Ninth American Air Force). Lieutenant-General Frederick A. M. Browning (hitherto Commander-in-Chief "Army Air Corps") has been appointed his deputy.'[4] The Germans naturally wanted to know what it was all about and immediately circulated their principal agents. On 15th August BRUTUS was asked: 'What do you know about the new command under Brereton and Browning? Which divisions belong to it? Are airborne operations now planned on a big scale?'[5] And to GARBO on the following day: 'According to news given by Daventry on 11th August, there has been created in England an Allied Airborne Army, Commander-in-Chief, Brereton, Deputy Commander Browning. We would like to know details about this army such as organisation, composition, disposition and tasks. . . . Has this army been created for a special important operation or is its appearance only the result of an organisation measure which has been diffused for reasons of propaganda?'[6]

For some time the Germans had been preoccupied with the idea that the Allies might be increasing the striking power of their airborne forces. Early in April when TRICYCLE went for his last interview in Lisbon he had been asked: 'Which English divisions are being formed into airborne divisions? Divisional numbers and localities.'[7] BRUTUS, being an airman himself, had taken several opportunities during the summer of playing on these fears. He suggested that airborne transport was becoming almost a normal form of conveyance in the American Army. 'A great part of the American troops carry out exercises in "Airborne" as a normal part of their training. So far as I can understand, regiments of glider pilots have

4. OKH Situation Report, dated 10th August, 1944.
5. BRUTUS Message received 1713 GMT, 15th August, 1944.
6. GARBO Message received 2111 and 2119 GMT, 16th August, 1944.
7. Questionnaire given to TRICYCLE in Lisbon at the beginning of April 1944.

been attached to the higher formations in order to render the divisions more mobile. These regiments are to play the same part towards the Americans as the transport companies play in the British Army.'[8] He also spoke of British gliders which were capable of carrying tanks, artillery and other weapons of war.[9] All this made a good foundation for the new airborne assault force. On 21st August BRUTUS said: 'With regard to General Brereton: a new force has been formed composed of all airborne divisions, of whom the Chief is General Brereton and his Second in Command General Browning. As reported, the Allies attach great importance to airborne operations in the future in the hope of bringing them under a joint command. In addition certain infantry divisions have undergone airborne training and can also be included in this type of operation.'[10] This found its reflection in the Intelligence Summary of 26th August. 'A further report from a particularly trusted source about the retention of the Allied Airborne Army for a big operational task deserves special notice. Concrete indications of the target are not available.'[11]

In order to give effect to the proposals outlined above it was decided to reorganise the deceptive forces in the following manner. The Ninth and Fourteenth Armies were to be detached from FUSAG and placed directly under SHAEF as a strategic reserve, the latter army moving forthwith from the Eastern counties to embarkation camps in the Southampton area. FUSAG would retain the Fourth British Army and would take command of the First Allied Airborne Army. The ground forces which it now controlled would concentrate north of the Thames where they would be more centrally placed for the amphibious operation.

3103 Signals Service Battalion, being now required overseas,[12] the Fourteenth Army went off the air on the 17th August, and from that day onwards information regarding its activities was made available

---

8. BRUTUS 1407 and 1412 GMT, 18th June, 1944.
9. BRUTUS 1252 GMT, 13th August, 1944.
10. BRUTUS 1714 and 1718 GMT, 21st August, 1944.
11. Appendix to Lagebericht West No. 1369, dated 26th August, 1944.
12. Three sections were left behind for a short time to represent the FUSAG Headquarters' links.

to the enemy through the reports of the controlled agents only. The move from East Anglia to the south coast was initiated by BRUTUS on 20th August. 'On returning to Wentworth I learned that there is great activity in the affairs of the Fourteenth American Army, as though it were a question of changing its location.'[13] Thereafter each division was seen off in the Eastern counties by agent 7 (7) and received on the south coast by agent 7 (4), the latter being assisted by BRUTUS, who visited Hampshire at the beginning of September. TATE, who lived at Radlett, was lucky enough to see several of the convoys travelling between Hatfield and Watford, while agent Three himself heard on 28th August that the Blackwall Tunnel under the Thames had been closed for three days for the passage of American troops. These were to be the Fourteenth Army's new locations:[14]

Fourteenth US Army:	Fareham.
XXXIII Corps:	Romsey.
17th US Infantry Division:	Brighton–Burgess Hill.
59th US Infantry Division:	Rolands Castle.
XXXVII Corps:	Worthing.
11th US Infantry Division:	Winchester.
48th US Infantry Division:	Brockenhurst.
25th US Armoured Division:	Tidworth.

All the moves were to be completed by 31st August.

On 31st August the German Intelligence Summary recorded: 'Parts of the Fourteenth American Army (XXXIII Army Corps) have, according to several reports, been transferred from their existing area, Ipswich–Cambridge, to the South. The 11th, 17th and 59th Infantry Divisions were reported in this connection. The 17th Infantry Division is said to have been moved to the Brighton area.'[15] By 12th

---

13. BRUTUS 1443 GMT, 20th August, 1944.
14. Special Means Interim Plan for the Movement of Fourteenth Army from East Anglia to the South Coast, dated 18th August, 1944.
15. Lagebericht West No. 1374, dated 31st August, 1944, a reflection of BRUTUS 1443 GMT, 20th August, GARBO 1950 GMT, 23rd August, and 2032 and 2040 GMT, 26th August, TATE 0603, 1818 and 0605 MET, 27th August, and GARBO 2034 and 2106 GMT, 28th August, 1944.

September they had become fully acquainted with the new situation. 'According to a report from a particularly trustworthy source the American Fourteenth Army with XXXIII and XXXVII Army Corps has been transferred from South-Eastern England to the south coast. According to this report the Headquarters of the Fourteenth Army is at Fareham (north-west of Portsmouth) while the American XXXIII Corps is in the Winchester area and the American XXXVII Corps with under command the 17th and 59th American Infantry Divisions is reported in the Worthing area. The transfer of the 11th and 48th American Infantry Divisions from the Cambridge area to the neighbourhood of Southampton is also reported by a good source.'[16] That the implications which lay behind the move were sufficiently well understood is shown by the following extract from the OKH Situation Report of 10th September. 'According to a message from a particularly trustworthy Abwehr source a large-scale concentration of American troops (some five infantry divisions and one armoured division partly from the East of England) seems to be taking place under XXXIII American Army Corps in the Southampton area. Simultaneously the Fourteenth American Army is said to have been transferred to this embarkation area. A move to France is probable and corresponds with the expectations which we have already expressed. This would mean the withdrawal of all American military formations from the South-East and South of England.'[17]

Even if we had wanted to do so it would have been impossible at this time to move the whole of the Fourth Army out of Kent so long as we wished to maintain its wireless traffic. The 55th, 61st, and 80th Infantry Divisions were obliged to remain. The two former were real training divisions and supplied their own links in the fictitious network. The 80th Division, an imaginary one, was represented on the air by signallers belonging to the 61st Infantry Division, who had to remain within a reasonable distance of their parent formation. In

---

16. Lagebericht West No. 1386, dated 12th September, 1944, a reflection of BRUTUS 2016, 2024, 2028 and 2032 GMT, 6th September, and 1715 and 1721 GMT, 7th September, 1944, and GARBO 2035, 2044 and 2052 GMT, 6th September, 1944.
17. OKH Situation Report West, dated 10th September, 1944.

these circumstances there was no object in moving 2nd British
Corps, which commanded the 55th and 61st Infantry Divisions.
Consequently it was only the Fourth Army Headquarters, 7th Corps
and the 58th Infantry Division which crossed the Thames. The 5th
British Armoured Division remained at Newmarket where it had
been all the time.[18] In order to bring the grouping of these formations into line with the new geographical dispositions, 7th Corps
now took all the divisions north of the Thames and 2nd Corps those
to the south. The 61st and 80th British Infantry Divisions thus went
from 7th Corps to 2nd Corps, while the 58th British Infantry
Division went from 2nd to 7th Corps.[19]

As the British formations of Fourth Army would be using many of
the billets that had previously been occupied by formations of the
American Fourteenth Army they could not begin their move to the
North until the Americans had left. The first news came from
GARBO on 9th September. '7 (7): Have not seen following US
units in this area since beginning of month: Fourteenth US Army,
XXXVII US Corps, 11th US Infantry Division, XXXIII US Corps.
Apart from some odd units, all US troops have left the area.
Innkeepers at Ipswich and Colchester have received orders from bil-
leting officers to continue to reserve accommodation previously
commandeered for arrival of further troops. Saw several staff cars in
Harwich and Ipswich with the sign of the Fourth British Army but
no troops or lorries seen. When in Colchester a week ago discovered

---

18. On 26th August, BRUTUS was asked: 'Of which brigades is the 5th British
    Armoured Division composed? Why is it at Newmarket if the corresponding
    corps is at Folkestone?' (Message received 1408 GMT). On 30th August,
    BRUTUS replied: 'With regard to the 5th British Armoured Division, it is sta-
    tioned in the area of Newmarket as this area is suitable for tank training units.
    It is considered normal to detach an armoured division from its corps in order
    to obtain good training conditions. . . . Composition: 37th Armoured Brigade
    and 43rd Infantry Brigade. According to one of my comrades the 37th Brigade
    took part in exercises with 7th Corps in Kent a few days ago.' (1711 and 1717
    GMT.) At the same time GARBO's sub-agent 7 (4) observed large armoured
    vehicles with the sign of the blue lobster, i.e. that of the 5th Armoured
    Division, south of Ashford. (2025 GMT, 26th August, 1944.)
19. SHAEF/24183/3/SM/Ops, dated 11th September, 1944. Special Means Plan
    for Move of part of Fourth Army from Kent to Essex. See Appendix X.

that all US troops had left. Large numbers of staff cars with the sign of Fourth British Army and 58th British Division seen outside Cups Hotel.'[20] On the next day TATE saw a convoy of the 7th Corps moving through London in a northerly direction.[21] Before 14th September 7 (4) had told GARBO that the 7th Corps had left Folkestone and the 58th Division Gravesend.[22] Subsequent messages from agents 7 (2) and 7 (7) located Fourth Army at Hatfield Peverel, the 58th Division at Colchester and 7th British Corps as being in the immediate neighbourhood. The German Intelligence Summary for 17th September contains the following paragraph: 'According to messages from a particularly trustworthy source, following on the withdrawal of the American divisions hitherto in the area north-east of London (County of Essex) parts of the Fourth English Army (hitherto 7th English Army Corps and 58th Infantry Division confirmed) have been moved into the area vacated. As part of this regrouping, the Headquarters of the Fourth English Army has moved to Colchester (north-east of London). It is probable that further divisions not yet named will follow this army.'[23] The Germans did not know about the wireless difficulty which prevented the 55th, 61st and 80th British Infantry Divisions from moving with the rest.

By 8th September the regrouping was accomplished. The Ninth and Fourteenth US Armies, the latter no longer represented by wireless, now formed the SHAEF strategic reserve and were about to embark for France. FUSAG, consisting of Fourth Army and the First Allied Airborne Army, were preparing for the great amphibious assault across the North Sea. FORTITUDE was ended. The new story is given in the directive of that date. 'After the Allied victories in Normandy and Brittany, General Eisenhower decided to make his main thrusts into Germany from that area. Subsequent exploitation of the successful Seine battle has made possible a rapid advance to the heart of Germany. In order to assist this advance and to prevent the escape of remnants of the German armies, Eisenhower has decided to retain a large airborne and amphibious striking force and a highly

---

20. GARBO 2032, 2048 and 2101 GMT, 9th September, 1944.
21. TATE 0604 MET, 10th September, 1944.
22. GARBO 1910 and 1916 GMT, 14th September, 1944.
23. Appendix to Lagebericht West No. 1391, dated 17th September, 1944.

trained strategic reserve in the United Kingdom. The tasks of this force will be to reinforce the Allied armies in France as the situation may demand, to carry out large-scale airborne operations anywhere on the enemy's lines of communication, to open new lines of communication from the United Kingdom against limited opposition and to occupy areas in the event of German withdrawal.'[24] This story had been made available to the Special Means Staff before the end of the month of August and the controlled agents had been taking steps to bring it to the enemy's notice for some time before FORTITUDE officially ended. The position was comprehensively summarised in a message sent by GARBO on the 31st August. At that time the race through Northern France had attained its full momentum. Montgomery had crossed the Belgian frontier and was heading north-west. Patton had reached the outskirts of Metz. Already the lines of supply had become abnormally stretched. In view of this GARBO's case officer asked which was to be the main thrust, for now would be the moment to bring the full weight of Special Means in support of the feint and thus draw German forces away from the true line of advance. Although it was not possible to give an answer to that question, there could be no objection to preparing the ground. On 31st August agent Three addressed the Germans in these terms. 'Important! The following obtained at meeting between myself, GARBO and 4 (3) yesterday, in reply to your questionnaire about airborne army and also explains the move of the Fourteenth US Army from the east coast. 4 (3): He says that the original FUSAG plan for attacking Pas de Calais has been definitely cancelled and the FUSAG forces are again being reorganised in the following way: The Fourteenth US Army and the Ninth US Army are now under the direct command of SHAEF, as SHAEF strategic reserve. This force will be at the disposal of SHAEF for Eisenhower to be able to reinforce the Allied armies in France if they want assistance in the advance which is now about to be driven to prevent the German Army from escaping to Germany. The Fourteenth US Army is being replaced in FUSAG by the new airborne army which has now been given the name of the First Allied Airborne Army. With

---

24. SHAEF/19011/Ops (B) (Fwd). GCT/370.28–202/Ops (B), dated 8th September, 1944. Current Cover and Deception Policy. See Appendix IX.

this rearrangement a great part of FUSAG is now composed of airborne troops and will be used for special operations, in fact FUSAG will become a sort of modern version of Combined Operations. For instance they will carry out large-scale airborne operations anywhere in France, Belgium, Holland or Germany to attack the enemy lines of communication. They will also be used to occupy any areas or countries which the Germans give up unexpectedly and this will avoid the necessity of having to make sudden dispersals of forces in the battle at the expense of carrying out their original plans. Following just arrived, urgently, from GARBO. This morning I happened to be present at an interview between J (3) and a war press correspondent of SHAEF, at M of I. He told us, in confidence, that a large attack in France is imminent. He was recently at advanced HQ of SHAEF in France where he learnt about the following discussions. 21 Army Group demands that Patton's advance should stop. They want him to make a feint attack towards the East, keeping back the weight of his forces to turn north to attack the German flank whilst the 21 Army Group, reinforced by FUSAG, makes a definite attack against the Pas de Calais, to occupy that zone. On the other hand Patton requests that all reinforcements and supplies are put at his disposal to attack into the centre of Germany, asking, at the same time, that the British Armies should make a deceptive attack against the Pas de Calais to maintain all the German forces there, leaving Patton's troops with freedom of action. The correspondent said that it would, therefore, be absurd to speculate without knowing what personal decision Eisenhower will eventually take as to which of the two attacks is the feint attack and which is the one destined to make the advance.'[25] On 2nd September the German Intelligence Summary contained the following appreciation. 'According to a report from a hitherto particularly trustworthy source the Ninth and Fourteenth American Armies have been parted from FUSAG and have come under the direct command of Eisenhower. (The strength of these two armies in Great Britain is at present to be taken as some eight infantry and two armoured divisions.) The object of this measure is said to be the creation of a large strategic reserve for Eisenhower in order to give him the opportunity of exploiting his successes in

25. GARBO 2046 to 2150 GMT, 31st August, 1944.

France by deploying new armies. The withdrawal of American formations from the South-East of England which was already reported in the "Short Appreciation for the West" of 31st August is thus confirmed. We must therefore reckon with a considerable influx of forces into France and the setting up of new higher formation staffs, and in this connection we must count on the *immediate* shipment of further formations from the United States to complete the Ninth and Fourteenth Armies. FUSAG, which is still held ready in England, is thus composed after reorganisation of the strong Fourth English Army (some twenty divisions) and the First Allied Airborne Army (six airborne divisions). This source suggests widespread use of this airborne army against rear lines of communication, while it does not express an opinion on the probable employment or the significance of the Fourteenth (?Fourth) English Army. The double change in the direction of the American Army Group which has been observed since the thrust forward from the area south of Paris particularly on the part of the Third American Army is attributed by the agent mentioned above to differences of opinion in the command. Montgomery is said to have demanded only a *deceptive* attack towards the East by the Third American Amy so as to enable him to envelop the German flank from the South with the *mass* of the American formations, while Patton wanted to press forward directly towards Germany and demanded for this purpose all available reinforcements of the whole of the supply arrangements for himself. It is not yet clear in which direction the *decisive* effort will finally be made since particularly the employment of the mass of the First American Army is at present not clear. But it must be assumed that with the further successes of the Americans in an easterly direction Patton's view has carried the day.'[26] This appreciation probably marks the zenith of GARBO's influence on the German High Command. At this moment, however, Allied policy did not require that his powers should be put to the test. On 12th September, nearly a fortnight after GARBO's message had gone, 21 Army Group submitted to SHAEF a cover plan with the object of making the enemy reinforce the Metz and Nancy fronts at the expense of the Northern front. The following story was proposed. '21 Army Group and the

---

26. Appendix to Lagebericht West No. 1376, dated 2nd September, 1944.

First US Army of Twelfth Army Group, having advanced as far as the Dutch and German frontiers, have now outrun their supplies. The failure of the Allies to capture Brest, Le Havre, as well as Calais and Boulogne, has caused an administrative crisis in the two army groups. General Eisenhower has, therefore, decided to hold with the Second British Army and First US Army whilst the Canadian Army deals with the ports of Le Havre, Boulogne and Calais, and to concentrate his administrative resources in order to enable the reinforced army under command General Patton to drive through the Metz–Nancy gap towards Saarbrucken. It is estimated that Second British Army and First US Army are likely to remain inactive until the first week of October.'[27] On 15th September the Twelfth Army Group notified SHAEF that the suggested plan was acceptable. On 16th September SHAEF informed 21 Army Group that it was not considered desirable to put into effect the proposed cover plan because the date of Arnhem had been advanced since this proposal had been submitted and because Third Army's operations around Nancy and Metz were producing actual threats in place of the proposed notional threats.[28]

The termination of FORTITUDE made it possible to release most of the troops and technical resources which had hitherto been employed on strategic deception in the United Kingdom. 5 Wireless Group had already joined 21 Army Group on the Continent. Units of 3103 Signals Service Battalion were now on their way. Only 12th Reserve Unit remained. Owing to the withdrawal of the German forces in Western Europe, it was now considered most unlikely that they would be able clearly to pick up low-powered wireless traffic. 12th Reserve Unit therefore issued a new signals programme which provided that there should be no further exercises, that the static wireless links of Fourth Army should be maintained down to and including divisional and independent brigade headquarters and that there should be no further restriction on the use of wireless in the signals training of the 55th and 61st Divisions.[29]

---

27. Appendix A to 21 AGP/00/272/2/G (R), dated 12th September, 1944.
28. Fwd 15007, dated 16th September, 1944. SHAEF Fwd to 21 Army Group.
29. G (O)/1523, dated 17th September, 1944. Fourth Army Directive No. 5.

Of the three naval wireless deception units, Force 'F' at Harwich and Sheerness was to close down on 5th September and Forces 'M' and 'N', located respectively at Gosport and Studland, on the 7th. The last two were to reappear for a few days in the Humber and Firth of Forth. This would help to emphasise the fact that the old FOR-TITUDE assault force had been dispersed and would place them conveniently should they be required to take part in the new operation. The dummy landing craft had been manned throughout the period of their display by two infantry battalions, the 4th Northants and the 10th Worcester. Dismantling of these craft was begun on 25th August and completed by the end of September. The 4th Northants were released on 21st August and the 10th Worcester on 15th September, the work of dismantling being taken over by the 24th Armoured Brigade, a formation specially trained in camouflage which had recently returned from the Middle East. After 25th August the use of other forms of camouflage such as dummy camps and signposts was discontinued. The remaining security regulations which had been imposed to help FORTITUDE were also removed.

XXXII

Arnhem

It has already been explained how Dr Kraemer, the German journalist who ran the twin agents JOSEPHINE and HECTOR in
Stockholm, had access to the German intelligence reports, which
were now so largely based on information supplied by British-controlled agents, and how he used them when making up their traffic.
It does not matter very much whether Kraemer himself believed in
FORTITUDE. The point is that he knew the Germans believed in
it and that it was therefore safe to dish it up a second time. It will be
remembered that before D Day we avoided, as far as we could,
making any very concrete prophecies regarding the invasion, prefer-
ring to confine ourselves to building up the false army group.
Consequently the uncontrolled agents held the stage at that time.
Between 1st January and 6th June, 1944, Krummacher's two files
contain sixty-five messages from JOSEPHINE, twelve from OSTRO
and only one each from GARBO and BRUTUS. All through May
GARBO's and BRUTUS's detailed reports were filling the OKH
Intelligence Summaries, but neither Krummacher nor the RSHA
found such minutiæ appropriate for inclusion in a body of documents which was evidently compiled for Hitler and his immediate
advisers. Strategic intentions and matters of high policy were what
they required and before 6th June only the uncontrolled agents could
provide such things. In the month immediately following D Day the
position changed. Now GARBO and BRUTUS had entered the
field of high strategy. During this short period Krummacher's two
files are found to contain twenty-five messages from JOSEPHINE,
ten from GARBO and nine each from OSTRO and BRUTUS. But

whereas JOSEPHINE's and OSTRO's messages had hitherto been vague and contradictory, GARBO's and BRUTUS's were precise and consistent. They would therefore have had no difficulty in having their views accepted in preference to those of the uncontrolled agents had the latter continued to report as erratically as they had done during the first six months of the year. But now they had FORTI-TUDE to guide them and JOSEPHINE, at any rate, far from contradicting our story, was confirming it in ever-increasing measure. His notable message of 9th June foretelling a second assault was presumably no more than a reasonable deduction from the reports of troop concentrations in South-East England which we had given to the Germans during May and the first week of June. On 19th June he gave Patton as the Commander of FUSAG. By the beginning of August he seems to have acquired a thorough grasp of the plot. 'FUSAG was originally to have been used for a second large-scale landing operation. As the timing of the Normandy invasion went completely wrong, it was decided not to undertake this second landing, which had been planned for the end of June; and formations from FUSAG were steadily transferred to France.'[1]

Like ourselves Dr Kraemer saw that something would have to be done with FUSAG after the Fifteenth Army had left the Pas de Calais. He also saw the likelihood of the Allies carrying out an amphibious attack on the German right flank. Or was it the threat of such an attack that he foresaw? Accordingly he made FUSAG move, but he made it move rather too far. 'Increased troop transports from South and Central England to Northern England are being associated with movements of parts of FUSAG. Operations in North and Central Norway, starting from England, are not expected, but landings in Jutland and Southern Norway.'[2] When Dr Kraemer sent that message our Fourth Army had not started to move. We have no record of the German answer, but they appear to

---

1. German Security HO Mil. (RSHA Mil.) B/L 11102/8 of 8th August, 1944, quoted in Luftwaffe Fuehrungsstab Ic Fremde Luftwaffen West No. 109/45 g. Kdos (A), dated 6th January, 1945. Assessment of Reports from Confidential Agents.
2. German Security HO Mil. B/L 13869 of 29th August, 1944, quoted in above-mentioned document.

have found it necessary to make some further enquiry which slightly shook the doctor. 'I was expecting your further enquiry, as my own suspicions had also been aroused at once. All sources however confirm that FUSAG formations have been stationed as far as the Humber. In addition there are individual reports about troop transports to Northern England/Scotland. . . . It is quite clear that either a large-scale decoy manœuvre is planned, to cover the employment of FUSAG in Belgium, Holland and the Heligoland Bight, or that an operation against Denmark is actually intended.'[3] The German Intelligence Summary of 9th September, having alluded to the withdrawal of Fourteenth US Army to the south coast, goes on to say: 'There are at present no reports of transfers or movements of *British formations* so there is no concrete evidence provided by the distribution of forces in England to support the reports which have been accumulating about imminent landings in Jutland or the German Bight. It must, however, be emphasised that such reports can, in general, only be checked by detailed air reconnaissance of the relevant invasion ports.'[4] The first British-controlled report of the move of British formations was not made until after this passage had been written.[5] So it looks as if Dr Kraemer's story had not been accepted even though he had modified it in his second message by suggesting that the FUSAG formations had not gone further than the Humber and by hedging his bet on Jutland and Southern Norway with the suggestion that the whole business might be deception.

We had no idea at the time that Kraemer was playing with our toys. Having built up the whole of FUSAG from nothing we naturally supposed that we had the undivided control of it, and on this assumption a plan was devised for the future employment of Fourth Army and the First Allied Airborne Army. About this time the airborne operation against Arnhem was decided upon. The Deception Staff were asked to cover that operation by suggesting an airborne drop on the same date but in a far removed area. If in the process we

---

3. German Security HO (RSHA)/10031 of 1st September, 1944, quoted in Luftwaffe Fuehrungsstab Ic Fremde Luftwaffen West No. 109/45 g. Kdos (A), dated 6th January, 1945. Assessment of Reports from Confidential Agents.
4. Appendix to Lagebericht West No. 1383, dated 9th September, 1944.
5. GARBO 2032, 2048 and 2101 GMT, 9th September, 1944.

could increase the threat to the German northern flank which the policy directive of 8th September required, a double advantage would be gained. In his original message about the First Allied Airborne Army sent on 21st and 22nd August, BRUTUS had suggested that airborne divisions would be taken from the Airborne Army and 'attached to armies or groups of armies for particular tasks, as for example in our Order of Battle there are three airborne divisions, notably the 9th and 21st American and 2nd British'.[6] On 10th September BRUTUS reported: 'The Allied Airborne Army is now under FUSAG. Confirm that airborne divisions can be detached and that a task force consisting of four airborne divisions[7] has already been posted to take part in the operation in conjunction with the Fourth Army. . . . From these changes one can suppose that the FUSAG operations will be preceded by an airborne attack which can be carried out even at long range. An attack against the North of Germany in the region of Bremen or Kiel is not excluded.'[8] We now have Fourth Army operating with a task force comprising four imaginary airborne divisions. The next move in the game was to induce a belief in the existence of a second task force. Once the Germans were told that there were two airborne task forces, one could assume that they would draw the conclusion that the second force consisted of the real airborne divisions in England about which they already knew. We were already required to say that a large airborne attack was impending elsewhere; all that BRUTUS now, therefore, had to do was to report that Kiel was about to be attacked by the fictitious task force. (Let us call this Task Force 'A'.) This provided a cover for the real attack. After the real assault had been made BRUTUS would merely have to point out that the assault on Arnhem by the real task force (Task Force 'B') had taken place before the attack on Kiel with Task Force 'A'. He had supposed that the operations would have been carried out in the reverse order. But he had at least given the date of the first operation correctly. Seeing that

6. BRUTUS 1725 GMT, 21st August, 1944.
7. He had added the real and newly arrived 17th American Airborne Division to the 9th and 21st American and 2nd British Airborne Divisions in a message sent on 1st September, 1944.
8. BRUTUS 1714 and 1724 GMT, 10th September, 1944.

the formations comprised in the real Task Force 'B' would be identified in battle at Arnhem, and would coincide with BRUTUS's
previous descriptions of the First Allied Airborne Army, the Germans
would, after the assault, be likely to have their belief strengthened not
only in the existence of the false Task Force 'A', but also in our intention to carry out a subsequent attack on the more remote objective.
In pursuance of this plan BRUTUS on 14th September, three days
before the Arnhem assault, sent the following message: 'I have just
learnt that there has recently been great activity at the headquarters
of the Allied Airborne Army and that they have even formed a
second task force. In view of the general situation, there is talk in our
headquarters that in three or four days one should expect an airborne
attack against Denmark, Kiel Canal or against ports in Northern
Germany. This appears to confirm my own opinion, already transmitted several days ago, especially when I learned of the move of the
Fourth Army into the Essex–Kent region. In my opinion the attack
can be undertaken by the special task force which I have already
reported as being attached to the Fourth Army.'[9] And on 20th
September, three days after the Arnhem landing: 'Regarding the airborne attacks: I have learnt that it is a question of the 1st British
Airborne Corps and the XVIII American Airborne Corps and not the
task force as supposed by me. As far as I know, this task force is still
ready for the operation with the Fourth Army. It includes the 9th,
17th and 21st American Airborne Divisions and the 2nd British
Airborne Division.'[10]

Before examining the German reactions to BRUTUS's plot, let us
see how Dr Kraemer was taking it. BRUTUS's message of 10th
September had told the Germans that an attack might be expected
against the North of Germany in the region of Bremen or Kiel. Dr
Kraemer had given Jutland and Southern Norway. It seems fairly
clear that he must have seen BRUTUS's message of the 10th and felt
a desire to fall into line, for on the 15th he told the Germans:
'FUSAG continues in Eastern England as far as the Humber.
Formations in Northern England and Scotland do not belong to
FUSAG.' And a little later: 'Air Vice-Marshal Trafford stated in

9. BRUTUS 1835, 1840 and 1846 GMT, 14th September, 1944.
10. BRUTUS 2122 and 2144 GMT, 20th September, 1944.

London on 11th and 12th September to a reliable informant that
FUSAG is not to be employed in Jutland, Southern Norway, but that
it is to be used in connection with operations of the Second English,
First American and First Canadian Armies. The Second English
Army will be advanced on a broad front as far as the Meuse and if
possible even as far as the Waal by 24th September. After that the
employment of powerful airborne forces in Eastern and Northern
Holland and the German frontier region is planned. Immediately on
completion of the air-landing action, which is intended to eliminate
German river positions in the rear, it is intended to use FUSAG in
Eastern Holland and the Heligoland Bight.' Finally, in order to
explain away his previous references to Norway and Denmark: 'In
the entourage of the exiled Norwegian and Danish Governments
information is being deliberately given out to the effect that a
FUSAG operation is projected in the North; moreover, in Denmark
and Norway these reports are also being given by the said
Governments to their own resistance movements.'[11] Dr Kraemer's
new operation was more detailed than anything we had offered and
his airborne drop was now unpleasantly near to Arnhem, but his
main FUSAG objective of Eastern Holland and the Heligoland Bight
might be said to approximately to BRUTUS's Kiel–Bremen target.

The first German reports on Arnhem suggested that British divisions only were being employed. 'An airborne landing which began
at mid-day on 17th September in the area of the Dutch Lower Rhine
comprises, according to reports so far available, some two to three
presumably British airborne divisions. All available English airborne
divisions from England are believed to have been engaged. . . . If the
assumption is confirmed that all the airborne formations employed
were *English* then the enemy command still has some four American
airborne divisions at its disposal and their employment may well be
expected in the sector of the American army group. Nevertheless, the
employment of the First Allied Airborne Army as a whole in the present landing area is not to be excluded. Concrete evidence for this is
not available.'[12] For some reason JOSEPHINE's message of the 15th

---

11. Quoted in Enclosure 3 to Luftwaffe Fuehrungsstab Ic No. 109/45 g. Kdos,
    dated 6th January, 1945.
12. Appendix to Lagebericht West No. 1391, dated 17th September, 1944.

had not reached Berlin until the early afternoon of the 17th.[13] The Intelligence Summary of the 17th continues: 'In connection with the air landings which have taken place, particular attention is deserved for an agent's report which has only just come in and which predicted these air landings correctly. In this report we are told that immediately after the air landing a landing operation by Fourth English Army (some fifteen divisions) would take place against Holland and the German Bight. The agent mentioned above considers that reports emanating particularly from diplomatic circles about landing intentions against Norway and Denmark are deliberate camouflage. Although the latest photographic reconnaissances of the Southern England ports showed no landing ships, we must reckon on their arrival at short notice in the presumed invasion ports of the Fourth English Army. Continuous watch from the air is required.' By the next day the correct Order of Battle had been established: 'The confirmation of the forces engaged, namely so far about three airborne divisions, shows that they are composed of two battle-tried American airborne divisions (82nd and 101st) and the 1st English Airborne Division in action for the first time, to which the Polish and Dutch parachute units, which are also engaged according to the English wireless, may belong. . . . The fact that the only two battle-tried American airborne divisions were dropped in front of the *English* sector makes it seem improbable that a *second large-scale* airborne operation is planned for the American sector. Rather we must deduce that the main effort of the whole operation lies in the sector of the Second English Army. According to our present picture of the battle, the main objective of the airborne operation is the capture of the crossings along the Eindhoven–Arnhem line in order to facilitate a quick thrust by the main forces of the Second English Army through Holland to form a bridgehead at Arnhem. This confirms the intention already suspected to cut off the German forces in Holland and at the same time to win a base from which to continue the operation east of the Rhine.'[14]

---

13. This delay resulted in a certain amount of enquiry and recrimination. It is not clear whether it was caused by a failure of communications or whether Dr Kraemer was merely playing the well-known trick of backing the winner after the race was over.

14. Appendix to Lagebericht West No. 1392, dated 18th September, 1944.

BRUTUS's message of 14th September seems to have suffered a similar delay; at any rate it was not until the 19th, two days after the landing, that any reference was made to it in the Intelligence Summary. 'The possibility of a *new landing operation* in conjunction with planned airborne operations is suggested by a further report from a very trustworthy agent, according to whom the present airborne operations should be coupled with future plans for Fourth English Army; the agent mentions in this connection the already reported moves of formations of the Fourth English Army to the Essex–Kent area. There is still no sure evidence[15] of such plans.[16] There is little reason to suppose that BRUTUS's message helped to divert the attention of the Germans from Arnhem, but that we emerged with the belief in our imaginary task force and in the impending attack on the German Bight enhanced, is shown by an appreciation of 23rd September. 'From various reports by prudent agents, the following picture of the present airborne operations and of future plans emerges; it is shown that three airborne corps were included in the First Allied Airborne Army; the 1st English Airborne Corps and the XVIII American Airborne Corps so far engaged comprise the 1st English, 82nd and 101st American Airborne Divisions, one Polish parachute brigade as well as possibly the 17th American Airborne Division, and here it is not yet finally clear whether the last-named is the 17th American Infantry Division (Airborne) though there are some indications of this. The allotment of further formations and smaller airborne army units is probable. To the airborne corps still in Great Britain belong presumably the 2nd English, 21st, 9th and 11th American Airborne Divisions and possibly the 59th American Infantry Division equipped for transport by air. The last-named having repeatedly been mentioned in this connection should also appear as an "assault division". This corps is said to be destined for employment as part of *landing operations by Fourth English Army* which are predicted against the German Bight in the sector Wiesemunde–Emden. The reports mentioned above make a convincing impression and have been partially confirmed by the course of operations and by troop identifications in recent days. . . . On the

---

15. 'Sure source' (*sichere quelle*) meant wireless intercept.
16. Appendix to Lagebericht West No. 1393, dated 19th September, 1944.

basis of the above reports, therefore, *new landings, coupled with strong airborne landings must be expected in the area of the German Bight.* We have so far no information as to the date of such undertakings. It must, however, be assumed that these intentions will only be capable of execution when a bridgehead has been successfully created at Arnhem and further operations from this bridgehead seem to the enemy command to be assured of success. The seasonal weather conditions in the Channel which are deteriorating will, however, set a time limit to these plans and will, therefore, tend to advance them.'[17]

It was important for the enemy to know what was happening in the east coast ports. On 29th September GARBO received these instructions: 'Please send somebody to the principal ports of the east and north-east coast as soon as possible under the present circumstances in order to investigate movements and troops in these ports; also it would be interesting if you could get news about destination of forthcoming operations of British Fourth Army.'[18] On the 30th TATE was asked: 'What are the anchorages or bases of aircraft-carriers or auxiliary aircraft-carriers on the east coast of Great Britain between Thames and Scapa? Can you find out if and where on the English and Scottish east coast, invasion preparations are taking place? Are invasion materials being assembled?'[19] On 3rd October BRUTUS also was asked to report on the ports of the east coast of England.[20]

---

17. Appendix to Lagebericht West No. 1397, dated 23rd September, 1944.
18. GARBO Message received 1910 GMT, 29th September, 1944.
19. TATE Message received 1911 and 1917 MET, 30th September, 1944 Another typical question for the farm-hand.
20. BRUTUS Message received 2144 GMT, 3rd October, 1944.

XXXIII

The Control of Deception Overseas

Before the invasion began much effort was expended in trying to visualise what the position would be when we had armies fighting in France. Two things were regarded as fairly certain; first, that we should capture a number of German 'stay-behind' agents in the country that was overrun and that some of these would be turned round and used for strategic deception;[1] second, that deception in

---

1. At this time we meant to send BRUTUS to France so as to have one really good agent on each side of the Channel. On 11th June, he asked the Germans to hide a transmitting set for him in France, which, he explained, he would be able to pick up when he went abroad. 'I can suppose that FUSAG may leave at any moment and I can lose radio contact with you. (2130 GMT). After three weeks the Germans answered: 'We thank you for the suggestion about installing concealed apparatus in France. Help us to realise this project by giving us as soon as possible date and place of future landing.' (Message received 1607 GMT, 2nd July, 1944). This placed us in a dilemma. If we suggested somewhere in the neighbourhood of the cover objective we would not get the wireless set. If, on the other hand, we told them to leave it where we knew we were going, it would spoil the cover story. As it seemed clearly more important to substantiate FORTITUDE, BRUTUS replied on 6th July: 'With regard to radio transmitters: I suppose that Arras, Lille and Ghent would be good places because it seems certain that FUSAG will attack east of the region at present occupied by 21 Army Group' (2025 GMT). Nothing happened until 6th October, when all idea of sending BRUTUS abroad had long since been abandoned and he had given up his appointment at FUSAG. 'The apparatus with 50,000 francs is buried between Claye and Meaux, on the north side of the National Highway No. 3, between Paris and Meaux, on the edge of the ditch, one metre below the grass. From the kilometre sign: Meaux

support of current operations would continue to be a function of SHAEF. This would require little less than a duplication of the Deception Staff. Cover plans might well have to be executed simultaneously in London and at Supreme Headquarters in France, while provision would certainly have to be made for controlling agents on both sides of the Channel. With this in view a new war establishment for the Sub-Section was approved in June.[2] In the event neither of the expectations which called this establishment into being were ever fulfilled. Nevertheless, when the Deception Staff went overseas in September 1944,[3] it was reorganised in such a way that the rear headquarters in London and the main headquarters in France were both practically self-supporting.

Before the invasion Most Secret Sources and other intelligence channels had made it clear that the Germans were setting up an elaborate network of 'stay-behind' gents in Belgium and France. In many instances their names and addresses, as well as the tasks which they were expected to fulfil, were already known to us. It was therefore necessary to build up a reserve of case officers who could take charge of these agents when they fell into our hands. For that purpose, three Security Counter-Intelligence Units, known as SCI Units, were formed. 104 SCI Unit was attached to 21 Army Group, 106 SCI Unit was to remain with SHAEF and would provide a pool of British case officers which could be drawn on when required,[4] while the American 'SCI Unit France' was to supply officers for all United States' needs, including those of the Sixth

---

12 Km. 4, Claye 2 Km. 3, respectively, you must walk straight ahead five metres in the ditch' (Message received 1808 GMT, 6th October, and 1804 GMT, 9th October, 1944). When this message was received, the American SCI Unit in Paris was anxious to provide one of the newly captured controlled agents, who happened to be in the vicinity of Meaux, with a transmitting set, but could not touch it until authorised to do so by the Germans. Eventually, when they became resigned to the fact that BRUTUS was not going abroad, they did what we hoped they would and told the new agent where it was. It was then possible to dig it up and put it into use.

2. Amendment No. 13 to WE VIII/457/5 w.e.f., 9th June, 1944.
3. An advance party had already gone overseas in August.
4. The officers of this section were mainly occupied in controlling agents in the 21 Army Group communication zone.

and Twelfth Army Groups and of the American communication zone.

Co-operation with the French in the running of controlled agents was a matter much discussed in the pre-invasion days. Should we let them into all our secrets? On the other hand, it was quite clear that whatever we might say the Deuxième Bureau would run the agents that they caught and it was better that they should do so with our knowledge and approval than without it. Without our help they could hardly avoid sending reports which would contravene deception policy and endanger operational security. It was therefore decided at the outset that co-operation with the Deuxième Bureau in these matters should be full and free.

The first German agent in France who came over to us after the invasion had been launched was captured in Cherbourg at the end of June shortly after the fall of that place. A lull of some weeks ensued, but in August, when the Allied advance became rapid and widespread, members of the German 'stay-behind' network began to give themselves up at an alarming rate. On 21st August a committee of officers belonging to the British and American army groups were formed to consider the running of these captured agents and met for the first time at Domfront. Combining the designations of the two army groups it was known as the 212 Committee and at this meeting its objects were defined as being to approve 'foodstuff' for controlled agents operating in the theatre, to direct the deception policy governing the traffic of controlled agents and to authorise the use of controlled agents for particular operations. SHAEF was invited to send an observer to watch proceedings. It was realised that these newly captured agents were not yet in a fit state to be used for deception, but it was hoped to select one or two of the more promising ones and build them up over a period, at the same time manœuvring them into the situations best suited for the tasks which they would later be required to perform. The remainder, so it was felt, could be usefully employed in a counter-espionage role. As these agents continued to come in, the difficulties and dangers of trying to use any of them for deception became increasingly apparent. Apart from the normal and unavoidable risk of line crossers, the ramifications of the German networks seemed to be endless. While this raised their worth as counter-espionage agents it reduced their value as potential vehicles of deception. On 18th September the Committee was taken over by SHAEF.

It had been agreed at the Domfront meeting on 21st August that the 212 Committee should be the approving authority for the traffic of controlled agents in France. With the rapid advance of the Allied armies and the capture of agents in widely separated districts, a more flexible system for approving traffic became necessary. It must always rest primarily with the case officer to decide what requires approval. Once it has been found necessary to constitute more than one approving authority the case officer must be given some direction as to whom he should approach. With this in view an instruction was issued on 25th September.[5] Henceforth army groups were authorised to approve military traffic affecting their own operations. Naval and air matters were to go respectively to ANCXF and AEAF, while messages dealing with higher strategy or affecting the communication zone as well as those with a political implication would go to SHAEF. SHAEF was also to receive confirmatory copies of all traffic to ensure that the agents were not working at cross purposes. Approval at each of these headquarters remained the responsibility of the operational staffs. So long as deception was being practised at all this was a necessary precaution, in spite of the fact that by far the greater part of the 'foodstuff' provided required higher approval from a security standpoint only. In the last weeks of the war, when deception had practically ceased, the responsibility for approving controlled agents' traffic at SHAEF was assumed by the Intelligence branch.

It has been said that our expectation of continuing strategic deception on the Continent was not fulfilled. Let us see why this was so. In order to make any plans of strategic deception effective two conditions must be satisfied. First the operation must be regarded by the enemy as a feasible one; second, it must be a containing operation in the true sense of the term, that is to say there must be a recognised and accepted intention to draw enemy forces in front of the threatened sector and to hold them there for a reasonable period, for even under the most favourable conditions one must assume that it will

5. SHAEF/24300/SM/Ops (B), dated 25th September, 1944.

take at least a fortnight to develop a strategic threat and not less than another fortnight to dissipate it.

Throughout the campaign the capture of the Ruhr remained the primary Allied objective. Bearing in mind the ever-present danger that unexpected developments in the real campaign might bring the true and the false operations into conflict, the Deception Staff at once sought to play a useful part by confining their efforts to sectors which might reasonably be expected to remain inactive during the coming months. Accordingly at the beginning of October a plan was drafted which suggested that the stiffening German resistance had caused the Allies to change their strategy and that in consequence the main axis of the Allied advance would be on Munich through the Black Forest, while an amphibious operation would be mounted in the United Kingdom against Norway. This plan was disapproved on the ground that it failed to fulfil the first condition, namely, that it would not be regarded by the enemy as feasible. In fact threats against both these sectors were maintained in a modified form throughout the latter months of the war, but they were not co-ordinated in an all-embracing strategic plan. The threat in the South became a part of Sixth Army Group's deceptive operations. The latent threat across the North Sea was kept alive by the continued presence of Fourth British Army in the United Kingdom.

Strategic deception being thus precluded from operating against the extremities of the front, consideration was now given to the creation of a threat in the more active sectors. As the crossing of the lower Rhine and the capture of the Ruhr retained the first priority, this in fact meant a threat to the Frankfurt area through the Metz gap. Between the beginning of October 1944 and the crossing of the Rhine in March 1945 numerous plans were written which aimed to convince the Germans that our main line of advance would be in the direction of Frankfurt. They all failed to receive approval because, although the Ruhr continued to be at all times the first Allied objective, it also remained a fixed principle of Allied strategy that no positive step should be taken to draw German forces in front of the central sector. Glancing through the bulky files of abortive plans that were written during this period of vain endeavour, one comes across such comments as these: 'I do not think this will work. We are setting Ops (B) a very difficult if not impossible task, but we must be sure that we have exhausted every possibility before we throw our hand in.'[6] 'The more I consider this matter the more convinced I am that the actual operations we intend to execute obviate the necessity for, and desirability of, a cover and deception plan.'[7]

When the German line stabilised at the end of September 1944 the day of strategic deception was over. Even if a continuation of strategic planning had been possible, a further difficulty would have arisen through the absence of suitable forces to carry out the deceptive operations. It was at no time the policy of SHAEF to hold a large reserve. When formations arrived in France they were assigned almost immediately to army groups. Thus when the Germans launched their offensive in the Ardennes on 16th December there were only two divisions in the SHAEF reserve, namely, the 82nd and 101st US Airborne Divisions. The only other immediately available formation was the 11th Armoured Division which had just landed. At the same time the opinion was gaining ground that to hold a large strategic reserve of imaginary formations in France would be fraught with danger. In August and early September, when the war seemed to be drawing to a close, we had no hesitation in arranging for the transfer of the Fourteenth Army to France because we did not think that the Germans would have time to discover that it was not really there, but to sustain a belief in its continued presence for many months with all the attendant risks of leakage and when none of its formations appeared in the front line might soon convince the enemy that it never had existed, with fatal consequences to strategic deception as a whole, and to the good name of our best agents. An argument against the continuation of strategic deception sometimes advanced at that time was that the Germans had no reserve themselves and could not therefore react. Subsequent events showed that this argument was hardly a good one, at any rate until after the Ardennes offensive had run its course.

The initiative had in truth passed to the army groups, who could still find scope for deception in support of the operations within their own sectors. In view of the larger part which the army groups were now being called upon to play in this field, it was thought advisable

---

6. DAC of S G-3 to Chief of Ops, 12th February, 1945.
7. Chief of Ops to DAC of S G-3, 24th February, 1945.

at the end of August[8] to define their powers more precisely, and on the 28th and 31st of that month appropriate instructions were issued by SHAEF. 'Supreme Headquarters AEF will plan and control over-all cover and deception operations. The groups of armies, in conjunction with their associated naval forces and air forces, and the communication zone, will plan and carry out such part of these operations as may be allotted to them.

'In order to assist operations in their own spheres, groups of armies are authorised to initiate cover and deception operations. Plans for these operations will be forwarded to this headquarters without delay to ensure co-ordination.'[9] On the other hand all Special Means requirements were to be submitted to SHAEF.[10] This precaution was considered necessary since all intelligence of that nature would be likely to go direct to the OKW for evaluation, so that inconsistencies would become more easily apparent than was the case with the other deception channels. Single control was therefore deemed to be essential. As long as we were only employing the controlled agents in the United Kingdom for deception, this arrangement could, incidentally, cause no added inconvenience, since requirements would in any case have to be canalised through SHAEF. Two months later, however, a difficulty arose. Quite legitimately the army groups were employing visual deception within their zones. But this raised the issue of the control of Special Means. If, for example, the insignia of some imaginary formation was paraded in the streets of Brussels it

---

8. At this time the Special Plans Section ceased to be under command of ETOUSA and was assigned to Twelfth Army Group.

9. SHAEF/19008/Ops (B) (Fwd), dated 28th August, 1944. Subject: Cover and Deception. Signed W. B. Smith, Lieut.-General US Army, Chief of Staff. The first paragraph shows that at this date we still believed that strategic deception had a future.

10. GBI/CI/370-2(SHAEF/CI/400x), dated 31st August, 1944. Subject: Cover and Deception. Signed W. B. Smith, Lieut.-General US Army, Chief of Staff. This instruction implicitly reversed the decision made only ten days before by the 212 Committee, that it should itself 'direct the deception policy governing the traffic of controlled agents and authorise the use of controlled agents for particular operations.' During the ensuing months, however, as the reader will presently see, the operational control of double-cross agents in France was in a large measure delegated to the army groups.

would be impossible for a controlled agent living in that city to fail
to observe those things which were being displayed for the benefit of
real German agents and which it was to be presumed were being
reported by the latter to the Germans. It was therefore ruled on 13th
November that 'any military information which was supported by
physical means should be classed as true and should, therefore, be put
over by army groups'.[11] In effect this gave to the army groups the
right to use controlled agents operating in their own zones for deception. On 5th December this right was confirmed. 'Cover planning
staffs at army groups are authorised to approve operational traffic of
all special agents within their own zones, providing such traffic concerns their own operations exclusively.'[12] It was of course still
obligatory for the army groups to obtain the approval of SHAEF
where other interests were affected. SHAEF also remained the channel for obtaining the services of the agents in the United Kingdom.
When enlisting the support of the British agents care was always
taken to avoid associating their reports too closely with those furnished by the agents abroad, who were still regarded as being more or
less unreliable. To have allowed such an association to develop would
have been to run the risk of discrediting our best channels through
the collapse of one of the Continental agents. This was why we
decided in the end not to send BRUTUS to France.

No attempt is made here to describe the cover plans which the army
groups initiated in support of their own operations, since these form
the subject of reports prepared by the deception staffs of the headquarters concerned. Suffice it to say that it was only in the zone of
Sixth Army Group that deceptive threats were sustained for any considerable period of time. Early in October, in answer to a request
from the Supreme Commander Mediterranean Theatre, a cover
operation was directed against the Franco-Italian frontier, and succeeded in holding the three German divisions stationed there until
the end of the war. When this army group reached the Rhine, a
second threat was initiated with the object of containing enemy

---

11. Minutes of the 212 Committee of 13th November, 1944, para. 4.
12. GBI/CI/211.1(Agents)/SHAEF/CI/57x, dated 5th December, 1944. Subject:
    Approval of Special Agents' Traffic in the North-West European Theatre.

forces in the Black Forest area. By a series of deceptive operations this threat was also kept alive until the time of Germany's final collapse.

The cover plans of the other two army groups, in the Central and Northern zones, were mainly of a short-term character designed to support specific operations within their own sectors, the assistance of the London-controlled agents being enlisted from time to time through SHAEF. Only one of these, a cover operation initiated by 21 Army Group in November 1944 and known as TROLLEYCAR, need be considered in this report because it became linked with the larger strategic programme in circumstances that will be described in a later chapter.

XXXIV

The End of FUSAG

Even if there now seemed to be no future for strategic deception, we still had in the United Kingdom a full complement of imaginary formations as well as a team of controlled agents actively engaged in operational deception. If the final scene of this lengthy drama was now drawing to a close, and the curtain was about to fall, some means would have to be found of disposing of the actors and the stage properties. Let us cast our minds back to the beginning of September. At that time the end of the war seemed very near. In a fortnight's time the enemy's Rhine defence was to be breached at Arnhem, leading to the encirclement of the Ruhr from the North and so to the total surrender of Germany. To assist these operations FUSAG had been reconstituted as an amphibious force comprising Fourth British Army and the First Allied Airborne Army which was to threaten an attack against the North-West German ports, thus drawing German reserves away from the line of the Allied advance across North-West Germany, while the Ninth and Fourteenth Armies had been withdrawn to form a strategic reserve which could support the overland advance of the Allies.

The failure of the Arnhem operation to achieve a major breakthrough and the subsequent stabilisation of the German line effected a radical change in the situation. As has already been stated, with the end of the war only a few weeks away one could send imaginary formations to France without much risk of the Germans finding out that they were being deceived, but if the war were going to drag on for many months these risks would be greatly increased. In the changed circumstances we therefore had to decide whether it was still worthwhile sending overseas imaginary formations which had been used in FORTITUDE. It also became necessary to reconsider the role of FUSAG. Since we had not succeeded in crossing the Rhine at Arnhem and since the capture of the Ruhr remained the first Allied objective, the continued exercise of a threat by FUSAG against the Dutch or German coast might draw German reserves into the Northern sector which was where we least wanted them.

Of the two armies comprised in the fictitious SHAEF strategic reserve, the Ninth, being real, had gone overseas at the beginning of September and was thus no longer at our disposal. The Fourteenth Army, it will be remembered, was last heard of in the Southampton area awaiting embarkation. On 14th September GARBO had reported: 'The Fourteenth US Army is remaining on the SHAEF reserve in southern embarkation areas pending further developments in the battle against Germany. 4 (3) does not think there is any likelihood that this army will go overseas for the present as all supply routes which have had to be monopolised by SOS are already working to capacity.'[1] That was a temporising measure. The effect of Arnhem and the stabilisation of the line upon deception policy was not immediate. A little time passed before the danger of reinforcing groups of armies in France with FORTITUDE formations was fully realised. At a meeting in Brussels on 25th September army groups were invited to state their requirements in respect of imaginary reinforcements. 21 Army Group asked for 2nd British Corps, while Twelfth Army Group applied, as a first instalment, for XXXVII Corps with under command the 25th US Armoured Division and the 59th US Infantry Division.[2] The rest of fourteenth Army would follow later. In compliance with this request, GARBO, at the beginning of October,[3] reported the departure of the American formations. This message found its reflection in the German

---

1. GARBO 1943 and 1950 GMT, 14th September, 1944.
2. This requirement could only be satisfied by an interchange of divisions between XXXIII and XXXVII Corps. This left XXXIII Corps with the 11th, 17th and 48th Infantry Divisions.
3. Through an oversight this message was omitted from the summary of GARBO's traffic. The date and time of its transmission is not, therefore, recorded.

Intelligence Summary of 7th October. 'The 59th American Infantry Division and the 25th American Armoured Division as well as the staff of the XXXVII American Army Corps are said to have been transferred to France.'[4] On 9th October BRUTUS reported: 'I have just heard that the headquarters of the 2nd British Corps, which was at Tunbridge Wells, left two weeks ago to take command of divisions already in France.'[5]

Early in October the decision to use FORTITUDE formations overseas was reversed. The question which now presented itself was how to get rid of Fourteenth Army. At the time that this reversal of policy occurred the 2nd British Corps was already operating under 21 Army Group in Belgium. On the other hand permission to employ XXXVII Corps and its two subsidiary divisions in the forward area had not yet been given to Twelfth Army Group. The ultimate destination of XXXVII Corps was never resolved. It had sailed from Southampton with the 25th Armoured and 59th Infantry Divisions at the end of September, apparently for France, but after that was never heard of again. Perhaps it was transferred to another theatre.

Shortly afterwards XXXIII Corps was disbanded and its three divisions were placed under command of the British Base Section.[6] The 11th and 17th Divisions were moved to South Wales at the end of October, where they were given a draft-finding role. 'According to a report from a credible source the 11th and 17th American Infantry Divisions are confirmed afresh as being in England and are said to be at the moment being drawn upon for reinforcements for the American divisions engaged in France. Both divisions are said to have been moved to the areas of Gloucester and South Wales where the training areas were repeatedly occupied by American troops before the invasion.'[7] It was not so easy to destroy imaginary formations as it had been to create them, for the summary goes on to say: 'The fact that the 11th and 17th American Infantry Divisions, which

---

4. Lagebericht West No. 1411, dated 7th October, 1944.
5. BRUTUS 1807 GMT, 9th October, 1944.
6. An American headquarters controlling and administering US troops stationed in the United Kingdom.
7. Lagebericht West No. 1460, dated 25th November, 1944.

have been for some time located in Great Britain, have not been used on the Western front, finds it explanation in the report of a good agent according to whom these divisions are being used for draft finding. It must, however, be pointed out that repeated experience shows that so called "draft finding divisions" can, if necessary, often be *made ready for battle by the Americans at short notice* and can then be sent to the front. These two divisions must therefore continue to be regarded as an operational reserve in the hands of Eisenhower.'[8] The 48th Division continued to carry out the airborne training upon which it had now been engaged for some months. 'The 48th American Infantry Division, also accepted in Great Britain, has been repeatedly reported as "airborne".'[9] Now that XXXIII and XXXVII Corps had been dispersed, Fourteenth Army Headquarters became redundant. It was never specifically disbanded since it would have been unrealistic for the controlled agents to discover everything. On 31st January, 1945, GARBO was asked: 'Can you find out what has become of the Fourteenth US Army, last reported by 7 (4) several months ago. Please give to this question your special attention, instructing your agents accordingly. An early reply will be highly appreciated.'[10] On 12th March he replied: 'Despite diligent enquiries no traces found of Fourteenth US Army.'[11]

We have now seen how the SHAEF strategic reserve was disposed of. The other problem which faced us was the future employment of FUSAG. The most obvious solution was to disband it too. Mention has already been made of the adverse effect which its continued presence in England might have upon the disposition of German reserves. There was a second reason for wishing to do away with the imaginary formations which still remained in the United Kingdom. British front-line divisions, such as the 50th and 59th, were being broken up to replace casualties, while American divisions were being used to reinforce 21 Army Group, yet in German eyes a whole British army remained uncommitted in the United Kingdom. In addition the imaginary airborne formations stayed at home while the real ones

---

8. Appendix to Lagebericht West No. 1460, dated 25th November, 1944.
9. Appendix to Lagebericht West No. 1460, dated 25th November, 1944.
10. GARBO Message received 1914 GMT, 31st January, 1945.
11. GARBO 2028 GMT, 12th March, 1945.

engaged in successive operations. This created a very unreal situation which was liable to provoke the Germans to ask why these British divisions were being withheld. In these circumstances it seemed best to disband all the remaining FORTITUDE formations and rely upon newly created ones should the need for strategic deception ever arise in the future. An extract from the Intelligence Summary for 27th October shows that this estimate of enemy reactions was not wide of the mark. 'With the efforts of the English Command to keep the existing field formations fully reinforced even during heavy campaigns we may conclude from these reflections that the formation of new divisions is not to be anticipated. It has, on the contrary, become evident that existing formations and units have been disbanded for the purpose of supplying other formations with battle experienced reinforcements to keep them up to strength. The recent engagement of an American division (104th Infantry) in the area of the First Canadian Army, as well as the continued presence of the 82nd and 101st American Airborne Divisions on the Second English Army front, are further proofs of the limited state of the English strength, and also of the anxiety to economise so far as possible with the forces still available and to spare English blood where possible. There is, so far, no information regarding the proposed use of the fourteen active English divisions (exclusive of independent brigades) which are known with certainty still to be in Great Britain. It is, however, to be assumed that the English Command is at pains, in view of the exacting requirements in personnel which are to be expected, to keep these last reserves in the home country for so long as possible.'[12] The solution which they found a month later, without any assistance from us, for this wholly incomprehensible state of affairs, must be regarded as an unmerited piece of good fortune. 'There are still no reports or other indications of the transfer of fresh British units to the Continent or of preparations for embarkation. The British formations assumed to be in Great Britain must, therefore, all continue to be accepted there. The striking retention of these forces can now only be explained by psychological–political factors. Noteworthy in this connection is Churchill's White Paper, published in recent days, in which the British war effort in all military and civilian spheres is set out in particularly impressive

---

12. Appendix to Lagebericht West No. 1431, dated 27th October, 1944.

form, and in which the conclusion is made that the contribution of the British Empire to the war so far is greater than that of any other belligerent country. This statement can, in a sense, be regarded as justification for the retention of troops which we now observe.'[13]

In spite of the arguments put forward by Ops (B) for the disbandment of all the remaining imaginary formations in the United Kingdom, the Operations Staff at SHAEF was unwilling to agree to the dispersal of the entire force. It was felt that a time might come in the near future when the amphibious threat across the North Sea might be played again with useful results. At the same time it was considered that for this purpose an army corps and an airborne task force would suffice. This decision enabled us at least to carry out a partial disbandment. All that we now had to do was to scale down the Fourth Army to the size of a corps, and First Allied Airborne Army to that of an appropriate task force, retaining Fourth Army Headquarters to command the two.

With Fourteenth US Army disposed of and Fourth Army thus reduced, FUSAG itself could now go. Before the end of October the Germans had learnt of its disbandment: 'A proven source reports from Great Britain that the staff of the First American Army Group (FUSAG) has been disbanded. The same source reports that the English Fourth Army, which has hitherto been under the command of FUSAG, is now directly under the Commander-in-Chief of the Allied invasion forces (General Eisenhower).'[14]

The reduction of Fourth Army and of First Allied Airborne Army was effected in the following manner. 2nd British Corps had already been sent to France. The 55th and 61st British Infantry Divisions, being real formations, were allowed to revert to their factual role as training divisions under command GHQ, Home Forces, while the survivors, that is to say 7th British Corps, the 58th and 80th British Infantry Divisions and the 5th British Armoured Division, all imaginary, were retained for future use. The 58th Infantry and 5th Armoured Divisions were already under command 7th British Corps and were located in the Eastern counties. The 80th Infantry Division, it will be

---

13. Appendix to Lagebericht West No. 1464, dated 29th November, 1944.
14. Lagebericht West No. 1425, dated 21st October, 1944, based on BRUTUS 1815 GMT, 17th October, 1944.

remembered, had, in the September reorganisation, been obliged to remain at Canterbury owing to its dependence on the signals of the 61st Infantry Division, and for this reason it had been brought under command of the 2nd British Corps at Tunbridge Wells. Now that low-powered wireless traffic had been dispensed with, it was free to move, and about the middle of October it reverted to 7th Corps and transferred to Claydon in Suffolk. 'A proven source confirms the 7th English Army Corps Headquarters and the 80th English Infantry Division, the latter now believed to be in the area of north of London.'[15]

To complete this regrouping of forces, the First Allied Airborne Army and the real formations belonging to it reverted to SHAEF, while the fictitious increment remained to form the new airborne task force. The imaginary airborne formations which thus became available to Fourth Army comprised one British and one American corps, the 19th and XVII. The former contained the British airborne divisions, that is to say the imaginary 2nd and the real 6th, which was still in England at that time; the latter contained the two imaginary American airborne divisions, the 9th and 21st, as well as the real 17th, which had not yet gone to France. Even this reduced force was felt to be larger than the circumstances demanded. It was therefore decided to disband the American element, thus making the Fourth Army wholly British. When this decision was made the existence of the XVII Airborne Corps had not yet been disclosed to the Germans. The 17th US Airborne Division was shortly to engage in real operations. It only remained, therefore, to dispose of the 9th and 21st US Airborne Divisions. Of these BRUTUS said on 29th November: 'Nottingham: I was able to learn that the 9th and 21st Airborne Divisions have been greatly reduced by reinforcements for other divisions and that from these two divisions they are going to form a single one. I was also told that there is now a new division in the Order of Battle of the Allied Airborne Army, namely, the 13th Division, and I can suppose that it is this division which has been formed from the other two divisions which left this region some time ago.'[16] The 13th US Airborne Division had in fact just arrived from America.

---

15. Lagebericht West No. 1434, dated 30th October, 1944, based on BRUTUS 1803 and 1808 GMT, 24th October, 1944.
16. BRUTUS 1743 and 1750 GMT, 29th November, 1944.

XXXV

TROLLEYCAR and the Move to Yorkshire

In order that Fourth Army might be conveniently placed to embark from the Humber and other northern ports should it be necessary to resuscitate the threat, it was now decided to move it to Yorkshire, where the Army Headquarters could become merged with Northern Command. The object of the latter arrangement was twofold: first, to allay German fears and make it appear that an operation was not intended in the immediate future; second, to help us to give direction to the threat when we wanted to revive it. '7 (7) reports from Yorkshire . . . that Fourth Army and Northern Command are being amalgamated and will control any future landing in Germany . . . in the same way as other commands have been given similar roles; for instance, Norway in the case of Scottish Command and the Channel Islands in the case of Southern Command.'[1]

All these arrangements were provided for in a paper dated 6th November and entitled 'Regrouping of the Notional Order of Battle in the United Kingdom'.[2] Here the following story is given to account for the changes. 'The capture of the Pas de Calais by 21 Army Group rendered the seaborne assault by First United States Army Group unnecessary. During the first weeks of September it appeared that the total defeat of Germany was imminent. First United States Army Group was therefore allotted a new role in support of the final breakthrough. First Allied Airborne Army was placed under

---

1. GARBO 1915 and 1924 GMT, 2nd December, 1944. Southern Command had in fact been instructed to prepare a plan for the reoccupation of the Channel Islands.
2. SHAEF/24309/SM/Ops (B), dated 6th November, 1944. See Appendix XI.

command First United States Army Group and Fourteenth United States Army reverted to SHAEF control. The airborne attack on Arnhem constituted the first phase of a major assault from the United Kingdom. Had this attack succeeded, a combined airborne and seaborne assault would have been launched by Fourth British Army supported by the remaining airborne divisions of First Allied Airborne Army, the whole force operating under the control of First United States Army Group. After the setback at Arnhem and the general stabilisation on the Western front, it was realised that an Allied victory in 1944 was unattainable. In these circumstances the operation of Fourth British Army and the special airborne force was held in suspense.'

No sooner had the decision to move Fourth Army to Yorkshire been made than the request, already referred to, from 21 Army Group in connection with their cover operation TROLLEYCAR was received. TROLLEYCAR sought to contain certain of the enemy's lay-back reinforcing divisions, mainly in Holland, by convincing the Germans that an attack would be made by the First Canadian Army west of Arnhem in conjunction with a sea and airborne attack from the United Kingdom. In these circumstances it seemed as if the move to Yorkshire might be made to serve two purposes. It could first be allowed to appear that the formations were moving to embarkation in the east coast ports, thus providing the threat required by TROLLEYCAR; later it could be discovered that they were merely proceeding from one home station to another.

Before observing the effect of Fourth Army's move, a few general remarks on the German fear of an amphibious attack across the North Sea may be useful. During the latter months of the war the Germans seem to have been haunted by this fear in an ever-increasing degree.[3]

---

3. On 18th January, the Oberkommando der Kriegsmarine analysed all the reports which had been received since the time of the invasion forecasting assaults on Norway, Denmark and the German Bight. These reports were graded X for true, XX for possible and XXX for false. The conclusions drawn here as to German contemporary beliefs regarding an assault across the North Sea are based principally on this document. It may be of passing interest to note that 66 messages were received from 47 sources. Of these messages OSTRO sent 8, JOSEPHINE 7 and BRUTUS 2. Of the remainder, 4 sources supplied two messages each and the remaining 40 only one apiece. Unfortunately we have no evidence to show what sustained these fears of an amphibious attack after January 1945.

Between the invasion and Arnhem practically all reports of impending attacks on Scandinavia were regarded as false. JOSEPHINE scored
rather heavily by saying that such attacks were *not* contemplated. But
he went down with his message of 28th August in which he forecast
the assault on Denmark and Norway which has already been referred
to in connection with the Arnhem operation. This report was
regarded as false. The first affirmative report which the Germans
marked as true was that of BRUTUS sent on 14th September, also in
connection with Arnhem. Two uncontrolled messages[4] which followed shortly after that of BRUTUS also received full marks. They
probably derived an adventitious benefit from the British-controlled
report. Thereafter their belief in the North Sea assault seems to have
waned as most of the messages are classified once more as false.[5]

Such was the position when TROLLEYCAR and the move of
Fourth Army to Yorkshire became a factor in the case. This move was
effected between the 10th and 20th November. It was conveyed to
the Germans in the usual way by messages from GARBO, BRUTUS,
TATE and BRONX.[6] Early in November, in conformity with the
requirements of TROLLEYCAR, certain wireless links had been
opened between 21 Army Group and the airborne forces in the
United Kingdom. On 17th November BRUTUS reported: 'As a
result of my personal observations and conversations with my colleagues, I can confirm that your fears about the airborne attack are
justified. From one of my airborne colleagues it is thought that the

---

4 20th September report from V-man DORETTE that invasion of Denmark
was likely and 22nd September report from KdM Hamburg that a landing in
North Germany and Denmark would take place in connection with the
Western offensive.

5. Towards the end of October, OSTRO and JOSEPHINE, in messages which
bear a curious similarity, put forward the story of an impending attack on
Northern Norway to forestall the advance of the Russians, which gained cre-
dence for a short time.

6. As was our custom, we started the operation by confirming the formations in
their previous locations. On this occasion that task was performed by
BRUTUS and so we read in the German Intelligence Summary of 19th
November: 'According to a report from a good source the 7th English Army
Corps as well as the 58th and 80th English Infantry Divisions and the 5th
Armoured Division have been confirmed in their old areas in Great Britain.'
(Lagebericht West No. 1454, dated 19th November, 1944.)

attack will take place against the region of Emden to capture the coastal installations in this region. It will be preceded, according to him, by a heavy attack by the Canadians in the North. I now regret very much that I was unable to visit the headquarters of the Fourth Army during my visit to Colchester, but nevertheless this plan is confirmed by the information which I received that the Fourth Army has begun to move towards the North, probably towards the region of embarkation.'[7] And two days later: 'Urgent: From an officer of the British 19th Airborne Corps, which has its headquarters at Salisbury, this corps includes the 2nd British Airborne Division which is in a high state of preparedness for departure.'[8] BRUTUS's first message was regarded as possible and given XX. After this, reports of Fourth Army's move began to come in. The Germans were obviously puzzled. 'The move, several times reported, of the formations of the 7th English Army Corps (38th [58th?] and 80th Infantry Divisions, 5th Armoured Division) from their previous locations in the South-East of the Island to Central England seems to be confirmed, though the reason for these moves is not clear. Since, however, for the present there is no sign of a move to port areas, we cannot yet speak of any impending embarkation of this division (*sic* corps).'[9] A fortnight later they were still somewhat perplexed. 'There is no fresh information regarding the shipment of formations to France; the presence of the Fourth English Army is again confirmed by a useful source. The apparently still uncompleted move of the 7th English Army Corps with the 58th Infantry and 5th Armoured Divisions from South-Eastern England to the neighbourhood of the Humber estuary is striking and the reasons for this are still not clear. Any new landing intentions (Denmark, German Bight) can, however, not be deduced from this move, particularly as they could not be in any way operationally connected with recognisable objectives in France. The

---

7. BRUTUS 1739, 1810 and 1828 GMT, 17th November, 1944.
8. BRUTUS 2157 GMT, 19th November, 1944.
9. Appendix to Lagebericht West No. 1460, dated 25th November, 1944, based on BRUTUS 1749, 1757 and 1801 GMT, 13th November, 1944, GARBO 1935 and 1945 GMT, 19th November, 1944, TATE 0750 and 1910 MET, 20th November, 1944, and GARBO 1858 and 1928 GMT, 23rd November, 1944.

possible concentration of landing craft in the Humber area must be investigated by air reconnaissance.'[10] By the 14th it had become fairly clear that no operation was imminent and that the move of Fourth Army had no special significance. 'From England there have come in no important messages during the last days, in particular we have been unable to obtain any fresh information regarding the purpose behind the move of the 7th English Army Corps, which has now been joined by the 80th English Infantry Division (now accepted in the Catterick area, north-west of Hull). In any case we *cannot accept* the intention to transfer these formations to the Western front in the near future after their withdrawal from South-Eastern England. Similarly, the fact that the 80th English Infantry Division belonging to the 7th English Army Corps was *not* placed in the area of a port when it was moved North gives reason to suppose that no imminent new landing operation is planned which would include this formation.'[11] Nevertheless, it would have been unsafe to leave anything to chance and so GARBO was told on 14th December: 'I should be very pleased if you could arrange that either you, 7 (2) or another of the sub-agents will make regular trips to the North and East of Scotland, once or twice monthly, in order to keep control over this district and its ports as we must always be prepared for the possibility of new landing operation which could have its bases of concentration in the North.'[12]

---

10. Appendix to Lagebericht West No. 1474, dated 9th December, 1944.
11. Appendix to Lagebericht West No. 1479, dated 14th December, 1944, based on GARBO 1915, 1924 and 1944 GMT, 2nd December, 1944, BRUTUS 1759 GMT, 4th December, 1944, GARBO 2000 GMT, 6th December, 1944, and GARBO 2018 GMT, 8th December, 1944.
12. GARBO Message received 1804 GMT, 14th December, 1944.

XXXVI
The Closing Scene

Once the requirements of TROLLEYCAR had been satisfied, it was agreed that we might complete the disbandment of the fictitious airborne task force. The real 6th British Airborne Division had already gone to France. Of the 2nd British Airborne Division the Germans had remarked on 17th November: 'The 2nd English Airborne Division, hitherto accepted in Great Britain, has apparently been used currently to find drafts for replacing losses of airborne troops already engaged. Presumably recourse has been had to parts of the 2nd English Airborne Division in the reconstitution of the 1st English Airborne Division destroyed at Arnhem, since the 1st Airborne Division is to be ready for battle again by the middle of December. In Great Britain, therefore, only two English airborne divisions (1st reforming and 6th) are accepted.'[1] In fact this belief in the dissolution of the 2nd British Airborne Division was not prompted by us at all, but must be attributed to an uncontrolled report. When we discovered at the end of the month, through Most Secret Sources, that they held this belief and since we now wished to disband the formation, we allowed BRUTUS to send a confirmatory message on 7th December. 'The 2nd Division will be used for giving reinforcements to the 1st and 6th British Airborne Divisions. I think that it will have been disbanded.'[2] At the same time he told the Germans that the 19th Airborne Corps at Salisbury was formed 'only as an administrative unit'.

---

1. Lagebericht West No. 1452, dated 17th November, 1944.
2. BRUTUS 1754 GMT, 7th December, and 1746 GMT, 8th December, 1944.

At the end of the year we were thus left with the Fourth Army Headquarters, already amalgamated with Northern Command, 7th British Corps, the 5th British Armoured Division and the 58th and 80th British Infantry Divisions. By the middle of January the chance of requiring even this reduced force seemed so remote that it was decided to carry the process of disbandment a stage further and to retain only the 58th and 80th British Infantry Divisions.[3] These further changes were summarised for the Germans in a message sent by agent Three on 2nd February. '7 (7) York: Have managed to get following complete story about Fourth Army from a Canadian offi-cer attached to 21 Army Group Headquarters. He is here on a mission and I have been cultivating him carefully. He tells me that Fourth Army and 7th British Corps have been disbanded. We already know from my previous investigations that the 5th Armoured Division has also been disbanded. According to this offi-cer, Montgomery had preferred to keep his reserves in England rather than behind the front line as he had always planned that Fourth Army should make an amphibious attack against Germany in support of a ground attack by 21 Army Group. This he had intended to make had not Arnhem failed. The heavy losses after Arnhem and during the Antwerp campaign, apart from the surprise German attack before Christmas, liquidated all plans for an attack by Fourth Army which had existed prior to their move to Yorkshire. Instead of this, it became necessary to draw on divisions under the Fourth Army to reinforce existing divisions. Montgomery preferred this course to the alternative of sending over the Fourth Army and with-drawing his mauled divisions, as the arrival of new formations of the Fourth Army in the battle front would have been observed by the Germans and have constituted a threat which would have drawn additional German reserves against 21 Army Group front. In reply to my question as to how the Allies would attempt another landing if it became necessary, he told me that the small British forces now in England were quite incapable of staging any operation, in fact he assured me that there were not sufficient British troops available even to occupy Norway should the Germans withdraw, as all avail-able forces would be held as strategic reserve for the final offensive

---

3. SHAEF/24309/SM/Ops (B), dated 19th January, 1945. See Appendix XII.

against Germany proper.'[4] Besides giving the enemy particulars of the disbandment of Fourth Army, this report sought to explain why these British divisions had been kept in England during the autumn, for a message received by GARBO on 12th January showed that this matter was still exercising the enemy's mind.[5] We did not, of course, at that time know about the 'psychological–political' argument which they themselves had put forward, but which they had evidently come to regard as not altogether satisfactory.

Soon after this the 58th and 80th Divisions moved South, the former to Hitchin and the latter to St Neots. These two last survivors were disbanded in April and the Germans were so informed in messages sent by GARBO on the 18th and 27th of that month.[6] Until the end they were represented on the air by 12th Reserve Unit which continued to operate after the New Year on a reduced establishment.

In January the Germans had come to the conclusion that the seaborne assault would only be launched in association with the main overland advance of the Allied armies. Northern Germany and Denmark were both, therefore, regarded as possible objectives, an attack on the former being the more immediate danger. Any attack on Norway would be purely diversionary in character. From this point onwards we have no way of feeling the German pulse except through the messages which they sent to the British-controlled agents. These showed increased anxiety during the spring of 1945. This was not to be attributed to anything which the British-controlled agents told them. Indeed during the period of Fourth Army's disbandment GARBO did everything in his power to allay their fears. But the events of the previous autumn had given the story a momentum which could not now be arrested. 'It is of very great

4. GARBO 1855, 1902, 1909, 1916 and 1924 GMT, 2nd February, 1945.
5. 'In order to get a clear idea of the English and US divisions stationed actually in Great Britain, please instruct your agents to investigate carefully about this question, transmitting to us all details which you and the agents may obtain. At the same time try and find out for which reasons the English and US divisions which still remain in Great Britain are not moved to the front in France and Belgium.' GARBO Message received 1918 GMT, 12th January, 1945.
6. GARBO 1814 and 1818 GMT, 18th April, and 1804 and 1809 GMT, 27th April, 1945.

importance to investigate by all means if there are any signs of preparations for a new operation to be carried out from Great Britain. Please send somebody to the important embarkation ports of the estuaries of the Thames and Humber and . . . further North on the east coast in order to find out if there exist troop concentrations in areas near to these ports or if landing craft and transport vessels are being assembled. Although 7 (7) in his last reports did not mention any special preparations, situation may have changed recently.'[7] And on the same day TATE was asked: 'Can you travel in the area of Bristol, Reading, Southampton, *possibly also in Humber district?*'[8] On 19th February GARBO was asked to send weekly reports 'even if this would be only to confirm that there has been no change of importance'.[9] He continued to assure them that there was no cause for alarm and on 2nd March went so far as to say: 'Any information you have to the contrary should be regarded with suspicion. An air reconnaissance by you would confirm this and relieve you of your anxiety.'[10] He hoped in this way to deal a blow at those uncontrolled agents who were still backing the story, but it was of no avail. On 12th March BRONX received a code similar to the one which she had used to tell the Germans about IRONSIDE. 'When we should expect a new invasion, either by landing or by parachute, let us know in the following code: Send. I have need for my dentist. . . . Landing South of Sweden £30, landing in Norway £40, landing in Denmark £50, landing in the German Bay £60, landing and parachuting in the German Bay £70. Parachuting to the west of Berlin £80, parachuting to the west of Berlin and landing in the German Bay £100.'[11] The fear of this attack seems to have remained with them until the end of the war. Under interrogation Colonel Meyer-Detring, who had been on Field-Marshal Von Rundstedt's staff at the time of the invasion and was later transferred to the OKW, stated that during the autumn of 1944 there had been various changes in the organisation of the

---

7. GARBO Message received 1850 and 1902 GMT, 31st January, 1945.
8. TATE Message received 1845 MET, 31st January, 1945.
9. GARBO Message received 2027, GMT, 19th February, 1945.
10. GARBO 1901 GMT, 2nd March, 1945.
11. BRONX Letter No. 14 from Lisbon, dated 7th March and received 12th March, 1945.

forces and of the command boundaries in North-West Germany, all of which were connected with the fear of a possible sea and airborne assault against the North-West German ports. He agreed that the German Admiralty had not taken this threat seriously owing to the naval difficulties involved, but added that the OKW had counted on the possibility of such an operation until the advancing Allied armies crossed the line of the Weser. Since the war ended the writer has been informed by Danes living in the west of Jutland that work on the coastal defences there was intensified during the last months of the war.

XXXVII

The Agents Take Their Leave

The disbandment of the 58th and 80th British Infantry Divisions in April 1945 constituted the last step in the dissolution of FORTITUDE's imaginary armies. It remains to see how each of the controlled agents took his leave. The only letter writers who engaged in operational deception during the latter months of the war were GELATINE and BRONX. The former had been showing signs of anxiety and depression for some time. At the beginning of April she saw that defeat was near and on the 7th complained to the Germans: 'I must know when to stop as I do not want to endanger my position at the last moment. And what happens after that?'[1] Her last letter was posted on 30th April. BRONX kept her head until the end and on 3rd May wrote: 'Events succeed each other so quickly that everyone here thinks of the war as being over, but no one knows who is really in command in Germany. It seems to me useless to send you military information, but I think I could, from time to time, send you political observations which would be of use to you in the reconstruction of Germany once this terrible period is over.'[2]

Of the three surviving wireless agents TATE, whose performances had been so disappointing in the summer, was beginning to receive some slight indication of recognition before FORTITUDE ended.[3]

---

1. GELATINE Letter No. 35, dated 7th April, 1945.
2. BRONX Letter No. 17, dated 3rd May, 1945.
3. The German Intelligence Summary (No. 1372) of 29th August, 1944, located the 17th US Infantry Division in the vicinity of Cambridge. This was almost certainly the result of a message sent by TATE at 1804 MET on 28th July,

In November he ceased to operate on our behalf, devoting himself thereafter to naval deception, in which employment he achieved some striking successes.

BRUTUS left FUSAG on 21st August and returned to the Polish Air Headquarters at the Rubens Hotel. He had already expressed some concern about the future of Poland and the treatment of Polish subjects by the Germans. This and the fact that he was no longer at the army group headquarters evidently made the Germans fear that they might soon lose him. They therefore did their best to impress him with the great value which they placed upon his services. 'We thank you profoundly for your excellent work and would like you to thank your friend CHOPIN also, who, despite his age, works so well. Tell him please that once the war is over he will have no further financial difficulties.'[4] These encouraging words did not remove the agent's anxiety regarding developments in his own country. On 11th September he told his masters: 'I am very much depressed. The news of former atrocities committed at the camp at Lublin have recently received much publicity in the press and have the appearance of being too true. . . . I believe that I have the right to ask for a true statement of your general policy towards my country.'[5] The Germans were quick to reassure him: 'Once again I thank you with all my heart for your excellent work. I implore you not to imagine that I have done nothing for you. I have passed on all your political propositions, especially concerning your country, recommending them to accept them.'[6] A little later BRUTUS pointed out how difficult it was for him to continue. 'My present work at my headquarters takes up a very great deal of time and I have not the same freedom of movement as before. The search for information and the lengthy enciphering still further reduces the time available.'[7] After this date

---

1944. A report sent by TATE on 5th October (0755 MET), at the request of Sixth Army Group, that a corps consisting of one armoured division and two infantry divisions was on its way from New York to Marseilles finds its counterpart in Appendix to Lagebericht West No. 1411, dated 7th October, and Lagebericht West No. 1430, dated 26th October, 1944.

4. BRUTUS Message received 1703 GMT, 31 August, 1944.
5. BRUTUS 1720 GMT, 11th September, 1944.
6. BRUTUS Message received 1713 GMT, 12th September, 1944.
7. BRUTUS 1832 GMT, 29th September, 1944.

his communications became very infrequent. His last message was
sent on 2nd January, 1945, when he announced that he was about to
pay a visit to 2nd TAF in the Neighbourhood of Brussels.

This leaves us with GARBO. As a result of his arrest in July he had
already handed over the active direction of the network to agent
Three. At the beginning of August he was assailed by a new trouble.
As the defeat of Germany drew nearer a certain number of German
collaborators living in neutral countries sought to reinsure their position by offering their services to the Allies. One of these, an Abwehr
agent in Madrid, approached the British Secret Service there and
offered, in consideration of their protection and a safe passage to
England, to disclose details of a German espionage network in the
United Kingdom. We had reason to believe that the information
which he desired to impart related to the GARBO organisation and
that the Germans were aware that he had acquired some knowledge
of this valued source of intelligence. Had he been allowed to unbur-
den himself of his secret, it would have meant closing the GARBO
case, for if we had continued to employ him in a double-cross role
after it was known to the enemy that we had been told of his activities in this country, it would merely have proved to them that he was
operating under control. GARBO's case officer therefore devised a
way of overcoming this most embarrassing problem. The manœuvre
adopted was full of complexities and took many months to achieve
its object; here it can be given only in bare outline. GARBO told the
Germans that the courier had heard through a third party, on one of
his visits to Lisbon, of the Spanish agent's intended defection. In spite
of this treacherous action GARBO begged his maters not to take any
action against him, but simply to let him know that their master spy
had escaped from England and was now in hiding in Spain. In this
way, GARBO pointed out, he would be robbed of his bargaining
counter and the English, if the information came to their ears, would
be induced to give up any enquiries which they might have initiated
as a result of these preliminary conversations.

With this added danger it now became essential for GARBO to go
into hiding. For this purpose he chose the cottage in South Wales
which had been occupied by Four after his escape from Hiltingbury
Camp at the time of the invasion. He found the life there very
monotonous and on 3rd October he gave the following account of

his surroundings: 'There are three of us, the Welsh couple and a Belgian. The former are both fairly old, each of about sixty years of age. They work all day long in the fields looking after the farm which consists of four head of cattle and about a hundred fowls. The house is miserable and poor and it only has electricity through a miracle, since the electricity supply happens to pass through some mountains and goes to a village which is only ten miles away. The old man is a Welsh Nationalist who, in his youth, worked a great deal for the Party. His English is worse than mine and I mostly do not understand what he says. They speak Welsh when they are talking together. He is now no longer mixed up in politics. He is a friend of 7 (2) and it was in this farm that the group which was formed by those who are now working for us used to print their propaganda leaflets. Here they used to hide their documents; they had, and still have, a secret cellar which leads out of the basement of the house. It is a sort of shelter where the Belgian and I would hide should there be an unexpected visit from one of the neighbours. This, however, is very unlikely, since in this corner of the world no one will ever turn up and, secondly, because the nearest neighbour lives two and a half miles away from the farm. The Belgian is a man who is a little simple. I do not know whether his brains are atrophied. On studying him he seems to be abnormal. We spend the day on our own, listening to the radio and reading books.'[8]

The Germans at once fell in with GARBO's proposals to defeat this treacherous act. To complete the story Madrid was told that during the months of October and November Mrs GARBO had been visited constantly by the Police and interrogated as to the whereabouts of her husband, her answer of course being that he had gone to Spain. In order to confirm this GARBO wrote letters to his wife which purported to have been written by him in Spain. These were taken, supposedly by the courier, to Madrid and delivered to the Germans, who, playing their part in the ruse posted the letters on to Mrs GARBO, thus providing her with evidence to support her statement that her husband had left the country.

Madrid showed itself to be very sympathetic towards GARBO in his new misfortunes and appreciative of his stoical courage in the

---

8. GARBO Letter No. 30, dated 3rd October, 1944.

face of such overwhelming difficulties. At Christmas he received
the following letter:

'My dear friend and colleague,

'The days are approaching which, in normal times, would be
days of good cheer for all of us. We are living through the decisive hours for the future of humanity and the civilisation of
Europe and surely for the whole world, and the thoughts of the
tremendous unhappiness which this evolution has, to some
extent, brought with it for millions of human beings do not
allow conscientious people to enter into the good atmosphere of
these festive moments. Thus, during these days we will devote
ourselves with more intensity, if this should be possible, to
thinking about our companions who, in the performance of
their duty and in the defence of their ideals, are now in a dangerous situation, terrible and very disagreeable. I should like to
be a writer in order that I should have facility to find the words
which might fully give you to understand the high esteem
which we all have for you and the desire we and our headquarters have to collaborate with you.

'We have, in your personality, your character, your valour, all
these virtues which become a gentleman. I hope, nevertheless,
that from what I have written to you, you will have been able to
feel that which perhaps through lack of ability to express myself
in the written word I have been unable to impress adequately.
We here, in the very small circle of colleagues who know your
story and that of your organisation, talk so often about you that
it often seems as if we were living the incidents which you relate
to us and we most certainly share, to the full, your worries. On
account of them I know that with the approach of Christmas
you will be suffering many bitter moments at having to spend
these days separated from the people who mean most in your
life. I trust, nevertheless, that the satisfaction at being able to
contribute, through the mediation of the organisation which
you have created, to a sacred cause which is that of the struggle
for the maintenance of order and salvation in our Continent
will give you comfort and moral strength to be able to go ahead
with us until we have overcome all obstacles.

At the termination of this year of truly extraordinary struggles I wish to express to you our firm and absolute conviction that next year will bring us further along our none too easy road, at the end of which we will find that which has been awaiting us as a worthy recompense for all the sacrifices which this temporary task has imposed upon us.

'For you, personally, my dear friend, you already know that my greatest wish is to see you soon free from your present critical situation and united once more with your family. We pray to the Almighty that He may give them and you His protection as He has done up till now and that He may inspire those who direct the destination of countries to avoid the final catastrophe in the world. What is now taking place in many countries in Europe is perhaps the first ray of light which He has shown us to illuminate and demonstrate what would occur if wise judgment is not shown in time in order that it should be appreciated where the true danger lies.

'These thoughts are also, to some extent, directed to all the companions of your organisation. I trust that it will be possible for you to pass to them our thoughts, our good wishes, and our gratitude for the magnificent work, and, in particular, to those who have helped you to resolve the present situation as true friends, to Three, Seven, the Courier, 7 (2), &c. We hope very sincerely that one of these days it will be possible for us to express to them all our feelings in a more concrete form.

'I know, my dear friend, that it is not possible to recompense materially all that you and your organisation are doing, nevertheless I wish very sincerely that all your colleagues should have the possibility of being able to do something during the days of Christmas which will remind them that our thoughts are with you. Were it possible, I would send from here something to each one of them as a small token. In view of the circumstances, I have no alternative but to confine myself to money which, I trust, they will all be able to accept as an expression of personal attention. I should be grateful to you, therefore, if you would take the necessary measures to effect this and I leave it to your judgment to decide the amount which should be given to each of them in accordance with your knowledge of the various friends. I think that maybe the equivalent of a month's payment might be suitable, but as I have already said, you have absolute freedom to take the decision in this connection.

'I purposely have not dealt with service matters in this letter. This I shall do when I have received your personal letter which, I hope, will give me details about your plan for escaping which I asked for by message, which will enable me, forthwith, to reply regarding all the possibilities in this connection.

'I enclose, with this letter, a remittance of $3,000.

'With our most cordial regards and a firm handshake.'[9]

Meanwhile, as the last paragraph of the Christmas letter discloses, GARBO was turning over in his mind means of escaping from the country and this formed the basis of much correspondence during the last months of the war. In these letters, as a security measure, GARBO was always referred to in the third person as 'the friend'. In March he decided, for purposes of disguise, to grow a beard and sent a photograph of himself to the Germans to see if they approved. The German answer is worth recording. 'Having examined the photographs of the friend I must assure you that I find the camouflage perfect. On the other hand, if I am to be quite frank in expressing my opinion I must say that this camouflage presents quite a lot of difficulties on account of the by no means usual shape of the friend's beard, since I think I can say with certainty that one can see very few people nowadays who wear a beard of that shape with the exception of those beards which are rather more developed and one connects with people advanced in years.'[10]

Before going any further we must see what had become of all the sub-agents. At the beginning of August when GARBO had reorganised the network, the position was as follows: the system of communication remained as heretofore. J (1) continued to act as courier and 4 (1) as the wireless operator. Of the unconscious collaborators, J (3) and J (5), with their ministerial connections, and 4 (3), the useful American

---

9. GARBO Letter from Lisbon, dated 12th December, 1944, and received 1st January, 1945.
10. GARBO Letter from Lisbon, dated 20th March, 1945, and received 1st April, 1945.

sergeant, were still valuable sources of intelligence. Agent Three, the deputy chief, was virtually in charge of the network, while his sub-agent 3 (3) continued to keep watch in Scotland. Four was still in hiding in South Wales. Seven had just retired from the service, had rejoined the Merchant Service and was hoping to arrange for Four's passage to Canada, where he would be able to join agent Five. Of Seven's sub-network, 7 (3), the Wren, had gone to India, 7 (5) and 7 (6) had dropped out, while 7 (2), 7 (4) and 7 (7), the faithful Donny, Dick and Dorick, continued to carry the main burden of the day. At the end of August Madrid sent GARBO an assessment of the sub-agents. It is of such interest that it is quoted in full.

'It has, for a long while past, been my desire to deal in brief with your various collaborators or, that is to say, to let you know how we here judge the quality and importance of their reports.

'I can say with satisfaction that all of these who are regular informants show that they have understood their mission owing to the logic of the good instructions which they have received from you. Outstanding in importance are the reports of your friend 4 (3), who, owing to the position he occupies, is the best placed for facilitating details with regard to the organisation of the army in general, about its large units and its composition, the arrival of new American divisions, plans of the High Command, &c. Though I imagine that in this connection you are dealing with an unconscious collaborator, it is necessary to cultivate this friendship by all possible means as you yourself have pointed out. The last report of this friend of yours about the reorganisation of FUSAG was excellent. Nevertheless, it is necessary to proceed with the greatest care so as not to arouse his suspicion through the questions you ask him.

'The informants 7 (2), 7 (4) and 7 (7) we consider to be perfect military observers and we have no further observation to make. If they continue to work as they have done up till now, then we are more than satisfied!

'As to 7 (1), it is a long time since we had news of him, possibly you can get some information through this channel about the present location of the 9th British Division, a matter which interests us as we have already stated by message.

'The work of 7 (5) did not last long and we could not judge his good qualities. We are happy that the difficulties he experienced did not bring more serious consequences. I realise that this agent must have been influenced by this incident. Nevertheless, I consider the Swansea area to be of great importance. Even though there are not, at present, large contingents of troops there, it is from other aspects of war of interest and therefore I do not think that you should break contact altogether with this agent. I think you should use him for work which is not dangerous as I do not think that he will be able to work free from fear, but he might be of some minor use. I leave the final decision to you.

'I am completely in agreement with your decision with regard to agent 7 (6), who has shown no signs of intelligence. We have had practically no news about 7 (3) since she has been in your employment. We hope for good results from her new place of residence.

'Seven is the one who has the greater merits, since he has organised his large network and has at the same time acted himself as an observer and military informant of great precision and accuracy. He has also supplied us with several reports of extraordinary merit. We should be very upset should we ever have to lose this friend who has overcome so many difficult situations. It was undoubtedly he who gave so much help in cases which had to be resolved with urgency such as the case of Four after he had left the camp. I hope, therefore, that we will be able to continue to count on the collaboration of Seven and should he not wish to remain here, we would like to have him in the new organisation in Canada which I will deal with more fully later in this letter.

'With regard to Three, who is undoubtedly your best collaborator, there is no need for me to say anything more since we have expressed, above, our opinion of him.

'As to 3 (1) and 3 (2), it is a long time since we have had news of them. (Possibly your friend who was in contact with them is no longer able to maintain this contact.) If this is the case, please let us know so that we can remove them from our list.

'The same applies to 3 (3) as has been said about 7 (2), 7 (4) and 7 (7), though I think that this is a case where the informant might intensify his work a little since it is undoubtedly the case that a lot of important military activities are taking place in the North, in spite of the fact that the possibility of an embarkation from there appears, for the moment, to have disappeared.

'I shall deal more fully with Four, together with the Canadian project. The effort which he made when the invasion was about to take place merits the highest recognition and praise. I perfectly well understand that what he is doing now and his present situation must be intolerable, and I consider that we should please him as quickly as possible.

'4 (1) continues to carry out his mission with all perfection and reliability. He has acquired a great deal of practice since he has been transmitting. The transmissions have sometimes been very difficult owing to atmospheric conditions and other disturbances. Should he be able to modify his set, increasing the frequency band from 5,000 to 9,000 Kcs. for example, we should be able to adapt more favourable frequencies to the general conditions and times of transmission. If he cannot do it, it does not matter, because we have managed to get along like this and will continue to do so.

'4 (2) is another of the agents about whom we have had no news for some time. I therefore hope that you will be also let me know in this connection whether we may remove him from our list or whether this agent is collaborating with you in some other connection.

'With regard to your friends J (3) and J (5), I do not think they call for any special mention. The information from the MOI, which you have obtained through J (3), has on many occasions made it possible for us to be able to draw important conclusions and this friend has, furthermore, served your cover magnificently.

'With reference to J (1), I can tell you that the sending of correspondence has worked recently to perfection. Some letters have been in my possession within a week.'[11]

By the beginning of October Four had left with Seven for Canada. In November 3 (3) resigned. In February 1945 GARBO decided to pay off 7 (5) and 7 (6). As they had done nothing for a long time he said he would give them £100 each. At the beginning of April Three went to see GARBO in South Wales as it was becoming evident that the end was near and agent Seven's organisation in particular was becoming restive. As GARBO pointed out to his masters:

---

11. GARBO Letter from Lisbon, dated 31st August, 1944, and received 9th September, 1944.

'These individuals are inspired by other ideas and their ends are different from ours. They have helped us because they believe and hope that with the assistance that they were giving us we would one day be able to help them and the ends of their Party. Now that they see that our situation is itself difficult and they cannot hope for anything from us, they wish to get out without compromise from the promise of loyalty which they have expressed.'[12] 7 (7) could not see how their work was going to benefit the Welsh Nationalist Movement. 7 (4) frankly admitted that he had only got mixed up in this business because of his mistress and intended to return to India when the war was over. 7 (2), though willing to continue, was suffering from asthma. Three himself was prepared to go on in the face of all difficulties. During the next few weeks the situation deteriorated fast, and on 1st May the Germans recommended to GARBO that he should wind up the whole organisation. 'The rapid course of events and the confusion reigning all over the world makes it impossible to see ahead with clarity the future developments of the general situation or to take decisions in this connection. We thank you with all our heart for the offer from Three and yourself for your continued future collaboration, understanding and fully appreciating the motives which animated this. On the other hand, you will understand that in a situation which does not allow one to look ahead it is our greatest wish and duty as colleagues to arrange matters in such a way, taking as a basis the present events, so as to ensure generally for your safety and that of the collaborators, giving them an opportunity to return to their private activities.'[13]

On 3rd May GARBO joined agent Three in London. A message sent on that day with a request to the Germans to destroy his papers ended on an optimistic note. 'I have absolute confidence, in spite of the present crisis which is very hard, that our struggle will not terminate with the present phase and that we are entering into what is developing into a world civil war which will result in the disintegration of our enemies.'[14] On the 6th the Germans replied: 'Grateful for your latest messages and, especially, your offers of unconditional

---

12. GARBO Letter No. 39, dated 8th April, 1945.
13. GARBO Message received 2025 and 2032 GMT, 1st May, 1945.
14. GARBO 1826 GMT, 3rd May, 1945.

collaboration. The heroic death of our Fuehrer clearly points the course which must be followed. All future work and efforts, should they be carried out, must be directed exclusively against the danger which is threatened by a coalition with the East. Only a close union of all the sane peoples of Europe and America can counteract this tremendous danger against which all other questions become unimportant. You will understand that in view of the very rapid evolution of the situation during the past week, it has become completely impossible for us to be able to tell you now whether we will later on be able to dedicate ourselves to the work, the basis of which is indicated above. Should we do so, we hope that we will be able to count on your proven friendship and enormous experience in service matters. We, therefore, fully approve your plan to return to Spain where, when once you have arrived, the plan for a new organisation directed against the East can be dealt with.'[15] On the 8th GARBO was told that if he should succeed in reaching Madrid he was to frequent the Café Bar La Modrena, 141 Calle Alcala, every Monday between eight and half-past eight in the evening starting on 4th June. He was to be seated at the end of the café and to be carrying the newspaper, *London News*. A person would meet him there who would say that he had come on behalf of Fernando Gomez.[16] On the same day GARBO sent his last message: 'I understand the present situation and the lack of guidance due to the unexpected end of the military struggle. News of the death of our dear Chief shocks our profound faith in the destiny which awaits our poor Europe, but his deeds and the story of his sacrifice to save the world from the danger of anarchy which threatens us will last for ever in the hearts of all men of goodwill. His memory, as you say, will guide us on our course and today, more than ever, I affirm my confidence in my beliefs and I am certain that the day will arrive in the not too distant future when the noble struggle will be revived, which was started by him to save us from a period of chaotic barbarism which is now approaching.'[17]

Soon after the war ended GARBO made his way to Spain. He eventually found Kuehlenthal, his master, in the small town of Avila.

---

15. GARBO Message received 1812, 1833 and 1841 GMT, 6th May, 1945.
16. GARBO Message received 1932 GMT, 8th May, 1945.
17. GARBO 1910, 1919 and 1925 GMT, 8th May, 1945.

'Kuehlenthal was overcome by emotion when he welcomed GARBO to his sitting-room. He told him how he had visualised this reunion and marvelled at GARBO's ability to overcome the apparently impossible obstacles which must have been in his way.' During the conversation which followed – it lasted for more than three hours – Kuehlenthal made it abundantly clear not only that he still believed in the genuineness of GARBO, but that he looked upon him as a superman. He was afraid of being repatriated to Germany and asked GARBO whether he could not, with his long experience, devise some means for his escape. The latter said that he would see what he could do and when he had made a suitable plan would communicate it through one of the agents, perhaps Three or Seven. Before he took his leave Kuehlenthal asked him where he was going next, to which GARBO replied: 'Portugal for a start.' 'How', asked Kuehlenthal, 'do you propose to get from Spain to Portugal?' 'Clandestinely,' GARBO replied.

XXXVIII

Conclusion

It is always unsafe to apply too literally the experiences of one war to the changed circumstances of another, especially so where one is concerned with the art of deception whose successful practice must, in any circumstances, depend on qualities of mind rather than on some fixed code of rules. The conclusions reached in this final chapter are therefore only offered with that important reservation. The most striking object lesson of FORTITUDE is its revelation of the capabilities and limitations of the different channels that were used to deceive the enemy. In 1943 it was supposed that the story would be told by physical and confirmed by special means. In fact the result was obtained by a process almost diametrically opposite. On reflection, it is hard to see how this could have been otherwise. Visual misdirection conveys its message by inference. On the field of battle such methods may suffice. The group of dummy tanks or the simulated noise of a mechanised column may well draw the enemy to the wrong flank. But where the sphere of one's activities extends over half a continent and one is operating from a base far removed from the enemy's centres of intelligence, something more is needed. Even here visual misdirection may in certain cases exert a positive influence. The bombing programme of the Allied Air Forces on the Pas de Calais achieved an undoubted success. Similarly one was justified in hoping that the display of dummy craft might have advanced the interests of FORTITUDE to some extent, although in the event this hope was not fulfilled. Generally speaking, however, mere physical misrepresentation on the ground placed there for the benefit of the hostile spy or reconnoitring aircraft allows of too many alternative interpretations to provide a satisfactory vehicle for the conveyance of elaborate strategic intentions, even if the spies and aircraft are there to look. Indeed it is not easy to imagine how certain vital aspects of a story of this nature, the disclosure of commanders' names for example, can be imparted at all by such means. At first sight one would say that wireless deception was subject to none of these limitations, but here again, in practice, certain difficulties arise. Even if one has the resources and the skill to disclose false intentions by controlled leakage, one can scarcely hope that the enemy will always be listening at the right moment, nor can one be sure that faulty reception may not prevent him from hearing if he is listening. The lesser special means channels, based on the spreading of rumour, are, as we have already seen, too diffuse to be relied upon. There is only one method which combines the qualities of precision, certainty and speed necessary for the conduct of strategic deception at long range and over an extended period, and that is the double-cross agent. He can tell his story in detail and without shadow of equivocation, knowing that it will reach its destination quickly and unaltered. By destroying the enemy's spy system in this country, thus establishing a degree of security which made the operation of controlled agents possible, and by setting up in their place GARBO, BRUTUS and their fellows, the British Security Service laid the foundation for all that FORTITUDE achieved. One is indeed driven to the conclusion that until these conditions are secured, it will be useless to embark upon a project of the magnitude and duration of FORTITUDE. Nor can one regard this initial task as completed when one has overcome the danger of serious leakage and persuaded a number of enemy spies to change their allegiance. As with other forms of attack, deception requires its vanguard. GARBO's case officer always held that it was not merely Kuehlenthal in Madrid, but the Abwehr in Berlin that he sought to win and through them the OKW. Once a man has sponsored the deception of his opponent, he will hesitate to admit his mistake even after his suspicions have been aroused. In this way a silent body of support is built up in the enemy camp as, one by one in ascending scale, the members of the opposing hierarchy accept the credibility of their renegade agents. This process can be more easily accomplished if one happens to be at war with a country which labours under a tyrannical government, where all loyalties are suspect and genuine error may be visited with dire penalties.

Although FORTITUDE would in the event have worked just as well if there had been no physical deception at all, it would be unwise to assume that such devices can be dispensed with in the strategic field. The majority of them should, however, be regarded less as instruments of deception than as security measures to be taken at those points where there is a danger of the enemy breaking through the security ring, so that if he does he will find nothing to contradict and if possible something to confirm the story which is being told by the controlled agents. It is a matter of insurance and in this as in all cases where risks are run, one is not necessarily justified in allowing a policy to lapse because no claim has been made. On the other hand there is everything to be said against over-insuring, for physical deception is far more costly than special means, yet it is the latter which carries the main burden of the operation. Furthermore, it lets many more into the secret and so magnifies one's security problems. An accurate estimate of the risks involved is thus of the utmost value in framing a deception policy and the services and ministries affected should be prepared to assess these risks and revise their assessments from time to time, remembering when they do so that the temptation to over-insure is always great, for while an over-estimate and the waste to which it gives rise will usually pass unnoticed, an under-estimate will, if things go wrong, receive the censure which is accorded to any miscalculation in war.

We may ask ourselves, in passing, why the German Intelligence proved so remarkably ineffective in the late war where the British Isles were concerned. As we have already seen, those measures which brought GARBO and BRUTUS into existence at the same time removed the real German spy from the scene. Absence of air reconnaissance can be explained by the decisive Allied superiority in that element. The failure of wireless intercept is more difficult to understand. Unfortunately, in spite of prolonged search, no trace has been found of the records of the German intercept service in the Western European theatre. Should these ever be discovered, they would undoubtedly throw valuable light on the subject. As it is one can only fall back on conjecture. Two possible explanations have been offered for the poor results obtained. On the one hand it has been suggested that the enemy concentrated the bulk of his intercept apparatus on the battle fronts where it operated at short range, with the result that the United Kingdom was not adequately 'covered', and on the other that the enormous volume of wireless traffic in this country presented a pattern so confused as to make intercept extremely difficult.

Given the conditions which governed the conduct of FORTITUDE, is there anything useful which our recent experience can teach us about the writing of the deception plan? Since it will presumably fall to the lot of special means to play the leading role, it becomes a matter of the first importance to see that the plan does not compel the controlled agents to say things which will impair their credit while the operation is still in progress. It should therefore provide them in advance with explanations upon which they can fall back when their initial forecasts have been disproved by events, as is always bound to occur with deception. As we have already seen, an 'escape clause' is not so essential where physical devices alone are employed since the enemy may attribute the misinformation to imperfections in his own intelligence machine. Thus the original FORTITUDE plans, written mainly from the point of view of the physical deceiver, paid scant attention to the future well-being of the controlled agents. Witness the proposed employment of the 3rd British Infantry Division in FORTITUDE NORTH, which would have placed the whole framework of deception in jeopardy as soon as that formation landed on D Day. Contrast this with Fourth Army's move to Yorkshire during the following autumn in support of TROLLEY-CAR. By that time we had come to realise the dominant part which the double-cross agents were playing in the execution of the plan and the consequent importance of safeguarding their position. On that occasion, before the Fourth Army had left the Eastern counties, we had already devised an alternative story to account for the move after it had become apparent that no embarkation from the Humber was intended. Looking back on the broader aspects of the operation, we find in FORTITUDE SOUTH II a sufficient release from the embarrassments created by FORTITUDE SOUTH I. Yet the new plan was evolved late in the day and long after the original one had been set in motion. A new commander was brought to Europe in time to replace Patton only through the very prompt co-operation of General Marshall, while the arrival of Fourteenth Army had to be ante-dated by more than a month, a procedure which, unless handled with care, may place some strain upon the enemy's credulity. It should always be one's aim to compose the lie and the 'let out' at the same time, so that from the moment that the plan begins to operate, every action can be so devised as to be capable, in retrospect, of alternative interpretations.

A further lesson which FORTITUDE brings home is the danger of treating a deceptive operation too literally. What is or is not possible matters less than what the enemy believes to be possible. We have a good example in the decision to use the Western Scottish ports for embarking the troops which were to take part in FORTI-TUDE NORTH. It is perfectly true that the Eastern ports had not the necessary capacity for the shipping required, but the Germans do not seem to have been aware of the fact. By abandoning the more obvious proposal in deference to our own administrative staff we removed the threat altogether. One is always inclined to credit the enemy with knowing as much about one's own affairs as one does oneself, but if the conditions precedent to the running of double-cross agents obtain, this will be far from the truth. A reasonable and straightforward story, even if it involves manœuvres which cannot in reality be performed, is often to be preferred to a more complex one which is capable of execution, but whose objects cannot readily be discerned.

If obscurity of aim is to be avoided in the preparation of a plan, this applies with still greater force to its execution. It is very easy to fall into the habit of mind which assumes that one's own is the only voice heard by the enemy, when in fact it is but one of many. If one is to be heard above the others, it can only be by saying what one has to say with clarity and conviction. At the same time one must seek, wherever possible, to silence one's rivals, not only because they pollute one's own stream, but because they may stumble on the truth and perhaps also for the more unexpected reason that they may, by clumsy repetition, cause the enemy to disbelieve one's own story. Both of the last named dangers were realised during the latter part of the war.[1] Deception thus demands that while our false intentions are being disclosed to the enemy in plain terms by the agents that we do control, those that we do not should at the first opportunity be won over to our side; failing which they must, in the euphemistic language of our times, be 'liquidated'.

Experience gained during the invasion has also taught us something about the technical handling of the various weapons of deception. When disclosing an elaborate story to the enemy it is not only easier, but usually safer and more effective, to use a few proved channels rather than divide it between a wide variety of agencies whose value is not known. By adopting the latter course one makes it less certain that the entire plot will be brought to the notice of the enemy and, what is worse, one suspect channel may bring discredit not only on the story itself but also on all the other means that one is employing

---

1. On 31st May, 1944, OSTRO gave a correct forecast of the invasion. There is no evidence to show that his message was based on anything more solid than his own imagination. In the autumn of 1944 an enquiry was initiated at the headquarters of the Fremde Luftwaffen West into the traffic of JOSEPHINE, HECTOR and OSTRO, which led to the surprising conclusion that all three agents were controlled by the Allies. This conclusion was based partly on the fact that they had failed to answer satisfactorily a number of catch questions which had been put to them, partly on certain similarities which were observed in their traffic, due, no doubt, to the fact that both Kraemer and Fidrmuc had been relying upon the same German intelligence summaries, but more particularly, in the case of JOSEPHINE, upon an ingenious analysis of FORTITUDE SOUTH which revealed all its weaknesses and roundly declared that the story had been false from start to finish. Fortunately the traffic of our own controlled agents was not submitted for examination, and since the part which they were playing in strategic deception had now practically ceased, they escaped castigation. The prime mover in this investigation appears to have been a junior officer named Count Posadowski. It is not without interest to observe that one of the first of his reports in which he cast doubt upon the credibility of these agents bears the marginal comment: 'This note was handed over personally by Lieutenant Count Posadowski to Lieutenant-Colonel von Dewitz, who was so annoyed that he read barely half of it. Thenceforward the former very intimate relations were broken off. There was no factual discussion of the matter.' Such is the fate of those who venture to suggest that geese are not swans after all. The Fremde Luftwaffen West evaluation of JOSEPHINE's reports on FUSAG is given at Appendix XIV.

to divulge it. This rule applies in the selection of controlled agents. The reader will remember how a part of the story was lost by giving it to the unproved TATE. He will also recall the reason why we refrained from associating the tried British agents with the less reliable ones in France. Deception staffs must be prepared to resist the pleas of case officers who will always seek to obtain the plums for their own protégés. More than half-a-dozen agents shared in the execution of FORTITUDE, but its success was due to two only, and those two we had recognised, at any rate by the summer of 1944, to be the star performers of the team. This is not to say that one should not use the lesser channels, whose credibility is reasonably assured, to provide independent confirmation. But here again there are pitfalls to avoid. It is natural that certain types of information should come into the hands of more than one spy acting independently. Identifications of the same troops and fixed installations, for example, which are or could be there for all to see, will not excite suspicion if they reach the enemy from several unconnected sources.[2] On the other hand, the discovery of highly secret operational intentions by more than one enemy agent is hardly true to life. The case of the air exercise in Kent on 29th May, 1944, has already been cited. An even graver risk was run in July of that year when, through a misunderstanding, GARBO and BRUTUS reported the whole of the FORTITUDE SOUTH II story in almost identical terms. When this occurs, one of two things will happen. Either the enemy will assume that both agents are operating under control, or he will take the second message as confirmation of the first and so become more firmly convinced of the truth of the report. Fortunately, in the last-named instance, the Germans took the latter view. But the danger of pursuing such a course far outweighs any possible advantage that may be gained.

It is necessary at this point to draw attention once more to a curious misconception which persisted throughout the continuance of FORTITUDE. At all times, the Political Warfare Executive, in its capacity as propaganda machine of the British Government, and on

---

2. During FORTITUDE a map was kept on which were marked imaginary installations which had been reported to the Germans, so that the controlled agents, when visiting the places where they were supposed to be situated, would not forget to observe them.

occasion the public statements of senior commanders and states-men,[3] were accounted as available channels for implanting falsehoods on the enemy. It is right that those at the head of affairs or who are responsible for framing the policy of national propaganda should be informed of current deception plans so that they may be prevented from saying anything that is at variance with them. But to make a channel which is known by the enemy to be officially inspired the mouthpiece of positive deception must surely run the risk of exciting suspicion. However imbued a deception staff may be with the advantages of a 'double bluff', no commander would ever allow particulars of an impending real operation to be broadcast to the world, and any intelligent enemy would be aware of this.

One hesitates to express any opinion on methods adopted during FORTITUDE in the handling of physical devices, for these were never really put to the test. The arguments which have been advanced on either side in the matter of dummy traffic and controlled leakage on the wireless have already been set out in an earlier chapter. Where visual misdirection is concerned it may be useful to reassert that in an island such as ours unmistakable evidence of an intention to invade is likely to become apparent only at a very late stage. It was the Germans themselves who, on 5th May, 1944, observed in reference to shipping on the south coast of England: 'We must, however, suppose that without doubt a considerable proportion, particularly of landing craft, have remained *unobserved* since these are, as we know from experience, well camouflaged and are hidden, withdrawn from sight into the numerous bays and waterways along the south coast.' Here at any rate the deceiver may find scope for economy of resources, for anything which cannot be seen until the last moment need not be represented at all.[4]

We now pass to the difficult matter of command and control. It is submitted that the control of a deceptive operation must be decided

---

3. These remarks do not apply to the allusion to FABIUS which Mr Churchill made in his speech of 29th March, 1944, for here there was a sufficient element of truth to remove it from the category to which reference is now being made.

4. The writer always contended that moorings, suitably placed and brought to the notice of the enemy by the controlled agents, would have been as effective and far less costly than a large fleet of dummy craft.

upon the self-evident principle that no two people can safely tell the same lie to the same person except by closely concerted action. We must therefore determine the scope of the operation. This will tell us who will be affected, which channels are likely to be used, and what agency is best fitted to correlate the activities of all concerned. The solitary scout behind the hedgerow can formulate and execute his own cover plan without reference to higher authority because he acts alone. At the other end of the scale we have the grand deception of FORTITUDE which bore upon every activity in the United Kingdom. It was therefore right that the directive of 26th February, 1944, should have left it to the Supreme Commander to 'co-ordinate and control the execution of the plan as a whole' and should have reserved to him 'the implementation of the plan by special means'. Whether it was equally right to place upon the Joint Commanders the responsibility for 'directing towards the Pas de Calais the threat created by the forces under their control' (which included the bulk of the physical means of deception) and for 'making preparations to continue the threat against the Pas de Calais after NEPTUNE D Day' is open to debate, for this amounted in effect to nothing less than a delegation to them of the conduct of FORTITUDE SOUTH I, the essential cover plan for OVER-LORD. The reader will remember that this delegation was made with the object of unifying control. The detailed planning and physical execution of both real and false operations were to be placed in the same hands. In fact, this course tended to divide rather than to unify. The implications of FORTITUDE SOUTH I inevitably extended into fields which lay beyond the purview of the Joint Commanders; furthermore, the principal executants, the controlled agents, remained under SHAEF, the senior command, an anomolous situation and one which gave rise to some inconvenience through the physical separation of the two headquarters. It is also hard to see what SHAEF gained by divesting itself of the command of specialist troops engaged in deception. If one is going to make the best use of one's inevitably limited resources, it seems reasonable to suggest that the agency best fitted to conduct the operation as a whole, and therefore most suitably placed to weigh the relative importance of conflicting demands throughout the theatres, should also command all specialist troops. These can always be allotted to subordinate commanders in such proportions and for such periods as the occasion demands.

This brings us to a consideration of staff organisation. Here the lesson of FORTITUDE is very clear. Reversing the practice of the Middle East, the deception staff at SHAEF was made a sub-section of the Operations Division, because it was said that only in this way would it be able to remain in 'the operational picture'. In fact, with an immense headquarters staff, it takes a long time for vital decisions to percolate to its lower levels. But strategic deception, if it is to succeed, must be in constant touch with the commander's thoughts. Furthermore, the current flows in both directions. Intelligence reaching the deception staff through the double-cross agents may be of immediate value to the commander. FORTITUDE achieved what it did because the conditions which governed its execution remained constant. The ineffectiveness of strategic deception during the latter months of the war may be partly explained by the isolation of the deception staff from the real centre of control. It is sometimes argued that while the deception staff should remain a part of the operations division, its head should have direct access to the commander.[5] But this gives rise to a situation more unorthodox than the stigmatised 'private army', and in practice the head of the deception staff may hesitate to exercise a right which involves the passing by of his immediate superior. Furthermore, it still leaves him outside the immediate current of events. Another reason for bringing the commander and the deceptive machine into close touch lies in the fact that deception may otherwise be given tasks to carry out which it is not well fitted to perform. There is a tendency on the part of those who are constantly at grips with compelling realities to regard deception as a swift panacea to be invoked when other remedies have failed. Although there may be occasions when its services can usefully be enlisted to give immediate aid,[6] it is generally more correct to regard

---

5. See COSSAC recommendation at page 29, para. 2.
6. For example, on 7th June, 1944, in order to help the American troops who had met opposition on the beaches, 21 Army Group asked the Special Means Staff at SHAEF to tell the enemy that the Guards Armoured Division was to sail on D + 3. It was not really due to leave until some days later, but it was

it as a method which achieves its results by a slow and gradual process rather than by lightning strokes. Like the fly-wheel of an engine it requires time to gain momentum and time again to lose it. By employing it at the eleventh hour one may be too late to do any good and merely succeed in bringing one's influence to bear at a time when it is in conflict with the real plan. Is it an exaggeration to say that a commander should be as closely and as constantly informed about his shadow armies as he is about his real ones? Reality and deception are but the reverse sides of the same coin, and the latter may bring benefits out of all proportion to the cost involved. This much events have proved.

Yet, when all is said, one is left with a sense of astonishment that men in such responsible positions as were those who controlled the destinies of Germany during the late war, could have been so fatally misled on such slender evidence. One can only suppose that strategic deception derives its capacity for giving life to this fairy-tale world from the circumstance that it operates in a field into which the enemy can seldom effectively penetrate and where the opposing forces never meet in battle. Dangers which lurk in this *terra incognita* thus tend to be magnified, and such information as is gleaned to be accepted too readily at its face value. Fear of the unknown is at all times apt to breed strange fancies. Thus it is that strategic deception finds its opportunity of changing the fortunes of war.

---

hoped that this false report might draw German forces in front of the British and Canadians and so relieve the position on the American beaches. At 0006 hours on 8th June, GARBO reported that the Guards Armoured Division was about to leave and in the same message told the enemy that the 3rd British Infantry Division had already taken part in the assault. The latter statement was true, and by including it we hoped to make them believe the other part of the message which was not. Madrid regarded this item of intelligence as being of such importance as to justify sending it direct to Paris, and on 9th June an urgent message from Paris to KO Spain stated that the information concerning the part played by the 3rd British Infantry Division in the assault was correct and added that the report of the impending departure of the Guards Armoured Division had been described by Von Rundstedt as especially important and that the latter had asked for further reports of a similar nature (History of the GARBO Case, chapter 24B, FORTITUDE (Phase II), pages 194, 199 and 200).

APPENDIX I

Plan BODYGUARD

Overall Deception Policy for the War against Germany

COS (43) 779 (O) (Revise)
25th December, 1943

Intention of this Paper

1. The intention of this paper is to formulate an overall deception policy for the war against Germany in accordance with CCS 426/1 of 6th December, 1943, paragraph 9 (*e*).

Object

2. To induce the enemy to make faulty strategic dispositions in relation to operations by the United Nations against Germany agreed upon at EUREKA.[1]

Present Situation

3. The German General Staff will this winter be considering the strategic disposition of their forces to meet offensive operations by the United Nations in 1944. Though they will be forced to maintain the bulk of their forces on the Russian front, they already suspect that large-scale Anglo-American operations will be undertaken in Western Europe some time in 1944. It is, however, doubtful whether they have at present sufficient information regarding the timing and scope of this threat to justify any immediate changes in their strategic dispositions.

4. At a later stage, however, preparations for OVERLORD[2] and

---

1. Cairo Conference.
2. Cross-Channel invasion.

to a lesser degree for ANVIL[3] will be on such a scale and of such a type that the enemy cannot fail to appreciate our intention to carry out a cross-Channel operation and an amphibious operation in the Western Mediterranean.

Deception Problem

5. The problem to be solved is twofold:

(*a*) *Overall Problem*

We must persuade the enemy to dispose his forces in areas where they can cause the least interference with operations OVER-LORD and ANVIL and with operations on the Russian Front.

(*b*) *Tactical Problem*

As soon as our preparations for OVERLORD and ANVIL clearly indicate to the enemy our intention to undertake a cross-Channel operation and an amphibious operation in the Western Mediterranean, Theatre Commanders concerned must implement their tactical cover plans to deceive the enemy as to the strength, objective and timing of OVERLORD and ANVIL.

Choice of Areas in which to Contain Enemy Forces

6. In view of SEXTANT[4] decisions our overall deception policy should be to contain enemy forces in areas where they will interfere as little as possible with operations on the Russian Front and with OVERLORD and ANVIL. Such areas are:

(*a*) *Northern Italy and Southern Germany*

It should be possible by means of real operations and feints to contain a number of first quality divisions in this area.

POINTBLANK[5] operations from Italy should also help to contain enemy fighter forces.

(*b*) *South-East Europe*

The JIC appreciate* that the enemy will do his utmost to hold

---

* JIC (43) 385 (O).
3. Proposed attack against French Mediterranean coast.
4. Teheran Conference.
5. Long-range bombing attacks.

South-East Europe, though limited withdrawals from the islands and Southern Greece might be undertaken. Provided that we can persuade the enemy to believe that considerable forces and landing craft are being concentrated in the Eastern Mediterranean it should be possible to contain enemy forces in the Balkans. Our chances of success would be increased if Turkey joined the Allies, but even if she refused we might still induce the enemy to fear the results of our continued infiltration. The deception plan would be assisted to a marked degree if the Russian General Staff staged an amphibious threat to the Bulgarian–Roumanian coasts across the Black Sea.

(c) *Scandinavia*

A threatened attack against Scandinavia should help to contain some first-quality divisions and limited naval and air forces. Such a deception plan would be assisted if the Germans were induced to believe that Sweden was prepared to co-operate with the Allies and if the Russians mounted a threat against enemy-occupied territory in the Arctic.

Allied Preparation for OVERLORD and ANVIL

7. (a) OVERLORD

It will be impossible wholly to conceal the gradual build-up of Allied forces and other preparations in the United Kingdom during the next few months. In addition the enemy will appreciate that considerable American forces in the United States are available for transfer to Europe.

In these circumstances our best chance of deceiving the enemy would be to indicate that Anglo-American strategy is dictated by caution and that we have no intention of undertaking the invasion of the Continent until we had assembled an overwhelming force and the necessary landing craft; these would not be available until the late summer. To support this story we must try to indicate that the assault and follow-up forces at present available in the United Kingdom are less than they in fact are, and that during the next few months we could re-enter the Continent against little or no opposition.

(b) ANVIL

Preparations and the build-up for ANVIL should not be so apparent in the early stages, therefore the tactical cover plan eventually put into operation by Allied Commander-in-Chief, Mediterranean Theatre, should suffice to cover this assault.

In the Mediterranean Theatre the enemy has in the past been induced to overestimate Allied forces by 20 to 30 per cent. It would be an advantage if such exaggeration could be maintained especially in the Eastern Mediterranean.

Russian Front

8. The Russian offensive will presumably be continued during the next few months but it would be of assistance to our plans if we could lead the enemy to believe that the Russian main summer offensive would not start before the end of June.

It would be plausible that this operation should thus precede OVERLORD and ANVIL thereby rendering the maximum assistance to these far more hazardous seaborne assaults.

Factors Against the Achievement of the Object

9. (a) Preparations for OVERLORD during the next few months and any announcements of the appointment of prominent commanders in the United Kingdom will indicate to the enemy *that our main strategy is switching from the Mediterranean to North-Western Europe.*

(b) Statements both in the press and on the radio and the platform may continue to emphasise the likelihood of operations in 1944 from the United Kingdom against North-Western Europe.

Factors For the Achievement of the Object

10. (a) Germany's armed forces are dangerously stretched by current operations and provided we can induce her to retain surplus forces in Scandinavia, Italy and the Balkans, she will find it difficult simultaneously to provide adequate forces for Russia, France and the Low Countries.

(b) Germany's defensive commitments are likely to be increased since:

    (i) The political and economic situation in Germany and occupied countries is deteriorating and may necessitate the maintenance of strong garrison forces in these areas.

    (iii) The attitude of neutrals and satellites may move further in favour of the Allies and compel Germany to dispose reserves to meet unfavourable developments.

(*c*) The assembly of the Rosyth force in North-East Scotland will reinforce the threat to Scandinavia.

Overall Deception Policy

11. The following Overall Deception Policy is based upon the considerations outlined above.

12. *Allied Intentions. We should induce the enemy to believe* that the following is the Allied plan for 1944.

(*a*) POINTBLANK operations were seriously affecting the enemy's war potential and, if continued and increased, might well bring about his total collapse. Consequently, reinforcement of the United Kingdom and the Mediterranean by long-range American bombers was to have first priority.

(*b*) The Allies must be prepared to take advantage of any serious German weakening or withdrawal in Western Europe and preparations to this end must be put in hand forthwith.

(*c*) To concert in spring an attack on *Northern Norway* with Russia with the immediate object of opening up a supply route to Sweden. Thereafter to enlist the active co-operation of Sweden for the establishment of air bases in Southern Sweden· to cover an amphibious assault on Denmark from the United Kingdom in the summer.

(*d*) Since no large-scale cross-Channel operation would be possible till late summer, the main Allied effort in the spring of 1944 should be against the Balkans, by means of—

    (i) An Anglo-American assault against the Dalmatian coast.

    (ii) A British assault against Greece.

    (iii) A Russian amphibious operation against the Bulgarian–Roumanian coast.

(iv) In addition, Turkey will be invited to join the Allies to provide operational facilities including aerodromes to cover operations against the Ægean Islands as a prerequisite to the invasion of Greece. her refusal would not materially modify the Allied intentions.

(v) Pressure against the satellites to induce them to abandon Germany.

(*e*) Anglo-American operations in Italy would be continued, and in order to hasten their progress, amphibious operations against the north-west and north-east coast of Italy would be carried out. Provided these were successful, 15 Army Group would later advance eastwards through Istria in support of the operations mentioned in (*d*) above.

NOTE. The operations in (*c*) (*d*) and (*e*) above would enable us to employ our amphibious forces and retain the initiative until preparations for the final assault in the later summer were completed.

(*f*) Though Russian operations would presumably be continued this winter it would not be possible for them to launch their summer offensive before the end of June.

(*g*) In view of the formidable character of German coastal defences and the present enemy strength in France and the Low Countries, a minimum of twelve Anglo-American Divisions afloat in the initial assault and a total force of about fifty divisions would be required for a cross-Channel assault. This operation would not be launched until the late summer (*i.e.* after the opening of the Russian summer offensive).

Allied Strength and Dispositions

13. We should induce the enemy to believe the following information regarding Allied strength and dispositions.

(*a*) *United Kingdom*

(i) Shortage of man-power has obliged the British Army in the United Kingdom to resort to cannibalisation, while several of their formations are on a lower establishment, or still lack their administrative and supply units. The number of Anglo-American Divisions in the United Kingdom available for offensive operations is less than is, in fact, the case. Some United States Divisions arriving in the United Kingdom have not yet completed their training.

(ii) Personnel of certain Anglo-American Divisions in the Mediterranean with long service overseas are being relieved by fresh divisions from the United Kingdom and United States. The former will, on relief, return to the United Kingdom where they will re-form and be utilised for training inexperienced formations.

(iii) Invasion craft remains the principal bottleneck and the full number required for the initial assault cannot be made available from home production and the United States before summer.

(*b*) *Mediterranean*

(i) Anglo-American forces in the Mediterranean, especially in Eastern Mediterranean, are greater than is, in fact, the case.

(ii) French forces are taking over responsibility for the defence of North Africa, thus leaving Anglo-American forces free for offensive operations elsewhere in the spring of 1944.

(iii) Certain British Divisions and landing craft are being transferred from India to the Middle East.

(iv) Fresh divisions from the United Kingdom and United States are expected to arrive in the Mediterranean.

Tactical Cover Plan

14. (*a*) *United Kingdom*

When the enemy realises that cross-Channel operations are imminent, the story indicating that no cross-Channel attack will occur until late summer, will tend to lose plausibility. *At this juncture the tactical cover plan prepared by Supreme Commander, Allied Expeditionary Force, will come into force with a view to deceiving the enemy as to the timing, direction and weight of OVERLORD.*

(*b*) *Mediterranean*

In due course the enemy will probably appreciate, especially from air reconnaissance, that an amphibious operation is being mounted in North African ports and Western Mediterranean Islands. At this stage, a tactical cover plan prepared by Allied Commander-in-Chief, Mediterranean Theatre, will come into force with a view to deceiving the enemy as regard the timing, direction and weight of ANVIL.

Timing

15. The selection of the D Day of all cover and deception plans mentioned above is a question to be decided by Supreme Commander, Allied Expeditionary Force. In this connection, it is recommended that the dates chosen should, in each case, be later than OVERLORD or ANVIL D Days, with a view to delaying the despatch of enemy reinforcements for as long as possible.

Supreme Commander, Allied Expeditionary Force, and Allied Commander-in-Chief, Mediterranean Theatre, should in consultation with the Controlling Officer decide the tempo of the OVERLORD and ANVIL tactical cover plans.

Means of Implementation

16. (*a*) *Physical Means*

Implementation by means of movements of forces, camouflage devices, W/T deception and other activities will be carried out in accordance with detailed plans prepared by Supreme Commander, Allied Expeditionary Force and Allied Commander-in-Chief, Mediterranean Theatre.

(*b*) *Diplomatic Means*

Genuine diplomatic approaches will be required to lead the enemy to believe that we intend persuading Sweden to join the Allies and assist us in operations in Scandinavia.

Even if Turkey refused to join the Allies in the near future, the enemy should be led to believe that our continued infiltration may give the Allies important opportunities in connection with a Balkan campaign.

(*c*) *Special Means*

Implementation by means of leakage and rumours in support of plans prepared by Theatre Commanders will be *co-ordinated* by the London Controlling Section.

(*d*) *Political Warfare*

The Political Warfare plan while not departing from its main purpose should conform to the above general policy.

(*e*) *Security*

Plan BODYGUARD cannot succeed unless the strictest security precautions are taken to conceal the true nature of OVERLORD and ANVIL preparations.

APPENDIX II

Plan FORTITUDE

SHAEF (44) 13
23rd February, 1944

INTRODUCTION

1. With the object of inducing the enemy to make faulty strategic dispositions in relation to operations by the United Nations

against Germany in 1944, Plan BODYGUARD outlined the cover and deceptive policy for the European Theatre as given in para. 2 below.

2. The enemy should be induced to believe:

(*a*) That forces are being held in readiness in the United Kingdom for a return to Western Europe at any time in the event of a serious German weakening or withdrawal.

(*b*) That an operation would be carried out in conjunction with Russia in the spring with the immediate object of opening a supply route through Northern Norway to Sweden, thereafter enlisting the active co-operation of Sweden for the establishment of air bases in Southern Sweden to cover an assault on Denmark from the United Kingdom in the summer.

(*c*) That a large-scale cross-Channel operation with a minimum force of fifty divisions and with craft and shipping for twelve divisions would be carried out in late summer.

3. Plan BODYGUARD also indicated that a tactical cover plan designed to deceive the enemy as to the timing, direction and weight of NEPTUNE should be executed when the imminence of cross-Channel operations indicated that invasion was likely to take place before late summer.

4. Within the framework of BODYGUARD, Plan FORTITUDE outlines the cover and deception policy for North-West Europe, based on the following assumptions:

(*a*) That the target date for NEPTUNE will be 1st June, 1944.

(*b*) That NO real operations, other than RANKIN, will be carried out in Norway before D Day NEPTUNE.

5. To induce the enemy to make faulty dispositions in North-West Europe before and after the NEPTUNE assault, thus:

(*a*) Reducing the rate and weight of reinforcement of the target area.

(*b*) Inducing him to expend his available effort on fortifications in areas other than the target area.

(*c*) Lowering his vigilance in France during the build-up and mounting of the NEPTUNE forces in the United Kingdom.

(*d*) Retaining forces in areas as far removed as possible from the target area before and after the NEPTUNE assault.

CONSIDERATIONS

Areas

6. Plan BODYGUARD indicates Scandinavia as the most suitable area against which to maintain a long-term threat, Northern Norway being an intermediate objective to the establishment of air bases in Southern Sweden. Sweden would be unlikely to concede her Southern airfields to the Allies with Germany still in occupation of Southern Norway. An assault on Denmark demands the prior occupation of the Stavanger–Oslo area, therefore the target for a deceptive operation should be extended to include this area.

7. As the NEPTUNE preparations proceed, the significance of the threat against NORWAY will tend to decrease and, for the sake of plausibility, should not be over-emphasised. At this stage the character and location of the NEPTUNE forces will become increasingly evident to the enemy and a cover target area, as far removed as possible from the real assault area, should be threatened. The Pas de Calais best fulfils the conditions of plausibility.

Timing

8. Climatic conditions do not normally allow operations in Southern Norway before 1st April, and in Northern Norway before 1st May. As it would take at least three months to occupy Southern Norway and to establish air bases in Southern Sweden, the enemy would expect us to assault Norway as early as possible if Denmark were to be invaded in the same year. Furthermore, to contain German forces in Scandinavia, a threat should be fully developed about one month before the target date of NEPTUNE. It would further assist NEPTUNE to continue the threat for as long as possible after D Day NEPTUNE. The amphibious training essential to an assault on Northern Norway cannot be completed to enable an assault to be undertaken before NEPTUNE D minus 17.

9. The threat to Southern Norway should therefore be developed by NEPTUNE D minus 30; the threat to Northern Norway and the full development of the Scandinavian threat being achieved by

NEPTUNE D minus 17 and maintained thereafter.

10. It would be plausible for the enemy to believe that the hazards of a cross-Channel operation demand the maximum assistance from all other fronts and in particular from the Russian front. As the enemy might well be led to believe that large enough forces cannot be assembled in the United Kingdom in time to take advantage of the Russian winter offensive, the cross-Channel operation should be timed to take advantage of the summer offensive. Climatic conditions on the Southern Russian front allow this offensive to start early in May and be extended to the whole front by the end of May. The enemy should be led to believe that we intend to allow this offensive to develop for six weeks until about NEPTUNE D plus 45, before launching large-scale cross-Channel operations.

11. By NEPTUNE D minus 30, the movement and administrative preparations and the concentration of air forces will be nearly complete and the concentration of craft and shipping will be between 70 and 80 per cent complete for NEPTUNE. These preparations, and the type and location of the forces will begin to threaten the NEPTUNE area only, unless preparations for the concentration of similar forces are made in East and South-East England. In order, however, to minimise our state of preparedness as a whole, the long-term preparations in the East and South-East should indicate a later target date.

12. If before NEPTUNE D Day, however, it becomes evident that the enemy does NOT believe in the later target date, preparations in the East and South-East should be accelerated and the threat to the Pas de Calais be fully developed.

Strength of Forces

13. A total of about fifty-eight divisions would be required for the deceptive operations; that is, two to Northern Norway, six to Southern Norway and fifty to the cross-Channel operation.

14. At the present rate of build-up in the United Kingdom there would only be about fifty-three divisions, with craft and shipping for twelve, available for operations by NEPTUNE D plus 45. We should, therefore, induce the enemy to believe that the deficiency of about five divisions will be made up from the United States during

the operation. At the same time, in order to emphasise the later target date, we should minimise the state of preparedness of the NEPTUNE forces by misleading the enemy about their state of training, organisation, equipment and their location.

Story A
From now until the NEPTUNE Assault

15. The enemy should be induced to believe that the Allies will carry out the following operations in North-West Europe in 1944.

Occupation Operations

16. From 1st February, 1944, balanced forces are being held in readiness to occupy any part of North-West Europe in the event of German withdrawal or collapse.

Southern Norway

17. With a target date of NEPTUNE D minus 30 an operation will be mounted from northern ports to invade Southern Norway. The assault will be made in the Stavanger area by one infantry division supported by parachute troops and commandos, followed up by one infantry division.

18. The force will be built up to a total of six divisions within three months, a proportion of this force being mountain trained. An advance to Oslo will be made along the coast by a series of mutually supporting land and amphibious operations, involving the use of landing craft sufficient to lift one brigade group.

19. Allied naval forces will escort the convoys and support the assault and subsequent amphibious operations. The assault will also be supported by carrier-borne aircraft. Long-range fighters will be flown in from the United Kingdom as soon as airfields are captured.

Northern Norway

20. With a target date of NEPTUNE D minus 17, an operation will be mounted in conjunction with Russian forces against Northern Norway to open road and railway communications with Sweden. The operation will be supported by Anglo-American naval forces, including aircraft carriers.

Change of Target Date

21. On or about NEPTUNE D minus 30, the enemy should be led to believe that the Southern Norway force is mounted and held in readiness to be launched at short notice; similar conditions will apply to the Northern Norway force on or about NEPTUNE D minus 17.

Denmark

22. As soon as the Allies are firmly established in Southern Norway with Allied air forces operating from there and Southern Sweden, an assault will be launched on Denmark.

Pas de Calais

23. With a target date of NEPTUNE D plus 45, a cross-Channel operation will be carried out by a total force of fifty divisions with craft and shipping for twelve divisions. The assault will be made in the Pas de Calais area by six divisions, two east and four south of Cap Gris Nez. The follow-up and immediate build-up will be a further six divisions. The force will be built up to the total of fifty divisions at the rate of about three divisions per day.

24. The first phase of the operation will be the establishment of a bridgehead which must include the major port of Antwerp and the communication centre of Brussels. From this bridgehead large-scale operations will be conducted against the Ruhr with the final object of occupying Germany.

25. The operation will be mounted as follows:

> Two assault and one follow-up divisions from the Wash to Deal.
> Four assault and one follow-up divisions from the south coast.
> One follow-up division from Bristol Channel.
> Two build-up divisions from the Humber and Tyne.
> One build-up division from the Mersey and Clyde.

Change of Target Date

26. (If at any time before NEPTUNE D Day it is discovered that the enemy does not believe in the later cover target date, the threat to the Pas de Calais will be rapidly developed.)

STORY B

FROM NEPTUNE D DAY

27. After D Day of NEPTUNE and for as long as possible, the enemy should be induced to believe that subsequent operations will be carried out as given below.

Pas de Calais (Maintenance of the threat)

28. The operation in the NEPTUNE area is designed to draw German reserves away from the Pas de Calais and Belgium. Craft and shipping for at least two assault divisions are assembled in the Thames Estuary and south-east coast ports; four more assault divisions are held in readiness in the Portsmouth area and will be mounted in craft and shipping from NEPTUNE. When the German reserves have been committed to the NEPTUNE area, the main Allied attack will be made between the Somme and Ostend with these six divisions in the assault.

Scandinavia

29. The operations in Norway and Sweden (see STORY A) will be carried out against resistance as soon as sufficient shipping is available from NEPTUNE, the assault on Denmark being postponed until spring 1945. If, however, there is any weakening of the German forces in Norway these operations will be launched on a reduced scale to take immediate advantage of the situation.

APPENDIX III

FORTITUDE Directive

SHAEF (44) 21
26th February, 1944

To—

Admiral Sir Bertram H. Ramsay, K.C.B., K.B.E., M.V.O.,
  Allied Naval Commander, Expeditionary Force.
General Sir Bernard L. Montgomery, K.C.B., D.S.O.,
  Commander-in-Chief, 21 Army Group.
Air Chief Marshal Sir Trafford L. Leigh-Mallory, K.C.B., D.S.O.,
  Air Commander-in-Chief, Allied Expeditionary Air Force.

Reference SHAEF (44)13, dated 23rd February, 1944, and COSSAC (44) 4, dated 7th January, 1944, paragraph 26.

General

1. The object of Plan FORTITUDE is to induce the enemy to make faulty dispositions in North-West Europe before and after the NEPTUNE assault.

Present Situation

2. Certain measures giving effect to Plan FORTITUDE have already been initiated by the Supreme Commander. These measures, which are listed at Appendix A, are subject to adjustment as a result of detailed planning.

Execution of the Plan

3. The Supreme Commander is to co-ordinate and control the execution of the plan as a whole and is to be responsible for the following arrangements:

(*a*) The implementation of the plan by special means.

(*b*) Political warfare and propaganda.

(*c*) The Occupation and Scandinavian operations (SHAEF (44) 13 paragraphs 16–22 and 29).

4. The Allied Naval Commander, Expeditionary Force, the Commander-in-Chief, 21 Army Group, and the Air Commander-in-Chief, Allied Expeditionary Air Force, will be responsible to the Supreme Commander for directing towards the Pas de Calais the threat created by the forces under their control and for concealing the state of readiness of these forces so as to indicate NEPTUNE D plus 45 as the real target date.

5. They will also be responsible for making preparations to continue the threat against the Pas de Calais after NEPTUNE D Day.

6. They will adhere to the broad design of Plan FORTITUDE.

Allotment of Wireless Deception Units and Major Equipments

7. The allotment of the wireless deception units and of the major equipments likely to be available is at Appendix B.

For the Supreme Commander,

F. E. MORGAN,

for W. B. SMITH,

Lieutenant-General, US Army,

Chief of Staff.

APPENDIX A TO FORTITUDE DIRECTIVE
PRESENT SITUATION

Camouflage and Concealment

1. Instructions were issued on 22nd September, 1943, directing maximum concealment in the South and West of all operational preparation, concentration and movement, and also directing discreet display in the East and South-East.

Wireless Security

2. Periodic wireless silence and intense activity was ordered on 9th December, 1943, as a security measure necessary to cover final

embarkation. Period 25th December, 1943, to 28th December, 1943, was observed; period 24th January, 1944, to 27th January, 1944, was broken at the request of 21 Army Group to allow 1 Corps exercises.

Deceptive and Decoy Lighting

3. Provision action for the installation of deceptive and decoy lighting at hards has been taken. These installations are mobile and can be adjusted to the requirements of detailed planning at about seven days' notice.

Movement and Administrative Preparations

4. General direction on the movement and administrative preparations necessary to support the Pas de Calais threat has been issued to the War Office, which is interpreting this direction in detail to Commands through General Headquarters, Home Forces, Q (Ops) and Q (M) channels.

Special Means

5. Implementation by Special Means within the framework of Plan FORTITUDE has been started.

Relevant Papers

Paragraphs

1. COSSAC/00/6/3/1/Ops, dated 22nd September, 1943.
   GHQ.HF.S/00/355/1/G(O), dated 25th January, 1944.
   SHAEF/18205/Ops, dated 7th February, 1944.
2. COSSAC/2355/Ops, dated 9th December, 1943.
3. COSSAC/3140/11/Sec, dated 18th December, 1943.
   COSSAC/18210/Ops, dated 27th January, 1944.
4. SHAEF/18201/4/Ops, dated 9th February, 1944.

APPENDIX B TO FORTITUDE DIRECTIVE
ALLOTMENT OF WIRELESS DECEPTION UNITS
AND MAJOR EQUIPMENTS

Supreme Commander

Wireless Deception Units
One static monitoring section, 5 Wireless Group.
One divisional section, 5 Wireless Group.
One monitoring section, 5 Wireless Group.

Military Equipments
100 Bigbobs (Inflatable).

Allied Naval Commander, Expeditionary Force,
Commander-in-Chief, 21 Army Group, and
Air Commander-in-Chief, Allied Expeditionary Air Force.

Wireless Deception Units
3103 Signal Service Battalion (US).
Two divisional sections, 5 Wireless Group.
One mobile monitoring section, 5 Wireless Group.

Military Equipments
150 Bigbobs Mk II (Rigid).
165 Bigbobs Mk V (Rigid).
50 Bigbobs Mk V (Inflatable).
150 Wetbobs (Rigid).
145 Wetbobs (Inflatable).

Air Equipments
36 Squadrons dummy aircraft (Spitfire type).
20 Squadrons dummy aircraft (P 51 type).

APPENDIX IV

FORTITUDE SOUTH

Joint Commanders' Plan

Ref. No.
NJC/00/261/33

CONTENTS

PART I. COVER PLAN FORTITUDE (SOUTH)

Introduction

1. The Allied Naval Commander-in-Chief Expeditionary Force, the Commander-in-Chief 21 Army Group and the Air Commander-in-Chief Allied Expeditionary Air Force have been charged by the Supreme Commander with the responsibility for

---

* These were short-term diversionary operations 'forming an integral part of operation NEPTUNE', and therefore omitted.

directing towards the Pas de Calais the threat created by the forces under their control and for concealing the state of readiness of these forces so as to indicate NEPTUNE D plus 45 as the real target date. The three Commanders-in-Chief are also responsible for continuing the threat against the Pas de Calais after NEPTUNE D Day. Further they will adhere to the broad design of Plan FORTITUDE.

Story

2. The story on which Plan FORTITUDE is based falls naturally into two phases:

> Phase (i) – Pre D Day.
> Phase (ii) – Post D Day.

(*a*) *Phase (i)*

The main Allied assault is to be made against the Pas de Calais area.

In the first place, the notional date for the operation will be D Day plus 45. There will come a time, however, when as D Day approaches our preparations will indicate the imminence of the assault, and when the enemy will realise the approximate date of our attack. When it is estimated that this period has been reached, the imminence of an attack will be confirmed by special means, but the area of the main attack will remain the Pas de Calais area.

(*b*) *Phase (ii)*

NEPTUNE is a preliminary and diversionary operation, designed to draw German reserves away from the Pas de Calais and Belgium. Once the main German reserves have been committed to the NEPTUNE battle, the main Allied attack against the Pas de Calais will take place.

The enemy will be induced to believe for as long as possible after NEPTUNE D Day that the main threat to the Pas de Calais is still to be carried out.

3. The code-word QUICKSILVER is used to cover the various operations which implement the threat to the Pas de Calais area either before or after D Day.

QUICKSILVER I

(a) *Phase (i)* *(Before D Day)*

4. The Supreme Commander has under command two Army Groups, the 21 Army Group, and the First United States Army Group, which consists of the First Canadian Army with under command 2 Canadian and VIII US Corps, and the Third United States Army with under command XX Corps and XII Corps.*

The First United States Army Group is located in the East and South-East of England.

The Air Force associated with the First United States Army is the Ninth United States Air Force stationed in the South and South-East.

(b) *Phase (ii)* *(After D Day)*

The First United States Army Group and a proportion of its associated Air Force is ready to attack the Pas de Calais. Once the forces under command 21 Army Group have enticed the enemy reserves in the Pas de Calais area towards the NEPTUNE bridgehead, the Supreme Commander intends to assault the area Pas de Calais with another Army Group.

Before the final assault a series of large-scale exercises will take place (of which the mounting of the assault on NEPTUNE is one).

QUICKSILVER II

W.T. Plan

5. *(a)* Appendix A shows the notional Order of Battle of the First United States Army Group, and at Appendix B is shown the diagram of the wireless communications of this Army Group.

(b) These stations, as shown in the diagram, will commence to operate from 24th April.

(c) Two notional combined exercises, the first DRYSHOD, the second WETSHOD, will be held by the 4 Canadian Infantry Brigade assisted by Force G. These exercises will take place on about 16th and 25th April.

---

* Amended on 5th June, XII being substituted for VIII Corps and XXXVII for XII Corps (21 AGP/00/272/2, dated 5th June, 1944).

QUICKSILVER III

Craft Indication

6. (*a*) In order that the threat supported by the wireless traffic of the notional First United States Army Group should be substantiated by the result of enemy aerial reconnaissance dummy landing craft will be erected and maintained in accordance with the table at Appendix C.

(*b*) Naval wireless traffic proportionate to the number of craft will be simulated in the mooring areas, appropriate Army wireless traffic being linked to these flotillas as far as possible.

(*c*) The signing of roads and special areas consistent with the story of the embarkation of the force will be carried out in Eastern and South-Eastern Commands.

QUICKSILVER IV

Air Plan

7. (*a*) The details of the Air Plan for the threat to Pas de Calais is contained in the general Air Plan for FORTITUDE which is attached at Appendix D.

(*b*) In additional a short programme against the beach area in the area Pas de Calais will be carried out immediately prior to D Day of OVERLORD. This will be supported by the tactical railway bombing plan which includes attacks on rail targets in the cover area.

QUICKSILVER V

Increase of Activity at Dover

8. In order to show the correct increase in activity in the area of Combined Headquarters Dover (Headquarters of 2 Canadian Corps) special work will be carried out to give the impression of extra tunnelling and the erection of further wireless stations being undertaken.

Appropriate new wireless circuits will be opened up.

QUICKSILVER VI

Night Lighting

9. In order to show activity at night in the areas where dummy craft are indicated, night lighting installations simulating vehicle lights and beach lighting will be erected in accordance with the table at Appendix E. These installations will be operative from mid-May onwards.

APPENDIX A TO PART I OF JOINT COMMANDERS' PLAN

(The notional Order of Battle of the First United States Army Group is given at page 92).

APPENDIX B TO PART I OF JOINT COMMANDERS' PLAN

(The wireless communications closely followed the lines of the Order of Battle referred to at Appendix A; the diagram is therefore omitted.

APPENDIX C TO PART I OF JOINT COMMANDERS' PLAN

Serial		Place and Area of Berthing	Approx. Quantity of Craft
1	Yarmouth	Breydon Water	50
		Ref. OS 1″ to 1 mile, Sheet 67.	
2	Lowestoft	Harbour 992105–996105	20
		Ref. OS 1″ to 1 mile, Sheet 77.	
3	Waldringfield	R. Deben	66
		R. Deben.	
		Ref. OS 1″ to 1 mile, Sheet 87.	
4	Wolverstone	R. Orwell	70
		Cathouse,	
		R. Orwell.	
		Ref. OS 1″ to 1 mile, Sheet 87.	
5	Dover	Dover Harbour	46
		Ref. OS 1″ to 1 mile, Sheet 117A.	
6	Folkestone	Folkestone Harbour	18
		Ref. OS 1″ to 1 mile, Sheet 117A.	
		Total	270

APPENDIX D TO PART I OF JOINT COMMANDERS' PLAN
AIR PLAN
STORY A

1. The main large-scale threat will be mounted by the actual forces in the South of England and the enemy will be induced to believe that the main attack will be at a later date than NEPTUNE D Day, and directed against the Pas de Calais area. This threat will be implemented by air forces by:

(i) Long-term preparations in South-East England indicating a target date of NEPTUNE D plus 45.

(ii) Carrying out training flying in the South-East by fighter type squadrons based in the South. This will indicate that familiarisation training for these squadrons is being undertaken prior to an assault against the Pas de Calais.

(iii) Carrying out training by High Speed Air Sea Rescue launches in the South-East. The use of two launches can simulate training of much larger numbers. Air Sea Rescue Squadrons will also carry out training in this area.

(iv) Carrying out a large-scale air operation, on or about NEPTUNE D minus 3 with fighters and a large force of bombers. A proportion of the fighter squadrons will be flown, on the days of this operation from airfields in the South, to advanced bases in the South-East from which they will operate. The aim of the operation will be to test the efficiency of operating fighter squadrons in 'shuttle service' from advanced bases whose position gives tactical advantage. The use of a large bomber force gives a good 'cover' excuse for staging this test. The movement of aircraft from the South of the Thames Estuary and Kent will be arranged to give the impression of a desire to conceal the operation. This will involve the careful manipulation of call-signs, the arrangement of deliberate indiscretions by R/T and very strict orders as to the height at which aircraft are to fly.

(v) Commencing the construction of additional dummy hard standings on airfields in the South-East to strengthen the impression of incomplete preparation already given by normal construction being carried out on these airfields.

(vi) Undertaking small-scale operations of the same nature as that referred to in sub-paragraph (iv) at frequent intervals with small air forces operating under the control of Sectors in the South-East. This will involve artistic disclosure of such operations by deliberate indiscretions on R/T and manipulation of call-signs.

STORY B

2. After NEPTUNE D Day, it will be evident to the enemy that a major attack has been launched. It will, therefore, be necessary to maintain the threat against the Pas de Calais. This will be implemented by:

(i) Disclosing to the enemy by special means the function of the US Air Forces located in South-East England.

(ii) One or two exercises in the South-East designed to simulate normal Army/Air Force co-operation.

REAL OPERATIONS

3. The bombing programme as designed does not compromise NEPTUNE and assists the Cover Plan.

Operations which indicate the NEPTUNE area will be compensated by 'Cover' flights against the 'Cover' area.

CULMINATION OF THREAT

4. It may become necessary for the threat against the Pas de Calais to culminate in order to contain or delay enemy forces which might be employed in areas where their presence would be embarrassing. It is estimated that the most likely period for this culmination would be from NEPTUNE D Day to D plus 14. If and when it is decided that the threat should culminate, concentrated close support bombing attacks, consistent with the time, size and scope of the operation, should be undertaken.

APPENDIX E TO PART I OF JOINT COMMANDERS' PLAN
NIGHT LIGHTING INSTALLATIONS

Dummy Craft Indication Area	Site of Night Lighting Installations	Ref. Map 1" to 1 mile Sheets 67, 77, 87, 98
1. Great Yarmouth	Breydon Water	(67/954246)
2. Lowestoft	Oulton Broad	(77/957109)
3. Lowestoft	Benacre Ness	(77/992011)
4. Deben River	Whitehall Farm	(87/742613)
5. " "	Kirton Creek	(87/745596)
6. " "	Falkenham Marshes	(87/762571)
7. Orwell River	Long Reach	(87/675557)
8. " "	Trimley Marshes	(98/703540)

APPENDIX V

FORTITUDE SOUTH

Outline Plan for Special Means*

SHAEF/24132/4/SM/OPS
6th May, 1944

---

* This system of writing 'Special Means' plans was devised in the summer of 1943 when it became the task of the Deception Staff at COSSAC to supply the TWIST Committee with the essential features of the COCKADE plans and with the dates on which individual releases could be made. It was found a convenient method of presenting the story to the controlled agents and was adopted in subsequent plans. Column (*b*) gives the facts on which the story was to be based; Column (*c*) gives the dates on which the events referred to in Column (*b*) would occur; Column (*d*) gives the story, based on the facts contained in Column (*b*), which was to be told by the controlled agents; Column (*e*) gives the date on which the story was to reach the enemy. So far as possible the serials were arranged chronologically in the order in which each item was to be disclosed to the Germans.

Long-term preparations for OVERLORD   F†
MULBERRY   G
Security measures permanently in force   H
Final preparations for NEPTUNE   J†
FORTITUDE (SOUTH)Military Order of Battle, forecast
    for D plus 10   K

Maps

Location of OVERLORD military forces before concentration
    (approximately Y minus 60)   MA
Location of OVERLORD military forces after concentration
    (Y minus 30 to Y minus 15)   MB
Location of FORTITUDE military forces after concentration   MC

NOTE. Marshalling areas and sub areas, camps, hards and traffic routes
are shown on maps held in Ops B War Room.

Appendix D, the 'phased programme for identification and grouping of
military forces – 1st May to NEPTUNE D Day', was designed to guide the
controlled agents when reporting the moves to concentration, real and false,
which occurred during that period. Similar programmes were prepared for
subsequent troop movements.

FORTITUDE SOUTH I employed real formations only, the basis of the
deception being to give them false concentration areas. The true locations
before concentration, given at map MA, are therefore the same for OVER-
LORD and FORTITUDE. Map MB gives the real OVERLORD
concentration, while map MC gives the false FORTITUDE concentration.

Appendices, A, B, C, E, G, H and K are omitted as most of the information
which they contain is to be found in other parts of this report. Appendices F
and J were never issued.

The Special Means plan of 6th May, 1944, was written before the change of
policy caused by the arrest of ARTIST took effect.

† Will be issued later.

FORTITUDE (SOUTH) – OUTLINE PLAN FOR SPECIAL MEANS

(a) Serial	(b) Fact	(c) Date	(d) Story	(e) Target Date	(f) Remarks
			Phase I Concentration period for NEPTUNE		
1	An Anglo-American force will carry out OVERLORD on NEPTUNE D Day. (Order of Battle is at Appendix A.)	NEPTUNE D Day	An Anglo-American force will carry out FORTITUDE in the Pas de Calais area. (Order of Battle is at Appendix B.)	Now onwards	It will be necessary to reduce the interval of 45 days between NEPTUNE D Day and FORTITUDE D Day, as now laid down in Plan FORTITUDE.
2	Locations of OVERLORD military forces in the UK as at 1st April, 1944, are at map MA.	1st April	Locations of FORTITUDE military forces as at 1st April, 1944, are identical with OVERLORD locations as shown at map MA.	By 1st May	Assembly of Naval forces is continuous. Day-to-day position shown on map in Ops B War Room. Main Air Force concentration completed on this date, and shown on map in Ops B War Room.

(a) Serial	(b) Fact	(c) Date	(d) Story	(e) Target Date	(f) Remarks
3	OVERLORD military forces move to concentration. (Map MB.) (FUSAG) FORTITUDE wireless net is established in concentration areas. (Appendix C.)	For dates of concentration of military forces see Appendix C. FORTITUDE (FUSAG) wireless net fully established 27th April.	FORTITUDE military forces move to concentration. (Map MC.)	Military forces to be identified in new locations, and grouping to be determined, in accordance with phased programme at Appendix D.	For concentration of Naval and Air Forces see serial 2, column (f).
4	Exercise FABIUS takes place in the English Channel. (Appendix E.)	25th April to 7th May	A naval exercise takes place in the English Channel to practise crews in embarkation, disembarkation and the handling of assault craft. 21 Army Group provides the troops for the Exercise.	Appendix E	
5	Long-term preparations, visible to air or ground observation, are being completed in the coastal belt Wash–Land's End and in South Wales. (Appendix F.)	Continuous	The completion of long-term preparations is being pressed forward in East and South-East England.	Continuous	The preparations should be reported accurately, with exception of those in South-West England which should be lightly dealt with. The Germans will probably believe that it is an invasion.

6	Concentrations of MULBERRY units are at Appendix G.	See Appendix G	See column (f)		Await any enemy reaction. If enemy appreciation correct, report for use in areas north and south of Boulogne.
7	Security measures permanently in force are at Appendix H.		Security restrictions have been imposed early to avoid drawing attention to NEPTUNE D Day.	Continuous	
8	All Service leave stopped.	6th April	Service leave is continuing, though frequently interrupted by large-scale exercises.		
			PHASE II NEPTUNE		
9	Final preparations for NEPTUNE undertaken. (Appendix J.)	See Appendix J	See remarks		Preparations in South and South-West should be minimised. Those in the East and South-East should be exaggerated. If pressed for an answer, NEPTUNE preparations should be described as an exercise.
10	NEPTUNE assault.	NEPTUNE D Day	Formations of 21 Army Group have launched the first stage in the re-entry to the Continent against the NEPTUNE area. The main assault will be made by FUSAG, when the	D Day to D plus 10	

(a) Serial	(b) Fact	(c) Date	(d) Story	(e) Target Date	(f) Remarks
			Germans are committed in the NEPTUNE area.		
			PHASE III Post-NEPTUNE		
11	First Canadian Army moves from South-East England to take part in NEPTUNE. Forces simulating 2 (British) Corps move from Scotland to locations vacated by First (Canadian) Army.	NEPTUNE	NEPTUNE having failed to draw the German reserves from the Pas de Calais, First Canadian Army has been placed under command of 21 Army Group and will be employed in the NEPTUNE area. At the same time, 2 (British) Corps has been placed under command FUSAG, and is moving from Scotland to the locations vacated by First Canadian Army. (New FUSAG Order of Battle is at Appendix K.)	NEPTUNE D plus 10 onwards	2 (British) Corps may have 1 Polish Armoured Division and 2 French Armoured Division placed under command, thereby increasing the threat of an armoured breakthrough in the Pas de Calais. The threat to the Pas de Calais is thus maintained.
12	VIII (US) Corps moves from East England to take part in NEPTUNE.	NEPTUNE D plus 10	It has been found necessary to send further reinforcements to the NEPTUNE area in order to draw German reserves from Pas de Calais.	NEPTUNE D plus 10	As for serial 10, column (f).

Appendix D to Outline Plan for Special Means

Phased programme for identification and grouping of military forces – 1st May to NEPTUNE D Day

(a) Serial	(b) Formation	(c) Factual locations and movements from 1st March, 1944	(d) Identified — Old location	(d) Identified — Date	(d) Identified — En route	(d) Identified — Date	Concentration area	Release date	(e) Grouping — Association with higher formation	(e) Grouping — Date	(f) Remarks
1	SHAEF	Moved from Norfolk House to Widewings [Bushy Park] – 1st March to 15th April. Move completed by latter date.	London	Continue reports							Continue to report in London area.
2	21 Army Group	Main Headquarters moved from Hammersmith to Southwick, 26th April. Rear Headquarters remains at Hammersmith.	West London	Continue reports until NEPTUNE D Day (see remarks).					SHAEF	Already implied in press reports.	Notional location of Main Headquarters subject to periodical review.
3	First (US) Army	Located at Clifton, near Bristol since beginning of period.	Bristol	Continue reports.					21 Army Group	7th May	The association of First (US) Army and 21 Army Group is necessary if the Germans are to believe that First Canadian Army is under command FUSAG.

(a) Serial	(b) Formation	(c) Factual locations and movements from 1st March, 1944	(d) Identified						(e) Grouping		(f) Remarks
			Old location	Date	En route	Date	Concentration area	Release date	Association with higher formation	Date	
4	V (US) Corps	Moved from Taunton to Norton Manor, near Salisbury. Move completed by 14th April.	Taunton	Already reported.			Norton Manor	10th May	First (British) Army	1st May	
5	First (US) Infantry Division	Located at Dorchester since beginning of period.					Slapton Dorset	3rd May 4th May	Should not be grouped with any higher formation.		First to be identified as complete formation during FABIUS assault at Slapton. To be reported subsequently returning in an easterly direction to concentration area. Thereafter, should not be mentioned.
6	2 (US) Infantry Division	Moved from Armagh (Northern Ireland) to Tenby. Move completed end of April.	Northern Ireland	Already reported.					Should not be grouped with any higher formation.		Arrival in England should not be mentioned.
7	29 (US) Infantry	Located at Tavistock since beginning of period.					Tavistock	Continue reports.	V (US) Corps	1st May	References to this Division should, from now onwards, be less frequent.

No.	Unit	Remarks		Location	Date	Grouping	Date	Remarks
8	VII (US) Corps	Located at Braemore (Hampshire) since beginning of period.		Braemore	15th May	First (US) Army	1st May	
9	4 (US) Infantry Division	Located at Tiverton since beginning of period.		Tiverton	Already reported (see remarks).	VII (US) Corps	1st May	Troops of this Division have been reported at Exeter and Torquay. Its location should not be stressed.
10	9 (US) Infantry Division	Located at Winchester since beginning of period.		Winchester	2nd May	Should not be grouped with any higher formation.		Released FOYNES Division.
11	90 (US) Infantry Division	Arrived Birmingham from US during March.	Should not be mentioned during period.					
12	XIX (US) Corps	Located at Warminster from beginning of period.	Should not be mentioned during period.					
13	30 (US) Infantry Division	Arrived Chichester from US early March. Move to Chesham completed by 15th April.		Chesham	10th May	Should not be grouped with any higher formation.		
14	2 (US) Armoured Division	Located at Tidworth since beginning of period.		Tidworth	20th May	Should not be grouped with any higher formation.		Training on Salisbury Plain should be emphasised.

(a) Serial	(b) Formation	(c) Factual locations and movements from 1st March, 1944	(d) Identified						(e) Grouping		(f) Remarks
			Old location	Date	En route	Date	Concentration area	Release date	Association with higher formation	Date	
15	3 (US) Armoured Division	Located at Wincanton since beginning of period.					Wincanton	Continue reports (see remarks).	First (US) Army. Should not be grouped with XIX (US) Corps.	10th May	References to this Division should, from now onwards, be less frequent.
16	82 (US) Airborne Division	Located at Leicester since beginning of period. Moved from Northern Ireland during February.	Should not be mentioned during period.								FOYNES Division, not released.
17	101 (US) Airborne Division	Located at Newbury since beginning of period.					Newbury	Continue reports (see remarks).	Should not be grouped with any higher formation.		Reports should continue on present scale.
18	Second (British) Army	Move from Oxford completed 23rd April. Main Headquarters – Southwick. Rear Headquarters – Purbrook. Static Headquarters – London.	Oxford	Already mentioned (see remarks).					21 Army Group	5th May	No further reference should be made to location of Second (British) Army. This, however, should be subject to periodical review.

19	1 (British) Corps	Located at Cobham since beginning of period.	Cobham	Continue reports.			Should not be grouped with any higher formation.
20	3 (British) Infantry Division	Move from Inverness to Denmead completed 15th April.	Inverness	Already reported.	Denmead		Should not be grouped with any higher formation.
21	27 (British) Armoured Brigade	Move from Moy (Inverness) to Petworth reported 14th April.		Should not be mentioned during period.			
22	3 (Canadian) Infantry Division	Move from Brockenhurst to Winchester reported 8th April.	Brocken-hurst	Already reported.	Winchester	10th May	Should not be grouped with any higher formation.
23	2 (Canadian) Armoured Brigade	Move from Burley to Fareham reported 3rd April.		Should not be mentioned during period.			
24	51 (British) Infantry Division	Moved Chesham to Bury St Edmunds end March-beginning April. Will move to Portsmouth area during May.	Newmarket	Continue reports until NEPTUNE D Day minus 5.			
25	4 (British) Armoured Brigade	Located at Worthing since beginning of period.		Should not be mentioned during period.			

(a) Serial	(b) Formation	(c) Factual locations and movements from 1st March, 1944	(d) Identified — Old location	Date	En route	Date	Concentration area	Release date	(e) Grouping — Association with higher formation	Date	(f) Remarks
26	8 (British) Corps	Move from Sandhutton to Worth Priory reported 17th April.	Sandhutton	Already reported.			Wakehurst	20th May	Should not be grouped with any higher formation.		
27	Guards Armoured Division	Moves from Brompton (Yorkshire) to Hove 30th April to 11th May.	Brompton	Already reported.			Hove. Units to be seen at Newhaven.	20th May 28th May	8 (British) Corps	15th May	
28	11 (British) Armoured Division	Move from Dalton to Aldershot completed by 10th April.	Dalton	Already reported.			Should not be mentioned during period.				
29	15 (British) Infantry Division	Move from Leeds to West Grinstead completed 26th April.	Leeds	Already reported.			West Grinstead	15th May	8 (British) Corps	20th May	
30	6 (Guards) Tank Brigade	Moves from Welbeck to Ashford 27th April to 3rd May.			Dorking	2nd May	Ashford	10th May			
31	12 (British) Corps	Located at Tunbridge Wells since beginning of period.					Tunbridge Wells	Continue reports (see remarks).	2 (British) Army	10th May	Mention rather more frequently.

No	Unit	Status	Location / Mention	Reports	Corps	Done	Notes
32	43 (British) Infantry Division	Located at Tenterden since beginning of period.	Tenterden	Continue reports.	12 (British) Corps	Already done	
33	53 (British) Infantry Division	Located at Hollingbourne since beginning of period.	Hollingbourne	Continue reports.	12 (British) Corps	Already done.	
34	59 (British) Infantry Division	Located at Canterbury since beginning of period.	Canterbury	Continue reports.	12 (British) Corps	Already done.	
35	34 (British) Armoured Brigade	Move from Canterbury to Aldershot completed 24th April.	Should not be mentioned during period.				
36	30 (British) Corps	Move from Newmarket to Three Bridges reported 30th April.	Should not be mentioned during period.				
37	7 (British) Armoured Division	Located at Didlington since beginning of period.	Should not be mentioned during period.				FOYNES Division not released.
38	50 (British) Infantry Division	Move from Bury St Edmunds to Brockenhurst reported 12th April.	Should not be mentioned during period.				Released FOYNES Division subject to periodical review.
39	8 (British) Armoured Brigade	Move from Fordham (Norfolk) to Burley. Thence to Lymington 6th to 14th April.	Should not be mentioned during period.				

(a) Serial	(b) Formation	(c) Factual locations and movements from 1st March, 1944	(d) Identified				Concentration area	Release date	(e) Grouping		(f) Remarks
			Old location	Date	En route	Date			Association with higher formation	Date	
40	49 (British) Infantry Division	Located at Norwich since beginning of period. May move to Tilbury area before NEPTUNE D Day.	Norwich	Continue reports.			Tilbury	27th May	Should not be grouped with any higher formation.		Report intensive training.
41	1 (British) Airborne Division	Located at Fulbeck since beginning of period.	Fulbeck	15th May					Should not be grouped with any higher formation.		Released FOYNES Division.
42	6 (British) Airborne Division	Located at Bulford since beginning of period.	Bulford	Continue reports.							Report training for operations during moonless periods.
43	FUSAG	Located in London since beginning of period. Represented by wireless traffic at Wentworth since 22nd April.					Wentworth	5th May	SHAEF	Already implied in press reports.	
44	First (Canadian) Army	Located at Leatherhead since beginning of period.					Leatherhead	Continue reports.	FUSAG	21st April	
45	2 (Canadian) Corps	Move from Three Bridges to Dover reported 24th April.	Three Bridges	Already reported.			Dover	1st May	First (Canadian) Army	21st April	

#	Formation		Location				Location		Formation		Remarks
46	2 (Canadian) Infantry Division	Move from West Grinstead to Dover reported 21st April.	West Grinstead	Already reported.			Dover	1st May	2 (Canadian) Corps	1st May	Should be reported as assault trained.
47	4 (Canadian) Armoured Division	Located at East Grinstead since beginning of period.							2 (Canadian) Corps	1st May	
48	VIII (US) Corps	Located at Marbury (Cheshire) since arrival from US during first half of April. Represented by wireless traffic at Folkestone since 25th April.					Folkestone	15th May	First (Canadian) Army	15th May	
49	79 (US) Infantry Division	Located at Northwich since arrival from US during first half of April. Represented by wireless traffic at Heathfield since 26th April.	Northwich	Already reported.			Heathfield	20th May	VIII (US) Corps	20th May	
50	28 (US) Infantry Division	Moved from Tenby to Chiseldon mid-April Represented by wireless traffic at Tenterden since 27th April.	Tenby	Already reported.	South Wales, Bristol	25th April 26th April	Tenterden	1st May	VIII (US) Corps	15th May	Should be reported as assault trained.
51	83 (US) Infantry Division	Located at Newcastle-under-Lyme since arrival from US during first half of April. Represented by wireless traffic at Elham (Kent) since 26th April.					Elham	10th May	VIII (US) Corps	20th May	

(a) Serial	(b) Formation	(c) Factual locations and movements from 1st March, 1944	(d) Identified				Concentration area	Release date	(e) Grouping		(f) Remarks
			Old location	Date	En route	Date			Association with higher formation	Date	
52	Third (US) Army	Located at Mobberley since arrival from US in March. Represented by wireless traffic at Chelmsford since 24th April.	Mobberley	Already reported.	Chelmsford	29th April	Chelmsford	7th May	FUSAG	5th May	
53	XII (US) Corps	Located at Bewdley since arrival from US during first half of April. Represented by wireless traffic at Chelmsford since 26th April.					Chelmsford	8th May	Third (US) Army	10th May	
54	80 (US) Infantry Division	Expected to arrive in UK from US during May. Will be represented by wireless traffic at Hadleigh (Suffolk) on arrival.					Hadleigh	On arrival in UK.	XII (US) Corps	On arrival in UK.	
55	7 (US) Armoured Division	Expected to arrive in UK from US early May. It will be represented by wireless traffic at Hatfield Peverel on arrival.					Hatfield Peverel	On arrival in UK.	XII (US) Corps	On arrival in UK.	

No.	Formation	Remarks	Location	Date	Location	Date	Location	On arrival in UK.	Higher formation	On arrival in UK.	Remarks
56	35 (US) Infantry Division	Expected to arrive in UK from US during May. It will be represented by wireless traffic at Brentwood on arrival.					Brentwood		XII (US) Corps		
57	XX (US) Corps	Located at Marlborough since beginning of period. Represented by wireless traffic at Bury St Edmunds since 25th April.	Marlborough	26th April			Bury St Edmunds	5th May	Third (US) Army	5th May	
58	4 (US) Armoured Division	Located at Chippenham since beginning of period. Represented by wireless traffic at Bury St Edmunds since 25th April.			Oxford, High Wycombe	20th April, 1st May	Bury St Edmunds		XX (US) Corps	10th May	
59	5 (US) Armoured Division	Arrived Chisledon from US early March. Move to Ogbourne completed by 22nd April. Represented by wireless traffic at East Dereham from 25th April.					East Dereham	12th May	XX (US) Corps	15th May	Division being dispersed for SOS duties.
60	6 (US) Armoured Division	Arrived Batsford from US early March. Represented by wireless traffic at Ipswich from 25th April.	Batsford	26th April	Ipswich	1st May	Woodbridge	1st May			
61	9 (US) Airborne Division										
62	2 (British) Airborne Division										

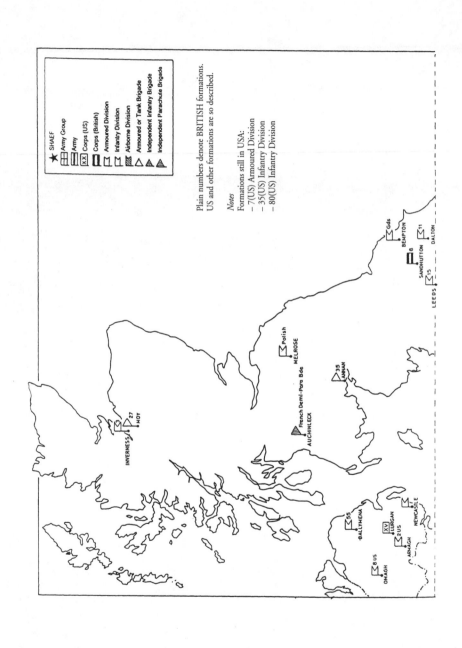

Plain numbers denote BRITISH formations.
US and other formations are so described.

Notes

Formations still in USA:
- 7(US) Armoured Division
- 35(US) Infantry Division
- 80(US) Infantry Division

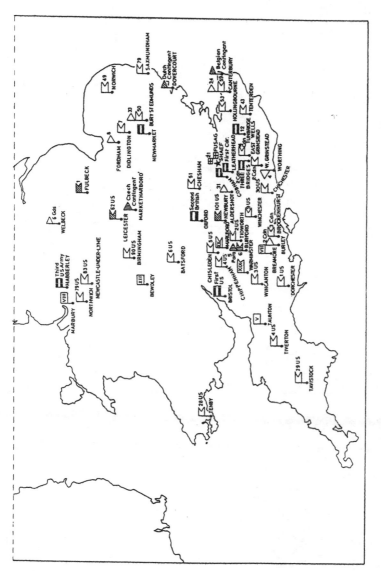

Location of OVERLORD military forces before concentration (approximately *Y* minus 60).

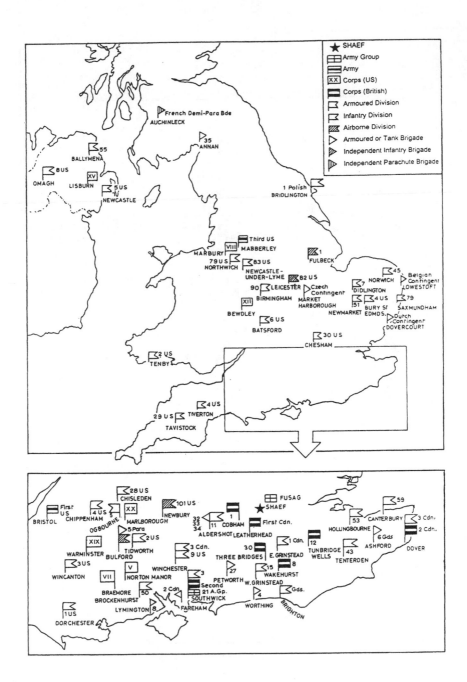

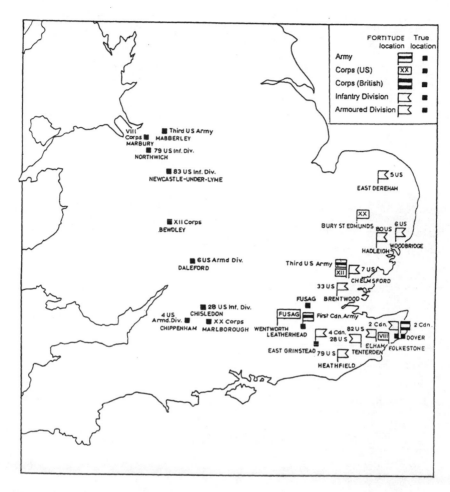

Location of FORTITUDE (SOUTH) military forces after concentration.

Opposite: Location of OVERLORD military forces after concentration (Y minus 30 to Y minus 15). Plain numbers denote BRITISH formations. US and other Allied formations are so described.

Notes

1. 51 (BRITISH) Infantry Division will move from NEWMARKET to PORTSMOUTH during May.
2. 49 (BRITISH) Infantry Division may move from NORWICH to TILBURY area during May.
3. 7 Armoured Division moves to concentration area within EASTCO on 7th and 8th May.
4. The following formations are still in the USA: 7(US) Armd. Div., 35(US) Inf. Div., 80(US) Inf. Div.

APPENDIX VI

Plan FORTITUDE SOUTH II

SHAEF/18250/Ops (B)
19th July, 1944

APPENDICES

SCOPE OF PLAN

1. In the light of circumstances prevailing at about D plus 20 and within the framework of Plan BODYGUARD, to formulate a plan for the continuation of threat to the Pas de Calais.

PRESENT SITUATION

2. The post D Day Story of the present plan is that operations in the NEPTUNE area are designed to draw German reserves away from the Pas de Calais and Belgium, and that when the German reserves have been committed to the NEPTUNE area the main Allied attack will be made between the Somme and Ostend. (See para. 28. Plan FORTITUDE, SHAEF (44) 13, dated 23rd February, 1944.)

3. The threat to the Pas de Calais has been maintained by a force located in the East and South-East of England which at the moment is composed as shown in Appendix 'A'. This force, a notional First US Army Group, has been associated with the XIX Tactical Air Command. Manipulation of air operations has shown that this force may also be supported by the remainder of the air forces under AEAF. The threat has been substantiated by considerable wireless

---

* As shown at page 222.
† As shown at page 244.

activity, as well as the display of some 250 dummy LCTs in the harbours and estuaries of East and South-Eastern England.

Change of Situation

4. From now onwards, formations which have been portrayed as belonging to First US Army Group and situated in the East and South-East England, will appear in the present bridgehead. It therefore follows that unless new formations are shown concentrated in the East and South-East England, the enemy will become aware that the Pas de Calais is no longer threatened, and will be at liberty to reinforce the present battle with forces at present deployed in the cover area. It is, therefore, necessary at this stage to formulate a new Story in order that the threat may be continued.

5. In order that some continuity of threat may be maintained, it has been decided to redesignate First US Army Group so that that Headquarters shall remain in this country so far as the enemy is concerned.

Object

6. To contain the maximum number of enemy forces in the Pas de Calais area for as long as possible.

Outline Story

7. General Eisenhower has already been forced to reinforce 21 Army Group with both American and Canadian forces from First US Army Group. To such a degree has this happened that he has decided that it is necessary for an American Army Group to be formed which shall take control of the American forces in the 21 Army Group area. This Army Group has, however, been subordinated to General Montgomery.

8. General Eisenhower has, therefore, instructed General Bradley to form Headquarters, Twelfth US Army Group, and has given him authority to call upon the resources of the First US Army Group to assist him in the quick formation of his new Headquarters.

9. The reinforcement of 21 Army Group has caused General Eisenhower to review the policy with regard to the forces which he is keeping in the East and South-East of England available for the assault in the Pas de Calais area. The future policy is to be as follows:

First US Army Group has been instructed to form a task force of at least 8 Divisions which will be kept available and unaltered for the assault on the Pas de Calais area. As reinforcements from the United States are received they will be added to the Order of Battle of First US Army Group. Should, however, the 21 Army Group sphere require further reinforcement, formations will be taken from the build-up divisions of the First US Army Group. Divisions transferred to 21 Army Group will normally be those who have been longest in England, in order that once divisions have been received from the United States they are kept inactive in this country for as short a time as possible.

10. General Eisenhower is in a position to reinforce the new bridgehead direct from the United States.

Outline Plan

Description of Operation

11. At Appendix 'B' is a description of the initial phase of the operation, which this outline plan is designed to support.

Naval

Ships and Craft

12. As far as durability and the rate of reconditioning allow, dummy craft will be displayed in the more sheltered south-east and east coast anchorages.

13. As far as operational and repair requirements allow, shipping and craft should be assembled in east and south-east coast ports and the disposition of any Force Headquarters ships due to be laid up or held in reserve should be made to support the location of notional assault force headquarters.

Training of Assault Forces

14. The training of three notional assault divisions will be simulated by wireless, divisional and RCT assault exercises being represented in normal assault training areas.

Combined Headquarters

15. Wireless activity from Supreme Headquarters to Combined Headquarters at Dover and Chatham will be maintained and naval wireless activity will be increased from these headquarters.

Military

Order of Battle

16. The Order of Battle at Appendix 'C' will be represented by wireless terminals at Army Group, Armies, Corps and Divisions. Permanent nets will be established by 26th July.

Location and Movement

17. Fourth British Army will move from Scotland to locations in South-Eastern Command between 14th July and 21st July.

18. From now until about 11th July, Fourteenth US Army will be located in Western and Southern Commands. Between 11th July and 21st July this army will move to concentration areas in Eastern Command.

Training

19. In addition to the assault training (para. 14) all formations will carry out CPX as far as resources permit.

Airborne Forces

20. The notional airborne forces will participate in assault training and CPX.

Special Force

21. Blocks of dummy warning messages will be broadcast by the BBC on French and Belgian programmes as required.

Mounting Preparations

22. Activity carried out for FORTITUDE SOUTH will continue.

Dummy Lighting at Ports and Hards

23. The present installations will remain available for illumination as required.

Air

Concentration of Air Forces

24. Ten groups of the Eighth US Fighter Command will be selected to act purely as a notional close support force for the First US Army Group.

Training of Air Forces

25. USSTAF will participate in the assault exercises and CPX as far as operational commitments allow.

Strategic Bombing

26. The strategic bombing programme already being carried out in support of FORTITUDE SOUTH will be continued.

COMMAND AND CONTROL

27. The Supreme Commander is to co-ordinate and control the execution of the plan.

28. Responsibility for giving effect to certain parts of the plan should be allotted as follows:

Paras 14, 16, 18, 19, 20: Deputy Theatre Commander, ETOUSA.

Paras 13, 14, 15: Allied Naval Commander, Expeditionary Force.

Paras 23: The Air Ministry.

Paras 12, 17, 22: Commander-in-Chief, Home Forces.

Appendix B to FORTITUDE SOUTH II
Description of Initial Phase of Operation

Target Dates

1. The military and air forces will be trained and concentrated by 26th July.

Mounting

2. The assault will be mounted from ports in the Southampton–Newhaven area.

Assault

3. The assault will be made by three infantry and three airborne divisions on the beaches exclusive River Somme to inclusive Boulogne.

Right: 55 British Division (2 Corps) and 2 British Airborne Division.

Centre: 59 US Division

Left: 17 US Division

} (XXXVII Corps) 9 and 21 Airborne Divisions.

Follow-up

4. *Right*: 58 British Division (2 Corps).

Left: 25 US Armoured Division (XXXIII Corps).

Build-up

5. The force will be followed up and built up from the Thames (US forces) and the Southampton area (British forces) at the rate of about one and a half divisions per day.

APPENDIX VII

FORTITUDE SOUTH II

Outline Plan for Special Means*

SHAEF/24183/3/SM/Ops
20th July, 1944

---

* The body of the Special Means plan for FORTITUDE SOUTH II is omitted since it consists of little more than a recapitulation of the outline plan contained in Appendix VI, arranged in chronological serials to suit the needs of the controlled agents. Appendices B, C, D and F are also omitted. Appendices G and H were never issued.

† Will be issued later.

NOTE. Marshalling areas and sub-areas, hards, &c., are shown on maps in Ops B War Room.

APPENDIX A TO FORTITUDE SOUTH II –
OUTLINE PLAN FOR SPECIAL MEANS

Sailing Dates of Formations included in FORTITUDE SOUTH Order of Battle

	Formation	Date of sailing
1.	79 (US) Infantry Division	14th June, 1944
2.	83 (US) Infantry Division	21st June, 1944
3.	Third (US) Army	6th July, 1944
4.	35 (US) Infantry Division	7th July, 1944
5.	First Canadian Army	9th July, 1944
6.	4 (US) Armoured Division	13th July, 1944
7.	6 (US) Armoured Division	18th July, 1944
8.	XII (US) Corps	19th July, 1944
9.	XX (US) Corps	19th July, 1944
10.	4 Canadian Armoured Division	20th July, 1944
11.	28 (US) Infantry Division	21st July, 1944
12.	7 (US) Armoured Division	15th August, 1944 ‡
13.	80 (US) Infantry Division	21st August, 1944 ‡
14.	5 (US) Armoured Division	27th August, 1944 ‡
15.	Twelfth Army Group	Not known

‡ Forecast.

APPENDIX E TO FORTITUDE SOUTH II – OUTLINE PLAN FOR SPECIAL MEANS

MOVES TO CONCENTRATION, AND OTHER RELATED TROOP MOVEMENTS

Note 1. Formations of First United States Army Group not shown below are already in concentration areas and therefore do not move.

2. All moves may be reported as stated subject to limitations set out in column (g).

3. Headquarters of 61 Infantry Division remains at Wye; formations and units under its command, hitherto employed as marshalling area staffs, notionally discontinue these duties 17th–20th July, and concentrate in Wye area for offensive training.

4. 4 Canadian Armoured Division moves in reality from concentration area (East Grinstead) to marshalling area 'S' on 18th July. No mention will be made of this movement.

(a) Serial	(b) Formation	(c) Old location	(d) Date of move	(e) Routes		(f) New location	(g) Remarks
				Rail	Road		
1	Fourteenth US Army	Mobberley	21st to 24th July	Entrain Wilmslow–Crewe–Rugby–Northampton–Bedford–Sandy–Cambridge–Bishops Stortford–Braintree–Witham–Chelmsford	Macclesfield–Derby–Leicester–Northampton–Bedford–Hitchin–Hertford–Chelmsford–Little Waltham	Little Waltham	Notional formation.

(a) Serial	(b) Formation	(c) Old location	(d) Date of move	(e) Routes — Rail	(e) Routes — Road	(f) New location	(g) Remarks
2	XXXIII Corps	Marbury	18th to 21st July	Entrain Hertford–Crewe–Rugby–Market Harborough–Seaton Junction–Peterborough–March–Ely–Newmarket–Bury St Edmunds	Macclesfield–Buxton–Nottingham–Stamford–Peterborough–Ely–Bury St Edmunds	Bury St Edmunds	Notional formation.
3	11 US Infantry Division	Northwich	15th to 18th July	Northwich–Altrincham–Cheadle–Derby–Nottingham–Melton Mowbray–Peterborough–Ely–Newmarket–Bury St Edmunds	Crewe–Stoke-on-Trent–Burton–Leicester–Kettering–Huntingdon–Cambridge–Bury St Edmunds	Bury St Edmunds	Notional formation.
4	48 US Infantry Division	Newcastle-under-Lyme	16th to 19th July	Newcastle-under-Lyme–Rugby–Market Harborough–Kettering– Huntingdon–Cambridge– Newmarket–Bury St Edmunds–Ipswich–Woodbridge	Stoke-on-Trent–Lichfield–Coventry–Northampton–Bedford–Royston–Sudbury–Ipswich–Woodbridge	Woodbridge	Notional formation.
5	25 US Armoured Division	Wincanton	19th to 22nd July	Wincanton–Radstock–Bath–Cheltenham–Birmingham–Leicester–Saxby–Bourne–South Lynn–Fakenham–East Dereham	Salisbury–Andover–Reading–Beaconsfield–Hitchin–Cambridge–Thetford–East Dereham	East Dereham	Notional formation.

6	17 US Infantry Division	Birmingham	17th to 20th July	Birmingham–Coventry–Rugby–Northampton–Bedford–Sandy–Cambridge–Bishops Stortford–Braintree–Witham–Hatfield Peverel	Coventry–Daventry–St Albans–Waltham Cross–Chelmsford–Hatfield Peverel	Hatfield Peverel	Notional formation. Notionally assault trained.
7	Fourth British Army	Ayr	18th to 20th July	Ayr–Dumfries–Carlisle–Crewe–Willesden Junction–Addison Road–Clapham Junction–Oxted–Eridge–Heathfield	Carlisle–Kendal–Preston–Stafford–Birmingham–Stratford–Oxford–Reading–Aldershot–Horsham–Haywards Heath–Heathfield	Heathfield	Notional formation.
8	2 British Corps	Dover	20th to 22nd July	Dover–Ashford–Tonbridge–Tunbridge Wells	Dover–Ashford–Cranbrook–Tunbridge Wells	Tunbridge Wells	Notional formation.
9	55 British Infantry Division	Broome Park	17th to 20th July	Dover–Ashford–Tonbridge–Redhill–Three Bridges	Dover–Ashford–Cranbrook–Tunbridge Wells–East Grinstead–Three Bridges	Three Bridges	Real formation. Factual location Three Bridges. Notionally assault trained, with notional 35 Tank Brigade, located at Hailsham, as its DD element.
10	58 British Infantry Division	Dover	14th to 17th July	Dover–Canterbury–Rochester–South Darenth–Gravesend	Dover–Canterbury–Rochester–Gravesend	Gravesend	Notional formation.

(a) Serial	(b) Formation	(c) Old location	(d) Date of move	(e) Routes		(f) New location	(g) Remarks
				Rail	Road		
11	7 British Corps	Beith	17th to 20th July	Beith–Kilmarnock–Dumfries–Carlisle–Hellifield–Leeds–Wakefield–Rotherham–Normanton–Nottingham–Loughborough–Leicester–Banbury–Oxford–Reading–Ash–Guildford–Redhill–Tonbridge–Ashford–Folkestone	Carlisle–Kendal–Leeds–Sheffield–Leicester–Northampton–Leighton Buzzard–Watford–Uxbridge–Staines–Leatherhead–Redhill–East Grinstead–Tunbridge Wells–Ashford–Folkestone	Folkestone	Notional formation.
12	5 British Armoured Division	Pembroke	21st to 24th July	Pembroke–Newport–Hereford–Birmingham–Leicester–Peterborough–Ely–Newmarket	Pembroke–Swansea–Newport–Gloucester–Oxford–Aylesbury–Baldock–Cambridge–Newmarket	Newmarket	Notional formation. Notionally located in the Midlands until June, when it went to South Wales for training in the Castle Martin area.
13	80 British Infantry Division	St Annes	22nd to 25th July	St Annes–Preston–Wigan–Warrington–Crewe–Stafford–Wolverhampton–Birmingham–Warwick–Banbury–Oxford–Reading–Guildford–Tonbridge–Ashford– Canterbury	Preston–Bolton–Macclesfield–Lichfield–Coventry–Banbury–Thame–Beaconsfield–Windsor–Croydon–Sevenoaks–Maidstone–Canterbury	Canterbury	Disbanded formation.

14	2 British Airborne Division	Grantham	20th to 23rd July	Grantham–Bottesford–Melton Mowbray–Market Harborough–Rugby–Leamington–Oxford–Reading–Basingstoke–Andover–Bulford	Grantham–Stamford–Northampton–Oxford–Hungerford–Bulford	Bulford	Notional formation.
15	Third US Army	Chelmsford	17th to 19th July	Chelmsford–Stratford–Willesden Junction–Richmond–Woking–Basingstoke–Salisbury–Fordingbridge	Epping–Watford–Windsor–Basingstoke–Salisbury–Fordingbridge	Braemore	Real formation. Factual location Braemore (Hampshire), moving to marshalling area 'C' approximately 29th June and sailing from Southampton approximately 6th July. No report of moves to marshalling area and embarkation.
16	XII US Corps	Folkestone	14th to 17th July	Folkestone–Ashford–Hastings–Lewes–Brighton–Havant–Eastleigh–Southampton	Folkestone–Ashford–Tunbridge Wells–Horsham–Arundel–Fareham–Southampton	Southampton	Real formation. Factual location Birmingham, moving to marshalling area 'C' approximately 14th July and sailing from Southampton approximately 19th July. No report beyond Ashford.

(a) Serial	(b) Formation	(c) Old location	(d) Date of move	(e) Routes — Rail	(e) Routes — Road	(f) New location	(g) Remarks
17	28 US Infantry Division	Tenterden	3rd to 8th July	Headcorn–Tonbridge–Redhill–Guildford–Reading–Didcot–Swindon	Tenterden–Tunbridge Wells–Horsham–Guildford–Basingstoke–Newbury–Chiseldon	Chiseldon	Real formation. Factual location Chiseldon, moving to marshalling area 'C' mid July and sailing from Southampton approximately 21st July. No report beyond Chiseldon.
18	80 US Infantry Division	Hadleigh	19th to 22nd July	Hadleigh–Brentwood–Stratford–Willesden Junction–Richmond–Woking–Basingstoke–Salisbury–Ringwood–Dorchester	Sudbury–Saffron Walden–Bishops Stortford–Hertford–St Albans–Maidenhead–Reading–Newbury–Andover–Salisbury–Blandford–Dorchester	Dorchester	Real formation. Factual location Sandiway. No report beyond Brentwood and Bishops Stortford.
19	7 US Armoured Division	Chelmsford	14th to 17th July	Chelmsford–Stratford–Willesden Junction–Richmond–Woking–Basingstoke–Andover	Waltham Cross–Watford–Windsor–Basingstoke–Andover	Tidworth	Real formation. Factual location Tidworth.
20	XX Corps	Bury St Edmunds	15th to 18th July	Bury St Edmunds–Cambridge–Bedford–Bletchley–Oxford–Didcot–Swindon	Bury St Edmunds–Cambridge–Bedford–Buckingham–Oxford–Swindon–Ogbourne	Ogbourne	Real formation. Factual location Ogbourne. No report beyond Cambridge. Moving to

							marshalling area 'C' approximately 15th July. Sailing approximately 19th July.
21	4 US Armoured Division	Bury St Edmunds	1st to 4th July	Bury St Edmunds–Cambridge–Bedford–Bletchley–Oxford–Didcot–Winchester–Southampton	Cambridge–Hitchin–Beaconsfield–Reading–Winchester–Marshalling areas 'C' and 'D'	Marshalling areas 'C' and 'D'	Real formation. Factual location Chippenham, until it moved to marshalling areas 'C' and 'D' early July, sailing from Southampton and Weymouth approximately 8th July. No report beyond Cambridge.
22	5 US Armoured Division	East Dereham	15th to 18th July	East Dereham–Kings Lynn–Melton Mowbray–Leicester–Rugby–Banbury–Oxford–Fairford	Wisbech–Peterborough–Kettering–Northampton–Banbury–Cirencester	Cirencester	Real formation. Headquarters of this division is in fact at Evesham, though parts of it are in Cirencester area.

(a) Serial	(b) Formation	(c) Old location	(d) Date of move	(e) Routes — Rail	(e) Routes — Road	(f) New location	(g) Remarks
23	6 US Armoured Division	Woodbridge	13th to 16th July	Woodbridge–Ipswich–Bury St Edmunds–Cambridge–Bedford–Bletchley–Oxford–Reading–Southampton	Woodbridge–Ipswich–Sudbury–Halstead–Bishops Stortford–St Albans–Aylesbury–Wallingford–Basingstoke–Winchester–Marshalling area 'C'	Marshalling area 'C'	Real formation. Factual location Moreton in the Marsh, moving to marshalling area 'C' mid July and sailing from Southampton approximately 20th July. No report beyond Ipswich.

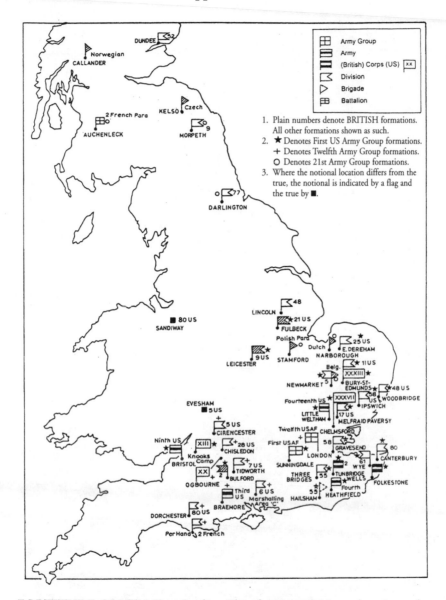

FORTITUDE SOUTH II – Outline Plan for Special Means locations after concentration.

9 Armoured Division and 38, 45, 47 and 61 Infantry Divisions continue, in fact, to be employed in marshalling and embarkation areas. 9 Armoured Division and 61 Infantry Division are notionally upgraded: the former is available to 21st Army Group for service overseas, the latter is included in First US Army Group Order of Battle. 38, 45 and 27 Infantry Divisions will continue, in fact, to be employed in static roles in the UNITED KINGDOM and will be so reported.

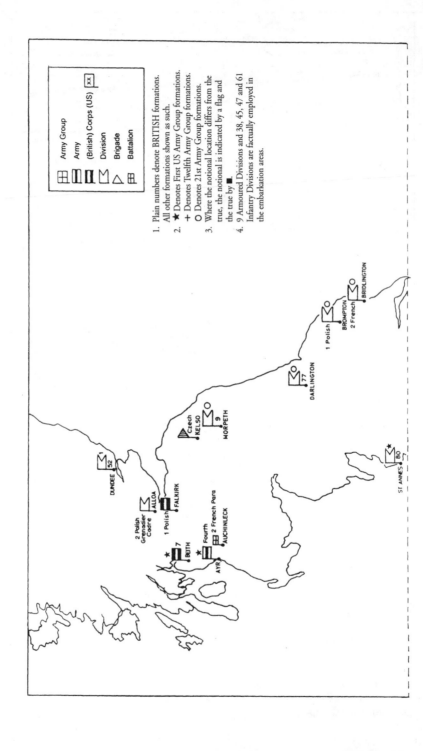

Legend:

⊞	Army Group
▮▮▮	Army
▮▮	(British) Corps (US)
⋀	Division
△	Brigade
⊞	Battalion
xx	

1. Plain numbers denote BRITISH formations. All other formations shown as such.
2. ★ Denotes First US Army Group formations.
   + Denotes Twelfth Army Group formations.
   O Denotes 21st Army Group formations.
3. Where the notional location differs from the true, the notional is indicated by a flag and the true by ■.
4. 9 Armoured Divisions and 38, 45, 47 and 61 Infantry Divisions are factually employed in the embarkation areas.

Map labels:

DUNDEE — 1, 52
2 Polish Grenadier Cadre — ALLOA
1 Polish — FALKIRK
AYR — 7, BOTH
Fourth — 2 French Para, AUCHINLECK
Czech — KELSO
9 — MORPETH
77 — DARLINGTON
1 Polish — BROMPTON
2 French — BRIDLINGTON
80 — ST ANNES

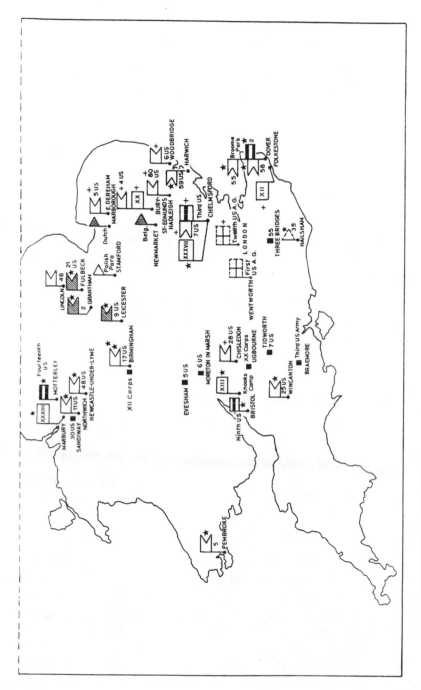

FORTITUDE SOUTH II – Outline plan for Special Means locations before concentration.

APPENDIX VIII

Special Means Interim Plan for the Movement of Fourteenth Army from East Anglia to the South Coast*

SHAEF/24183/3/SM/Ops
18th August, 1944

1. Fourteenth Army will move from its present locations to concentration areas on the south coast in accordance with the schedule at Appendix 'A'.

2. This movement will be disclosed in two phases:

(*a*) Reports will be made of the moves of the two assault divisions (17 and 59 US Infantry Divisions) and of the departure only of the two follow-up divisions (11 and 48 US Infantry Divisions). These will indicate a move to embarkation in accordance with FORTITUDE SOUTH II.

(*b*) Reports will be made of the entire move. These will indicate either:

(i) An impending attack against the Pas de Calais by First US Army Group, with the roles of the two armies reversed, United States forces being now on the right and British on the left, or

(ii) The transfer of Fourteenth Army to Normandy.

3. The timing of the two phases referred to in para. 2 above will depend upon the progress of events.

---

* As this and all subsequent troop movements in the United Kingdom depended almost entirely on reports from the controlled agents, no further outline 'operational' plans, if we exclude the Cover and Deception Policy Directive of 8th September, 1944 (Appendix IX), were issued. From now onwards all fictitious troop movements, disbandments and regroupings were the subject of Special Means plans only.

APPENDIX A TO SPECIAL MEANS PLAN DATED 18TH AUGUST, 1944

(a) Serial	(b) Formation	(c) Old location	(d) Date of move	(e) Routes Rail	(e) Routes Road	(f) New location	(g) Remarks
1	Fourteenth US Army	Little Waltham	28th to 30th Aug.	Chelmsford–Stratford–Willesden Junction–Addison Road–Guildford–Petersfield–Havant–Fareham	Epping–Barnet–Windsor–Aldershot–Alton–Fareham	Fareham	
2	XXXIII Corps	Bury St Edmunds	23rd to 25th Aug.	Bury St Edmunds–Cambridge–Bedford–Bletchley–Oxford–Reading–Basingstoke–Andover–Romsey	Cambridge–Hitchin–Beaconsfield–Reading–Winchester–Romsey	Romsey	
3	17 US Infantry Division	Hatfield Peverel	23rd to 26th Aug.	Chelmsford–Stratford–Willesden Junction–Addison Road–Reigate–Brighton	Chelmsford–Romford–Blackwall Tunnel–Croydon–Reigate–Brighton	Brighton–Burgess Hill area	
4	59 US Infantry Division	Ipswich	20th to 23rd Aug.	Ipswich–Stratford–Willesden Junction–Addison Road–Guildford–Petersfield–Rowlands Castle	Colchester–Chelmsford–Epping–Barnet–Windsor–Aldershot–Petersfield–Rowlands Castle	Rowlands Castle	

(a) Serial	(b) Formation	(c) Old location	(d) Date of move	(e) Routes Rail	(e) Routes Road	(f) New location	(g) Remarks
5	XXXVII Corps	Chelmsford	26th to 28th Aug.	Chelmsford–Stratford–Willesden Junction–Addison Road–Clapham Junction–Brighton–Worthing	Epping–Barnet–Denham–Staines–Leatherhead–Dorking–Horsham–Worthing	Worthing	
6	11 US Infantry Division	Bury St Edmunds	20th to 23rd Aug.	Bury St Edmunds–Cambridge–Bedford–Bletchley–Oxford–Diccot–Winchester	Cambridge–Hitchin–Beaconsfield–Reading–Winchester	Winchester	
7	48 US Infantry Division	Woodbridge	25th to 28th Aug.	Woodbridge–Ipswich–Bury St Edmunds–Cambridge–Bedford–Bletchley–Oxford–Reading–Southampton–Brockenhurst	Ipswich–Sudbury–Halstead–Bishops Stortford–St Albans–Aylesbury–Wallingford–Basingstoke–Winchester–Brockenhurst	Brockenhurst	
8	25 US Armoured Division	East Dereham	28th to 31st Aug.	East Dereham–Kings Lynn–Melton Mowbray–Leicester–Rugby–Banbury–Oxford–Reading–Hungerford–Tidworth	Cambridge–Bedford–Buckingham–Oxford–Wantage–Hungerford–Tidworth	Tidworth	

APPENDIX IX

Current Cover and Deception Policy

SHAEF/19011/Ops (B) (Fwd)
GCT/370.28–202/Ops (B)
8th September, 1944

Situation

1. The enemy is in retreat in the West in face of superior Allied forces. He is being compelled on all sectors to conform to the Allied manœuvres. It is considered that he is unlikely to react to any large-scale deceptive operations on the Allied front in the West, but that he may be susceptible to making faulty dispositions elsewhere, and is in a position where disintegration of control may take place at any time.

Policy

2. In view of this situation FORTITUDE SOUTH II is hereby terminated and replaced by the following overall deception policy:

(*a*) In order to extend further the enemy forces and accelerate his retreat, threats will be maintained against his rear communications and northern flank.

(*b*) In order to disrupt his system of control and undermine the enemy's will to fight, maximum assistance will be rendered to Allied Psychological Warfare.

(*c*) If the enemy offers serious resistance to the Allied advance into Germany, the Allies by deception methods should be in a position to assist the resumption of this advance with the full weight of the resources at their disposal.

Story

3. After the Allied victories in Normandy and Brittany, General Eisenhower decided to make his main thrust into Germany from that area. Subsequent exploitation of the successful Seine battle has made possible rapid advances to the heart of Germany. In order to assist these advances and to prevent the escape of remnants of the German Armies, Eisenhower has decided to retain large airborne and amphibious striking forces and a highly trained strategic reserve in the United Kingdom.

4. The tasks of these forces will be:

(*a*) To reinforce the Allied armies in France as the situation may demand.

(*b*) To carry out large-scale airborne operations anywhere on the enemy's lines of communication.

(*c*) To open new Ls of C from the United Kingdom against limited opposition.

(*d*) To occupy areas in the event of German withdrawal.

5. For these tasks, the forces in the United Kingdom will be regrouped as follows:

(*a*) *Prior to airborne operations by First Allied Airborne Army.* First US Army Group will be composed of Fourth British Army and First Allied Airborne Army, plus associated Naval and Air Forces; while Fourteenth US Army will come under direct control of Supreme Headquarters, forming the nucleus of a strategic reserve.

(*b*) *Subsequent to airborne operations.* First US Army Group will be disbanded as such, and this Headquarters will take command of the strategic reserve consisting of Fourteenth US and Fourth British Armies under administrative control of Communication Zone.

Allocation of Responsibility

6. Supreme Headquarters, Allied Expeditionary Force, is to give effect to the policy and story under paras 2, 3, 4 and 5.

7. 21 Army Group and Twelfth Army Group and the Communication Zone will submit their requirements for any additional forces necessary to give effect to para. 2 (*c*) of the Policy.

By Command of General Eisenhower:

W. B. SMITH,
Lieutenant-General, US Army,
Chief of Staff.

APPENDIX X

Special Means Plan for Move of Part of
Fourth Army from Kent to Essex

SHAEF/24183/3/SM/Ops
11th September, 1944

1. Moves of First US Army Group formations are taking place in accordance with movement table at Appendix 'A' and are being reported by Special Means.

2. Fourth Army will be regrouped as follows:

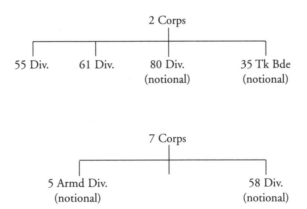

Note. The above regroupings will have taken effect during the wireless silence period 2nd–5th September.

APPENDIX A TO SPECIAL MEANS PLAN DATED 11TH SEPTEMBER, 1944

(a) Serial	(b) Formation	(c) Old location	(d) Date of move	(e) Routes		(f) New location	(g) Remarks
				Rail	Road		
1	58 Division	Gravesend	6th to 7th Sept.	Gravesend–Dartford–Clapham Junction–Addison Road–Willesden Junction–Stratford–Brentwood–Chelmsford–Colchester	Gravesend–Greenhithe–Dartford–Greenwich–Blackwall Tunnel–Hackney–Romford–Brentwood–Chelmsford–Hatfield Peverel	Colchester	
2	7 Corps	—	8th to 10th Sept.	Folkestone–Ashford–Maidstone–Oxford–Swanley Junction–Bromley–Clapham Junction–Addison Road–Willesden Junction–Broxbourne–Bishops Stortford–Saffron Walden–Bartlow–Clare	Folkestone–Ashford–Maidstone–Wrotham–Rochester–Dartford–Greenwich–Hackney–Epping–Bishops Stortford–Great Dunmow–Finchingfield–Clare	Clare	7 Corps trps road parties stage Epping Forest nights 8th–9th and 9th–10th September.
3	HQ Fourth Army	Heathfield	11th to 14th Sept.	Tunbridge Wells–Tonbridge–Redhill–Croydon–Addison Road–Willesden Junction–Stratford–Brentwood–Chelmsford–Hatfield Peverel	Heathfield–Tunbridge Wells–Sevenoaks–Farningham–Greenwich–Blackwall Tunnel–Hackney–Romford–Brentwood–Chelmsford–Hatfield Peverel	Hatfield Peverel	

APPENDIX XI

Regrouping of Notional Order of Battle in the United Kingdom*

SHAEF/24309/SM/Ops (B)
6th November, 1944

---

*1. Reference is made in this plan to a newly created 17th British Corps. This Corps was brought into being to command the 55th and 61st British Infantry Divisions when 2nd British Corps went abroad. Very soon afterwards it was decided to let the Germans know that 55th and 61st Divisions were under the control of GHQ, Home Forces, which was in fact the case, thus 17th Corps became superfluous. As its existence was never reported to the Germans, it is not referred to at all in the text of the report.

2. The 'story' at paragraph 7, refers to the possibility of British forces in the United Kingdom being sent to the Far East. This was to explain why these fresh divisions did not appear in France. In the event we did not make use of this part of the story.

Introduction

1. Fourth British Army was moved in July 1944 from Scotland to South-East England in order to support the threat to the Pas de Calais under FORTITUDE SOUTH II. The continued presence of Fourth British Army in South-East England, after the capture of the Pas de Calais at the beginning of September, coupled with the creation of a notional airborne force in the United Kingdom provided the latent threat of a combined airborne and seaborne operation against Denmark or the North-West German ports. As time passes it becomes increasingly difficult to explain why certain airborne divisions are employed in successive operations on the Continent while other fresh divisions in the United Kingdom remain uncommitted, also to explain why it should be necessary to reinforce 21 Army Group with American Divisions when there are still a number of British Field Divisions in the United Kingdom.

Future planning requires that a force should remain in the United Kingdom capable of exerting at short notice a threat against the North-West German ports. On the other hand a continuation of the *status quo* begins to present an unreal picture.

Object

2. To retain in the United Kingdom a force, plausible in the eyes of the Germans, and capable of exerting at short notice a threat to the North-West German ports.

Order of Battle

3. Notional order of battle of field forces in the United Kingdom supporting FORTITUDE SOUTH II is at Appendix 'A'.

4. On the termination of FORTITUDE SOUTH II on 8th September, 1944, Fourteenth United States Army ceased to be under command First United States Army Group and came under SHAEF control. First Allied Airborne Army with a notional increment came under command First United States Army Group. (Order of Battle is at Appendix 'B'.)

5. During the period 25th September–7th October the following regroupings occurred:

(*a*) 2 British Corps Headquarters came under command 21

Army Group and proceeded overseas, being replaced in the United
Kingdom by the newly formed 17 British Corps.

(*b*) XXXVII Corps with 25 United States Armoured Division
and 59 United States Infantry Division came under command
Twelfth Army Group and proceeded overseas.

(*c*) 17 United States Infantry Division came under command
XXXIII Corps (Order of Battle is at Appendix 'C').

6. During October, First United States Army Group was disbanded. First Allied Airborne Army and the real formations under
command reverted to SHAEF control, while the notional airborne
formations, under a notional airborne force Headquarters came
under command of Fourth British Army. As part of this regrouping
17 US Airborne Division ceased to be under command XVII Corps.
Shortly after the disbandment of First US Army Group, Fourteenth
US Army was also disbanded. (Order of Battle and locations are at
Appendix 'D'.) NOTE. See also last paragraph of story.

Story

7. The capture of the Pas de Calais by 21 Army Group rendered
the seaborne assault by First US Army Group unnecessary. During
the first weeks of September it appeared that the total defeat of
Germany was imminent. First United States Army Group was
therefore allotted a new role in support of the final breakthrough.
First Allied Airborne Army was placed under command First US
Army Group and Fourteenth US Army reverted to SHAEF control.
The airborne attack on Arnhem constituted the first phase of a
major assault from the United Kingdom. Had this attack succeeded, a combined airborne and seaborne assault would have been
launched by Fourth British Army supported by the remaining airborne divisions of First Allied Airborne Army, the whole force operating under the control of First US Army Group. After the setback
at Arnhem and the general stabilisation on the Western Front, it was
realised that an Allied victory in 1944 was unattainable. In these circumstances the operation of Fourth British Army and the Special
Airborne Force was held in suspense. At about this time certain
important policy decisions affecting the allocation of United States
and British forces in all theatres were made by the Combined Chiefs

of Staff. In view of impending British commitments in the Far East, a situation was envisaged where British forces might have to be withdrawn from the European Theatre, and replaced, if necessary, by additional United States forces. It was realised that this might involve an enlargement of the American and a reduction of the British zone. It was laid down that, so far as possible, formations which had no service overseas should be chosen for the Pacific Theatre.

In these circumstances a regrouping of forces is being carried out in the United Kingdom. 7 Corps will move to Yorkshire and there continue to train for the operations referred to above. It will also be available to satisfy British requirements in Burma and the Far East at short notice. 55 and 61 British Infantry Divisions will shortly come under control GHQ, Home Forces as draft-finding formations. When this occurs, 17 Corps Headquarters will become available for employment elsewhere. Special Airborne Force Headquarters and XVII US Airborne Corps will be disbanded. 9 and 21 US Airborne Divisions will be in part cannibalised, and in part will form the nucleus of a new airborne division. 19 British Airborne Corps will remain with under command 2 British Airborne Division and any other airborne formations that may subsequently be made available. Fourth British Army will be incorporated in Northern Command and will be available to command 7 Corps and 19 Airborne Corps, for the execution of the operation now held in suspense. The seaborne element in this force will sail from the Humber.

During October, certain other regroupings occurred which did not become known until November. These were as follows: XXXIII Corps was disbanded. 11, 17 and 48 US Infantry Divisions came under command British Base Section. The two former moved to the South Wales area and became draft-finding divisions, the latter will move shortly to Scotland and will continue its airborne training in the Dundee area.

Plan

8. Notional forces in the United Kingdom will be regrouped as shown at Appendix 'E' in accordance with the story at paragraph 7.

Appendix A to Special Means Plan dated 6th November, 1944
Order of Battle at 8th September, 1944

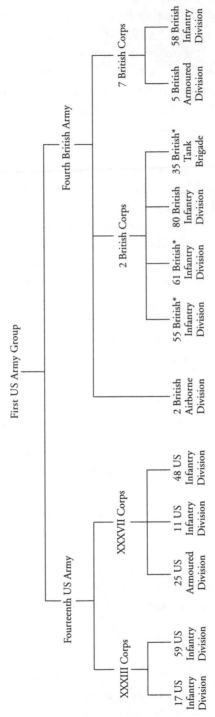

* Real formations.

APPENDIX B TO SPECIAL MEANS PLAN DATED 6TH NOVEMBER, 1944
ORDER OF BATTLE – 9TH SEPTEMBER–25TH SEPTEMBER, 1944

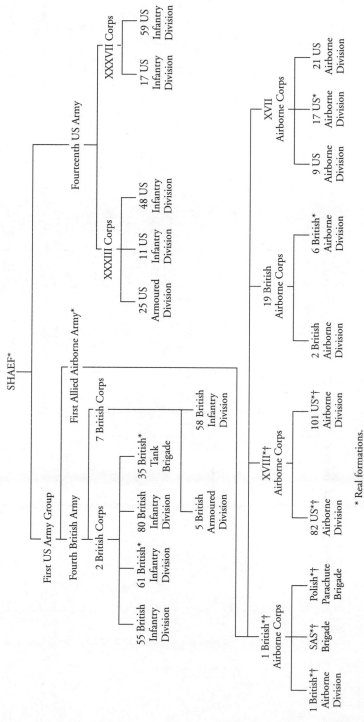

* Real formations.
† Formations factually placed under command 21 Army Group.

APPENDIX C TO SPECIAL MEANS PLAN DATED 6TH NOVEMBER, 1944
ORDER OF BATTLE AT 10TH OCTOBER, 1944

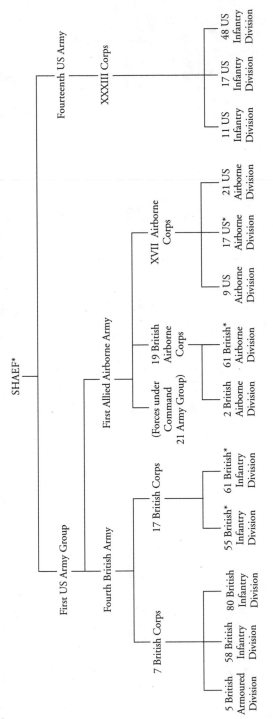

SHAEF*

First US Army Group

First Allied Airborne Army

Fourteenth US Army

Fourth British Army

(Forces under Command 21 Army Group)

19 British Airborne Corps

XVII Airborne Corps

XXXIII Corps

7 British Corps

17 British Corps

5 British Armoured Division

58 British Infantry Division

80 British Infantry Division

55 British* Infantry Division

61 British* Infantry Division

2 British Airborne Division

61 British* Airborne Division

9 US Airborne Division

17 US* Airborne Division

21 US Airborne Division

11 US Infantry Division

17 US Infantry Division

48 US Infantry Division

* Real formations.

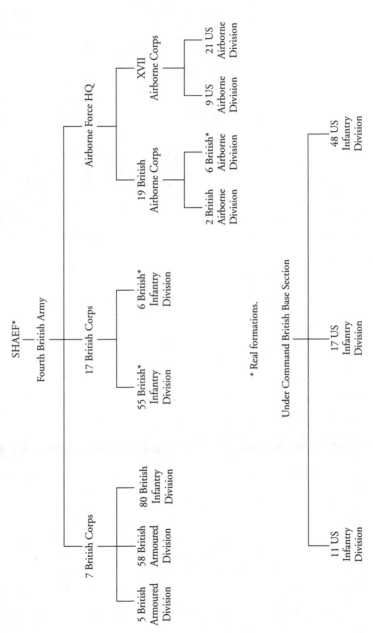

APPENDIX D TO SPECIAL MEANS PLAN DATED 6TH NOVEMBER, 1944
ORDER OF BATTLE AT 1ST NOVEMBER, 1944

SHAEF*

Fourth British Army

Airborne Force HQ

7 British Corps

17 British Corps

19 British Airborne Corps

XVII Airborne Corps

5 British Armoured Division

58 British Armoured Division

80 British Infantry Division

55 British* Infantry Division

6 British* Infantry Division

2 British Airborne Division

6 British* Airborne Division

9 US Airborne Division

21 US Airborne Division

* Real formations.

Under Command British Base Section

11 US Infantry Division

17 US Infantry Division

48 US Infantry Division

APPENDIX E TO SPECIAL MEANS PLAN DATED 6TH NOVEMBER, 1944
ORDER OF BATTLE AT 15TH NOVEMBER, 1944

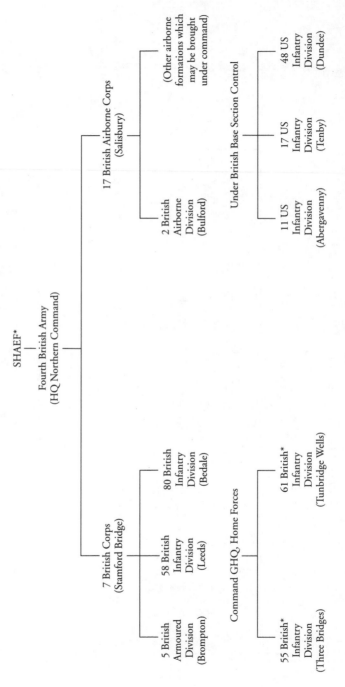

SHAEF*

Fourth British Army
(HQ Northern Command)

7 British Corps
(Stamford Bridge)

5 British Armoured Division
(Brompton)

58 British Infantry Division
(Leeds)

80 British Infantry Division
(Bedale)

17 British Airborne Corps
(Salisbury)

2 British Airborne Division
(Bulford)

(Other airborne formations which may be brought under command)

Command GHQ, Home Forces

55 British* Infantry Division
(Three Bridges)

61 British* Infantry Division
(Tunbridge Wells)

Under British Base Section Control

11 US Infantry Division
(Abergavenny)

17 US Infantry Division
(Tenby)

48 US Infantry Division
(Dundee)

* Real formations.

9. Forces will be located and notional troop movements will be carried out as shown at Appendix 'F'.

APPENDIX F TO SPECIAL MEANS PLAN DATED 6TH NOVEMBER, 1944
MOVEMENTS OF FORCES

(a) Serial	(b) Formation	(c) Old Location	(d) Date of Move	(e) New Location
1	80th British Infantry Division	Needham Market	10th–15th November	Bedale
2	7th British Corps	Clare	13th–16th November	Stamford Bridge
3	5th British Armoured Division	Newmarket	14th–19th November	Brompton
4	58th British Infantry Division	Colchester	15th–20th November	Leeds
5	Fourth British Army	Hatfield Peverel	17th–20th November	York
6	48th US Infantry Division	Newbury	1st–5th December	Dundee

APPENDIX XII

Disbandment or Reorganisation of Notional Forces in the United Kingdom

SHAEF/24309/SM/Ops (8)
19th January, 1945

Introduction

1. The notional forces remaining in the United Kingdom were extensively reported to the enemy during the past year by high-grade special agents as well-trained field formations. From captured documents we know that all have been accepted by the enemy as forming part of our Order of Battle, yet not one has been identified in the field.

2. To remedy this unreal situation, a partial solution was provided by a regrouping of forces put into effect on 6th November, 1944 (SHAEF/24309/SM/Ops (B) dated 6th November, 1944). This paper completes the process initiated on that date. The notional Order of Battle at 15th November, 1944 is at Appendix 'A'.

Object

3. To safeguard the position of high-grade special agents in the United Kingdom.

Factors affecting the Story

4. Notional formations in the United Kingdom cannot be retained as part of the field force without endangering the security of deception.

5. Events in the last six months should have led the enemy to regard the disbandment or down-grading of Allied field formations as a normal procedure at the present time (see Appendix 'B').

6. The notional forces required for future strategic deception can be provided by the creation of new formations.

Story

7. To meet the growing demand for reinforcements, a major reorganisation of Allied forces in the United Kingdom is being carried out with effect from 1st January, 1945. Details are at Appendix 'C'. Order of Battle at 1st February, 1945, is at Appendix 'D'.

Implementation

8. Implementation of the reorganisation referred to in paragraph 7 will be carried out by Special Means.

APPENDIX A TO SPECIAL MEANS PLAN DATED 19TH JANUARY, 1945
ORDER OF BATTLE AFTER 15TH NOVEMBER, 1944

This Order of Battle still obtains subject to the modifications provided for in the footnotes.

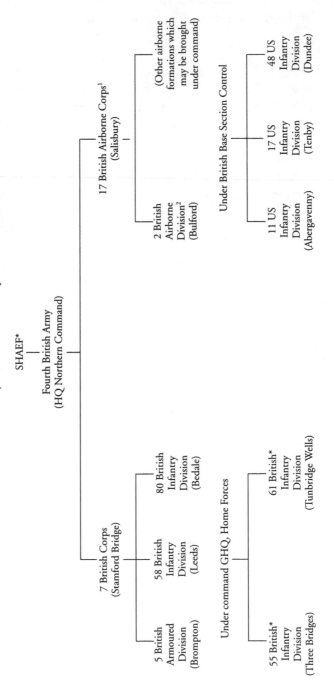

SHAEF*

Fourth British Army
(HQ Northern Command)

7 British Corps
(Stamford Bridge)

5 British Armoured Division (Brompton)

58 British Infantry Division (Leeds)

80 British Infantry Division (Bedale)

Under command GHQ, Home Forces

55 British* Infantry Division (Three Bridges)

61 British* Infantry Division (Tunbridge Wells)

17 British Airborne Corps[1]
(Salisbury)

2 British Airborne Division[2] (Bulford)

(Other airborne formations which may be brought under command)

Under British Base Section Control

11 US Infantry Division (Abergavenny)

17 US Infantry Division (Tenby)

48 US Infantry Division (Dundee)

* Real formations.

1. Absorbed into Hants and Dorset District HQ during December 1944, as an Administrative HQ.

2. Disbanded during December 1944, personnel being absorbed into 1 British Airborne Division.

APPENDIX B TO SPECIAL MEANS PLAN DATED 19TH JANUARY, 1945

1. During the first half of 1944 the following British infantry divisions were notionally established as HE formations:

38 Infantry Division.
45 Infantry Division.
47 Infantry Division.
55 Infantry Division.
61 Infantry Division.

During the second half of the year these formations were reported to the enemy as having been reorganised as static draft-finding divisions.

2. During the Autumn of 1944 59 British Infantry Division was factually disbanded, and 50 British Infantry Division was returned to the United Kingdom for reconstitution as a LE division. Of these two divisions 59 British Infantry Division has been used by 21 Army Group as a notional formation. It is likely, however, that the true facts may become known to the enemy regarding both these formations.

3. During October the reorganisation of notional 11 and 17 US Infantry Divisions as draft-finding formations was reported by Special Means and, in the following month, the cannibalisation of notional 9 and 21 US Airborne Divisions was announced.

APPENDIX C TO SPECIAL MEANS PLAN DATED 19TH JANUARY, 1945
REORGANISATION OF FORCES

Serial	Formation	Disposal	Remarks
1	(A) US FORCES 41 Infantry Division	Disbanded	No further reference should be made to this formation.
2	17 Infantry Division	Disbanded	No further reference should be made to this formation.
3	48 Infantry Division	Disbanded	Cadres of specialist troops will return to US for inclusion in a special force now being constituted in that country.

Serial	Formation	Disposal	Remarks
4	(B) BRITISH FORCES Fourth Army	HQ absorbed in Northern Command. Armed troops dispersed under arrangements made by GHQ, Home Forces	
5	7 Corps	Disbanded	
6	5 Armoured Division	Disbanded	Personnel should be observed in small numbers at Bovington Tank School, Keswick MT School and in other scattered parts of the United Kingdom during period 1st February–1st March, 1945.
7	58 Infantry Division	Converted to LE draft-finding division and will move to Hitchin under command GHQ, Home Forces.	If at a future date release of wireless operators becomes necessary this formation will be disbanded.
8	80 Infantry Division	Converted to LE draft-finding division and will move to St Neots under command GHQ, Home Forces.	If at a future date release of wireless operators becomes necessary this formation will be disbanded.
9	19 Airborne Corps	Disbanded	No further reference should be made to this formation.

APPENDIX D TO SPECIAL MEANS PLAN DATED 19TH JANUARY, 1945
ORDER OF BATTLE OF NOTIONAL FORMATIONS IN
THE UNITED KINGDOM AT 1ST FEBRUARY, 1945

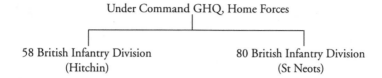

Under Command GHQ, Home Forces

| 58 British Infantry Division | 80 British Infantry Division |
| (Hitchin) | (St Neots) |

APPENDIX XIII

FORTITUDE SOUTH Order of Battle

British Controlled Agents' Share in Compiling German Intelligence Reports during the Year 1944

LBW – OKH Lagebericht West.
UBR – Ueberblick des Britishchen Reiches.

NOTE. Much information supplied by the controlled agents is also to be found in the Fremde Heere West maps giving locations of forces in the United Kingdom.

1. I could only identify one infantry division with the divisional sign of a white bear facing sideways on a black square. Headquarters probably in the region of Beccles. Region occupied, Norwich, Great Yarmouth and Southwold.	BRUTUS 1 Feb., 1944, 1814 GMT	LBW 1168 7 Feb., 1944. A credible Abwehr source has reported the 49th English Infantry Division in the Norwich-Lowestoft area (Eastern Command). . . . Divisional staff is probably at Beccles, 25 Km. south-east of Norwich.
2. The 45th Infantry Division here has swopped places with the 55th Infantry Division in Sussex.	PANDORA Letter to arrive not before 25th Jan., 1944.	LBW 1179 18 Feb., 1944. A good source reports that the 45th English Infantry Division is stationed in the South-Eastern Command and has relieved the 55th English Infantry Division employed on the coast. The 55th English Infantry Division is still in South-Eastern Command.
3. The region around Brighton seems to be occupied by units of the Division which carries the badge of the yellow drum . . . elements of a large force . . . with the badge of a white spearhead, erect on a red diamond, were in transit from North to South, moving in the general direction of Shoreham by sea.	BRUTUS 20 Feb., 1944. 1653 GMT	App. to LBW 1187 26 Feb., 1944. According to a credible Abwehr message we must reckon with the possibility that the 1st English Army Corps HQ, hitherto thought to be in Scotland, and 45th English Infantry Division believed to be in Northern Ireland, have been moved to the South of England (Brighton area).

Message	Source	Reference	Comment
4. (Reporting after tour of South and South-West England) an observation to which I give importance is that the distribution of the forces to date is all along the length of the coast and there is no concentration at special points.	GARBO 17 Feb., 1944. 2010 GMT	App. to LBW 1189 28 Feb., 1944.	Fresh confirmation is forthcoming from a well-regarded source that the English and American groups of forces are still in their same areas.
5. Portland. I saw some American soldiers with the number '1' in red on khaki ground, in the neighbourhood of the town.	GARBO Letter No. 15 posted 19 Feb., 1944.	App. to LBW 1189 28 Feb., 1944.	The reported appearance of traces of the 1st American Infantry Division, hitherto assumed to be in the Western Mediterranean, still lacks confirmation.
6. There is an airborne division in the region between Southampton, Bournemouth and Salisbury, with the sign of a blue Pegasus on a maroon rectangle. With regard to the number of the Airborne Division with the sign of a blue Pegasus on a maroon rectangle already reported in the region of Salisbury, this is the 6th Airborne Division.	BRUTUS 21 Feb., 1944. 1738 GMT BRUTUS 8 March, 1944. 1730 GMT	LBW 1215 25 March, 1944.	The English 6th Airborne Division has been confirmed in Great Britain through a captured document. Reports from Abwehr and from a sure source agree that the division is no longer in the area south of Hull (Northern Command) but in the neighbourhood of Salisbury (Southern Command).
7. 7 (7) Norwich. I saw a lot of troops and vehicles of the 9th Division. (This was intended for the 9th British Armoured Division.)	GARBO 13 April, 1944. 1847 GMT	LBW 1235 14 April, 1944.	A trustworthy Abwehr report states that the 9th American Infantry Division hitherto thought to be in the European theatre, but in an unknown location, is also in Great Britain.
8. 15th Infantry Division is north and west of Leeds; sign red lion rampant on yellow, in white circle. (Also given in numerous controlled reports from November 1943 onwards.)	FREAK 17 April, 1944. 1634 GMT	LBW 1246 25 April, 1944.	The presence of the 15th English Infantry Division believed to be in an unknown location in the Middle East has not been confirmed. According to several Abwehr messages, this division is in Great Britain in the Leeds area (Northern Command).
9. According to a conversation with an American officer in the first place the Headquarters of the XX American Army Corps is situated at Marlborough. In the second, the Sixth Armoured Division occupies the northern part of Gloucestershire.	BRUTUS 26 April, 1944. 1634 GMT	LBW 1255 4 May, 1944.	According to an unconfirmed Abwehr message, the American Armoured Division hitherto accepted in an unknown location in the Worcester area. This may possibly be the Sixth American Armoured Division.

10. Third US Army near Knutsford, Cheshire, located in Western Command where troops are usually stationed after arrival at Liverpool. 79th and 83rd Infantry Divisions in this army.	FREAK 26 April, 1944. 1125 GMT	LBW 1255 4 May, 1944.	The two American Divisions assumed to be in *Yorkshire* and *Norfolk* may according to a good Abwehr message be the 79*th* and 83*rd American Infantry Divisions.* Confirmation of this must be awaited.
11. Passing by Salisbury for Torquay, I was able to make out the area occupied by the First American Army; in the Salisbury district, the VII American Army Corps with the badge of the figure '7' in white on a blue shield.	BRUTUS 29 April, 1944. 1206 GMT	LBW 1255 4 May, 1944.	According to a credible message the VII American Army Corps is in the area north-west of Torquay.
12. 7 (2) Tenterden. The 28th American Infantry Division has arrived here. I saw officers of same in Dover and Folkestone. (GARBO). The 28th Division was reported by 7 (7) when he left the South Wales area.	GARBO 1 May, 1944. 1840 GMT	LBW 1256 5 May, 1944.	The 28th American Infantry Division was, according to a further Abwehr message, moved from its previous area around Swansea (South Wales) to the *Folkestone* area in South-East England.
13. 7 (7) Ipswich. Saw many troops in station and town. Armoured cars, tank transports and vehicles with the insignia of the 6th US Division.	GARBO 2 May, 1944. 1955 GMT	LBW 1256 5 May, 1944.	The 6th American Armoured Division, hitherto believed to be in the county of Worcester (see LBW 1255) is, according to an as yet unconfirmed Abwehr message, said to be in the East of England in the Ipswich area.
14. See serials 11, 12 and 13	BRUTUS 29 April, 1206 GMT GARBO 1 May, 1840 GMT 2 May, 1955 GMT	App. to LBW 1256 5 May, 1944.	The advance reported by good sources of the 6th American Armoured Division to Ipswich, of the 28th American Division to Folkestone (south-west of Dover) and of the VII Army Corps into the Torquay area points to the already known main concentration areas and further rounds off the picture of completed concentration.

15. 7 (2). I saw troops of the VIII US Corps in Folkestone with the insignia of the number '8' in an octagonal figure.	GARBO 1 May, 1944. 1840 GMT	App. to LBW 1263 12 May, 1944.	The observation by a useful source of the VIII American Army Corps in South-East England (probably in the Folkestone area) makes it seem probable that in that area there are, in addition to the 18th American Infantry Division already reported there, one or two further American formations hitherto not exactly located. The general picture therefore emerges that besides the strong Anglo-American group of forces in *South-Western* England, we must reckon with the employment of single American divisions from all the remaining jumping off areas.
16. 7 (4) Newhaven-Brighton. He deduced from conversations he had, that most of the troops embarked were of the Division with the inverted triangle, which he has reported recently as on the move. Alton, north-east of Winchester; some forty lorries with the badge of a black triangle with another red inverted triangle within it, the whole in a red circle. Fareham. In the town, vehicles, lorries and men with the sign of the two triangles. The 3rd English Infantry Division . . . is no longer in Scotland but at Newhaven, Sussex, and took part in exercises in the Channel last week.	GARBO 8 May, 1944. 2040 GMT BRUTUS 5 May, 1944. 1605 GMT BRUTUS 9 May, 1944. 1603 GMT FREAK 10 May, 1944. 1135 GMT	LBW 1263 12 May, 1944.	According to various credible Abwehr messages, the *3rd English Armoured Grenadier Division* is in the area north of Portsmouth. The Division seems to have transferred to the Southern Command at the conclusion of its training in Scotland, and took part in the large-scale landing exercises in the Isle of Wight/Portsmouth/Brighton area at the beginning of May.
17. Four, Hiltingbury Camp. 47th London Division is in a camp to the south of mine. Seven, Romsey. I saw vehicles with the insignia of the 47th London Division. Your question about 47th Division: it has definitely left Yorkshire. Think it is somewhere in the South of England, but exact location not yet known.	GARBO 30 April, 1944. 1918 GMT GARBO 11 May, 1944, 2037 GMT FREAK 12 May, 1944. 1216 GMT	LBW 1264 13 May, 1944.	According to several trustworthy Abwehr messages the 47th English Infantry Division hitherto accepted in Scarborough (Northern Command) has been for some time in the Southampton/Winchester area (Southern Command).

18. 51st English Division back from Italy. Many officers and men diverted to train other divisions. Re-formed 51st Division east of Newmarket. Returned without vehicles, replacement in progress.	FREAK 24 April, 1944. 1213 GMT	UBR 29 15 May, 1944.	The 51st English Infantry Division has been confirmed in Newmarket (east of Cambridge).
With regard to 51st Highland Division, according to my friends it has returned from Italy and is stationed in Suffolk.	BRUTUS 4 May, 1944. 1850 GMT		
19A. 38th Infantry Division in the Isle of Wight. It is a Home Defence Division, not organised for operations overseas. Seven. On the main Romsey-Ringwood road I saw one hundred and twenty-five military vehicles of all types, including bren gun carriers, with the insignia of the 54th Division.	FREAK 4 May, 1944. 1344 GMT GARBO 11 May, 1944. 2037 and 2043 GMT	UBR 29 15 May, 1944.	The 54th and 38th English Infantry Divisions have been confirmed in their areas. An Abwehr report that the latter is only capable of limited employment and is being used as a training division requires confirmation.
19B. 7 (4) Newhaven-Brighton. He has seen many troops and vehicles of the 61st and 45th Divisions, also South-Eastern Command, Commando 3 and Commando 6.	GARBO 8 May, 1944. 2049 GMT	UBR 29 15 May, 1944.	The 45th and 61st English Infantry Divisions as well as the 3rd and 6th English Commandos have been confirmed in their existing areas.
19C. Bury St Edmunds, east of Newmarket; headquarters of the American XX Army Corps; sign, two Roman figures 'X' interlaced in yellow on a blue shield, the shield outlined in borders of red and yellow. Many traces also in the town of the American 4th Armoured Division.	BRUTUS 9 May, 1944, 1730 and 1735 GMT	UBR 29 15 May, 1944.	In East Anglia, in the Bury St Edmunds area (some 50 km. south-west of Norwich) are situated, according to a well-regarded Abwehr source, the XX Army Corps as well as the 4th Armoured Division.
19D.	...	UBR 29 15 May, 1944.	*General Conclusion.* The main enemy concentration is showing itself ever more clearly to be in the South and South-East of the Island. This is supported by the transfer of two English Divisions into the Portsmouth area, and the recently observed introduction of American formations into the English group of forces in South-Eastern England (so far observed, one corps and one

			infantry division). The launching of single American infantry divisions from the other invasion areas is also to be reckoned with.
20. 15th English Infantry Division now moved to mid Sussex, composed of three infantry brigades, mainly Scottish troops.	FREAK 16 May, 1944. 1627 GMT	LBW 1271 20 May, 1944.	According to a proven Abwehr source, the 15th English Infantry Division, hitherto accepted in the Leeds area (Northern Command) has been transferred to Southern Command. The Division is situated in the county of Surrey, somewhere in the neighbourhood of Horsham.
21. Dorking. Saw some vehicles in transit belonging to the 11th English Armoured Division, with the sign of a black bull on a yellow triangle. Worthing. In transit, vehicles of the Guards Armoured Division with the sign of an eye on a black shield with a red border.	BRUTUS 25 May, 1944. 1836 GMT BRUTUS 26 May, 1944. 1605 GMT	LBW 1280 29 May, 1944.	According to several proven Abwehr sources, large parts of the English armoured formations hitherto assumed to be in Central England, have been transferred into the South-Eastern Command. The formations in question are the English Guards Armoured Division, parts of which were observed in the Dorking area on the march to the South, and the 11th English Armoured Division which has been identified in the neighbourhood of Worthing.
22. At Lewes many troops with sign of a knight with lance. Haywards Heath, north of Brighton; numerous soldiers and vehicles with the sign of white horseman on a red square, which seems to be the sign of the Army Corps stationed in this region.	GARBO 26 May, 1944. 2218 GMT BRUTUS 27 May, 1944. 1305 GMT	LBW 1280 29 May, 1944.	The 8th English Army Corps Headquarters is also believed to be in the same area* (hitherto Northern Command). * *i.e.* Sussex.
23. One and a half miles north of Shepherdswell station is a large car park under trees alongside road. A concrete track leads into the park which contains US lorries and vehicles belonging to the 83rd Division.	GARBO 27 May, 1944. 2215 GMT	LBW 1280 29 May, 1944.	According to a credible Abwehr message, the 83rd American Infantry Division is in the Dover/Deal area.

24. Seven, Ipswich. Have seen the sign of the Panda several times in the district.	GARBO 25 May, 1944. 2045 GMT	LBW 1285 3 June, 1944.	The 9th British Armoured Division, hitherto accepted in the Northern Command and whose move to the South was already apparent, has been credibly reported in the Ipswich area (Eastern Command).
25. Seven, Tilbury. Saw men and vehicles of the 9th Armoured Division.	GARBO 1 June, 1944. 2035 GMT	App. to LBW 1287 5 June, 1944.	Movements in the Lower Thames Estuary point to the transfer of formations (among them the 9th Armoured Division) to the suitably equipped harbours in that area which may be used to relieve the harbours on each side of Dover which lie within range of German gunfire.
26. FUSAG contains two armies: First Canadian Army, headquarters Leatherhead . . . and Third American Army, headquarters unknown. I also know that Third American Army includes the XX Corps, already reported at Bury St Edmunds. (Probably supported by previous messages of TREASURE, GARBO and, perhaps MULLET and PUPPET.)	BRUTUS 31 May, 1944. 2056 GMT BRUTUS 31 May, 1944. 2117 GMT	LBW 1288 6 June, 1944.	According to Abwehr messages which we consider to be reliable, the Headquarters of the Third American Army may be in the area south-west of Norwich. Confirmation must be awaited.
27. I am beginning a series of messages about First American Group of Armies, called FUSAG, C-in-C General Patton. . . . from what I know, the Allied Expeditionary Force, commander General Eisenhower, is composed of FUSAG and the 21 Army Group, commander General Montgomery. One can conclude that FUSAG gives the impression of being ready to take part in active operations in the near future. FUSAG contains two armies: the First Canadian Army, Headquarters at Leatherhead, Commander General Crerar . . . and the Third American Army, headquarters unknown.	BRUTUS 31 May, 1944. 1605, 2051 and 2056 GMT	App. to LBW 1288 6 June, 1944.	According to a reliable Abwehr message of 2nd June, the forces at present in the South of England are organised in two army groups (21st English and First American). It seems from this report that the American First Army Group contains the First Canadian Army (approximately thirteen divisions), known to be in Southern England, as well as the Third American Army between the Thames and the Wash (approximately twelve divisions). It is not yet clear whether they are under the command of General Bradley or General Patton. The 21 Army Group is commanded by General Montgomery.

	GARBO message	German reference	
28. 7 (7) Harwich. Sign, not previously seen, of a yellow shield with three blue mountain peaks outlined in white. This newly arrived division from USA.	GARBO 3 June, 1944. 2109 GMT	LBW 1288 6 June 1944.	The American 80th Division has been reported in the Harwich area. This may be one of the formations which arrived from the USA in April/May.
29. 3 (3) is in London having been called here by me by telegram. He says that the 52nd Division is at present in camps in the areas Saltcoats-Kilmarnock-Preswick and Ayr. The entire Division is concentrated here. He also saw there a large number of the insignia of the pilgrims' shell which he had previously mentioned in the area of Dundee.	GARBO 26 May, 1944. 1952 GMT	OKH Situation Report West 1290 8 June, 1944.	At the same time the 7 English Army Corps, hitherto assumed to be north of Dundee has been reported on the west coast of Scotland in the Greenock area.
30. 3 (3) having received news of the landing in Scotland of a large contingent of troops coming from Ireland, disregarded my instructions that he should not leave the Clyde in order to investigate this information. He discovered the entire division had, in fact, arrived and was encamped in the Dumfries-Lockerbie area. Insignia is the red rose on a white ground. He believes it is the 55th English Division.	GARBO 4 June, 1944. 1956 GMT	OKH Situation Report West 1290 8 June, 1944.	According to a credible Abwehr message the 2nd English Army Corps, hitherto reported in the Stirling area (Scottish Command), and the 58th English Infantry Division, stationed West of Edinburgh, were transferred at the beginning of the month to the Dumfries area (Solway Firth).
. . . Returning to Glasgow, on arrival at Motherwell he discovered that vehicles and men in full equipment in large numbers were assembling there and in the surroundings belonging to the stag's antlers division and the one with the sign of the fish in red on blue and white waves. The road in direction of Hamilton was controlled by CMP.	GARBO 4 June, 1944. 2002 GMT	LBW 1290 8 June, 1944.	The English 2nd Army Corps Headquarters, hitherto reported in the Stirling area (Scottish Command), and the English 58th Infantry Division west of Edinburgh, were, according to a credible Abwehr message, transferred to the Dumfries area (Solway Firth) at the beginning of the month.

Message	Source	Reference	German interpretation
31. I found Three awaiting me after a short interview he had had with 7 (4). Urgent points communicated; he learnt that the 3rd British Division landed in the first assault and has identified it as the one with the insignia of the inverted triangle. The Guards Armoured Division will enter in action three days after initiating the first attack. This division has left the area.	GARBO 8 June, 1944. 0006 GMT	LBW 1290 8 June, 1944.	A proven Abwehr source reports that the English Guards Armoured Division, at present situated in the Worthing area, will embark on the third day of the invasion in the port of Brighton. The appearance of this Armoured Division may therefore be expected in the near future.
32. The region in East Anglia is occupied by the Third American Army with headquarters at Chelmsford. It includes the XX US Armoured Corps, headquarters at Chelmsford. Composition of the XX Corps: 4th US Armoured Division, headquarters Bury St Edmunds; 5th US Armoured Division, headquarters East Dereham; 6th US Armoured Division, headquarters Woodbridge. A short time ago the Third Army included the XII American Corps recently reported at Folkestone under the First Canadian Army. At Brentwood I also saw a few soldiers of the 35th American Infantry Division. It has now been attached to the XII American Corps and sent to Kent. As already reported, the 28th Assault Division also forms part of the XII Corps. It is at present located at Harwich, where it has just completed amphibious exercises in conjunction with the Royal Navy.	BRUTUS 6 June, 1944. 2005 GMT BRUTUS 6 June, 1944. 2009 GMT BRUTUS 7 June, 1944. 1601 GMT BRUTUS 7 June, 1944. 1604 GMT BRUTUS 7 June, 1944. 1609 GMT	LBW 1292 10 June, 1044.	According to a reliable message the American 28th Infantry Division hitherto accepted in the Dover area, has been transferred to the Harwich area. The American Infantry Division hitherto believed to be in the Norwich area and whose number was unknown may, according to fresh evidence, be the 35th Infantry Division. According to a credible Abwehr message it is at present in the neighbourhood of Brentwood (about 30 kms. north-east of London). In addition the 5th American Armoured Division has been reported by a credible Abwehr source to be with the American group of forces in the Norwich and Ipswich area. This is presumably the American Armoured Division of unknown number previously assumed to be in Cornwall, but whose presence there had not been confirmed for a long time. The American XII Army Corps was named as a new headquarters in the Ipswich area.
33. 7 (7) . . . also saw, nearby, British troops with the sign of the 47th London Division. 7 (4) reports that the following divisions are to be found in his area without indication of embarking at present: . . . Southern	GARBO 31 May, 1944. 2049 GMT GARBO 9 June, 1944. 0052, 0058	LBW 1293 11 June, 1944.	The 47th English Infantry Division, hitherto assumed to be in the Portsmouth area, has, according to unanimous reports from various sources, been transferred at an unknown date to the Thames Estuary, to the neighbourhood of Southend.

Command: . . . 47th London Division . . . 7 (7) reports that the activity in his area has greatly increased, giving the following divisions stationed in the area without indication of embarking for the moment: . . . 47th London Division.	and 0104 GMT	
34. See serial 30 Doncaster; units with the sign of the 58th British Division and a few of the 2nd British Army Corps, lately reported by me in Scotland.	GARBO 4 June, 1944. 2002 GMT BRUTUS 7 June, 1944. 1625 GMT	The same source, whose reports about the location of English 2nd Army Corps Headquarters and 58th English Infantry Division in Scotland have so far been confirmed, reports these on 7th June in the Doncaster area (30 kms. north-east of Sheffield). Since a few days ago another trusted source observed both these formations north of the Solway Firth marching to the South, it can be accepted that they are in process of taking up their positions in concentration areas in the South or East of England. LBW 1293 11 June, 1944.
35. The 2nd British Airborne Division in the region of Grantham.	BRUTUS 7 June, 1944. 1620 GMT	According to an Abwehr source which has reported accurately for a long time, the 2nd English Airborne Division hitherto thought to be in the Western Mediterranean, location unknown, is now in the Grantham area (30 kms. east of Nottingham). LBW 1293 11 June, 1944.
36. Amplification and notes on the messages sent yesterday; looking over the messages, I see that I omitted to include, in the list of troops in the area of 7 (2), the units 2nd Canadian Division and 2nd Canadian Corps.	GARBO 9 June, 1944. 2047 GMT	A trusted Abwehr source reports as still being in Dover on 9th June, the 2nd Canadian Infantry Division, which was believed, according to a sure source to be in the Caen neighbourhood on 6th June. Since hitherto no further reports of this formation have been received from the bridgehead there exists the possibility that this division is still in Great Britain. Confirmation must be awaited. LBW 1293 11 June, 1944.

37. The British 2nd Corps is now included in FUSAG and has headquarters at Louth. It is composed of the 55th and 58th Divisions, with headquarters at Skegness and Horncastle respectively. I heard that they are due to leave shortly for Kent.	BRUTUS 14 June, 1944. 1629 GMT	App. to LBW 1299 17 June, 1944.	According to recent evidence the group of forces in Central England (Sheffield area) forming the 2nd English Army Corps with probably two divisions, also belongs to the American Army Group held ready in the South-East of England, which brings the total strength of the latter up to twenty-five to twenty-seven divisions.
38. 7 (4) Brighton; the situation has changed little with the following exceptions. Troops with the insignia of the knight on horseback have left the area. They left for Normandy.	GARBO 16 June, 1944. 2112 GMT	LBW 1300 18 June, 1944.	According to a proven Abwehr source the English 8th Corps Headquarters has left the Horsham area. There are various pointers to the employment of this headquarters in the bridgehead under the Second English Army.
39. US troops with the insignia of a blue circle cut in four have arrived in the area of Lewes. (GARBO.) This insignia was reported by 7 (7) on his last journey to London as having been seen in his area.	GARBO 16 June, 1944. 2146 GMT	LBW 1300 18 June, 1944.	According to a credible report the 35th American Infantry Division has been moved from the area south-west of Ipswich to the area north of Brighton.
40. 7 (2) has also seen some troops with the insignia of the red fish on waves and the stag's antlers. . . . (GARBO) I attach the greatest importance to the reference by this agent to these insignias as it is an indication that all the troop concentrations seen by Three in Motherwell may have been moved South.	GARBO 16 June, 1944. 2153 GMT GARBO 16 June, 1944. 2201 GMT	App. to LBW 1301 19 June, 1944.	From England there are further signs that the FUSAG formations are closing up towards the south-east coast. The hitherto unconfirmed transfer of the English 2nd Corps formations accepted in Central England to Kent fits in with this South East concentration.
41. 7 (7) communicates that the American division at present occupying the camps in which the 28th US Division had been before they left for the South, is the division which has the insignia of a serpent which the Americans call rattlesnake. This division recently arrived in England. In his letter he sets out in	GARBO 17 June, 1944. 1910 and 2110 GMT	LBW 1301 19 June, 1944.	According to credible reports the 28th American Infantry Division has been moved back to Kent from the Ipswich area where it is said to have been carrying out landing exercises. In the place of the 28th American Infantry Division there is said to be a new US division in the Ipswich area, which is alleged to have

Message	Source	Reference	German Comment
detail . . . the manoeuvres which the 28th US Division carried out on the beaches of Felixstowe.			arrived recently in England. This may be the 8th American Infantry Division. Confirmation must be awaited.
42. I have learnt that FUSAG will receive during the assault very strong support from the Ninth and Eighth Air forces, composed of heavy bombers. This last appears to indicate an attack against a strong position and the possibility of an attack across the Channel is discussed.	BRUTUS 18 June, 1944. 1015 GMT	App. to LBW 1301 19 June, 1944.	Attention is deserved by a report from a particularly trustworthy source according to which FUSAG will be supported in action by strong portions of the heavy bomber force, which points to its employment against strong fortifications and so fits in with our existing appreciation (Middle Channel coast).
43. 7 (7) has learnt through a well-informed channel that there are more than a hundred tank transport barges capable of transporting about five hundred tanks . . . which have gradually been concentrating in the ports of Yarmouth, Lowestoft and in the rivers of Debenham and Orwell.	GARBO 9 June, 1944. 0121 and 0137 GMT	App. to LBW 1304 22 June, 1944.	The reported concentration of landing craft in the harbours of the central east coast (Harwich-Yarmouth) also deserves attention.
44. See serial 40. I have written to the agent 7 (2) telling him that he should let me know urgently if he sees there . . . troops of the 55th Division which 3 (3) also reported in the concentration at Motherwell. 7 (2) says that he has seen troops . . . of the 55th Division in his area.	GARBO 16 June, 1944. 2153 , 2201 and 2206 GMT GARBO 20 June, 1944. 2110 and 2120 GMT	LBW 1306 24 June, 1944.	The 55th English Infantry Division hitherto accepted doubtfully north of Dungenness has been confirmed by the same source. This formation is seemingly subordinated to the 2nd English Army Corps.

Message	Reference	Comment
45. The XXXVII USA Corps recently included in the Third American Army, has its headquarters at Great Baddow, two kilometres south-east of Chelmsford; sign: on a yellow circle a diamond divided into two triangles, of which the top is white and the lower black. A third triangle, white, below, touches the black one at the apexes. Composition: the 7th US Armoured Division, the 59th American Division, at Chelmsford and the Harwich region respectively and another division of which the details are unknown to me. BRUTUS 24 June, 1944. 1846 and 1852 GMT	LBW 1307 25 June, 1944.	According to an unconfirmed agent's report the American XXXVII Army Corps is in the area around and south-west of Harwich, with under command the American 7th Armoured Division (Chelmsford area) and the American 59th Infantry Division (Harwich area). The 7th Armoured Division may be the armoured division of unknown number which on previous evidence was hitherto believed to be in the South-West of England. The 59th Infantry Division is probably the American Infantry Division of unknown number which hitherto for want of further information was believed to be in Scotland, but which had not been confirmed there for a long time.
46. 7 (7). In Ipswich saw sign of 80th Division. GARBO 3 July, 1944. 2006 GMT	LBW 1318 6 July, 1944.	According to a report from a proven source the 80th English Infantry Division, hitherto believed to be in North Wales, is in the Ipswich area.
47. FUSAG has three airborne divisions now in its Order of Battle of which one, namely the 21st American, is to be found in the Grantham area. BRUTUS 21 July, 1944. 1723 GMT	LBW 1334 22 July, 1944.	According to a credible report, the American Airborne Division hitherto shown in an unknown location and presumably with the number 11, is situated in the Grantham area (north-east of Leicester).
48. Montgomery demanded immediate reinforcements in Normandy in such a fashion that it was necessary to send units from FUSAG which were already in the South of England, notably the First Canadian Army and a large part of the Third American Army. The fresh units in FUSAG will take up the duties of the units which have been despatched. . . . The Fourteenth American Army has already removed towards East Anglia, to the area formerly occupied by the Third Army. The headquarters are at Little Waltham. BRUTUS 20 July, 1944. 2019, 2024 and 2144 GMT	LBW 1339 27 July, 1944.	According to captured documents confirmed by credible Abwehr reports, the American Third Army hitherto accepted in the area north of London, is said to have been transferred to Northern France as a second American Army Staff. In its place we are to assume the headquarters of the American Ninth Army hitherto shown with location unknown or a newly arrived Fourteenth Army.

49. I have learned that the 1st Polish Division has left for Aldershot on the 23rd and is due to go overseas in the near future.	BRUTUS 26 July, 1944. Message No. 920	LBW 1340 27 July, 1944.	According to a proven Abwehr source, the 1st Polish Armoured Division, last reported in the area north of Hull on the move southwards, is in the Aldershot area.
50. Composition of the Fourteenth Army: XXXIII and XXXVII American Corps, of which the headquarters are respectively at Bury St Edmunds and Chelmsford.	BRUTUS 28 July, 1944. 1804 GMT	LBW 1341 29 July, 1944.	According to credible Abwehr reports, in addition to the American Ninth Army, Fourteenth Army is also to be accepted under FUSAG. In addition the XXXIII Army Corps has been newly reported in Great Britain under the Fourteenth Army.
51. I have just learnt that several of our officers from FUSAG are at present in Normandy with the First Canadian Army and the 4th Canadian Armoured Division, which have recently arrived in France. They are attached as spectators, as McNair was anxious that they should be present at an attack before the FUSAG assault. One can therefore suppose that the First Canadian Army will attack in the near future.	BRUTUS 28 July, 1944. 2017 GMT	LBW 1341 29 July.	A very reliable Abwehr source reports the move of the staff of First Canadian Army and of 4th Canadian Armoured Division to the landing front in Normandy. The supposition that, following on the recently observed incorporation of the Fourth English Army in the First American Army Group (still in Great Britain) in place of the First Canadian Army, the First Canadian Army was now only destined for tasks of administration and organisation has, therefore, not been confirmed.
52. FUSAG, changes in the Command: I suppose that Eisenhower and Patton were not in agreement over the change in the Order of Battle because Patton has been replaced by General McNair as Commander-in-Chief of FUSAG.	BRUTUS 19 July, 1944. 1737 GMT	OKH Situation Report 4 Aug, 1944.	According to reliable reports Lt.-General L. J. McNair, until recently Commander-in-Chief of the Land Forces in the USA, who has since been killed while on a visit to the front, was destined to succeed Lt.-General Patton as Commander-in-Chief of the American First Army Group (England). It seems that Lt.-General Patton has now assumed command of the Third American Army in Normandy. No information is available about the new commander of the American First Army Group in Great Britain. It is thought that Lt.-General Bradley has taken command of the American Twelfth Army Group in Normandy. General Montgomery retains his overall command of the operations in Normandy and remains Commander-in-Chief of the English 21 Army Group.
Patton was removed from his command of FUSAG and given, instead, the command of the Third US Army, giving over the command of the Twelfth US Army Group to General Bradley, who is Eisenhower's 'Yes Man' who, at the same time, has the experience of the battles he has led in France. The command of FUSAG was unfilled for a few days and was then given over to another of Eisenhower's favourites called McNair, who has just recently arrived from America.	GARBO letter No. 22 dated 20 July, 1944.		

Patton is at present Commander-in-Chief of the Third American Army.	BRUTUS 22 July, 1944. 1712 GMT
The new American Army Group in Normandy is called 'Twelfth Army Group', Commander-in-Chief, General Bradley. It was formed at the end of the month of June but the formation was kept secret. Several of our officers from Wentworth are at present in the Twelfth Army Group.	BRUTUS 22 July, 1944. 1720 GMT
I have learnt that General McNair has been killed in Normandy where he had gone for a short visit to consult with General Montgomery and to inspect the coastal defences. This loss is considered here as very serious. It is thought that a successor will be appointed immediately to command the FUSAG operations.	BRUTUS 26 July, 1944. Message No. 921
I have found out through the press that General McNair has died by enemy action in Normandy.	GARBO 29 July, 1944. 2040 GMT
All American forces destined for the Normandy operation, namely the First and the Third American Armies, are included in the Twelfth Army Group, of which the head is General Bradley. There is also in Normandy the 21 Army Group composed of the First Canadian Army and the Second British Army. The chief is General Montgomery.	BRUTUS 1 Aug., 1944. 2033 GMT
Both Army Groups come directly under SHAEF, of which the supreme head is General Eisenhower. It is possible that, in practice, Montgomery commands both Army Groups on the battlefield.	BRUTUS 2 Aug., 1944. 1741 GMT
53. 7 (7). General impression: Decrease in number of US armoured troops but increase in number of US infantry troops.	GARBO 7 Aug., 1944. 2126 GMT
Norwich-Ipswich: There has been a reduction in American armoured divisions in this area (despatched to France) and an increase in American infantry divisions.	OKH Report 10 Aug, 1944.

54. FUSAG has three airborne divisions now in its Order of Battle of which one, namely the 21st American, is to be found in the Grantham area.	BRUTUS 21 July, 1944. 1723 GMT.	LBW 1360 17 July, 1944.	It appears from several credible reports that the American Airborne Division in the area east of Leicester is the 21st Airborne Division.
55. The XXXIII Corps at Marbury in Cheshire; composition: 11th and 48th US Divisions and an American armoured division. The 11th and 48th Divisions arrived during the month of June, well trained.	BRUTUS 10 July, 1944. 2014 GMT (*sic.*)	LBW 1360 17 Aug., 1944.	Several reliable Abwehr sources have given repeated reports of an 11th American Infantry Division in England in the Bury St Edmunds area. The existence of an 11th Infantry Division besides the 11th Airborne division seems therefore not impossible; confirmation must, however, be awaited.
11th Infantry Division. Headquarters in Delamer House near Norwich.	GARBO 28 July, 1944. Letter No. 23		
Just returned from trip to Cambridge, Norwich, Cromer and Leicester. Cambridge: Considerable troop movement, both road and rail, through the town. Road convoys of the 11th US Infantry Division travelling East.	TATE 28 July, 1944. 0630 MET		
Bury St Edmunds. In addition to the units of the XXXIII Corps there are also units of the 11th American Infantry Division, with the sign of a circle divided like the face of a clock. The segments are coloured alternately white/blue, with the exception of 11 o'clock, which is coloured black. It occupies the region formerly occupied by the 4th American Armoured Division.	BRUTUS 29 July, 1944. 2014 GMT		
Is the 11th US Division, reported by Seven, an airborne or disembarkation or infantry division?	GARBO 9 Aug., 1944. Received 2002 GMT		
Reply to questions: The 11th US Division is an infantry division, as you will have noticed from the vehicle markings given in Seven's reports sent by GARBO last month.	GARBO 14 Aug., 1944. 1950 GMT		

Message	Source	Reference	Assessment
56. With regard to General Brereton: A new force has been formed composed of all airborne divisions, of whom the chief is General Brereton and his second in command General Browning. As reported, the Allies attach great importance to airborne operations in the future in the hope of bringing them under a joint command. In addition certain infantry divisions have undergone airborne training and can also be included in this type of operation. . . . It is supposed that seaborne operations will no longer be possible after the late autumn, whereas airborne operations will always be possible. Furthermore, it is expected that the most important operations will take place on the Continent far from the sea, where surprise can only be obtained by airborne operations. Thus the Allies hope to use airborne divisions for delivering a decisive coup and to facilitate this they deem it necessary to create a new command.	BRUTUS 21 Aug, 1944. 1714, 1718 and 1725 GMT and 22 Aug, 1944. 1740 GMT	App. to LBW 1369 26 Aug, 1944. OKH Situation Report 27 Aug, 1944	A further report from a particularly trusted source about the retention of the Allied Airborne Army for a big operational task deserves special notice. Concrete indications of the target are not available. The newly reported message (from a particularly proved source) about the withdrawal of the Allied Airborne Army for a large-scale operational task deserves special attention. There are no concrete indications of the target.
57. I was told that the other Airborne Division has the number nine and is stationed in Leicestershire. It belongs to the Fourteenth Army. In Leicester troops of a US Airborne Division. Their sign was a white circle with blue ground. On this was a vertical yellow flash of lightning. Reference to Airborne Division: Believe it was the 9th but this is very uncertain. In our Order of Battle there are three airborne divisions, notably the 9th and 21st American and 2nd British.	BRUTUS 30 July, 1944. 1331 GMT TATE 31 July, 1944. 1808 MET TATE 6 Aug, 1944. 1803 MET BRUTUS 21 Aug, 1944. 1725 GMT	LBW 1370 27 Aug, 1944.	According to a reliable Abwehr report there is in Great Britain in addition to the 21st American Airborne Division, a 9th American Airborne Division. This may be the American Division hitherto shown in Great Britain as the 11th Airborne Division. Conformation must be awaited.

	Source	LBW	Commentary
58. Everything is now being done to prepare the Fourteenth Army as quickly as possible for its new task. I learned that it includes two American assault divisions, namely the 17th and 59th, which are at present undertaking exercises on the east coast.	BRUTUS 26 July, 1944. Messages No. 915 and 916	LBW 1372 28 Aug., 1944.	According to several credible reports the American Infantry Division accepted in the area north of Cambridge, may be the 17th Infantry Division.
At Cambridge station a troop train with soldiers of a US Division. Divisional sign: circle with white diagonal cross with red and blue ground.	TATE 28 July, 1944. 1804 MET		
XXXVII Corps still remains at Chelmsford. It has been transferred from the Third American Army. Sign: three triangles, already signalled. It includes the 17th and 59th Assault Divisions.	BRUTUS 28 July, 1944. 1815 GMT		
With regard to the 17th American Infantry Division: Sign, in a circle an oblique white cross, the vertical quadrants of the circle in red and horizontal ones in blue.	BRUTUS 15 Aug., 1944. 1806 GMT		
59. Great numbers of British troops, tanks and vehicles have disembarked with insignia, seen for the first time, of the letters 'GO' in black on a green circle.	GARBO 23 Aug., 1944. 2023 GMT	App. to LBW 1371 28 Aug., 1944.	A move reported by several proven sources of the 8th English Armoured Division from Egypt to England has probably taken place as a result of the extreme need for reinforcements in France. It shows too the anxiety of the enemy command to make good quickly the group of forces still in England which must recently have been weakened by the unexpected withdrawal from it of troops for France.
60. I also had an opportunity of passing two days at Bristol and Exeter to see the units of the Ninth American Army.	BRUTUS 10 Aug., 1944. 1810 GMT	LBW 1374 31 Aug., 1944.	The American Ninth Army, which hitherto was thought to be in the South East of England in the immediate neighbourhood of FUSAG is now, according to credible information, in the Bristol area. The subordination of the formations in the Salisbury area to this army command seems, therefore, a possibility.
7 (2) reports on return from south-west tour. Identified following units in Bristol area from vehicle markings: 691st Field Artillery Battalion, 193rd Field Artillery Battalion, 184th	GARBO 16 Aug., 1944. 2032, 2049 and 2055 GMT		

Parts of the Fourteenth American Army (XXXIII Army Corps) have, according to several reports, been transferred from their existing area, Ipswich-Cambridge, to the South. The 11th, 17th and 59th Infantry Divisions were reported in this connection. The 17th Infantry Division is said to have been moved to the Brighton area.

LBW 1374 31 Aug., 1944.

BRUTUS 20 Aug., 1944. 1443 GMT

GARBO 23 Aug., 1944. 1950 GMT

GARBO 26 Aug., 1944. 2032 and 2040 GMT

TATE 27 Aug., 1944. 0603, 1818 and 0605 MET (*sic*)

Medical Battalion and 172nd Engineer Battalion, all belonging to the Ninth US Army with the markings '99A' in addition to the unit number. Troops have no army insignia though, from conversations with a soldier, I was able to confirm that the Ninth Army identification is correct though he could not explain the reason for the absence of army insignia. Same contacts said that three more divisions are due to arrive from USA to be put under the command of the Ninth Army.

61. On returning to Wentworth, I learned that there is great activity in the affairs of the Fourteenth American Army, as though it were a question of changing its location. Will do my best to obtain details but have to return to our Air Headquarters in London on 21st August.

Urgent. 7 (7). The entire 59th, rattlesnake, American Division has started to leave Ipswich area, moving towards the South. Other divisions also preparing to leave. Agent is investigating and will send detailed reports soon as possible.

7 (4) Saw many units with sign of white St Andrew's cross on circular background in red and blue, which I discovered belongs to the 17th US Division which have been arriving in Brighton area. Headquarters of this division is at Stanmer Park, about four miles from Brighton on Lewes road. Have identified following units of this division: 293rd Infantry Regiment, 144th Engineering Battalion.

During the past few days large US convoys travelling between Hatfield and Watford in a westerly direction; divisional sign was a black snake on a circular blue ground. Saw further vehicles travelling in the same direction with the following sign, difficult to describe: two similar triangles with their points together (looks like an old-fashioned hour glass); the upper triangle is black the lower is white. On the upper black triangle there is a third triangle, the flat side against the flat side of the black triangle. The third triangle is white. The whole thing is on a circular, yellow ground.

7 (7). Numerous rumours that entire American Army in this area is leaving for South. Troops of 11th US Division, previously seen in Stowmarket, have left the district; few troops of XXXIII US Corps seen in Bury St Edmunds. Many troops of this Corps left recently for unknown destination. Many convoys of 17th US Division seen moving South. Advanced units of this division moved South some time ago. 7 (4) recently reported arrival in Brighton area of units of this division. 3 (*b*) Blackwall Tunnel, under the Thames, was closed for three days for passage of American troops.

GARBO 28 Aug., 1944. 2034 and 2106 GMT

62. To investigate your questionnaires about airborne and armoured troops, I sent 7 (2) for a short trip to Larkhill-Bulford area where airborne and armoured troops were located before the landing. He discovered the following troops in this area: 7 (2) 2nd British Airborne Division, with sign of winged horse, also saw American armoured troops and tanks of 25th US Armoured Division, just arrived from Norfolk also some men with sign of 8th US Armoured Division without vehicles. These both have usual US armoured divisional sign with the number superimposed to identify the division. Also saw US infantry troops and convoys with the following sign: A blue oval with the letter 'V' in white interlaced with the number '9' in red and a

GARBO 30 Aug., 1944. 1926, 1946 and 1958 GMT

According to a credible report, a further two American infantry divisions and one armoured division were moved from the United States to Great Britain during the second half of August. These may be the 94th and 95th Infantry Divisions and the 25th Armoured Division which are said to be in the area north of Salisbury.

LBW 1374 31 Aug., 1944.

	GARBO	App. to LBW	
circle divided diagonally, with the number '9' in black on white in the left semi-circle and the number '4' in white on black in the right semi-circle. Had no time to identify but believe latter is the 94th US Division. 63. *This message relates to the reorganisation of FUSAG and to the alleged rival policies of Field-Marshal Montgomery and of General Patton in France. It is quoted in full in Chapter 31.*	GARBO 31 Aug., 1944. 2046 to 2150 GMT.	App. to LBW 1376 2 Sept., 1944.	*This extract, which is also given in Chapter 31, repeats almost the whole of GARBO's message.*
64. 7 (2). Southampton and surrounding areas: Most military camps in the area are occupied by US troops. All roads extremely busy with large convoy movements. Saw following troops and vehicles: Fourteenth US Army, XXXIII US Corps, US division with the sign of the letter 'VV' in white interlaced with the number '9' on a blue oval, 11th US Infantry Division, SOS, SHAEF, 48th US Division, 59th US rattlesnake Division, 9th US Armoured Division, 25th US Armoured Division, 2nd British Airborne Division. General impression: great activity and movement of troops, vehicles, armour and supplies. Fourteenth US Army was recently reported by 7 (7) as having left his area. Fourteenth US Army has moved to the south coast for embarkation. 7 (2) recently reported that Fourteenth Army and other US troops are in the Southampton area.	GARBO 6 Sept., 1944. 2035 and 2044 GMT	App. to LBW 1383 9 Sept., 1944.	According to a report from a hitherto particularly trustworthy source, there are at present strong concentrations of American troops taking place in the Southampton area. In this connection the following are mentioned: the 25th and 95th Infantry Divisions and 9th Armoured Division, as well as the 11th, 48th and 59th American Infantry Divisions, with the staff of the American XXXIII Army Corps, which were hitherto believed to be in the area north-east of London and have several times been reported on the move to the South. The headquarters of the Fourteenth American Army is also said to have been transferred from the Ipswich area to Southampton.
	GARBO 9 Sept., 1944. 2101 GMT	OKH Situation Report 10 Sept., 1944.	According to a report from a particularly trustworthy Abwehr source a large-scale concentration of American troops (some five infantry divisions and one armoured division partly from the East of England) seems to be taking place under XXXIII American Army Corps in the Southampton area. Simultaneously the Fourteenth American Army is said to have been transferred to this embarkation area. A move to France is probable and corresponds with the expectations which we have already expressed. This would mean the withdrawal of all

Summary	Reference	Source	Message
American military formations from the South-East and South of England. According to a report from a particularly trustworthy source the American Fourteenth Army with XXXIII and XXXVII Army Corps has been transferred from South-Eastern England to the south coast. According to this report the headquarters of the Fourteenth Army is at Fareham (north-west of Portsmouth) while the American XXXIII Corps is in the Winchester area and the American XXXVII Corps with under command 17th and 59th American Infantry Divisions is reported in the Worthing area. The transfer of the 11th and 48th American Infantry Divisions from the Cambridge area to the neighbourhood of Southampton is also reported by a good source.	LBW 1386 12 Sept., 1944.	BRUTUS 6 Sept., 1944. 2016, 2024, 2028 and 2032 GMT. 7 Sept., 1944. 1715 and 1721 GMT GARBO 6 Sept., 1944. 2035 and 2044 GMT	65. I can confirm the arrival of the Fourteenth American Army from East Anglia. Throughout the region, atmosphere of activity. . . . The Fourteenth American Army, headquarters Fareham, appears to occupy the region as far as Worthing in the east but was unable to define the limit in the west. The XXXVII American Corps has its headquarters in the area of Worthing. The 17th Infantry Division and the 59th Division, both assault divisions. The XXXIII Corps probably occupies the area west of Fareham-Winchester. I did not have the possibility of checking. The 17th American Infantry Division appears to occupy the region to the north of Brighton. . . . The 59th American Infantry Division appears to have its headquarters at Rolands Castle. See serial 64
According to messages from a particularly trustworthy source, following on the withdrawal of the American divisions hitherto in the area north-east of London (County of Essex) parts of the Fourth English Army (hitherto 7th English Army Corps and 58th Infantry Division confirmed) have been moved into the area vacated. As part of this regrouping, the headquarters of the Fourth English Army has moved to Colchester (north-east of London). It is probable that further divisions not yet named will follow this army.	App. to LBW 1391 17 Sept., 1944.	GARBO 9 Sept., 1944. 2032, 2048 and 2101 GMT	66. 7 (7). . . . Apart from some odd units, all US troops have left the area. Innkeepers at Ipswich and Colchester have received orders from billeting officers to continue to reserve accommodation previously commandeered for arrival of further troops. Small hotel at Ipswich occupied by SOS officers recently evacuated. Saw several staff cars in Harwich and Ipswich with the sign of the Fourth British Army but no troops or lorries seen. . . . When in Colchester a week ago discovered that all US troops had left. Large numbers of staff cars with the sign of Fourth British Army and 58th British Division seen outside Cups Hotel. These belong to staff officers in transit.

The possibility of a *new landing operation* in conjunction with planned airborne operations is suggested by a further report from a very trustworthy agent, according to whom the present airborne operations should be coupled with future plans for the Fourth English Army; the agent mentions in this connection the already reported moves of operations of the Fourth English Army to the Essex/Kent area (see Short Appreciation for the West of the 17th September). There is still no *sure* evidence of such plans.

App. to LBW 1393 19 Sept., 1944.

GARBO 14 Sept., 1944. 1910 and 1916 GMT	Folkestone: 7th British Corps has left area. Canterbury: many troops and vehicles of 80th Division still seen. Wye: 61st Division seen. Three Bridges: 55th Division seen. 58th Division left Gravesend last week.
TATE 10 Sept., 1944. 0604 MET	Saw a large British convoy travelling in a northerly direction, through London, on 8th September. Had the sign of a yellow shell on a blue square.
BRUTUS 10 Sept., 1944. 1714 and 1724 GMT	67. Allied Airborne Army is now under FUSAG. Confirm that airborne divisions can be detached and that a task force, consisting of four airborne divisions, has already been posted to take part in the operation in conjunction with the Fourth Army. They will probably take the place of the 17th and 59th Assault Divisions which, up till now, remain in the Fourteenth American Army. From these changes one can suppose that the FUSAG operations will be preceded by an airborne attack which can be carried out even at long range. An attack against the North of Germany, in the regions of Bremen or Kiel is not excluded.
BRUTUS 14 Sept., 1944. 1728, 1835, 1840 and 1846 GMT	From one of my colleagues, I learn that the 1st British Parachute Brigade was due to take part in an airborne operation against the Pas de Calais on 3rd September and that the operation was cancelled on account of the rapid advance of 21 Army Group. There is great secrecy about airborne preparations and my informant did not even know the numbers of the units of the 1st British Airborne Corps. On the other hand I have just learned that there has recently been great activity at the headquarters of the Allied Airborne Army and that they have even formed a second task force. In view of the general situation, there is talk in our headquarters that in three or four days one

should expect an airborne attack against Denmark, Kiel Canal or against ports in Northern Germany. This appears to confirm my own opinion, already transmitted several days ago, especially when I learnt of the move of the Fourth Army into the Essex-Kent region. In my opinion, the attack can be undertaken by the special task force which I have already reported as being attached to the Fourth British Army.

BRUTUS 10 Sept., BRUTUS 20 Sept., 1944. 2122 and 2144 GMT

68. See serial 67

Regarding the airborne attacks, I have learned that it is a question of the 1st British Airborne Corps and the XVIII American Airborne Corps and not the task force as supposed by me. As far as I know, this task force is still ready for the operation with the Fourth Army. It includes the 9th, 17th and 21st American Airborne Divisions and the 2nd British Airborne Division.

App. to LBW 1397 23 Sept., 1944.

From various reports by prudent agents, the following picture of the present airborne operations and of future plans emerges; it is planned that three airborne corps were included in the First Allied Airborne Army; the 1st English Airborne Corps and the XVIII American Airborne Corps so far engaged comprise the 1st English, 82nd and 101st American Airborne Divisions, one Polish Parachute Brigade as well as possibly the 17th American Airborne Division and here it is not yet finally clear whether the last-named is the 17th American Infantry Division (Airborne) though there are some indications of this. The allotment of further formations and smaller airborne army units is probable. To the Airborne Corps still in Great Britain belong presumably the 2nd English, 21st, 9th and 11th American Airborne Divisions and possibly the 59th American Infantry Division equipped for transport by air. The last-named having repeatedly been mentioned in this connection should also appear as an 'assault division'. This Corps is said to be destined for employment as part of landing operations by Fourth English Army which are predicted against the German Bight in the sector Wiesemunde-Emden. The reports mentioned above make a convincing impression and have been partially confirmed by the course of operations and by troop identifications in recent days. There are so far no messages regarding the employment of the 6th English Airborne Division now to be assumed in Great Britain (at present probably still resting). The employment of this particularly battle-experienced airborne division must, however, be expected additionally in future airborne operations. On the basis of the above reports, therefore, new landings, coupled with strong airborne landings must be expected in the area of the German Bight. We have so far no information as to the date of such undertakings. It must, however, be assumed that these intentions will only be capable of execution when a bridgehead has been successfully created at Arnhem and further operations from this bridgehead seem to the enemy command to be assured of success. The seasonal weather conditions in the Channel which are deteriorating will, however, set a time limit to these plans and will, therefore, tend to advance them.

LBW 1404 30 Sept., 1944.

According to prisoners of war and various reliable Abwehr sources the presence of the 2nd English Airborne Division has repeatedly been confirmed in Great Britain. Since the 4th English Parachute Brigade, assumed to be in this formation (*i.e.* in 2nd Airborne Division) was identified with the 1st English Airborne Division in the landing area in Holland, the recent report from a proven Abwehr source according to which the 2nd English Airborne Division was made up of the 11th and 12th English Parachute Brigades and the English 13th Air Landing Brigade, may be regarded as credible. The Divisional Commander seems to be Major-General D'Arcy, formerly commander of the 9th English Armoured Division.

BRUTUS 13 Aug, 1944. 1307 and 1311 GMT

BRUTUS 24 Aug, 1944. Received 1723 GMT

69. The composition of the 2nd British Airborne Division: the 11th and 12th Parachute Brigades and 13th Air Landing Brigade. Each brigade is composed of three battalions. There is also an Air Landing Reconnaissance Squadron with the number '6' and an Air Landing Artillery Regiment. The Commander-in-Chief of the Division is Major-General D'Arcy, who formerly commanded the 9th Armoured Division.

How many aircraft and gliders can be reserved in Great Britain for air landing operations on a large scale? Airborne divisions are composed of an air landing and two parachute brigades; we do not, therefore, understand your message No. 988 of 20th August.

70. 44th US Infantry Division and 9th US Armoured Division have recently disembarked in Normandy. (Another message of about this date from GARBO reported the departure of XXXVII Corps and of the 59th US Infantry Division and the 25th US Armoured Division. By an oversight it was omitted from the Traffic Summary.)	GARBO 4 Oct., 1944. 2018 GMT	LBW 1411 7 Oct., 1944.	According to a proven Abwehr source besides the 44th American Infantry Division and the 49th American Armoured Division (see Lagebericht West No. 1409 of 5th October, 1944), the 59th American Infantry Division and the 25th American Armoured Division as well as the staff of the XXXVII American Army Corps are also said to have been transferred to France.
71. Heard from a good source that an American Corps is on its way from New York to Marseilles. It consists of one armoured division and two infantry divisions.	TATE 5 Oct., 1944. 0755 MET	App. to LBW 1411 7 Oct., 1944.	According to a report, hitherto unconfirmed, from a good source, shipment of troops will shortly take place from the USA to Marseilles for the Western front. In view of the fact that the Channel ports are not yet fully working, this report seems not improbable, particularly as the proposal would afford considerable relief to the road communications in Northern France.
		LBW 1430 26 Oct., 1944.	According to available reports we must reckon with the transfer, up to the end of October, of a further two infantry divisions and one armoured division from the USA to Europe.
72. Am sending details obtained at Wentworth. I was told that the 61st and 80th British Infantry Divisions have been withdrawn from 7th (sic) Corps but that they remain at Wye and Canterbury respectively. Headquarters of the 7th Corps are now somewhere to the south of Newmarket and include the 5th British Armoured Division and the 58th British Infantry Division. The Fourth Army has its headquarters in the region of Witham.	BRUTUS 5 Oct., 1944. 1809, 1813 and 1815 GMT	LBW 1413 9 Oct., 1944.	A proven Abwehr source has confirmed the following formations in their existing areas in Great Britain at the beginning of October, 58th, 61st and 80th English Infantry Divisions also 5th English Armoured Division as well as the staffs of the Fourth English Army and 7th English Army Corps.

73. Urgent. I met by chance my colleagues from FUSAG and as a result of the details which I have received I can state that FUSAG has been disbanded. The Fourth Army comes directly under SHAEF.	BRUTUS 17 Oct., 1944. 1815 GMT	LBW 1425 21 Oct., 1944.	A proven source reports from Great Britain that the staff of the First American Army Group (FUSAG) has been disbanded. The same source reports that the English Fourth Army which has hitherto been under the command of FUSAG, is now directly under the Commander-in-Chief of the Allied Invasion Forces (General Eisenhower).
74. The 2nd British Corps has been replaced by the 17th British Corps, of which the Commander-in-Chief is General Templer. I suppose that the headquarters are at Tunbridge Wells. It includes the 55th and 61st Divisions. I cannot understand what is happening to the 80th British Division. From what I am told it is at present north of London in the 7th British Corps (to be verified). (*Note.* The 17th British Corps only lasted about a week and this is the only time that it was mentioned. Before the end of the month, it was decided to say that the 55th and 61st British Infantry Divisions were under War Office control, which was in fact the case.)	BRUTUS 24 Oct., 1944. 1803 and 1808 GMT	LBW 1434 30 Oct., 1944.	A proven source continues to report the presence of the 2nd English Army Corps Headquarters in Tunbridge Wells (South-East England). The Commander of this Army Corps is Lt.-General G. W. R. Templer. The 55th and 61st Infantry Divisions are, with certainty, included in this Corps and are in their accepted areas. The same source confirms the 7th English Army Corps Headquarters and the 80th English Infantry Division, the latter now believed to be in the area north of London.
75. In the region of Witham much activity on the part of units of the Fourth British Army which appears to be preparing to leave for the North. . . . Detailed report: the region is occupied by the Fourth British Army and the 7th Corps with the sign of a sea shell, which appears to have its headquarters in the region of Sudbury. It includes the 5th Armoured Division, with the sign of a lobster, the 58th Division with the sign of a stag's head, and the 80th Division with the sign of a red steamship and a yellow sky. In the region of Witham and Hatfield Peverel, much activity;	BRUTUS 13 Nov., 1944, 1749, 1757 and 1801 GMT	LBW 1454 19 Nov., 1944.	According to a report from a good source the 7th English Army Corps as well as the 58th and 80th English Infantry Divisions and the 5th Armoured Division have been confirmed in their old areas in Great Britain.

vehicles of the Fourth Army, 7th Corps and a few of the 80th Division.

76A. 7 (4) Gloucester: following troops seen: SOS, Americans with armoured division sign number 11 also some troops of 11th US Infantry Division. Have learned that 11th US Infantry Division is now stationed at Abergavenny and that it is being used to provide reinforcements for other US divisions in France which have sustained heavy losses. Also learnt that 17th US Division passed through here and has gone to Wales but could not discover exact location. This division is being also used in the same way as 11th US Infantry Division.	GARBO 23 Nov., 1944. 1931 and 1940 GMT	According to a report from a credible source the 11th and 17th American Infantry Divisions are confirmed afresh as being in England and are said to be at the moment being drawn upon for reinforcements for the American divisions engaged in France. Both divisions are said to have been moved to the areas of Gloucester and South Wales where the training areas were repeatedly occupied by American troops before the invasion.
		LBW 1460 25 Nov., 1944.
76B. See serial 76A	GARBO 23 Nov., 1944.	The fact that the 11th and 17th American Infantry Divisions, which have been for some time located in Great Britain, have not been used on the Western front finds its explanation in the report of a good agent according to whom these divisions are being used for draft finding. It must, however, be pointed out that repeated experience shows that so called 'draft-finding divisions' can, if necessary, often be *made ready for battle by the Americans at short notice* and can then be sent to the front. These two divisions must therefore continue to be regarded as an operational reserve in the hands of Eisenhower.
		App. to LBW 1460 25 Nov., 1944.

	Source	Comment	Reference
77. See serial 75 7 (7) reports from Newmarket: Convoys of 7th Corps have continued to pass through daily since last reporting, all moving in northerly direction. Troops and armour of 5th Armoured Division are already starting to move out. Have learned from my contact that this division is moving to Yorkshire. Have been in Spalding, in Lincolnshire, for a few days. Saw a large British convoy passing through the town in the direction of Boston; had the sign of the 5th American Division. On the railway station there were many British troops with the sign of a yellow sea shell on a blue square. 7 (7) Sudbury: Saw large convoys of 58th Infantry Division moving direction of Cambridge. Three: this confirms that the troops of this division, seen by me in Glasgow, were on leave. . . . Have ascertained that 80th Infantry Division has been stationed in area between Ipswich and Stowmarket but that it left this district again between 10th and 15th of this month. Am proceeding to Yorkshire to investigate on basis of information received from my contact that 5th Armoured Division was moving to that county.	BRUTUS 13 Nov., 1944. GARBO 19 Nov., 1944. 1935 and 1945 GMT TATE 20 Nov., 1944. 0750 and 1910 MET GARBO 23 Nov., 1944. 1858 and 1928 GMT	The move, several times reported, of the formations of the 7th English Army Corps (38th (58th?) and 80th Infantry Divisions, 5th Armoured Division) from their previous locations in the South-East of the Island to Central England seems to be confirmed, though the reason for these moves is not clear. Since, however, for the present there is no sign of a move to port areas, we cannot yet speak of any impending embarkation of this division (*sic* corps).	App. to LBW 1460 25 Nov., 1944.
78. Reference divisions trained as airborne: as already reported, the 48th American Infantry Division has undergone this training. It was formerly included in the XXXIII American Corps, which appears to have been disbanded as this division, together with the 11th and 17th American Divisions, is under command of British Base Section.	BRUTUS 17 Nov., 1944. 1752 GMT	The 48th American Infantry Division, also accepted in Great Britain, has been repeatedly reported as 'airborne'. It must, however, be assumed that this division is destined for employment in connection with further planned airborne landings.	App. to LBW 1460 25 Nov., 1944.

Message	Source	Appreciation	Reference
79. *Location and further moves of Fourth British Army should be controlled carefully by your other agents.*			
7 (7) reports from York: has discovered that Fourth British Army has moved here but can find no sign of other divisions reported moving North in this area as yet. He is continuing investigations though he states there is no sign of preparations for embarkation and has been told that Fourth Army and Northern Command are being amalgamated and will control any future landings in Germany, whether to help the present offensive or to occupy areas which you abandon, in the same way as other Commands have been given similar roles, for instance Norway in the case of Scottish Command and the Channel Islands in the case of Southern Command. . . . 80th British Infantry Division has left Canterbury area. This confirms 7 (7) report.	GARBO 2 Dec., 1944. Received 1910 GMT GARBO 2 Dec., 1944. 1915, 1924 and 1944 GMT	There is no fresh information regarding the shipment of formations to France; the presence of the Fourth English Army is again confirmed by a useful source. The apparently still uncompleted move of the 7th English Army Corps with 58th Infantry and 5th Armoured Divisions from South-Eastern England to the neighbourhood of the Humber estuary is striking and the reasons for this are still not clear. Any new landing intentions (Denmark, German Bight) can, however, not be deduced from this move, particularly as they could not be in any way operationally connected with recognisable objectives in France. The possible concentration of landing craft in the Humber area must be investigated by air reconnaissance.	App. to LBW 1474 9 Dec., 1944.
Reference your message of 28th November. Confirmation that the Fourth Army is at present in Yorkshire. From what I was told I had supposed that it would already have left from the Humber region against the region of Emden. I believe that I was mistaken as to the date and that the operation has only been postponed.	BRUTUS 4 Dec., 1944. 1759 GMT		
7 (7) York: Agent has finally discovered that 58th Division is stationed in the areas surrounding Leeds. . . . He discovered this division by following the direction of very large convoy of brand new heavy trucks with divisional sign painted, which were being delivered to the division. . . .	GARBO 6 Dec., 1944. 2000 GMT		
7 (7). Have discovered that 80th Division is stationed in the areas of Bedale and Catterick. . . . Agent assures me there is no immediate danger of an embarkation since 80th Division is undergoing training.	GARBO 8 Dec., 1944. 2018 GMT	From England there have come in no important messages during the last days, in particular we have been unable to obtain any fresh information regarding the purpose behind the move of the 7th English Army Corps, which has now been joined by the 80th English Infantry Division (now accepted in the Catterick area, north-west of Hull). In any case we *cannot accept* the intention to transfer these formations to the Western front in the near future after their withdrawal from South-Eastern England. Similarly the fact that the 80th English Infantry Division belonging to the 7th English Army Corps was *not* placed in the area of a port when it was moved North gives reason to suppose that no imminent *new landing operation* is planned which would include this formation.	App. to LBW 1479 14 Dec., 1944.

80. The 6th Airborne Division is in the region of Salisbury.	BRUTUS 7 Dec., 1944. 1747 GMT	App. to LBW 1479 14 Dec., 1944.	The 6th English Airborne Division is probably still in the Salisbury area.
81. 7 (4) Bournemouth: Saw considerable number of newly arrived American troops which are starting to occupy camps near here. These wear the sign of red shield divided horizontally, the main, lower portion in red, the smaller, upper portion blue, superimposed on blue portion is white design like a telephone receiver. Have not been able to identify this yet but am continuing investigation.	GARBO 16 Dec., 1944.	LBW 1483 18 Dec., 1944.	The presence of the 76th American Infantry Division has been reported in a Southern English port by a trustworthy source. We must reckon with its early shipment to France.

APPENDIX XIV

JOSEPHINE and FUSAG

The following is an extract from a German document bearing the reference Luftwaffenfuehrungsstab Ic, Fremde Luftwaffen West, Nr. 109/45 g. Kdos (A), dated 6th January, 1945, which suggests that JOSEPHINE's messages about FUSAG were inspired by the Allies.

'JOSEPHINE's Reports on the First American Army Group (FUSAG)

1. FUSAG's existence was first notified on 9th January, 1944, and was regularly mentioned with certainty up to 17th June. In the spring of 1944 it was increasingly reported by agents and by the press.

2. In assessing JOSEPHINE's reports, the purport of all reports on FUSAG may be noted as follows:

(*a*) The Allied Armies under FUSAG's command kept on changing. Finally it was stated that one *English* and one Allied airborne army were under the command of FUSAG, *i.e.* of an American Army Group.

(*b*) Changes in the command of FUSAG were reported quite as frequently as changes in the formations subordinate to it.

(*c*) When the invasion began, FUSAG was generally put down as being a second great group of forces, for a second landing operation north of the first.

(*d*) After the continued withdrawal of divisions from the armies under FUSAG's command, to reinforce the invasion forces, reports were also received as to movements of FUSAG into Central and Northern England, in connection with landing operations against Jutland and Southern Norway, and later against the Heligoland Bight.

3. It may be seen from (2) that FUSAG was certainly used by the enemy as an "army in being".*

Technical adviser's personal impression is that FUSAG existed simply for this purpose.

4. During the second half of the year, reports from the agent JOSEPHINE conform to the enemy's decoy activities. Until the middle of October 1944, they did much to uphold the 'fiction' of FUSAG as a strong group of forces intended for further landings.

The first reports came in very late – according to records on file, not until 6th August. Like other agents JOSEPHINE reported (German Security H.O.Mil (RSHA Mil) B/L 11102/8 of 8th August, 1944):

(*a*) "FUSAG was originally to have been used for a second large-scale landing operation. As the timing of the Normandy invasion went completely wrong, it was decided not to undertake this second landing, which had been planned for the end of June; and formations from FUSAG were steadily transferred to France."

(*b*) As there was no longer any practical likelihood that FUSAG would be employed for a second landing, it was now mentioned in connection with a landing operation against Southern Norway and Denmark. (German Security H.O. Mil B/L 13869 of 29th August, 1944): "Increased troop transports from Southern and Central England to Northern England are being associated with movements of parts of FUSAG. Operations in Northern and Central Norway, starting from England, are not expected, but landings in Jutland and S. Norway."

Replying to further enquiry he stated (German Security H.O. (RSHA) 10031 of 1st September):

"I was expecting your further enquiry (!), as my own suspicions had already been aroused at once. All sources however confirm that FUSAG formations have been stationed as far as the Humber. In addition there are individual reports about troop

---

*Original phrase in English. The meaning of this expression is somewhat obscure.

transports to Northern England/Scotland. As reported, these were not observed previously. Resumption of Swedish air traffic to England refused, although conceded at end of August. It is quite clear that either a large-scale decoy manœuvre is planned, to cover the employment of FUSAG in Belgium–Holland–Heligoland Bight, or that an operation against Denmark is actually intended."

(*c*) Later on, the idea of connecting FUSAG with the movements of troops to Northern England was withdrawn, but the increasingly doubtful FUSAG was reported to be destined for a large-scale landing in the Heligoland Bight (GAF Ops Staff Ic. Attache Group 88087 of 15th September): "FUSAG continues in Eastern England as far as Humber. Formations in Northern England and Scotland do not belong to FUSAG. Employment of FUSAG in Eastern Holland and Heligoland Bight after strong airborne landing has been carried out in Eastern and Northern Holland."

5. In conclusion, it must be pointed out that JOSEPHINE was thus a participant in the enemy's decoy plans, which were aimed at holding down strong German forces for as long as possible at various points from Norway to France.'

It is of interest to note that the Germans, however nearly they came to appreciating the nature of the FORTITUDE deception, never seemed to realise that the threat relied upon the use of misplaced or else of wholly fictitious forces. The foregoing document, while suggesting that a large-scale deception had been put into effect by the Allies with the object of containing the Fifteenth German Army in the Pas de Calais, assumes that this was achieved by sending real troops into the Eastern and South-Eastern counties.

All the interrogations of senior German officers, which took place in Nuremberg after the war was over in order to assist in the writing of this report, were conducted on the basis that information was being sought on behalf of the official war historians. Dr Percy Schramm, the chronicler of the OKW War Diary, more astute than the rest, eyeing his interlocutor quizzically during the course of his interview, suddenly interposed the question: 'All this Patton business wasn't a trick, was it?' 'What do you mean by that?' came the reply.

'What I mean is this. Were all those divisions sent to South-East England simply to hold our forces in the Pas de Calais?' 'I certainly imagine', answered his interrogator, 'that if you had denuded the Pas de Calais, they would have been used to attack that place, but since you did not do so, they were equally available to reinforce Montgomery.' 'Ah, that is what we always thought,' said Dr Schramm with evident relief.

APPENDIX XV

Glossary

APPENDIX 'Y'.	Original cover plan for OVERLORD written during the autumn of 1943 and subsequently superseded by FORTITUDE.
'A' FORCE.	Force employed to plan and to execute deceptive operations in the Mediterranean theatre.
ANCXF.	Allied Naval Commander Expeditionary Force.
AEAF.	Allied Expeditionary Air Force.
AMT VI.	Secret Intelligence Branch of the RSHA.
ABWEHR.	Security and Intelligence Branch of the German fighting Services.
ABWEHRSTELLE.	Abwehr headquarters in German-occupied territory.
AGENT.	A spy.
—CONTROLLED.	See double-cross agent.
—DOUBLE CROSS.	A spy who works for the enemy but deceives his original employer into believing that he still acts in his interest.
—TRIPLE CROSS.	A spy who continues to work for his original employer but deceives the enemy into believing that he has betrayed his trust and is working for them.
—UNCONTROLLED.	A spy who furnishes his employer with information which he falsely claims to have acquired from genuine enemy sources.
—UNCONSCIOUS.	A person who by his indiscretions unwittingly provides the spy with information.
—STRAIGHT.	A bona fide spy.

B1A.	Sub-section of MI5 operating double-cross agents.
Big Bob.	Dummy landing craft.
COSSAC.	Chief of Staff to Supreme Allied Commander designate.
Controlling Officer.	Adviser to the British Chiefs of Staff on Deception in all theatres.
CLH Units.	Wireless Deception Units representing naval assault forces.
Case Officer.	Officer in personal charge of double-cross agent.
DD Tank.	'Duplex Drive', or amphibious tank.
Eins Heer.	Section of Abwehr responsible for military intelligence.
Fremde Heere West.	'Foreign Armies West' section of OKH Intelligence Staff.
G (R).	Deception staff at 21 Army Group.
Hard(s).	Hard standings to facilitate embarkation of vehicles into landing craft.
KO.	Kriegs Organization – Abwehr headquarters in neutral countries.
LCS.	London Controlling Section – see Controlling Officer.
Lagebericht West.	Intelligence Summary produced daily by OKH.
Ops (B).	Sub-section – Deception staff at SHAEF.
OKH.	Oberkommando des Heeres (Army High Command).
OKW.	Oberkommando der Wehrmacht. (Supreme Command of the Armed Forces).
PWE.	Political Warfare Executive.
PRU.	Photographic Reconnaissance Unit.
R Force.	Force of specialist troops in 21 Army Group employed for Deception.
RSHA.	Reichssicherheitshauptamt. Headquarters of German civil security service.
Special Means.	The name given to all forms of controlled leakage.
SIME.	Security Intelligence Middle East.

SPECIAL PLANS SECTION.	Deception Staff at Twelfth Army Group.
SOE.	Special Operations Executive. British sabotage organisation.
TWENTY COMMITTEE.	Committee appointed by British Directors of Intelligence to approve reports by double-cross agents.
WF ST.	Wehrmachtführungs stab. Controlling staff of the Wehrmacht.
Y SERVICE.	Wireless Intercept.

INDEX

(Imaginary formations are printed in italics.)

7/02   ⑨   6/02   PLC 5/12 Archival

12/05   ⑪   7/05

3/07   ⑪   7/05

10/18   ⑬   8/16